TAXING THE CHURCH

Taxing the Church

RELIGION, EXEMPTIONS, ENTANGLEMENT, AND THE CONSTITUTION

Edward A. Zelinsky

OXFORD
UNIVERSITY PRESS

OXFORD
UNIVERSITY PRESS

Oxford University Press is a department of the University of Oxford. It furthers the University's objective of excellence in research, scholarship, and education by publishing worldwide. Oxford is a registered trademark of Oxford University Press in the UK and certain other countries.

Published in the United States of America by Oxford University Press
198 Madison Avenue, New York, NY 10016, United States of America.

Library of Congress Cataloging-in-Publication Data

Names: Zelinsky, Edward A., author.
Title: Taxing the church : religion, exemptions, entanglement, and the constitution / Edward A. Zelinsky.
Description: New York : Oxford University Press, 2017. | Includes bibliographical references and index.
Identifiers: LCCN 2017021978 | ISBN 9780190853952 ((hardback) : alk. paper)
Subjects: LCSH: Church tax—Law and legislation—United States. | Clergy—Taxation—Law and legislation—United States. | Church and state—United States. | Religion and state—United States. | Constitutional law—United States.
Classification: LCC KF6442 .Z45 2017 | DDC 343.7306/6—dc23
LC record available at https://lccn.loc.gov/2017021978

9 8 7 6 5 4 3 2 1

Printed by Edwards Brothers Malloy, United States of America.

Note to Readers

This publication is designed to provide accurate and authoritative information in regard to the subject matter covered. It is based upon sources believed to be accurate and reliable and is intended to be current as of the time it was written. It is sold with the understanding that the publisher is not engaged in rendering legal, accounting, or other professional services. If legal advice or other expert assistance is required, the services of a competent professional person should be sought. Also, to confirm that the information has not been affected or changed by recent developments, traditional legal research techniques should be used, including checking primary sources where appropriate.

(Based on the Declaration of Principles jointly adopted by a Committee of the American Bar Association and a Committee of Publishers and Associations.)

This book is dedicated to the memories of two ladies,
each a heroine in her own way:
Lucille Brotman Zukerman Zelinsky
and
Sara Geizhals Dronski Twersky

Contents

Acknowledgments

I AM GRATEFUL to the individuals and institutions which have assisted me in writing this book.

First on the list is the Zelinsky family seminar. My children—Jacoba Urist, Aaron Zelinsky, Joshua Zelinsky, and Nathaniel Zelinsky—and their mother, my college sweetheart and wife, Doris, have read and criticized countless versions of this book. Perhaps even more important, they (and their wonderful friends and spouses) have spent hours over dinners debating the issues I discuss in this book. While this book is dedicated to the grandmothers of my children, it could just as properly have been dedicated to those children and their mother.

Institutionally, I presented the themes of this book both to my colleagues at the Benjamin N. Cardozo School of Law of Yeshiva University and to the 2016 Columbia Law School–Hebrew University Tax Conference. Participants in both of these faculty seminars made perceptive observations for which I am grateful.

I have spent much of my professional career thinking about the themes of this book. Two law journals deserve credit for allowing me to explore those themes in their pages, the *Cardozo Law Review* and the *Boston College Law Review*. In particular, chapter 6 (pertaining to the tax treatment of parsonages) derives from my article, "Do Religious Tax Exemptions Entangle in Violation of the Establishment Clause," 33 *Cardozo Law Review* 1633 (2012), while chapter 1 (pertaining to the U.S. Supreme Court's cases on taxes and the First Amendment) derives from "Are Tax

'Benefits' for Religious Institutions Constitutionally Dependent on Benefits for Secular Entities," 42 *Boston College Law Review* 805 (2001).

Finally, I have benefited from the research assistance of a fine group of Cardozo students: Rachel A. Azarow, Juliana Bleiberg, Harrison Braun, Aaron Bretter, Jonah Brill, Adam Brownstone, Alexandra Eisig, Antonio Fuertes, Nicole A. Kim, John Ludwig, Michael Maradi, Spencer Mayer, Natalia Pivovarova, Meir S. Polter, Ishara Quick, and Bansari Sheth.

The conventional caveat to this kind of acknowledgment is that any mistakes are my responsibility. In this case, that caveat is true.

Introduction

WHEN I TOLD a prominent judge that I was writing a book entitled *Taxing the Church*, the judge responded in a puzzled tone: "But churches are not taxed." The judge's comment confirmed my determination to write this book, which addresses the legal and tax policy issues that arise when churches and other religious institutions are taxed or exempted.

At one level, the judge's statement is quite sound: There are broad areas in which churches[1] and, more generally, religious organizations enjoy tax exemption. Houses of worship are, in every state of the union, exempt from property taxation and do not pay tax on the income generated by their basic religious activities. Churches are also exempt from other taxes such as unemployment compensation taxes.

But, beyond this initial generalization, matters are more complex: Churches and other religious entities pay more taxes than many believe. Churches and other religious organizations are treated quite diversely by different taxes and by different states. Sometimes churches and other religious entities are taxed in the same fashion as secular organizations and persons. Yet other taxes narrowly exempt churches while taxing secular philanthropic organizations.

The states' sales taxes, for example, vary in their respective approaches to religious institutions. In some states, churches and other religious organizations both pay

[1] For ease of exposition, I generally use the term "church" generically, to refer to all houses of worship, including synagogues and mosques.

sales tax on their retail purchases and collect tax on their retail sales. In other states, churches and other sectarian entities pay sales tax as retail buyers but do not collect tax as retail sellers. In yet other states, the pattern is reversed, with churches and religious organizations collecting taxes on their retail sales while they are exempted from the taxation of their retail purchases. In other states, churches are wholly immune from sales tax obligations as either buyers or sellers.

Within the broad consensus exempting churches from property taxation, there are notable differences among the states' particular approaches. The states, for example, disagree about the property tax status of parsonages in which clergy live. Some states exempt such parsonages from property taxation; others do not. In some states, housing occupied by supervising clergy qualifies as tax-exempt parsonages. In other states, it does not. Even though churches and other religious entities do not pay federal and state income taxes on their religious activities, these sectarian entities often pay state taxes on their unrelated business incomes and always pay federal taxes on such unrelated business income. In most states, churches are subject to taxes on real estate transfers.

In addition to the tax on unrelated business income, the Internal Revenue Code also imposes its payroll taxes on churches and religious organizations. In particular, sectarian institutions pay the employer's portion of the FICA taxes financing Social Security and Medicare for such institutions' nonclerical employees. Ministers[2] pay self-employment taxes to fund Social Security and Medicare. These federal payroll taxes can be considerable.

Thus, an empirical theme of this book is the diversity with which churches and other religious institutions are treated by the federal and state tax systems. Sectarian institutions pay more taxes than many believe. In important respects, the states differ among themselves in their respective approaches to the taxation of sectarian entities while the taxes imposed by the federal government treat churches differently. Sometimes the Internal Revenue Code exempts churches along with secular eleemosynary entities. Sometimes the Code taxes churches like nonreligious organizations. Sometimes the federal tax law narrowly exempts only churches.

The observation that churches and religious organizations, while exempt from many taxes, are subject to others raises the chief normative issue which this book confronts: Should churches be taxed?

Just as the empirical reality is more diverse than many believe—churches and religious institutions are subject to many taxes—my normative conclusions will disappoint those looking for simple, absolutist answers. Central to my analysis is the

---

[2] For ease of expression, I often use the term "minister" generically, to refer to all clergy, including priests, nuns, rabbis, cantors, and imams.

concern which has come to be called "entanglement": Either taxing or exempting churches and other sectarian entities entangles church and state. In the tax context, there are no disentangling alternatives. Some taxes entail more church-state entanglement than do other taxes. Different tax provisions entail different types and different quantities of entanglement risk.

I propose to denominate as "enforcement entanglement" the enmeshment of church and state which results when churches are taxed. I propose the label "borderline entanglement" for the church-state tussles which occur when churches and other sectarian actors are tax exempt. When churches (and other religious entities and actors) are tax exempt, they must claim exemption while tax collectors must police the boundaries of exemption and sometimes reject those claims. The upshot is church-state entanglement over the borders of exemption.

Taxing churches and religious institutions leads to church-state enforcement entanglement while exempting churches and sectarian entities leads to borderline entanglement over the boundaries of the exemption. When the modern government confronts the contemporary church, there is no disentangling alternative.

Enforcing ad valorem property taxation, for example, enmeshes taxpayers and tax collectors in difficult disputes about the valuation of property. Such taxation can also lead to enforcement entanglement when property owners lack the liquidity to pay tax. In cases where a property owner has no cash to discharge his property tax obligations, the tax collector must take action—typically foreclosure—to collect property taxes owed but unpaid. The taxes generating the greatest enforcement entanglement are those, like ad valorem property taxation, where the amount of the taxpayer's liability may be difficult to determine and where the taxpayer may lack the cash to pay the tax.

In contrast, sales taxation is a form of taxation less pregnant with possibilities for church-state enforcement entanglement. Most retail sales involve no valuation controversy as the purchaser usually pays an easily ascertainable cash price. Most taxable sales present no liquidity issues since the purchaser typically pays cash, including the sales tax owed on his purchase.

The taxes to which churches are more frequently subject—federal Social Security and Medicare taxes, state sales taxes, real estate conveyance levies—generally fall on the less entangling end of the spectrum. The taxes from which religious institutions are exempt—general income taxes, value-based property taxes, unemployment taxes—are typically taxes with the greatest potential for enforcement-related entanglement between church and state.

Tax policy invariably involves choices among conflicting goals, such as revenue-generation, administrability, public acceptability, economic neutrality, valuation considerations, and liquidity concerns. None of these goals can ever be achieved in toto. When tax laws impact churches and other sectarian entities, the minimization of church-state entanglement should be an important, often controlling, goal. In practice, it often is as Congress and the state legislatures generally exempt churches and religious institutions from the taxes with the greatest possibilities of enforcement-related entanglement. However, in the tax context, church-state entanglement can never be eliminated in its entirety, any more than any other legitimate objective of tax policy can ever be obtained perfectly.

To many, the choice to tax the church (or not) is straightforward. For some, tax exemption reflexively constitutes subsidization forbidden by the First Amendment. For others, tax exemption is always a reasonable (perhaps required) accommodation of the constitutionally recognized autonomy of religious institutions.

My analysis departs from both of these absolutist perspectives. The automatic equation of exemption with subsidization is unpersuasive: While it is economically better to be untaxed, exemption can serve the important nonsubsidizing goal of mitigating enforcement entanglement between church and state. Governments may legitimately exempt religious entities from taxation to acknowledge such entities' autonomy and to avoid the enforcement entanglement inherent in the relationship between the taxpayer and the tax collector. The autonomy of religious institutions and actors is an important facet of the constitutionally protected value of free exercise.

However, tax exemption itself entangles the state and sectarian entities and personnel at the borders of exemption as those entities and personnel claim eligibility for tax exemption and dispute with the state and its agents the boundaries of exemption. Tax exemption requires governments to forgo revenues they would otherwise collect.

Against this background of conflicting considerations, it is unpersuasive to label any tax exemption, deduction, or exclusion as a "subsidy" unless there is first agreement upon a normative tax base from which such exemption, deduction, or exclusion departs. Exemptions for religious actors and institutions can be legitimate, nonsubsidizing features of a normative tax base when such exemptions are used to minimize enforcement entanglement between church and state. In a world of imperfect choices between entangling alternatives, it is often a plausible, nonsubsidizing choice to exempt sectarian actors and institutions and thereby incur the problems of borderline entanglement rather than enmesh church and state in the difficulties of enforcement entanglement.

On the other side of the ledger, churches and other sectarian institutions utilize public services, often quite heavily. Such institutions are often wealthy and engage in economically significant transactions including the purchase and sale of real estate and the payment of wages. Such wealth and transactions reflect capacity to pay tax.

To the extent possible, taxation should be economically neutral among potential taxpayers and their comparable activities. Tax exemption forgoes revenues which could either finance public services or permit tax rate reductions.

Hence, taxing the church or exempting the church involves imperfect trade-offs among competing and legitimate values. On balance, our federal system of decentralized legislation makes these trade-offs reasonably, though not perfectly. For example, the sales tax obligations of churches and religious entities could be broadened without risk of significant additional church-state entanglement. Similarly, real estate conveyance taxes properly apply to the sales and purchases of sectarian entities since these are typically easily taxed cash transactions. As I discuss in chapter five, the contrast between real estate conveyance taxes and ad valorem property taxes is instructive: The former entail less threat of enforcement-related entanglement because there are no valuation or liquidity issues when there is a cash sale or purchase of religious property. Thus, looking at the enforcement entanglement generated by these two taxes, it is understandable that ad valorem property taxes which often entail valuation and liquidity challenges generally do not apply to churches while less entangling real estate conveyance taxes usually do.

Tax policy trade-offs are best made legislatively. Law professors (I am proud to be one) typically esteem courts and prioritize judicial decision-making. This high regard for the judiciary usually results in a predominant focus on decision-making in the courts. However, taxation is and should be primarily a product of the legislative process. The tax status of churches and other religious entities is, at its core, a status bestowed by federal and state statutes. Congress and the state legislatures should make the inherent trade-offs in taxing or exempting the church.

Prominent legal commentators tout the benefits of decentralized decision-making under our system of federalism.[3] According to Justice Brandeis' famous metaphor, the states serve as laboratories of experiment,[4] crafting different approaches to legal problems in light of local preferences and conditions. Public policymakers in the various states can make different trade-offs in light of the imperfect choices policymakers often confront.

As an empirical matter, the story which follows is in large measure an account of such federalism. As we shall see, the states' property and sales taxes treat sectarian

---

[3] *See, e.g.*, Heather K. Gerken, *Our Federalism(s)*, 53 WM. & MARY L. REV. 1549 (2012); Jeffrey S. Sutton, San Antonio Independent School District v. Rodriquez, *and Its Aftermath*, 94 VA. L. REV. 1963, 1984 (2008); Erwin Chemerinsky, *The Values of Federalism*, 47 FLA. L. REV. 499, 533–539 (1995); Larry Kramer, *Understanding Federalism*, 47 VAND. L. REV. 1485, 1500, 1511, 1513, 1514, 1521–1529, 1544–1545, 1556 (1994); Jenna Bednar & William N. Eskridge Jr., *Steadying the Court's "Unsteady Path": A Theory of Judicial Enforcement of Federalism*, 68 S. CAL. L. REV. 1447, 1467–1470 (1995).

[4] *New State Ice Co. v. Liebmann*, 285 U.S. 262, 311 (1932) (Brandeis, J., dissenting).

entities with a wide array of approaches. In a world of trade-offs and imperfect choices, this diversity is, as a normative matter, a strength of our federal system since multiple solutions emerging from state-by-state choices are often better than a single, uniform rule imposed nationally.

However, as we shall also see, in important instances, the Internal Revenue Code creates national norms which the states generally tend to follow when taxing or exempting the church. For example, every state emulates the Code by excusing from basic income taxation churches and other sectarian and secular eleemosynary entities—though eight states, reflecting the diversity which is the hallmark of federalism, disagree with the Code and do not tax the unrelated business incomes of such philanthropic entities.

The first four chapters of this book are empirical in nature, outlining the ways in which the federal and state governments tax and exempt the church and other religious institutions. The first chapter discusses the tax-related case law of the U.S. Supreme Court under the Establishment and Free Exercise Clauses of the First Amendment. This case law presages many of the themes of this book: The first of these themes is the significance of entanglement considerations in the taxation and exemption of religious entities and actors. Minimizing church-state entanglement should be a critical, often controlling, consideration in the decision to tax or exempt sectarian institutions. In practice, the minimization of entanglement helps to explain current patterns of taxing and exempting the church.

A second important lesson emerging from the Supreme Court's case law is the distinction between the enforcement-related entanglement which results from applying tax laws against sectarian entities and the borderline entanglement which flows from the need to police the boundaries of exemption. When it comes to taxing or exempting the church, there are no purely disentangling choices.

A third theme introduced by the Supreme Court's case law is the greater judicial willingness to accept the tax exemption of sectarian institutions and actors when exemption simultaneously extends to nonsectarian entities and individuals. A fourth teaching emerging from this case law is the often conclusory way in which the term "subsidy" is deployed to denounce tax exemptions. An exemption may serve a nonsubsidizing purpose and properly help to define the tax base.

The second chapter examines the states' respective constitutional provisions concerning churches and taxation. These state constitutional measures mandate property tax exemption for religious properties along with exemption for secular eleemosynary properties. However, there is important diversity within the states' constitutional consensus exempting sectarian properties. Some state constitutions exempt relatively narrowly, relieving from property taxation only "houses of worship." Other states define exempt property more broadly, extending constitutional tax immunity to any kind of "religious" property including, for example, sectarian summer camps sponsored by churches and parsonages in which clergy live. This state-by-state diversity in the tax treatment of religious persons and actors is an important theme of this book and an important strength of our federal system of taxation.

Chapter three examines the Internal Revenue Code's treatment of religious entities. The federal tax statute embodies three diverse approaches to taxing and exempting sectarian organizations and activities. Some provisions of the Code—the charitable deduction, the general income tax exemption for eleemosynary institutions, the federal unemployment tax—exempt religious entities along with other charitable, educational, and philanthropic institutions. Other provisions of the Code narrowly target churches for tax exemption. For example, the Code relieves churches of filing requirements with which nonchurch religious entities and other eleemosynary organizations must comply. Similarly, churches' retirement plans receive uniquely lenient treatment under the Code. Churches receive special procedural protections from IRS audits.

Yet other provisions of the Code tax churches just like secular entities. Churches generally pay the FICA taxes—the Social Security and Medicare payroll taxes—on the compensation paid to their nonclerical employees. These payroll taxes can be considerable. Churches also pay federal income taxes on their unrelated business incomes.

Chapter four completes the empirical portion of the book by examining the states' statutory approaches to taxing and exempting churches. Here too an important theme is diversity among different states and different taxes. Just as the Internal Revenue Code treats churches and sectarian entities diversely, the various states and their sundry taxes treat churches and other religious institutions diversely. Sometimes, churches and religious institutions are taxed like secular entities. In other contexts, sectarian entities and persons are tax-exempted along with secular eleemosynary institutions and actors. Yet other state tax provisions narrowly exempt churches and other religious organizations.

Chapter five begins the transition from empirical to normative concerns, explaining and evaluating the diverse pattern of taxing and exempting churches and other religious institutions. Entanglement concerns help to explain this diversity.

Chapter five identifies which taxes carry the greatest (and least) threat of church-state entanglement. Chapter five also discusses why entanglement should be an important—often controlling—consideration when deciding to tax or exempt religious institutions. Ultimately, either taxing or exempting churches and other sectarian entities involves entanglement. Taxing religious institutions enmeshes such institutions and the tax collector when the collector enforces the tax obligations of such institutions. Exempting sectarian entities entangles church and state at the borders of exemption, as individuals and entities claim exemption and as the tax collector polices such claims.

Central to this discussion are such generally accepted tax policy criteria as revenue, administrability, valuation concerns, taxpayer liquidity, public acceptability, and economic neutrality. The characterization of any tax exemption, exclusion, or deduction as a "subsidy" is only compelling in the context of these often conflicting criteria, none of which can be achieved in toto. The tax exemption of churches and other religious actors can serve the nonsubsidizing function of minimizing enforcement-related entanglement between church and state. If so, such exemption is not a subsidy but, rather, is a proper feature of a normative tax base.

On balance, the federal and state tax systems do a reasonable job of taxing churches where the possibilities for enforcement entanglement are least and of exempting churches where the prospects for enforcement-related entanglement are greatest. Our federal system of decentralized legislative decision-making works reasonably well to make the imperfect trade-offs inherent in taxing and exempting religious entities. However, as I discuss in the two chapters which follow, there is room for improvement in particular settings.

Chapter six revisits the tax status of parsonages and parsonage allowances. The tax treatment of parsonages and parsonage allowances is an important test case for many of the themes advanced in this book. Moreover, the tax status of clerical housing, in particular the income tax treatment of parsonages and parsonage allowances, will continue to be controversial in the years ahead.

Some states grant favorable property tax treatment to clerical residences, exempting them from taxation. Other states do not. The Internal Revenue Code excludes from ministers' gross incomes both the imputed rental value of parsonages provided in-kind and cash parsonage allowances. These income tax exclusions are constitutionally permitted, though not constitutionally compelled, to reduce church-state enforcement entanglement. Such minimization of church-state entanglement is a legitimately nonsubsidizing, secular purpose.

However, the Code's exclusion of cash housing allowances from ministers' incomes is not justified as a matter of tax policy. Such cash transactions are easily valued and give cash to the minister to pay income tax. Thus, considering the tax policy criteria of valuation and taxpayer liquidity, taxing cash parsonage allowances would entail less enforcement entanglement than would the taxation of housing provided to clergy in kind.

Chapter seven addresses another continuing controversy, the Internal Revenue Code's restrictions on the political activity of churches. Again, where others see a dichotomous choice framed in absolutist terms—keep churches out of politics, let the churches do whatever they want—I see contestable trade-offs among legitimate and competing values. Among the most important of these values is minimizing church-state entanglement. To advance this value, I propose a statutory safe harbor protecting churches' internal expressions of political sentiments. It is excessively entangling for the IRS and the state tax collectors to police speech on the pulpit or within a religious congregation.

In contrast, the ban on political activity by churches (and other tax-exempt entities) remains compelling when that activity is more resource-intensive, particularly when such activity is designed to reach beyond the membership of a particular congregation. Without such a ban, exempt institutions could be used to divert funds to political campaigns on a tax-deductible basis. The distinction between churches' internal expression and resource-diverting political activity is not without its interpretive problems—what important legal rule is not?—but it is a better trade-off among the competing values than is current law.

While the first part of chapter seven proposes to loosen an existing tax-related constraint on churches, the second part of that chapter identifies an area where additional taxation of churches is sensible: Sales taxes should apply more broadly to churches' purchases and sales since cash transactions carry less danger of church-state entanglement.

To those with an absolutist perspective, it undoubtedly seems paradoxical that I simultaneously seek to expand the sales tax liability of churches while I would afford greater protection from the tax collector for churches' internal expression. In conventional terms, it would be "anti-church" to enlarge churches' sales tax obligations, while it would be "pro-church" to protect the federal income tax exemptions of houses of worship which engage in internal political discussions. However, if (as I believe should be the case) entanglement considerations should be of critical importance, it is compelling to reduce the enforcement entanglement inherent in the IRS's policing of church deliberations while at the same time enlarging churches' obligations to collect and pay under the less entangling sales tax.

The eighth and final chapter places my analysis in the context of the extended scholarly debates about the First Amendment and the proper tax treatment of nonprofit entities. These debates include four constitutional controversies: the original understanding of the First Amendment, the relative merits of judicial and legislative decision-making in exempting churches from laws of general applicability, the criteria which should govern legislative exemptions from laws of general applicability, and the rhetoric of separationism under the First Amendment. In addition, I place my analysis in the context of two important tax policy controversies: the possible income taxation of nonprofit institutions and the future of the unrelated business income tax (UBIT). I address each of these debates in the context of taxing and exempting churches. The underlying theme of this final chapter is that discussion both of the First Amendment and of tax policy would be enhanced by greater attention to the considerations at play when taxing or exempting churches and to the various policies which Congress and the state legislatures have embraced in response to these considerations.

Even if the reader disagrees with some or all of my particular conclusions about current law or my prescriptions for the future, I hope that, by the end of this book, the reader will have been persuaded of the book's general themes: Churches and other religious institutions are treated diversely by the federal and state tax systems. Sectarian institutions pay more tax than many believe. In important respects, the states differ among themselves in their respective approaches to the taxation of sectarian entities. Either taxing or exempting churches and other sectarian entities entangles church and state. The taxes to which churches are more frequently subject—federal Social Security and Medicare taxes, sales taxes, real estate conveyance taxes—fall on the less entangling end of the spectrum. The taxes from which religious institutions are exempt—general income taxes, value-based property taxes, unemployment taxes—are typically taxes with the greatest potential for church-state enforcement entanglement. It is unpersuasive to reflexively denounce the tax exemption of religious actors and institutions as a subsidy. Tax exemption can implement the secular, nonsubsidizing goal of minimizing church-state enforcement entanglement and thus be regarded as part of a normative tax base.

Taxing the church or exempting the church involves often difficult trade-offs among competing and legitimate values. On balance, our federal system of decentralized legislation makes these legal and tax policy trade-offs reasonably, though there is room for improvement in particular settings.

1

THE FEDERAL CONSTITUTIONAL LAW ON TAXATION AND RELIGION

IN THIS CHAPTER, I explore the First Amendment decisions of the U.S. Supreme Court concerning taxes. In seven cases, the Court has grappled with the First Amendment implications of state and local taxes for religious entities and actors. Only once in its history has the U.S. Supreme Court confronted the First Amendment status of a federal tax. These Supreme Court decisions presage four themes of this book: the importance of entanglement considerations when deciding to tax or exempt the church, the distinction between enforcement entanglement and borderline entanglement, the greater judicial willingness to accept the tax exemption of sectarian institutions and actors when exemption simultaneously extends to nonsectarian entities and individuals, and the often conclusory way in which the term "subsidy" is deployed to denounce tax exemptions. The tax exemption of religious persons may serve the nonsubsidizing purpose of minimizing church-state enforcement entanglement and thereby properly define the tax base.

A. *MURDOCK* AND *FOLLETT*

In 1791, along with the rest of the Bill of Rights, the Establishment and Free Exercise Clauses of the First Amendment became part of the U.S. Constitution: "Congress shall make no law respecting an establishment of religion, or prohibiting the free exercise thereof . . ." Over a century and a half passed before the U.S. Supreme Court confronted the tax implications of the First Amendment in *Murdock v. Pennsylvania*[1] and *Follett v. Town of McCormick*.[2]

The Court's decisions in *Murdock* and *Follett*, like several of the Court's latter opinions on religion and taxation, split the Court. Besides indicating divisions which recur in judicial decisions in this area, *Murdock* and *Follett* identified key questions confronting the courts, policymakers, and commentators: Does the tax exemption of religious institutions and activity improperly subsidize the sectarian or is such exemption appropriate to avoid church-state entanglement? Must tax exemptions for religious entities and actors be part of broader exemptions for other eleemosynary institutions or may tax exemptions be fashioned more narrowly only for sectarian institutions and activity? Should the courts carve First Amendment exemptions from laws of general applicability?

Murdock and *Follett* were both decided 5–4, and both involved municipal ordinances imposing flat licensing fees on persons selling goods and merchandise in the community. As the dissenters pointed out, the challenged fees applied to all persons and were not proved to be excessive in amount.[3] Nevertheless, the *Murdock* Court held, in an opinion by Justice Douglas, that the First Amendment's Free Exercise Clause required exemption from these generally applicable local licensing fees for Jehovah's Witnesses' canvassing activities.

According to the Court's five-justice majority, the licensing fees imposed by the challenged ordinance imposed unacceptably intrusive burdens on the exercise of the religious rights of the Jehovah's Witnesses. It does not matter, for First Amendment purposes, that comparable burdens are imposed on commercial solicitation activity: "The constitutional rights of those spreading their religious beliefs through the spoken and printed word are not to be gauged by standards governing retailers or wholesalers of books."[4]

While "religious groups and the press" can be taxed to defray the costs of government, the flat license fee imposed constitutionally unacceptable burdens directly on the exercise of the Jehovah's Witnesses' First Amendment right to canvass: "It is one thing to impose a tax on the income or property of a preacher. It is quite another thing to exact a tax from him for the privilege of delivering a sermon."[5]

---

[1] 319 U.S. 105 (1943).

[2] 321 U.S. 573 (1944).

[3] *See Murdock*, 319 U.S. at 118 (Reed, J., dissenting).

[4] *Id.* at 111.

[5] *Id.* at 112.

The *Murdock* minority would have none of this. The challenged ordinance, they contended, imposed "nondiscriminatory, nonexcessive taxation."[6] The *Murdock* majority thus created "a tax subsidy" by holding the Jehovah's Witnesses immune from the solicitation fees imposed by the challenged municipal ordinance.[7]

A year later, *Follett* confirmed the Court's division. A majority concluded again that the First Amendment exempted Jehovah's Witnesses' religious solicitors from a municipality's flat license fee. The majority further denied that this conclusion "mean[s] that religious undertakings must be subsidized" or that religious groups and actors cannot be subject to taxation: "But to say that they, like other citizens, may be subject to general taxation does not mean that they can be required to pay a tax for the exercise of that which the First Amendment has made a high constitutional privilege."[8]

Concurring with Justice Douglas's opinion for the *Follett* Court, Justice Murphy took particular aim at the minority's claim "that the effect of our decision is to subsidize religion."[9] "[T]his is merely a harsh way of saying that to prohibit the taxation of religious activities is to give substance to the constitutional right of religious freedom."[10]

The Court's minority remained unconvinced. The challenged license fee was neither "discriminatory" nor "onerous."[11] As a result of the majority's decision exempting him from the municipal license fee, Mr. "Follett will enjoy a subsidy for his religion."[12]

Murdock and *Follett* identify fundamental questions raised by the choice to tax or exempt religious institutions and actors: Is tax exemption necessarily a subsidy? When (if ever) is exemption appropriate for nonsubsidizing purposes? As I discuss further in chapter five,[13] the label "tax subsidy" is often deployed problematically. It is only compelling to declare a tax exemption a subsidy after identifying the normative tax base from which such exemption is a departure. There is no subsidy if the activity excluded from taxation should not have been taxed in the first place.

The opinions of the *Murdock/Follett* minority further suggest why the Court's subsequent case law often focuses upon the simultaneous extension *vel non* of tax benefits to secular as well as religious institutions. If exemptions, exclusions, or deductions do constitute subsidies, subsidies restricted to religious entities and activities raise troubling Establishment Clause issues. Many would view a subsidy underwriting

---

[6] *Id.* at 121 (Reed, J., dissenting).

[7] *Id.* at 130.

[8] *Id.* at 578.

[9] *Id.* at 579 (Murphy, J., concurring).

[10] *Id.* at 579.

[11] *Id.* at 579–580 (Roberts, J., dissenting).

[12] *Id.* at 581.

[13] *See infra* at 148–152.

only religious activity as the paradigmatic target at which the Establishment Clause of the First Amendment is aimed. If, on the other hand, tax provisions characterized as subsidies extend to broad categories of nonprofit institutions, it is arguably not religion as such being subsidized, but eleemosynary activity more generally.

A final issue presaged in *Murdock* and *Follett* is whether the courts should carve First Amendment exceptions from laws of general applicability, an issue which remains contentious.[14]

B. *WALZ*

A generation later, in *Walz v. Commissioner*,[15] the U.S. Supreme Court confronted the First Amendment's implications for the property tax exemption of religious entities. While *Murdock* and *Follett* divided the Court, *Walz,* upholding New York's tax exemption for religious properties, was an 8–1 decision. However, the Court's near unanimity as to result did not reflect unanimity as to reasoning as two of the eight justices sustained the New York exemption on grounds different from those of their colleagues. Indeed, some justices participating in subsequent decisions have treated these concurrences, not the *Walz* majority opinion, as the controlling statement of the Court's jurisprudence in this area.

Writing for six members of the *Walz* majority, Chief Justice Burger upheld New York's real property tax exemption for religious institutions in terms of entanglement and accommodation. The goal of the Court's First Amendment jurisprudence, Chief Justice Burger wrote, is to find a path between the Establishment and Free Exercise Clauses "to avoid excessive entanglement" of government and religious institutions,[16] thereby "preventing the kind of involvement that would tip the balance toward government control of churches or government restraint on religious practice."[17] Given a constitutionally based concern with "the autonomy and freedom of religious bodies,"[18] it is plausible for New York and other states to determine that such bodies "should not be inhibited in their activities by property taxation or the hazard of loss of those properties for nonpayment of taxes."[19]

> Grants of exemption historically reflect the concern of authors of constitutions and statutes as to the latent dangers inherent in the imposition of property

[14] *See infra* at 223–229.

[15] 397 U.S. 664 (1970).

[16] *Walz*, 397 U.S. at 670.

[17] *Id.*

[18] *Id.* at 672.

[19] *Id.*

> taxes; exemption constitutes a reasonable and balanced attempt to guard against those dangers. . . .[20]
>
> Elimination of exemption would tend to expand the involvement of government by giving rise to tax valuation of church property, tax liens, tax foreclosures, and the direct confrontations and conflicts that follow in the train of those legal processes. . . .[21]
>
> The hazards of churches supporting government are hardly less in their potential than the hazards of government supporting churches. . . .[22]
>
> The exemption creates only a minimal and remote involvement between church and state and far less than taxation of churches. It restricts the fiscal relationship between church and state, and tends to complement and reinforce the desired separation insulating each from the other.[23]

There is an important distinction between the *Murdock/Follett* version of First Amendment doctrine articulated by Justice Douglas and the entanglement jurisprudence enunciated by Chief Justice Burger in *Walz*. In *Murdock* and *Follett*, the Court held tax exemption to be constitutionally required. This represents First Amendment concerns in their strongest possible form: Exemption is constitutionally compelled from a law of general applicability to separate church and state. In contrast, the *Walz* Court held tax exemption to be constitutionally "permissible state accommodation" of religious institutions, allowed but not required.[24]

While entanglement concerns constitute the crux of Chief Justice Burger's *Walz* opinion, the opinion expounds two subthemes, both of which have also become central to the question of taxing sectarian entities. First, Chief Justice Burger placed New York's exemption for religious institutions within the context of the Empire State's simultaneous exemption of the real property of secular eleemosynary institutions, "a broad class of property owned by nonprofit, quasi-public corporations which include hospitals, libraries, playgrounds, scientific, professional, historical, and patriotic groups."[25] New York thus does not exempt "churches as such."[26] Rather, New York "has an affirmative policy that considers these groups as beneficial and stabilizing influences in community life and finds this classification useful, desirable, and in the public interest."[27]

---

[20] *Id.* at 673.

[21] *Id.* at 674.

[22] *Id.* at 675.

[23] *Id.* at 676.

[24] *Id.* at 673.

[25] *Id.*

[26] *Id.*

[27] *Id.*

These observations do not fit comfortably with the entanglement/accommodation theory at the core of the Chief Justice's *Walz* opinion. There is, after all, no First Amendment restraint on government involvement with hospitals or playgrounds.

It is, accordingly, tempting to dismiss these observations as *dicta*. However, it is more compelling to read these comments as reflecting greater judicial acceptance of tax exemptions for churches and other religious institutions when exemption simultaneously extends as well to secular philanthropic activities and entities. It is also more persuasive to read the Chief Justice's observations as an answer to Justice Douglas's *Walz* dissent.[28] Justice Douglas indicted the New York property tax exemption as a subsidy. If there is a subsidy, Chief Justice Burger replied for the majority, it is not a subsidy of religion "as such" but a subsidy of eleemosynary activity more generally.

A second subtheme of the Chief Justice's *Walz* opinion is the legislative discretion to determine tax classifications. In *Gibbons v. District of Columbia*, the U.S. Supreme Court in 1886 confronted a federal statute for the District of Columbia which limited tax exemption to church buildings and the land underlying such buildings.[29] On the basis of this statute, the *Gibbons* Court denied exemption to church-owned property which had been left vacant in anticipation of it becoming income-producing.[30] In *Walz*, Chief Justice Burger quoted from the *Gibbons* decision:

> In the exercise of this (taxing) power, Congress, like any State legislature unrestricted by constitutional provisions, may at its discretion wholly exempt certain classes of property from taxation, or may tax them at a lower rate than other property.[31]

Chief Justice Burger cited this passage from *Gibbons* to demonstrate that the Court at that earlier time implicitly accepted the constitutionality of tax exemptions for religious institutions.[32] This reading is fair as far as it goes. However, the passage from *Gibbons* implies more than this: Congress "may at its discretion" tax certain properties at lower rates and may wholly exempt from taxation other kinds of properties.[33]

Read in the context of the original *Gibbons* opinion, this statement is consistent with the claim that legislatures possess great latitude in defining tax bases. That

---

[28] *Id.* at 700 (Douglas, J., dissenting).

[29] 116 U.S. 404 (1886).

[30] *Id.* at 408.

[31] *Walz*, 397 U.S. at 679–680 (quoting *Gibbons*, 116 U.S. at 408). The parenthetical was added to the language of *Gibbons* by the Chief Justice.

[32] *Id.* at 680.

[33] *Id.* at 679–680.

"discretion," in turn, suggests the challenge inherent in identifying normative tax bases and the consequent difficulty proclaiming any particular exclusion, exemption, or deduction as subsidizing rather than base-defining: There is no subsidy until there is a generally accepted normative base from which such exclusion, exemption, or deduction deviates. Since, however, legislatures have great discretion when defining tax bases, it is often problematic to label a tax provision as a subsidy rather than as a legitimate legislative decision to tax some persons and activities but not others. Moreover, since the definition of a tax base is primarily a legislative task, those seeking exemptions should primarily pursue such exemptions in the legislative process rather than in the courts.

Justice Brennan's concurrence in *Walz*, while supporting the majority's result, does not embrace its entanglement/accommodationist reasoning. Rather, Justice Brennan's opinion focuses upon the broad range of secular institutions and activities receiving the New York property tax exemption. Indeed, there is a straight line from Justice Brennan's *Walz* concurrence, supporting tax exemption for churches as part of a broad exemption for sectarian and secular eleemosynary property, to Justice Brennan's opinion two decades later for the *Texas Monthly* plurality, rejecting a sales tax exemption limited to religious publications.[34]

While Justice Brennan opined that "tax exemptions and general subsidies . . . are qualitatively different" from one another, his doctrinal support for the property tax exemption of religious property ultimately rests on subsidy grounds.[35] New York's exemption of church properties serves the secular purpose of encouraging churches'

> public service activities and of a pluralistic society. During their ordinary operations, most churches engage in activities of a secular nature that benefit the community; and all churches by their existence contribute to the diversity of association, viewpoint, and enterprise so highly valued by all of us.[36]

It was critical to Justice Brennan that this exemption covers both the properties of secular institutions and the properties in which churches conduct secular activities:

> These [religious] organizations are exempted because they, among a range of other private, nonprofit organizations contribute to the well-being of the community in a variety of nonreligious ways, and thereby bear burdens that would otherwise either have to be met by general taxation, or be left undone, to the

[34] *Texas Monthly v. Bullock*, 489 U.S. 1 (1989).
[35] *Walz*, 397 U.S. at 690.
[36] *Id.* at 692–693.

> detriment of the community. . . .[37] Government may properly include religious institutions among the variety of private, nonprofit groups that receive tax exemptions, for each group contributes to the diversity of association, viewpoint, and enterprise essential to a vigorous, pluralistic society.[38]

It is thus not surprising that, when *Texas Monthly* confronted the Court two decades later with a sales tax exemption limited to religious publications, Justice Brennan found that narrow exemption distinguishable from the broad exemption at issue in *Walz*.

Justice Harlan's *Walz* concurrence endorses Justice Brennan's emphasis on the breadth of the New York exemption.[39] Justice Harlan linked that breadth with entanglement concerns, concluding that there is less entanglement danger when an exemption is broad:

> In the instant case noninvolvement is further assured by the neutrality and breadth of the exemption. In the context of an exemption so sweeping as the one before us here its administration need not entangle government in difficult classifications of what is or is not religious, for any organization—although not religious in a customary sense—would qualify under the pervasive rubric of a group dedicated to the moral and cultural improvement of men. Obviously the more discriminating and complicated the basis of classification for an exemption—even a neutral one—the greater the potential for state involvement in evaluating the character of the organizations.[40]

Justice Harlan thus focused on the potential for entanglement at the borderlines of tax exemption, as different entities seek classification as religious institutions and the tax collector must police whether an entity claiming exemption is religious or not. I propose to call this borderline entanglement. This form of entanglement is minimized when (as is the case with New York's property tax exemption) the exemption also extends to nonreligious eleemosynary institutions. When that is the case, classification of an entity as religious *vel non* can often be avoided by categorizing that entity instead as a cultural, philanthropic, or educational institution and thus exempt on that alternative, secular basis.

---

[37] *Id.* at 687.

[38] *Id.* at 689.

[39] *Id.* at 697 (Harlan, J., concurring).

[40] *Id.* at 698–699.

In contrast, the concern of the *Follett, Murdock*, and *Walz* majorities is what I would denominate as enforcement entanglement, the enmeshment of church and state which results when government imposes and collects taxes from religious institutions and actors. These majority opinions focus upon the autonomy of religious organizations and actors and the need to protect such sectarian entities and personnel from taxation to avoid governmental intrusion upon their resources and autonomy. *Murdock* and *Follett* represent First Amendment concerns in their strongest form, compelling government to grant tax exemption to protect the autonomy of religious organizations and actors. In contrast, under *Walz*'s permissive/accommodationist approach, the state has latitude to grant tax exemption to religious persons because such exemption is understood as recognizing sectarian autonomy, protected by the First Amendment. However, the state is not required to exempt to avoid tax-related enforcement entanglement.

Justice Douglas, the author of *Murdock* and *Follett*, was the dissenter in *Walz*. Three aspects of Justice Douglas' *Walz* opinion are noteworthy. First, Justice Douglas based his dissent on the theory that "[a] tax exemption is a subsidy":[41] "I would suppose that in common understanding one of the best ways to 'establish' one or more religions is to subsidize them, which a tax exemption does."[42] Justice Brennan would later reprise this theme in *Texas Monthly*.[43]

Second, Justice Douglas rejected the contention, accepted by Justices Harlan and Brennan, that the subsidization of religious entities is constitutionally permissible when it is part of the broader subsidization of secular nonprofits:

> Government could provide or finance operas, hospitals, historical societies, and all the rest because they represent social welfare programs within the reach of the police power. In contrast, government may not provide or finance worship because of the Establishment Clause any more than it may single out "atheistic" or "agnostic" centers or groups and create or finance them.[44]

Finally, Justice Douglas not surprisingly felt compelled to reconcile his majority opinions in *Murdock* and *Follett* with his subsequent constitutional condemnation of New York's property tax exemption in *Walz*. *Murdock*, Justice Douglas noted, distinguished between a constitutionally forbidden tax imposed directly on

[41] *Id.* at 704 (Douglas, J., dissenting).

[42] *Id.*

[43] 489 U.S. 1 (1989).

[44] *Walz*, 397 U.S. at 708–709 (Douglas, J., dissenting).

religious activity and a constitutionally acceptable levy imposed on the income of religious actors or on the "property used or employed in connection with those activities."[45]

However, this observation, accurate as far as it goes, does not fully address the tension between, on the one hand, the exemption-as-subsidy argument embraced by Justice Douglas in *Walz* ("[a] tax exemption is a subsidy"[46]) and, on the other hand, the rejection of the subsidy label in *Murdock* and *Follett* (*Murdock* and *Follett* do not "mean that religious undertakings must be subsidized"[47]).

Walz plays an important role in this book as a seminal judicial statement warning about the possible dangers of "excessive entanglement"[48] when churches and other religious institutions are taxed. *Walz* also helps to distinguish between the enforcement-related entanglement which concerned Chief Justice Burger and the borderline entanglement which concerned Justice Harlan. *Walz* signals as well greater judicial acceptance of tax exemption for religious institutions and persons when exemption simultaneously extends to secular entities.

C. *TEXAS MONTHLY*

The divisions manifested in *Murdock, Follett*, and *Walz* reappeared in *Texas Monthly v. Bullock*.[49] Like *Walz, Texas Monthly* produced four separate opinions. However, unlike *Walz*, in *Texas Monthly*, no single opinion garnered the support of more than three justices. Quite aptly, Judge Noonan has labeled *Texas Monthly* an "enigma."[50]

Texas Monthly involved a Texas sales tax statute which applied to all secular publications but not to religious literature. In a plurality opinion joined by Justices Marshall and Stevens, Justice Brennan found this narrow sales tax exemption for religious publications distinguishable from the broad property tax exemption upheld in *Walz*. Hence, the Texas sales tax statute violated the Establishment Clause.

The central focus of Justice Brennan's *Texas Monthly* opinion is the same as the focus of his *Walz* concurrence: the breadth of the tax exemption. According to Justice Brennan, in *Walz*, it was critical that the property tax exemption sustained

[45] *Id.* at 707 (quoting *Murdock*, 319 U.S. at 112).
[46] *Id.* at 704.
[47] *Follett*, 321 U.S. at 577–578.
[48] *Walz*, 397 U.S. at 670.
[49] 489 U.S. 1 (1989).
[50] John T. Noonan Jr., The Lustre of Our Country: the American Experience of Religious Freedom 195 (2000).

by the Court excludes from taxation "real estate owned by a wide array of nonprofit organizations."[51]

> The breadth of New York's property tax exemption was essential to our holding that it was "not aimed at establishing, sponsoring, or supporting religion," but rather possessed the legitimate secular purpose and effect of contributing to the community's moral and intellectual diversity and encouraging private groups to undertake projects that advanced the community's well-being and that would otherwise have to be funded by tax revenues or left undone.[52]

As a summary of Justice Brennan's *Walz* concurrence, as well as Justice Harlan's separate opinion, this characterization is accurate. It is, however, not a convincing portrayal of Chief Justice Burger's majority opinion for himself and five of his colleagues, an entanglement-focused opinion which concentrates upon "the autonomy and freedom of religious bodies" and which only addresses the breadth of the New York exemption as a secondary theme.[53]

Justice Brennan's emphasis upon the broad reach of the New York property tax exemption, and the contrasting narrowness of the Texas sales tax exemption, is understandable in light of his other critical move in *Texas Monthly*: "Every tax exemption constitutes a subsidy."[54] It is a short step from this premise to the conclusion that "Texas' narrow exemption"[55] for sales of religious literature violates the Establishment Clause as a forbidden government subsidy of religion.

In assessing the Texas sales tax exemption at issue in *Texas Monthly*, it is critical which (if any) variant of entanglement doctrine applies. The *Murdock/Follett* rendition of entanglement theory indicates that Texas' sales tax exemption for religious literature is constitutionally mandated since religious actors cannot "be required to pay a tax for the exercise of that which the First Amendment has made a high constitutional privilege."[56] Justice Burger's accommodationist version of entanglement doctrine indicates that this exemption, while not required by the First Amendment, is constitutionally permitted "to avoid excessive entanglement" of government and religious institutions when such institutions pay tax and the government enforces the tax.[57] Justice Harlan's formulation of entanglement theory indicates that Texas's

---

[51] *Texas Monthly*, 489 U.S. at 11.

[52] *Id.* at 12 (internal citation omitted).

[53] *Walz*, 397 U.S. at 672.

[54] *Texas Monthly*, 489 U.S. at 14.

[55] *Id.* at 15.

[56] *Follett*, 321 U.S. at 578.

[57] *Walz*, 397 U.S. at 670.

narrow sales tax exemption is constitutionally forbidden as, at the borders of such exemption, the state must "evaluat[e] the character of the organizations" claiming the exemption to determine if such organizations are religious or not.[58] Justice Brennan, and his two colleagues who constituted the *Texas Monthly* plurality, opted for Justice Harlan's approach.

To nudge aside *Murdock, Follett,* and their strong form of entanglement theory, Justice Brennan in *Texas Monthly* deployed a dual strategy: to "disavow" parts of *Murdock* and *Follett* and to cabin what is subsequently left of those opinions into the particular factual circumstances of those cases.[59] The plurality's outcome in *Texas Monthly* is, Justice Brennan acknowledged, "admittedly in tension with some unnecessarily sweeping statements in" *Murdock* and *Follett*.[60] Indeed. The *Murdock* Court declared: "The constitutional rights of those spreading their religious beliefs through the spoken and printed word are not to be gauged by standards governing retailers or wholesalers of books."[61]

For the *Texas Monthly* plurality, precisely the opposite is true: Differential sales tax treatment for religious and nonreligious publications unacceptably subsidizes religion. Hence, to the extent *Murdock* and *Follett* say otherwise, Justice Brennan and his colleagues "disavowed" those opinions.[62]

Since Justice Brennan and his two colleagues did not overrule *Murdock* and *Follett*[63] (but just "disavowed" those opinions' "unnecessarily sweeping statements"), they sought to distinguish *Murdock* and *Follett* from *Texas Monthly* by emphasizing three aspects of the municipal license fees successfully challenged in those earlier cases. First, the local fees challenged in those cases were "occupation tax[es]" unlike the sales tax at issue in *Texas Monthly*.[64] Second, the *Murdock/Follett* municipal fees were "flat"[65] levies which imposed upon religious canvassers burdens "far from negligible."[66] Finally, the municipal taxes imposed in *Murdock* and *Follett* "restrain[ed] in advance"[67] by requiring payment before the Jehovah's Witnesses engaged in religious solicitation.

Little of this is persuasive. Why is it constitutionally relevant that the *Murdock/Follett* fees were labeled license fees on the occupation of soliciting while the Texas

---

[58] *Id.* at 699 (Harlan, J., concurring).

[59] *Texas Monthly*, 489 U.S. at 21.

[60] *Id.*

[61] *Murdock*, 319 U.S. at 111.

[62] *Texas Monthly*, 489 U.S. at 21.

[63] Indeed, it is unclear what it would mean for a three-justice plurality to overrule prior precedent.

[64] *Texas Monthly*, 489 U.S. at 22, 24.

[65] *Id.*

[66] *Id.* at 23.

[67] *Id.* at 24 (quoting *Murdock*, 319 U.S. at 114).

levy is denominated as a sales tax? Justice Brennan never explains why this formalistic distinction is relevant. The economic incidence of the two levies is the same. To the extent the taxes are passed onto purchasers, both increase the final price of religious materials. To the extent the taxes are absorbed by the sellers, both levies discourage the purveyors of religious materials. As a substantive matter, it makes no difference whether the tax is styled as an occupational fee on solicitation or as a sales tax.

It, moreover, rewrites *Murdock* and *Follett* to characterize the burdens imposed by the municipal ordinances as "far from negligible."[68] The *Murdock/Follett* dissenters consistently noted the absence of evidence that the challenged municipal license fees were onerous; the Court's majority never disagreed. It thus revises the story of *Murdock* and *Follett* to suggest that the Court invalidated the municipal fees as economically burdensome.

It is, finally, true that the license fees imposed in *Murdock* and *Follett* were payable prior to solicitation while the Texas tax was collected after the sale occurred when the seller had cash with which to pay the tax. From a cash flow perspective, a tax collected earlier, prior to the event giving rise to taxpayer liquidity, is tougher on the taxpayer than is a tax collected later, when the taxpayer has the cash with which to pay. It is, however, difficult to see that the broad constitutional assertions of *Murdock* and *Follett* come, in the final analysis, down to this.

In short, Justice Brennan's approach to *Murdock* and *Follett* is unpersuasive. However, by rejecting the *Murdock/Follett* version of First Amendment doctrine in its strong form, Justice Brennan set the groundwork for his embrace of the borderline version of entanglement theory exemplified by Justice Harlan's *Walz* concurrence. Under that theory, Texas' narrow exemption of religious publications from sales taxation "produce[s] greater state entanglement with religion than the denial of an exemption."[69] When a seller claimed eligibility for the restricted Texas sales tax exemption, the state was required to determine the borders of that exemption to see if the seller qualified as religious. Such an eligibility determination will enmesh the state in conflict with groups claiming the exemption.[70]

As the *Texas Monthly* dissenters noted,[71] Chief Justice Burger's *Walz* opinion offers an alternative view of entanglement, one which justifies a narrow tax exemption as accommodating the autonomy of religious actors. The *Texas Monthly* plurality assumes the answer to the critical question of that case, that is, whether a narrow

---

[68] *Id.* at 23.

[69] *Id.* at 20.

[70] *Id.* at 21.

[71] *Id.* at 29–45 (Scalia, J., dissenting).

tax exemption restricted to religious entities causes more entanglement (because of the need to define the exemption's borders) or less entanglement (because the state respects the autonomy of the religious entity by not enforcing the tax against it).

Embracing the borderline version of entanglement doctrine, Justice Brennan and his two colleagues reason that tax exclusions, deductions, and exemptions for religious institutions are, as a constitutional matter, dependent upon the extension of the same exclusions, deductions, and exemptions to secular entities. From this vantage, narrow exemptions limited to religious bodies and undertakings enmesh government and sectarian institutions in constitutionally unacceptable conflict over boundary definitions. This vantage also reflects the greater judicial acceptance of tax exemptions for churches and other sectarian entities when exemption simultaneously extends to secular institutions as well.

Justice White concurred in striking the Texas sales tax exemption, relying solely on the Press Clause of the First Amendment.[72] Hence, the critical fifth and sixth votes against the Texas exemption came from Justices Blackmun and O'Connor.

Writing for them both, Justice Blackmun was uncomfortable with the plurality's approach to *Follett* and *Murdock*. Ultimately, however, Justice Blackmun's concurrence comes to the same result as does Justice Brennan's plurality opinion: a narrow sales tax exemption restricted to religious publications violates the Establishment Clause; a broader exemption, for a larger class including religious literature, passes constitutional muster.

On the one hand, the *Texas Monthly* plurality, according to Justice Blackmun, unnecessarily "repudiat[ed] *Follett* and *Murdock*,"[73] both "longstanding precedents."[74] But "a tax exemption *limited to* the sale of religious literature by religious organizations violates the Establishment Clause."[75]

For Justice Blackmun, *Follett* and *Murdock* might be reconciled with an Establishment Clause prohibition on state sales taxes "exempting religious literature alone."[76] While the task of such reconciliation "may be left for another day,"[77] Justice Blackmun hinted that states must exempt religious literature from sales taxation but must also structure their sales tax exemptions broadly to include significant non-religious publications as well. Here, again, we see greater judicial receptivity to tax exemptions for religious institutions and actors when such exemptions accompany equivalent exemptions for secular eleemosynary entities.

---

72 *Id.* at 25 (White, J., concurring).

73 *Id.* at 27 (Blackmun, J., concurring).

74 *Id.*

75 *Id.* at 28 (emphasis in original).

76 *Id.* at 29.

77 *Id.* at 28.

In *Texas Monthly*, Justice Scalia dissented for himself, Chief Justice Rehnquist, and Justice Kennedy and denounced the opinions of Justices Brennan and Blackmun "as a judicial demolition project"[78] which invalidated not just the sales tax exemption at issue in *Texas Monthly* but a variety of narrow tax benefits which apply only to religious actors and activities. Such limited tax benefits "permeate the state and federal codes," including the federal income tax exclusion for parsonages and parsonage allowances.[79]

Citing *Walz* as an exemplar of the "accommodation principle,"[80] Justice Scalia correctly observed that Justice Brennan had conflated his and Justice Harlan's *Walz* concurrences with Chief Justice Burger's majority opinion.[81] While that majority opinion had noted the breadth of the New York property tax exemption, that breadth was not critical to the majority's reasoning.[82] Rather, the central theme of *Walz* was the "accommodation principle":[83] "The [*Walz*] Court did not approve an exemption for charities that happened to benefit religion; it approved an exemption for religion *as* an exemption for religion."[84]

Moreover, the Texas sales tax exemption, like the New York property tax exemption, reduces entanglement:

> [H]ere as in *Walz*, it is all but certain that elimination of the exemption will have the effect of *increasing* government's involvement with religion. The Court's invalidation of [the sales tax exemption] ensures that Texas churches selling publications that promulgate their religion will now be subject to numerous statutory and regulatory impositions, including audits, requirements for the filing of security, reporting requirements, writs of attachment without bond, tax liens, and the seizure and sale of property to satisfy tax delinquencies.[85]

Thus, concern about enforcement entanglement led Justice Scalia and his colleagues to condone tax exemptions restricted to religious institutions and actors. Such exemptions properly recognize the autonomy of religious institutions and do not depend upon the simultaneous exemption of secular entities and activities. Hence, the dissenters concluded, tax exemptions minimizing church-state enforcement

---

[78] *Id.* at 29 (Scalia, J., dissenting).
[79] *Id.* at 33.
[80] *Id.* at 39.
[81] *Id.* at 33.
[82] *Id.* at 36–37.
[83] *Id.* at 39–42.
[84] *Id.* at 38 (emphasis in original).
[85] *Id.* at 44 (emphasis in original; internal citations omitted).

entanglement are constitutional when limited to religious groups as was the Texas sales tax exemption.

The *Texas Monthly* dissenters also found greater force in *Follett* and *Murdock* than did Justice Brennan. *Follett* and *Murdock* "are narrowly distinguishable,"[86] wrote Justice Scalia. However, the Texas sales tax "exemption comes so close to being a constitutionally required accommodation, there is no doubt that it is at least a permissible one."[87]

In short, for the *Texas Monthly* dissenters, *Follett, Murdock*, and the "accommodation principle" articulated by Chief Justice Burger in *Walz* indicate that the Texas sales tax exemption for religious literature is, as a First Amendment matter, "not only permissible but perhaps required."[88]

Like *Walz, Texas Monthly* plays an important role in this book as we explore the issue of tax-related entanglement between church and state, the distinction between enforcement entanglement and borderline entanglement, the characterization *vel non* of exemptions as subsidies, and the greater judicial acceptance of tax exemptions when secular, as well as religious, persons are also exempted.

D. *JIMMY SWAGGART MINISTRIES*

Judge Noonan has characterized *Texas Monthly* as marking the end of the Supreme Court's "*Murdock* mind."[89] Perhaps so. But in *Texas Monthly*, two concurring justices struggled with the scope of the *Murdock/Follett* principle while the three dissenters professed their adherence to those earlier decisions.

It is therefore striking that the Court's subsequent decision in *Jimmy Swaggart Ministries v. Board of Equalization*[90] resulted in a single unanimous opinion which discounted *Murdock* and *Follett*, and which followed Justice Brennan's opinions in *Walz* and *Texas Monthly* as the Court's controlling doctrine.

California's sales tax statute requires churches and other religious entities in the Golden State to pay and collect taxes on retail sales.[91] This kind of sales taxation, discussed in chapter four,[92] belies the simple narrative that churches are not taxed. Jimmy Swaggart Ministries sold religious merchandise in California and

---

[86] *Id.* at 41.
[87] *Id.* at 42.
[88] *Id.* at 31.
[89] NOONAN, *supra* note 50, at 193.
[90] 493 U.S. 378 (1990).
[91] Cal. State Bd. of Equalization, Pub. 18, *Nonprofit Organizations* 5 (2016).
[92] *See infra* at 79–81.

claimed a constitutional right to sales tax exemption per *Murdock* and *Follett*. Justice O'Connor, writing for a unanimous Court, rejected this claim to constitutional exemption from California's sales tax.

Justice O'Connor, echoing Justice Brennan's *Texas Monthly* opinion, distinguished the California sales tax from the municipal license fees at issue in *Murdock* and *Follett* as the latter were flat and were paid before solicitation could occur.[93] In *Murdock* and *Follett*, Justice O'Connor wrote, the "primary vice of the ordinances at issue was that they operated as prior restraints of constitutionally protected conduct," that is, the right of the Jehovah's Witnesses to engage in religious solicitation without first paying a municipal license fee.[94] Such fees "acted as a *precondition* to the free exercise of religious beliefs" unlike the California sales tax, collected after a sale has occurred.[95] Moreover, the California sales tax is calibrated to the quantum of the taxpayer's sales; indeed, the tax "represents only a small fraction of any retail sale."[96]

In short, in *Follett* and *Murdock*, it was "the particular nature of the challenged taxes" which violated the Free Exercise Clause as these were "flat license taxes that operated as a prior restraint on the exercise of religious liberty."[97]

Justice O'Connor also concluded that the California sales tax, applied to Jimmy Swaggart Ministries, did not result in excessive entanglement of religion and government. In this context, Justice O'Connor used the term "administrative entanglement"[98] to advance a borderline definition of entanglement concerns:

> Most significantly, the imposition of the sales and use tax without an exemption for appellant does not require the State to inquire into the religious content of the items sold or the religious motivation for selling or purchasing the items, because the materials are subject to the tax regardless of content or motive. From the State's point of view, the critical question is not whether the materials are religious, but whether there is a sale or a use, a question which involves only a secular determination.[99]

This is Justice Harlan's entanglement concern, the avoidance of conflict and litigation over the boundaries of exemption. From this vantage, the sales taxation of churches entangles less than does an exemption limited to sales of religious items.

---

93 *Swaggart Ministries*, 493 U.S. at 387–389.
94 *Id.* at 387.
95 *Id.* (emphasis in original).
96 *Id.* at 389.
97 *Id.* at 386.
98 *Id.* at 393.
99 *Id.* at 396.

Such a narrow exemption limited to religious activity engenders problems at the boundary of exemption, determining who is (and is not) eligible for exemption under the rubric of "religion."

Indeed, once Justice O'Connor rejected the *Follett/Murdock* vision of constitutionally required exemption to avoid intrusion into religious activity, Justice Harlan's theory of borderline entanglement was the only approach available to her. The permissive, accommodationist version of entanglement doctrine articulated by Chief Justice Burger in *Walz* is inapplicable in a case like *Swaggart Ministries*, as California chooses against accommodation by adopting a sales tax statute with no religious exemptions.

Particularly significant is Justice O'Connor's observation, in the context of her *Swaggart Ministries* entanglement analysis, that *Walz* approved property tax exemption only "as part of a general exemption for nonprofit institutions."[100] This observation prioritizes the *Walz* concurrences of Justices Brennan and Harlan: Tax exemptions, exclusions, and deductions can only be granted to churches if such benefits simultaneously extend to a broad class of secular properties. While Justice O'Connor never formally uses the term "subsidy" in *Swaggart Ministries*, her opinion implicitly embraces Justice Brennan's perspective for the *Texas Monthly* plurality, a plurality Justice O'Connor had declined to join.

The conflict between *Swaggart Ministries* (which finds little life in *Follett* and *Murdock*) and the analysis of the *Texas Monthly* dissenters (which sees great vitality in those older decisions) leaves the reader wondering why those dissenters joined Justice O'Connor's opinion. At one level, the *Texas Monthly* dissent and *Swaggart Ministries* can be reconciled via the permissive nature of the accommodation principle articulated by Chief Justice Burger in *Walz*: That Texas may constitutionally exempt religious literature from sales taxation does not mean that California must exempt in this fashion. Under the First Amendment, accommodation by tax exemption is permitted, not required.

Moreover, as I discuss in chapter five,[101] sales taxation entails less enforcement entanglement than does ad valorem property taxation. Since most taxable sales are for cash consideration, sales taxation does not involve the valuation and liquidity challenges of property taxation. From this perspective, sales taxation poses less danger of church-state conflict than does property taxation—which explains why all nine justices approved California's imposition of its sales tax upon sectarian institutions.

---

[100] *Id.* at 393.

[101] *See infra* at 137–138.

E. *NYQUIST* AND *MUELLER*

In contrast to the unanimously decided *Swaggart Ministries*, the Court's earlier opinions in *Committee for Public Education v. Nyquist*[102] and *Mueller v. Allen*[103] split the Court. In *Nyquist*, a six-justice majority struck a package of New York State programs bolstering nonpublic elementary and secondary education. Among these programs was "a system for providing income tax benefits to parents of children attending New York's nonpublic schools."[104] The *Nyquist* majority struck these tax benefits under the Establishment Clause

> as such benefits render assistance to parents who send their children to sectarian schools [and thus] their purpose and inevitable effect are to aid and advance those religious institutions.[105]

The *Nyquist* Court rejected the proffered analogy between these tax benefits and the Empire State's property tax exemption upheld in *Walz*. Among the reasons that *Nyquist* rejects reliance on *Walz* is that New York's property tax "exemption covered all property devoted to religious, educational, or charitable purposes"[106] while the tax benefits challenged in *Nyquist* "flow primarily to the parents of children attending sectarian, nonpublic schools."[107] In light of "the narrowness of the benefited class,"[108] the New York State tax program entailed "potential divisiveness" along sectarian lines.[109] These observations reflect the greater judicial acceptance of tax exemptions for religious entities and persons when exemption extends as well to secular institutions and individuals and a corresponding skepticism of tax benefits awarded narrowly to churches and sectarian entities.

Chief Justice Burger, then-Justice Rehnquist, and Justice White dissented in *Nyquist* with each of the three writing an opinion joined by the other two. Chief Justice Burger's dissent emphasized that the New York tax benefits invalidated by the Court did not go directly to sectarian schools, but rather went to parents of children attending such schools. In First Amendment terms, the Chief Justice argued,

---

[102] 413 U.S. 756 (1973).

[103] 463 U.S. 388 (1983).

[104] *Nyquist*, 413 U.S. at 789. The Supreme Court concluded that it was unnecessary to describe "this hybrid benefit" as either an income tax deduction or an income tax credit since the benefit had features of both.

[105] *Id.* at 793.

[106] *Id.* at 794.

[107] *Id.*

[108] *Id.*

[109] *Id.*

"government aid to individuals generally stands on an entirely different footing from direct aid to religious institutions."[110] Justice Rehnquist asserted in dissent the similarity between the New York tax benefits invalidated in *Nyquist* and the New York property tax exemption sustained in *Walz*. The Empire State's tax benefit for parents sending their children to private schools "is still abstention from taxation" and thus valid under the Establishment Clause per *Walz*.[111] Justice White maintained that "the overriding consequence of" the New York tax benefits was "preserving the secular functions of these [nonpublic] schools" and that "the resulting, but incidental, benefit to religion should not invalidate" such benefits.[112]

Mueller reflected a 5–4 split among the justices. In *Mueller*, the Court sustained against First Amendment challenge a Minnesota income tax deduction for parents' expenses for their children's elementary and secondary educations. A critical factor for the five-justice majority was the facial breadth of the deduction, available not just to parents sending their children to sectarian schools but also available to parents educating their offspring in public schools and in secular private institutions. For example, the Minnesota deduction applies if a parent living in one public school district pays tuition to send her child to a public school in another district.[113] The deduction also applies if a public school parent pays for "certain summer school tuition."[114] The Minnesota deduction is specifically disallowed for the purchase of religious materials.[115]

The majority's principal doctrinal challenge in *Mueller* was to distinguish the Minnesota income tax deduction sustained in that case from the New York tax provision previously struck in *Nyquist*. Among the relevant distinctions, according to the *Mueller* Court, was the limited availability of the *Nyquist* tax benefits, obtainable only by "parents of children in *nonpublic* schools."[116] In contrast, the Minnesota "deduction is available for educational expenses incurred by *all* parents, including those whose children attend public schools and those whose children attend nonsectarian private schools or sectarian private schools."[117] Since Minnesota grants the deduction for educational outlays "neutrally" to a broad spectrum of citizens, that deduction "is not readily subject to challenge under the Establishment Clause."[118]

---

[110] *Id.* at 801 (Burger, C.J., dissenting).
[111] *Id.* at 810 (Rehnquist, J., dissenting).
[112] *Id.* at 823–824 (White, J., dissenting).
[113] *Mueller*, 463 U.S. at 391, n.2 (item 2).
[114] *Id.* (item 3).
[115] *Id.*, n.1 (reproducing MINN. STAT. § 290.09(22)).
[116] *Id.* at 398 (emphasis in original).
[117] *Id.* at 397 (emphasis in original).
[118] *Id.* at 398–399.

In response to the assertion that, in practice, "the bulk of deductions" are taken by Minnesota parents sending their children to religious schools, the *Mueller* majority pointed to the facial neutrality of the challenged statute.[119] Responding to the contention that the Minnesota deduction requires excessive entanglement as "state officials must determine whether particular textbooks qualify for a deduction" by virtue of their secular content, the majority, without extensive analysis, concluded that that determination is no more entangling than other similar judgments the Court had previously condoned under the First Amendment.[120] Finally, in language reminiscent of Chief Justice Burger's *Walz* opinion, the *Mueller* Court noted the "broad latitude" of the Minnesota legislature to design the state's income tax base.[121]

In sum, for the *Mueller* Court, the facial breadth of the Minnesota state income tax deduction, available to public school parents and to parents sending their children to secular private schools, immunized the deduction from Establishment Clause challenge. Thus, again, a tax provision benefiting religious entities and persons won judicial acceptance because, at least nominally, the provision assisted secular organizations and individuals as well.

The *Mueller* minority accepted none of this. For the four-justice minority, the Minnesota tax deduction is indistinguishable from the New York tax provision struck in *Nyquist*. Each constitutes a "subsidy" of sectarian education in violation of the Establishment Clause.[122] Moreover, in practice, this tax subsidy is focused upon parents who utilize religious schools because such parents constitute "the vast majority of the taxpayers who are eligible to receive the benefit" of the deduction.[123] Even if, in practice, the income tax deduction conferred benefits more broadly, according to the *Mueller* minority, the deduction would fail constitutional muster as furthering "the religious mission" of sectarian schools.[124]

In short, for the *Mueller* dissenters, the breadth of the Minnesota deduction is illusory and irrelevant. The Minnesota deduction is a subsidy that, as a practical matter, subsidizes religious schools. Even if the deduction in practice subsidized more broadly, it would, for these dissenters, violate the Establishment Clause as subventing religious instruction.

119 *Id.* at 401.

120 *Id.* at 403.

121 *Id.* at 396 (quoting *Regan v. Taxation with Representation of Wash.*, 461 U.S. 540, 547 (1983)).

122 *Id.* at 408–409 (Marshall, J., dissenting).

123 *Id.* at 405.

124 *Id.* at 409, n.2.

F. *LEE*

In contrast to the divisions manifested in decisions such as *Follett, Murdock, Texas Monthly, Nyquist,* and *Mueller, United States v. Lee,*[125] like *Swaggart Ministries,* was decided unanimously. Whereas the Court's other decisions scrutinized state and local taxes under the First Amendment, *Lee* is the only case in which the U.S. Supreme Court has subjected a federal tax to such constitutional scrutiny. The federal tax was upheld.

Mr. Lee, a member of the Old Order Amish religion, employed other members of his faith to work on his farm and in his carpentry shop.[126] He did not pay the FICA payroll tax[127] imposed on employers nor did he withhold the FICA tax[128] employers are required to retain from their employees' wages. Mr. Lee's noncompliance with the FICA taxes stemmed from his religious beliefs forbidding participation in and the financing of public insurance like the Social Security system funded by the FICA taxes paid by employers and employees.[129]

Ruling against Mr. Lee, the U.S. Supreme Court held that the federal "Government's interest in assuring mandatory and continuous participation in and contribution to the social security system is very high."[130] That interest, the *Lee* Court concluded, outweighed Mr. Lee's offsetting interest in protecting his religious convictions:

> Because the broad public interest in maintaining a sound tax system is of such a high order, religious belief in conflict with the payment of taxes affords no basis for resisting the tax.[131]

If Mr. Lee had no employees, he would have qualified for Internal Revenue Code Section 1402(g)[132] and its exemption from the self-employment tax financing Social Security and Medicare benefits. Section 1402(g), the Court concluded, was

---

[125] 455 U.S. 252 (1982).

[126] *Id.* at 254.

[127] I.R.C. § 3101, 26 U.S.C. § 3101.

[128] I.R.C. § 3111, 26 U.S.C. § 3111.

[129] *Lee*, 455 U.S. at 257.

[130] *Id.* at 258–259.

[131] *Id.* at 260. In *Employment Division, Department of Human Resources of Oregon v. Smith*, 494 U.S. 872, 880 (1990), the Court cited *Lee* for the proposition that the First Amendment does not require exemption from "a neutral, generally applicable regulatory law that compel[s] activity forbidden by an individual's religion."

[132] I.R.C. § 1402(g), 26 U.S.C. § 1402(g).

a congressional "effort toward accommodation"[133] which plausibly "drew a line"[134] between, on the one hand, employers who religiously oppose Social Security but must pay FICA tax and, on the other, self-employed persons who similarly reject Social Security on religious ground and are consequently excused from paying the self-employment tax.

Lee, written by Chief Justice Burger for himself and seven of his colleagues,[135] follows the trail of permissive accommodation marked by *Walz*. In Mr. Lee's case, Congress elected not to accommodate. In *Burwell v. Hobby Lobby*,[136] the Court subsequently characterized *Lee* as "turn[ing] primarily on the special problems associated with a national system of taxation," namely, that it is "untenable to allow individuals to seek exemptions from taxes based on religious objections to particular Government expenditures . . ." As we shall see in chapter three,[137] Congress subsequently reassessed and granted FICA tax exemption to employers like Mr. Lee.

G. CONCLUSION

The Supreme Court's seven First Amendment decisions on religion and taxation identify several themes which are central to this book. Chief among these are concern about tax-related entanglement between church and state, the difference between enforcement-related entanglement and borderline entanglement, and the greater judicial willingness to accept the tax exemption of sectarian institutions and actors when exemption simultaneously extends to secular entities and individuals.

The Court's decisions also confront (though they do not resolve) the question whether tax exemptions for religious institutions and actors improperly subsidize the sectarian or whether such exemptions serve the nonsubsidizing purpose of disentangling church and state and are thus part of a normative tax base. As we explore further the taxation and tax exemption of churches and of other religious institutions and actors, these themes are central to the story.

[133] *Lee*, 455 U.S. at 260, n. 11.

[134] *Id.* at 261.

[135] Justice Stevens concurred in a separate opinion. *Id.* at 261.

[136] 134 S. Ct. 2751, 2784 (2014).

[137] *See infra* at 56.

As we shall see, other cases, such as *Bob Jones University v. United States*,[138] *Hernandez v. Commissioner of Internal Revenue*,[139] *Lemon v. Kurtzman*,[140] *Employment Division, Department of Human Resources of Oregon v. Smith*,[141] and *Christian Echoes National Ministry, Inc. v. U.S.A.*,[142] also play important roles in the story which follows. However, the U.S. Supreme Court decisions explored in this first chapter help frame important themes relevant to taxing and exempting churches and other religious entities.

---

[138] 461 U.S. 574 (1983).

[139] 490 U.S. 680 (1989).

[140] 403 U.S. 602 (1971).

[141] 494 U.S. 872 (1990).

[142] 470 F.2d 849 (10th Cir. 1972).

2

STATE CONSTITUTIONS ON RELIGION AND TAXATION

THIRTY-FOUR STATES' constitutions explicitly address the tax-exempt status of religious property.[1] These state constitutional provisions fall into three patterns: The strongest state constitutional provisions guarantee property tax exemptions for "religious" institutions and uses. Other state constitutions permit, but do not compel, property tax exemptions for religious entities and activities. A third category of state constitutional provisions narrowly exempts from property taxation "churches" or places of "worship" rather than the broader category of "religious" properties. All of these state constitutions simultaneously grant or permit tax exemptions to secular eleemosynary properties as well.

No state constitution addresses the income or sales tax treatment of religious institutions or activity. As a historical matter, this is not surprising: Most state constitutions were drafted when property taxation was the dominant revenue source of state and local governments, and the modern income and sales taxes had not yet been implemented.[2]

---

[1] W. Cole Durham & Robert Smith, 4 Religious Organizations and the Law §17:78.

[2] John Witte Jr., *Tax Exemption of Church Property: Historical Anomaly or Valid Constitutional Practice?*, 64 S. Cal. L. Rev. 363, 389 (1991).

The state constitutions reflect a consensus that churches are property tax exempt along with other secular eleemosynary properties. Within that broad consensus, there is greater diversity than many recognize with respect to particular kinds of sectarian holdings such as parsonages and nonchurch religious properties. These properties are tax exempt in some states but not in others. This diversity is a virtue of our system of decentralized, federalist decision-making since, in a world of imperfect choices, different states can and do make different trade-offs in the taxation and exemption of religious institutions and actors.

A. STATE CONSTITUTIONAL EXEMPTIONS FROM PROPERTY TAXATION

Eleven states' constitutions guarantee property tax exemptions for "religious" entities and activities. These guarantees extend to various categories of secular, philanthropic properties as well.

Among the constitutional provisions mandating the tax-free status of religious property is the New York State property tax exemption upheld in *Walz*. The Empire State's constitution requires tax exemption for

> real or personal property used exclusively for religious, educational or charitable purposes as defined by law and owned by any corporation or association organized or conducted exclusively for one or more of such purposes and not operating for profit.[3]

In this same vein, Alaska's constitution provides in mandatory terms that

> [a]ll, or any portion of, property used exclusively for non-profit religious, charitable, cemetery, or educational purposes, as defined by law, shall be exempt from taxation.[4]

---

[3] N.Y. CONST. art. XVI, § 1.

[4] ALASKA CONST. art. IX, § 4.

The constitutions of Kansas,[5] Kentucky,[6] Michigan,[7] New Jersey,[8] North Dakota,[9] Oklahoma,[10] South Dakota,[11] and Utah[12] similarly compel tax exemption for religious properties. Louisiana's constitution[13] decrees the exemption of "[p]roperty owned by a nonprofit corporation or association organized and operated exclusively for religious, dedicated places of burial, charitable, health, welfare, fraternal, or educational purposes, no part of the net earnings of which inure to the benefit of any private shareholder or member thereof and which is declared to be exempt from federal or state income tax." In these eleven states, the constitutional guarantee of tax exemption extends to secular eleemosynary properties as well as to religious properties.

The constitutions of eight states permit, but do not require, the state legislature to exempt religious properties along with secular philanthropic properties. For example, Florida's constitution provides that "[s]uch portions of property as are used

[5] KAN. CONST. art. XI, § 1(b) ("All property used exclusively for state, county, municipal, literary, educational, scientific, religious, benevolent and charitable purposes . . . shall be exempted from property taxation.").

[6] KY. CONST. § 170 ("There shall be exempt from taxation public property used for public purposes . . . real property owned and occupied by, and personal property both tangible and intangible owned by, institutions of religion; institutions of purely public charity . . ."). Prior to amendment in 1990, the Kentucky Constitution was similar to the constitutions of Virginia and Wyoming in that it extended property tax exemption to "places actually used for religious worship" and to "parsonages or residences owned by any religious society, and occupied as a home, . . . by the minister of any religion . . ."). *See Mordecai F. Ham Evangelistic Association v. Matthews*, 300 Ky. 402 (1945) (applying the pre-1990 version of § 170 of the Kentucky Constitution).

[7] MICH. CONST. art. IX, § 4 ("Property owned and occupied by non-profit religious or educational organizations and used exclusively for religious or educational purposes, as defined by law, shall be exempt from real and personal property taxes.").

[8] N.J. CONST. art. VIII, § 1, ¶ 2 ("Exemption from taxation may be granted only by general laws . . . Exemptions from taxation may be altered or repealed, except those exempting real and personal property used exclusively for religious, educational, charitable or cemetery purposes, as defined by law, and owned by any corporation or association organized and conducted exclusively for one or more of such purposes and not operating for profit.").

[9] N.D. CONST. art. X, § 5 ("[P]roperty used exclusively for schools, religious, cemetery, charitable or other public purposes shall be exempt from taxation.").

[10] OKLA. CONST. art. X, § 6 ("[A]ll property used exclusively for religious and charitable purposes . . . shall be exempt from taxation . . .").

[11] S.D. CONST. art. XI, § 6 ("The Legislature shall, by general law, exempt from taxation, property used exclusively for agricultural and horticultural societies, for school, religious, cemetery and charitable purposes . . .").

[12] UTAH CONST. art. XIII, § 3(1)(f) ("The following are exempt from property tax: [P]roperty owned by a nonprofit entity used exclusively for religious, charitable, or educational purposes . . .").

[13] LA. CONST. art. VII, §21B(1)(a)(i).

predominantly for . . . religious or charitable purposes may be exempted by general law from taxation."[14] Similarly, Illinois' constitution provides:

> The General Assembly by law may exempt from taxation only the property of the State, units of local government and school districts and property used exclusively for agricultural and horticultural societies, and for school, religious, cemetery and charitable purposes . . .[15]

Also along these permissive lines are the constitutions of Arizona,[16] Indiana,[17] Nebraska,[18] North Carolina,[19] Tennessee,[20] and West Virginia,[21] which authorize, but do not mandate, the tax exemption of religious properties and other secular, eleemosynary properties. In practice, each of these states' legislatures has accepted the invitation of its respective state constitution by adopting a statute exempting religious and other eleemosynary properties from taxation.

The third type of state constitutional provision grants property tax exemption narrowly to "churches" or to places of "worship" rather than to the broader category of "religious" properties. These more limited exemption provisions are sometimes mandatory and sometimes permissive. For example, Alabama's constitution[22] requires the tax exemption of properties "used exclusively for religious worship . . . or for purposes purely charitable." In this same vein, Arkansas's constitution mandates the property tax exemption of "churches used as such,"[23] while California's

[14] Fla. Const. art. VII, § 3(a).

[15] Ill. Const. art. IX, § 6.

[16] Ariz. Const. art. IX, § 2(2) ("Property of educational, charitable and religious associations or institutions not used or held for profit may be exempt from taxation by law.").

[17] Ind. Const. art. X, § 1(c)(1) ("The General Assembly may exempt from property taxation any property in any of the following classes: Property being used for . . . religious or charitable purposes.").

[18] Neb. Const. art. VIII, § 2(2) ("[T]he Legislature by general law may classify and exempt from taxation property owned by and used exclusively for agricultural and horticultural societies and property owned and used exclusively for educational, religious, charitable, or cemetery purposes, when such property is not owned or used for financial gain or profit to either the owner or user . . .").

[19] N.C. Const. art. V, § 2(3) ("The General Assembly may exempt . . . property held for educational, scientific, literary, cultural, charitable, or religious purposes, and, to a value not exceeding $300, any personal property.").

[20] Tenn. Const. art. II, § 28 ("[A]ll property real, personal or mixed shall be subject to taxation, but the Legislature may except such as may be held by the State, by Counties, Cities or Towns, and used exclusively for public or corporation purposes, and such as may be held and used for purposes purely religious, charitable, scientific, literary or educational . . .").

[21] W. Va. Const. art. X, § 1 ("[B]ut property used for educational, literary, scientific, religious or charitable purposes . . . may by law be exempted from taxation . . .").

[22] Ala. Const. art. IV, § 91.

[23] Ark. Const. art. XVI, § 5(b).

constitution exempts from taxation "[b]uildings, land on which they are situated, and equipment used exclusively for religious worship."[24]

Ohio's constitution permits the property tax exemption of "houses used exclusively for public worship."[25] Similarly, the constitutions of Colorado,[26] Minnesota,[27] Missouri,[28] Montana,[29] New Mexico,[30] and Pennsylvania[31] permit or require the exemption of property described as "church" property or as property devoted to "worship." The constitutions of South Carolina,[32] Virginia,[33] Texas,[34] and Wyoming[35] exempt from property taxation parsonages as well as church property.

The constitution of Georgia addresses the property tax status of religious properties in a unique fashion. Georgia's constitution provides that "[a]ny law which reduces or repeals exemptions granted to religious or burial grounds or institutions of purely public charity must be approved by two-thirds of the members elected to each branch of the General Assembly."[36]

---

[24] Cal. Const. art. XIII, § 3(f).

[25] Ohio Const. art. XII, § 2.

[26] Colo. Const. art. X, § 5 ("Property, real and personal, that is used solely and exclusively for religious worship, for schools or for strictly charitable purposes . . . shall be exempt from taxation, unless otherwise provided by general law.").

[27] Minn. Const. art. X, § 1 ("Taxes shall be uniform upon the same class of subjects and shall be levied and collected for public purposes, but . . . all churches, church property, houses of worship, institutions of purely public charity, and public property used exclusively for any public purpose, shall be exempt from taxation except as provided in this section . . . The legislature by law may define or limit the property exempt under this section other than churches, houses of worship, and property solely used for educational purposes by academies, colleges, universities and seminaries of learning.").

[28] Mo. Const. art. X, § 6(1) ("[A]ll property, real and personal, not held for private or corporate profit and used exclusively for religious worship, for schools and colleges, for purposes purely charitable . . . may be exempted from taxation by general law . . .").

[29] Mont. Const. art. VIII, § 5(1)(b) ("The legislature may exempt from taxation . . . Institutions of purely public charity, hospitals and places of burial not used or held for private or corporate profit, places for actual religious worship, and property used exclusively for educational purposes.").

[30] N.M. Const. art. VIII, § 3 ("[A]ll church property not used for commercial purposes, all property used for educational or charitable purposes . . . shall be exempt from taxation.").

[31] Pa. Const. art. VIII, § 2(a)(i) ("The General Assembly may by law exempt from taxation: Actual places of regularly stated religious worship.").

[32] S.C. Const. art. X, § 3(c) ("There shall be exempt from ad valorem taxation: all property of all public libraries, churches, parsonages and burying grounds . . .").

[33] Va. Const. art. X, § 6(a)(2) ("Real estate and personal property owned and exclusively occupied or used by churches or religious bodies for religious worship or for the residences of their ministers.").

[34] Tex. Const. art. VIII, § 2(a) ("[T]he legislature may, by general laws, exempt from taxation . . . actual places of religious worship, also any property owned by a church or by a strictly religious society for the exclusive use as a dwelling place for the ministry of such church or religious society . . .")

[35] Wyo. Const. art. XV, § 12 ("The property of the United States, the state, counties, cities, towns, school districts and municipal corporations, when used primarily for a governmental purpose, and public libraries, lots with the buildings thereon used exclusively for religious worship, church parsonages, church schools and public cemeteries, shall be exempt from taxation, and such other property as the legislature may by general law provide.").

[36] Ga. Const. art. VII, § 2, ¶ IV.

These thirty-four state constitutional provisions reflect a broad consensus that religious as well as secular eleemosynary properties should be tax exempt. All states with constitutional provisions which permit (but do not require) tax exemptions for religious property in practice exempt by statute in the same fashion as do the states in which the property tax exemption of religious property is constitutionally mandated. Likewise, as we shall see in chapter four,[37] all states with constitutions which are silent on the subject of religious property tax exemptions grant such exemptions by statute. Thus, at one level, it does not matter that some state constitutions require property tax exemptions for religious properties while other state constitutions do not. All states exempt some religious property from taxation even if such exemption is not constitutionally compelled.

Moreover, no state constitution requires income tax exemptions for religious institutions even though, as I discuss in chapter four, such exemptions are universally extended by state statutes.[38] Just as state legislatures grant property tax exemptions even when their respective constitutions do not require such exemptions, all state legislatures extend income tax exemptions to religious entities though none of their respective state constitutions explicitly require them to grant such income tax exemptions.

B. INTERPRETING "CHURCH" FOR PROPERTY TAX EXEMPTION PURPOSES

States with narrow constitutional exemptions for "church" properties or "houses of worship" sometimes interpret expansively their parallel tax exemptions for "educational" and "charitable" properties. When this happens, properties which are exempted in some states as "religious" are instead exempted in these other states as educational or charitable. In such cases, the practical result is the same—the tax exemption of religious property—whether the state's constitutional exemption is phrased expansively or more narrowly.

Instructive is the decision of the Ohio Supreme Court in *Hubbard Press v. Glander, Tax Commissioner*.[39] Ohio's constitutional provision is limited, permitting property tax exemption of "houses used exclusively for public worship."[40] The Ohio Constitution also permits the property tax exemption of "institutions used exclusively for charitable purposes."[41] The Ohio General Assembly has by statute

---

[37] *See infra* at 67–77.

[38] *See infra* at 97–99.

[39] 156 Ohio St. (1951).

[40] OHIO CONST. art. XII, § 2.

[41] *Id.*

elected to implement both of these exemptions, adhering to the constitution's precise terminology.[42]

The Hubbard Press was a nonprofit corporation controlled by the Presbyterian Church which printed "offering envelopes, pledge cards, forms for accounts, financial records, statements and other supplies for use by churches and congregations."[43] Hubbard Press's factory, with its extensive manufacturing machinery, was not a location at which "public worship" occurred. Nevertheless, the Buckeye State's supreme court upheld property tax exemption on the grounds that the Hubbard Press was a charitable institution:

> [A] nonprofit corporation, a branch of a great Church, engaged in exclusively furnishing supplies without profit to that Church as an essential means for not only carrying on its great religious and benevolent activities but for preserving its very life, comes squarely within the tax exemption [for charitable institutions].[44]

The Ohio Court thus surmounted the more circumscribed phrasing of the Buckeye State's constitutional tax exemption for "houses used exclusively for public worship"[45] by reading into the property tax exemption for charitable property an exemption for religious property such as the Hubbard Press facility, which itself was not devoted to worship.

In this same vein, *Wholistic Life Church, Inc. v. Christerson*[46] involved a camp-style facility operated by a nonprofit religious corporation. The facility encompassed a variety of buildings including a clinic, a kitchen and dining hall, exercise and music rooms, a library, a swimming pool, and housing for staff and attendees.[47] Missouri exempts from taxation property used "exclusively for religious worship,"[48] a standard which these facilities could not satisfy. On the other hand, the Missouri appeals court held this facility tax exempt as used for charitable purposes. The court was influenced by the homeless clientele the facility served and the availability of the facility's services to those who could not pay.[49]

---

42 Ohio Rev. Code Ann. §§ 5709.07(A)(2) ("The following property shall be exempt from taxation: (2) Houses used exclusively for public worship . . .") and 5709.12(B) ("[R]eal and tangible personal property belonging to institutions that is used exclusively for charitable purposes shall be exempt from taxation . . .").

43 156 Ohio St. at 171.

44 *Id.* at 177.

45 Ohio Const. art. XII, § 2.

46 968 S.W.2d 190 (Mo. Ct. App. 1998).

47 *Id.* at 191.

48 Mo. Const. art X, § 6(1); Mo. Ann. Stat. §137.100.

49 968 S.W.2d at 194–95.

Flathead Lake Methodist Camp v. Webb[50] involved Montana's property tax exemption "for educational purposes [and] places for actual religious worship."[51] In the face of the narrow term "actual religious worship," Montana's supreme court upheld a religious camp's tax exemption through an expansive notion of what constitutes education:

> [T]he clear purpose and achievement of the camp is to teach children how to relax, how to be better citizens, how to assert a Christian influence on their home communities, how to appreciate God and morality through closeness to nature, and how to grow to maturity. Qualities of character and a good sense of moral values must be learned. They may or may not be being taught to them in their homes, but it certainly is being taught to them at this camp. The fact that the children's day is so carefully planned to include instruction is the most crucial aspect of our decision that the camp fulfills an educational purpose.[52]

The Hubbard Press, Wholistic Life Church, and *Flathead Lake Methodist Camp* indicate that, in the face of more restrictive exemptions limited to church properties, some state courts interpret their constitutional exemptions for charitable and educational properties broadly to reach results similar to those obtained in states with more expansive constitutional exemptions for religious properties.

Some states with narrow constitutional exemptions for churches push the boundaries of those exemptions by statute. For example, Colorado's constitution provides for the tax exemption of property "that is used solely and exclusively for religious worship . . ."[53] Colorado's legislature, by statute, initially broadened the concept of tax-exempt property used for worship to include "land which is essential" to structures used for worship, as well as land for "parking" for worship and "houses used primarily for religious reflection."[54] Under this standard, the Colorado Supreme Court upheld the property tax exemption of a summer camp operated by a religious entity on the grounds that the camp's secular "activities were necessarily incidental to the religious worship and reflection purposes" animating the camp.[55] Colorado's legislature

[50] 144 Mont. 565 (1965).

[51] MONT. CONST. art. VIII, § 1(b).

[52] *Flathead Lake*, 144 Mont. at 572. *See also Cincinnati Community Kollel v. Levin, Tax Commissioner*, 113 Ohio St.3d 138 (2007) (holding that a Jewish kollel, an institute for the advanced study of Jewish texts, qualifies as an educational entity for property tax exemption purposes).

[53] COLO. CONST. art. 10, § 5.

[54] *Maurer v. Young Life*, 779 P.2d 1317, 1330 (1989) (quoting prior version of COLO. REV. STAT. ANN. § 39-3-101(1)(e)).

[55] *Id.* at 1331.

eventually liberalized the property tax exemption statute to include any property "owned and used solely and exclusively for religious purposes."[56] Under this broader statutory test, Colorado's court of appeals extended property tax exemption to a YMCA camp on the grounds that "recreational activities including hiking, fishing, biking, horseback riding, cross-country skiing, tennis, roller skating, ropes courses and fitness rooms"[57] "furthered [the YMCA's] religious mission and purposes."[58]

In short, when property tax exemption is constitutionally limited to "churches" or places of "worship," the tax exemption of religious property is sometimes in practice broader as a result of case law or statutes extending tax-exempt status to nonchurch religious properties as charitable or educational institutions.

C. THE PROPERTY TAX STATUS OF PARSONAGES

The differing terminology of particular states' constitutional exemptions can drive different outcomes in specific cases. Such differences are most apparent in the states' varied approaches to the property tax exemption of parsonages. Some state constitutions explicitly provide for the property tax exemption of the homes in which ministers[59] live. Other states exempt parsonages through statutes which deem parsonages to be "religious" or "church" properties. Yet other states classify ministers' homes as tax-exempt religious holdings through case law interpretations of constitutional and statutory exemptions of religious properties. Finally, other states deny property tax exemption to parsonages. The upshot is significant diversity in the states' property tax treatments of clerical residences.

In the first category come states like South Carolina. The constitution of the Palmetto State expressly exempts from property taxation "churches" and "parsonages."[60] Similarly, Virginia's constitutional property tax exemption for "churches or religious bodies for religious worship" also explicitly exempts from taxation "the residence of their ministers."[61] In this same vein, Wyoming's constitutional exemption includes "church parsonages."[62] Texas' constitution authorizes the legislature to exempt from property taxation "any property owned by a church or by a strictly

[56] Colo. Rev. Stat. Ann. § 39-3-106(1).

[57] *Grand County Board of Commissioners v. Colorado Property Tax Administrator*, 2016 COA 02, para. 4.

[58] *Id.* at para. 36.

[59] In this and similar contexts, I use the term "minister" generically to refer to all clergy including priests, nuns, rabbis, cantors, and imams.

[60] S.C. Const. art. X, §3(c).

[61] Va. Const. art. X, §6(a)(2).

[62] Wyo. Const. art. XV, § 12.

religious society for the exclusive use as a dwelling place for the ministry of such church or religious society . . ."[63] These state constitutions leave no doubt that "parsonages" are or can be declared property tax exempt.

Alaska is emblematic of the second approach under which state statutes declare parsonages to be tax-exempt religious properties. Alaska's constitution mandates tax exemption for "property used exclusively for non-profit religious . . . purposes."[64] By statute, Alaska has defined exempt religious property to include "the residence of an educator in a private religious or parochial school or a bishop, pastor, priest, rabbi, minister, or religious order of a recognized religious organization . . ."[65] Similarly, Arkansas's state constitution grants property tax exemption to "churches used as such."[66] Statutorily, Arkansas has declared that this exemption applies to "[p]arsonages owned by churches and used as homes for pastors . . ."[67] West Virginia's constitution permits the property tax exemption of "religious" properties.[68] Statutorily, West Virginia extends this exemption to "[p]arsonages and the household goods and furniture pertaining thereto."[69] The Kansas legislature has also granted tax exemption to parsonages,[70] thereby overturning the earlier decision of the Sunflower State's supreme court[71] that parsonages do not merit such exemption.

Nebraska exemplifies the third approach of exempting parsonages from property taxation through case law interpretation of exemptions for "religious" properties. Both Nebraska's constitution[72] and its property tax statute[73] exempt from taxation property "used exclusively for . . . religious . . . purposes." Against this constitutional and statutory background, the Cornhusker State's supreme court held that parsonages are property tax exempt:

> [A] parsonage owned by a church, which parsonage houses a pastor who is engaged in full-time ministerial work, which parsonage is provided to him for the convenience of the church and parishioners, and which parsonage services

---

[63] Tex. Const. art. VIII, § 2(a).

[64] Alaska Const. art. IX, § 4.

[65] Alaska Stat. Ann. § 29.45.030(b)(1). *See also Evangelical Covenant Church v. Nome*, 394 P.2d 882, 885–886 (1964) (holding that a church's second home used by an "assistant or lay pastor" qualifies as property tax parsonage).

[66] Ark. Const. art. XVI, § 5.

[67] Ark. Code Ann. §26-3-303.

[68] W. Va. Const. art. X, § 1 ("[B]ut property used for educational, literary, scientific, religious or charitable purposes . . . may by law be exempted from taxation . . .").

[69] W. Va. Code Ann. § 11-3-9(a)(6).

[70] Kan. Stat. Ann. § 79–201.

[71] *Vail v. Beach*, 10 Kan. 214 (1872).

[72] Neb. Const. art. VIII, §2.

[73] Neb. Rev. Stat. § 77–202(1)(d).

> numerous religious purposes, is property used exclusively for religious purposes and exempt from taxation.[74]

In other states, the limited language of the state's property tax exemption has led the courts to declare parsonages as taxable. As we have seen, Ohio's constitution permits the property tax exemption of "houses used exclusively for public worship."[75] Ohio's legislature has, by statute, implemented this authority in similarly narrow terms. Ohio's exemption statute incorporates the constitutional language by declaring as property exempt from taxation "[h]ouses used exclusively for public worship . . ."[76]

Ohio's courts have held that this circumscribed definition of exempt property does not include parsonages. As early as 1874, the Buckeye State's supreme court ruled that a minister's home is not property tax exempt as a place of public worship:

> [A] parsonage, although built on ground which might otherwise be exempt as attached to the church edifice, does not come within the exemption. The ground in such case is appropriated to a new and different use. Instead of its being used exclusively for public worship, it becomes a place of private residence. Nor does it make any difference that, by the usages of the church, the presence of a priest or pastor is essential to conduct the services of public worship. Other persons are necessary to carry on public worship as well as a minister to conduct the services. There must be a laity or congregation as well as a minister or preacher, and it is equally necessary that they should have places of abode; yet it would not be claimed that their residences could be exempt.[77]

This remains the law of Ohio today.[78] On the other hand, Ohio's courts have upheld the property tax exemption of a church custodian's apartment as "incidental to the primary use of the building for public worship."[79]

The law of Pennsylvania is similar. Pennsylvania's constitution permits the General Assembly of the Keystone State to exempt from property taxation "[a]ctual places of regularly stated religious worship."[80] The statute implementing this exemption defines the category of religiously exempted properties as "[a]ll churches,

---

[74] *Nebraska Annual Conference of United Methodist Church v. Scotts Bluff County Board of Equalization*, 243 Neb. 412, 419 (1993).

[75] OHIO CONST. art. XII, § 2.

[76] OHIO REV. CODE ANN. § 5709.07(A)(2).

[77] *Gerke v. Purcell*, 25 Ohio St. 229, 248–249 (1874).

[78] *Faith Fellowship Ministries, Inc. v. Limbach*, 32 Ohio St. 3d 432, 435 (1987).

[79] *In re Bond Hill-Roselawn Hebrew School*, 151 Ohio St. 70, 75 (1949). *See also St. Paul's Evangelical Lutheran Church v. Board of Tax Appeals*, 114 Ohio App. 330 (1955).

[80] PA. CONST. art. VIII, § 2(a)(i).

meeting-houses, or other actual places of regularly stated religious worship, with the ground thereto annexed necessary for the occupancy and enjoyment of the same."[81] Under these constitutional and statutory standards, Pennsylvania's courts have held that parsonages are not exempt from property taxation as they are not places at which "worship" actually occurs.[82]

Similarly, the supreme court of Utah held that parsonages were not property tax exempt when Utah's constitutional standard for exemption was property "used exclusively for . . . religious worship . . ."[83] Utah subsequently amended its constitution to more broadly require the property tax exemption of "religious" property.[84] Utah's courts have not revisited the property tax status of parsonages under this more expansive terminology.

In short, while the broad outlines of religious tax exemptions transcend particular constitutional language, in specific cases (such as the exemption *vel non* of parsonages), different constitutional language can lead to divergent tax treatment of religious properties. When a state constitution explicitly enumerates "parsonages" as a form of tax-exempt property, the results often differ from when the state constitution limits religious-based property tax exemption to places of worship.

D. OTHER STATE CONSTITUTIONAL PROVISIONS

In addition to provisions permitting or requiring the tax exemption of religious properties, other state constitutional provisions are potentially relevant to the tax status of religious institutions and entities. However, these state constitutional texts have so far played insignificant roles in the tax arena.

Every state constitution has a passage guaranteeing religious liberty. These clauses run the gamut from clones of the First Amendment to more detailed articulations of constitutional protections for religious practice and doctrine. At one end of the spectrum, the constitutions of Alaska,[85] Hawaii,[86] Louisiana,[87] Montana,[88] and

[81] 72 PA. STAT. ANN. § 5020.204.

[82] *See, e.g., Connellsville Street Church of Christ v. Fayette County Board of Assessment Appeals*, 838 A.2d 848 (2003).

[83] *Salt Lake County v. Tax Commission*, 548 P.2d 630 (1976).

[84] UTAH CONST. art. XIII, § 3(1)(f).

[85] ALASKA CONST. art. I, § 4 ("No law shall be made respecting an establishment of religion, or prohibiting the free exercise thereof.").

[86] HAWAII CONST. art. I, § 4 ("No law shall be enacted respecting an establishment of religion, or prohibiting the free exercise thereof . . .").

[87] LA. CONST. art. I, § 8 ("No law shall be enacted respecting an establishment of religion or prohibiting the free exercise thereof.").

[88] MONT. CONST. art. II, § 5 ("The state shall make no law respecting an establishment of religion or prohibiting the free exercise thereof.").

South Carolina[89] track the language of the First Amendment. At the other end of the spectrum, Missouri's constitution contains the most detailed statement of religious freedom in a state constitution:

> That all men and women have a natural and indefeasible right to worship Almighty God according to the dictates of their own consciences; that no human authority can control or interfere with the rights of conscience; that no person shall, on account of his or her religious persuasion or belief, be rendered ineligible [for public office, as a witness, or as a juror], or be molested in his or her person or estate; that to secure a citizen's right to acknowledge Almighty God according to the dictates of his or her own conscience, neither the state nor any of its political subdivisions shall establish any official religion, nor shall a citizen's right to pray or express his or her religious beliefs be infringed; that the state shall not coerce any person to participate in any prayer or other religious activity, but shall ensure that any person shall have the right to pray individually or corporately in a private or public setting so long as such prayer does not result in disturbance of the peace or disruption of a public meeting or assembly; that [all] shall have the right to pray on government premises and public property so long as such prayers abide within the same parameters placed upon any other free speech under similar circumstances; that the [governing bodies] may extend to ministers, clergypersons, and other individuals the privilege to offer invocations or other prayers at meetings [of] governing bodies; that students may express their beliefs about religion in written and oral assignments free from discrimination based on the religious content of their work; that no student shall be compelled to perform or participate in academic assignments or educational presentations that violate his or her religious beliefs; that the state shall ensure public school students their right to free exercise of religious expression without interference, as long as such prayer or other expression is private and voluntary, whether individually or corporately, and in a manner that is not disruptive and as long as such prayers or expressions abide within the same parameters placed upon any other free speech under similar circumstances; and, to emphasize the right to free exercise of religious expression, that all free public schools receiving state appropriations shall display, in a conspicuous and legible manner, the text of the Bill of Rights of the Constitution of the United States; [public safety exception].[90]

---

[89] S.C. Const. art. I, § 2 ("The General Assembly shall make no law respecting an establishment of religion or prohibiting the free exercise thereof . . .").

[90] Mo. Const. art. I, § 5.

These state constitutional clauses have had little impact on the taxation or exemption of religious properties. In *Book Agents of the Methodist Episcopal Church, South v. State Board of Equalization*,[91] local government agencies invoked the religious liberty clause of the Tennessee Constitution, claiming that that clause precluded tax exemption for religious properties. The Tennessee Constitution provides

> [t]hat all men have a natural and indefeasible right to worship Almighty God according to the dictates of their own conscience; that no man can of right be compelled to attend, erect, or support any place of worship, or to maintain any minister against his consent; that no human authority can, in any case whatever, control or interfere with the rights of conscience; and that no preference shall ever be given, by law, to any religious establishment or mode of worship.[92]

The supreme court of the Volunteer State dismissed the constitutional challenge to religious properties' tax exemption on two grounds.[93] First, the Tennessee Constitution explicitly authorizes the tax exemption of properties "held and used for purposes purely religious."[94] Second, the Tennessee Supreme Court cited *Walz* for the proposition that "there are significant differences in terms of the religious liberty clauses" between "subsidies and exemptions."[95]

It is understandable that Tennessee's supreme court held that one provision of that state's constitution, guaranteeing religious liberty, did not implicitly repeal another constitutional clause, authorizing property tax exemption for religious properties. On the other hand, the income and sales tax exemption of religious entities is not constitutionally grounded. A state constitution's religious liberty clause might carry greater weight in the context of challenges to such purely statutory exemptions.

The decision of the North Carolina Supreme Court in *The Appeal of Springmoor, Inc.*[96] also demonstrates the limited impact of the states' constitutional religious liberty clauses in the context of religious property tax exemptions. The North Carolina property tax statute exempted "home[s] for the aged, sick, or infirm" only if such homes were sponsored by a "Masonic organization" or were religiously operated.[97] The supreme court of the Tar Heel State held that this exemption, limited to Masonic and religious facilities, "violate[d] the constitutional prohibition

---

[91] 513 S.W.2d 514 (1974).

[92] TENN. CONST. art. I, § 3.

[93] 513 S.W.2d at 525–526.

[94] TENN. CONST. art. II, § 28.

[95] 513 S.W.2d at 526.

[96] 348 N.C. 1 (1998).

[97] *Id.* at 3–4 (discussing N.C. GEN. STAT. § 105–275(32)).

against the establishment of religion as found in both the federal and state constitutions."[98] While the North Carolina court invoked the state constitution to buttress its conclusion, the state constitution provided no independent weight for the court's decision. The court's opinion in *Springmoor, Inc.* is grounded in the U.S. Supreme Court's First Amendment decisions in *Texas Monthly* and *Lemon v. Kurtzman*.[99]

It was thus unnecessary for the North Carolina Supreme Court to find independent substance in the North Carolina Constitution's religious liberty provisions since the U.S. Supreme Court's First Amendment case law, the court concluded, was controlling. However, in the future, state supreme courts might ascribe greater weight to their states' respective religious liberty clauses if there is no controlling federal case law, if that case law points in a direction which the state courts find unappealing, or if limitations on taxpayer standing in the federal courts[100] channel into the state courts more challenges against state tax exemptions for religious actors and institutions.

In addition to religious liberty provisions, many state constitutions also have what are often designated as "Blaine" amendments. These state constitutional provisions derive from the political controversy in the last half of the nineteenth century over the growth of the Catholic Church and its holdings.[101] No less a figure than President Ulysses S. Grant stimulated the debate, observing that "there is scarcely a limit to the wealth that may be acquired by corporations, religious or otherwise, if allowed to retain real estate without taxation."[102] Simultaneously, Catholic leaders claimed that public schools were *de facto* Protestant institutions and that Catholics should not be required to pay taxes to fund such institutions. Seeking the Republican nomination for the presidency, Rep. James Blaine of Maine proposed to amend the U.S. Constitution to apply the Free Exercise and Establishment Clauses to the states and to further provide that

> no money raised by taxation in any State for the support of public schools, or derived from any public fund therefore, nor any public lands devoted thereto,

---

98 *Id.* at 12. The religious liberty clauses of the North Carolina Constitution do not actually incorporate the term "establishment." Rather those clauses prevent any "human authority" from "control[ling] or interfer[ing] with the rights of conscience" and protect persons from "discrimination by the State because of . . . religion." N.C. Const. art. I, §§ 13 and 19.

99 348 N.C. at 10–11.

100 Edward A. Zelinsky, *Putting State Courts in the Constitutional Driver's Seat: State Taxpayer Standing After* Cuno *and* Winn, 40 Hastings Const. L.Q. 1 (2012); Laurence H. Winer & Nina J. Crimm, God, Schools, and Government Funding: First Amendment Conundrums 194–221 (2015).

101 Joseph O. Oluwole & Preston C. Green III, *School Vouchers and Tax Benefits in Federal and State Judicial Constitutional Analysis*, 65 Am. U. L. Rev. 1335, 1389–1393 (2016); Winer & Crimm, *supra* note 100, at 45–48.

102 Quoted in Edward A. Zelinsky, *Are Tax "Benefits" for Religious Institutions Constitutionally Dependent on Benefits for Secular Entities?*, 42 B.C.L. Rev. 805, 808 (2001).

> shall ever be under the control of any religious sect, nor shall any money so raised or lands so devoted be divided between religious sects or denominations.[103]

Blaine's proposed amendment was neither added to the U.S. Constitution nor did it secure the White House for Blaine. However, Blaine's proposal spawned "Blaine" amendments to many state constitutions.

While the texts of these amendments vary from state to state, they propound the basic theme that public funds cannot be used for sectarian purposes, particularly parochial schools. The Blaine amendment of Florida's constitution is typical:

> No revenue of the state or any political subdivision or agency thereof shall ever be taken from the public treasury directly or indirectly in aid of any church, sect, or religious denomination or in aid of any sectarian institution.[104]

Florida's Blaine Amendment, like the comparable amendments of other states, has played little role in determining the contours of state taxation. Florida's court of appeal, for example, concluded that the Sunshine State's Blaine Amendment does not preclude the tax exemption of religious institutions because such exemption "does not involve a disbursement from the public treasury."[105]

Many states have adopted Religious Freedom Restoration Acts (RFRAs).[106] While these are statutes, the state RFRAs are quasi-constitutional in nature and purport to override other state statutes when such statutes unacceptably impinge upon religious belief and practice. To date, the state RFRAs have had no impact upon the taxation or exemption of churches or other religious entities. However, the federal courts are now largely foreclosed on standing grounds from hearing constitutional challenges to state tax subsidies and exemptions.[107] We can thus expect more challenges in the state courts, under both the federal and state constitutions and, possibly, state RFRAs.

---

[103] Quoted in Mark Edward DeForrest, *An Overview and Evaluation of State Blaine Amendments: Origins, Scope, and First Amendment Concerns*, 26 Harv. J.L. & Pub. Pol'y 551, 556 (2003).

[104] Fla. Const. art. I, § 3.

[105] *McCall v. Scott*, 199 So. 3d 359, 370 (Fla. Dist. Ct. App. 2016).

[106] *See, e.g.*, Connecticut Act Concerning Religious Freedom (CACRF), Conn. Gen. Stat. § 52–571b. *See also* Winer & Crimm, *supra* note 100, at 260–261; Marci A. Hamilton, God vs. the Gavel: Religion and the Rule of Law 182–185 (2005). For the general public, the best known RFRA controversy occurred in Indiana. *See* Edward A. Zelinsky, *Indiana's RFRA Statute: A Plea for Civil Discourse* (Apr. 6, 2015), http://blog.oup.com/2015/04/indiana-rfra-statute-civil-discourse/.

[107] Zelinsky, *supra* note 100 at 1; Winer & Crimm, *supra* note 100, at 194–221.

E. CONCLUSION

The state constitutions reflect a consensus that churches are property tax exempt along with other secular eleemosynary properties. Within that broad consensus, there is greater diversity than many recognize with respect to particular kinds of sectarian holdings such as parsonages and nonchurch religious properties. These properties are tax exempt in some states but not in others. This diversity is a virtue of our system of decentralized, federalist decision-making since, in a world of imperfect choices, different states can and do make different trade-offs in the taxation and exemption of religious institutions and actors.

3

THE INTERNAL REVENUE CODE AND RELIGIOUS INSTITUTIONS

THE INTERNAL REVENUE Code treats religious entities in three different ways. Sometimes, the Code bestows favorable treatment upon religious organizations along with other, secular eleemosynary institutions. In other cases, the Code contains special exemptions limited to churches. In yet other instances, the Code taxes churches and sectarian institutions in the same fashion as secular and profit-making entities.

The first category—Code provisions which broadly bestow favorable income tax treatment upon sectarian entities and actors along with secular philanthropic organizations and persons—includes the income tax deduction for contributions to both religious and nonreligious eleemosynary institutions and the income tax exemption for such institutions. Also in this first category is the exemption from the federal unemployment tax, an exemption which applies to both religious and nonreligious eleemosynary employers.

In contrast to these provisions which apply alike to sectarian and secular eleemosynary entities, the Code also extends some tax benefits narrowly just to religious organizations and persons. Among the federal tax advantages limited to religious actors are the special income tax treatment of parsonages and parsonage allowances, procedural protections only for churches, and the Code's lenient treatment of churches' retirement plans for their employees.

Taxing the Church. Edward A. Zelinsky.

In the third approach to churches and religious entities, many provisions of the Internal Revenue Code tax them like secular organizations. Most prominent in this category is the FICA employment-based tax and the self-employment tax which together finance the Social Security system. These taxes apply to most churches, to other sectarian employers, and to the employees of such churches and religious employers. The FICA payroll taxes contain narrow religious exemptions for individuals and churches which do not believe in social insurance. However, religious employers and individuals are largely subject to the employment and self-employment taxes supporting the Social Security system. The often considerable burden these levies impose belie the simple narrative that churches do not pay taxes. The Code also taxes the unrelated business income of churches and other religious entities along with the unrelated business income of secular nonprofit entities. The Code similarly imposes regulatory taxes on otherwise exempt entities, including churches and other sectarian and secular institutions, when they engage in activity incompatible with such entities' tax-exempt status.

The Patient Protection and Affordable Care Act (PPACA)[1] and the Health Care and Education Reconciliation Act of 2010 (HCERA)[2] (colloquially known as "Obamacare") added to the Internal Revenue Code tax-based individual and employer mandates. Reflecting this third pattern, churches and their employees are generally subject to these tax-based federal health care mandates in the same fashion as are for-profit and secular nonprofit employers.

A. THE FEDERAL INCOME TAX

With important qualifications, the federal income tax treats churches and other religious institutions favorably along with secular eleemosynary entities. Like secular eleemosynary entities, churches and other religious institutions do not pay basic federal income taxes. Donors to churches and other sectarian entities receive the same charitable income tax deduction as do contributors to secular nonprofit entities.

These favorable income tax treatments are qualified in important respects. Along with secular eleemosynary institutions, churches and religious organizations are subject to the federal tax on their unrelated business incomes. Churches and sectarian entities are also subject to the Code's regulatory network of penalty taxes which apply to secular, nonprofit organizations as well. These regulatory taxes, along

[1] Pub. L. No. 111-148, 124 Stat. 119 (2010) (PPACA).

[2] Pub. L. No. 111-152, 124 Stat. 1029 (2010) (HCERA).

with the Code's tax on unrelated business income, contravene the uncomplicated characterization of churches as paying no taxes.

Among the key provisions of the Internal Revenue Code affecting religion are the income tax contribution deduction of Code Section 170[3] and the income tax exemption extended by Code Section 501(c)(3).[4] Unlike Code provisions more narrowly targeted at religious institutions and actors, the contribution deduction and income tax exemption apply to a broad range of nonprofit institutions, including religious, charitable, and educational organizations.

Under Code Section 170, a taxpayer may deduct contributions to a domestic, nonprofit "corporation, trust, or community chest, fund, or foundation" which is "organized and operated exclusively for religious, charitable, scientific, literary, or educational purposes."[5] Section 170 also requires that a nonprofit, domestic entity receiving a deductible contribution not be "disqualified for tax exemption under section 501(c)(3) by reason of attempting to influence legislation" and must "not participate in, or intervene in (including the publishing or distributing of statements), any political campaign on behalf of (or in opposition to) any candidate for public office."[6] This provision is sometimes denoted as the "Johnson Amendment" since it was proposed by then-Senator Lyndon B. Johnson in 1954.[7] As we shall see in chapter seven,[8] this prohibition has been a point of contention between certain churches and those who oppose such churches' political activity.

Code Section 501(c)(3) tracks Code Section 170 and its grant of an income tax deduction for donations to qualifying eleemosynary entities. Section 501(c)(3) guarantees those same entities immunity from basic federal income taxes. Together, Code Sections 170 and 501(c)(3), by providing income tax deductions for donors to religious entities and by relieving those entities of federal income taxes, treat churches and other sectarian organizations with the same generosity extended simultaneously to secular eleemosynary institutions.

Some of the sharpest controversies under these Code provisions have dealt with religious organizations and their donors, in particular, the U.S. Supreme Court's

[3] I.R.C. § 170, 26 U.S.C. § 170.

[4] I.R.C. § 501(c)(3), 26 U.S.C. § 501(c)(3). Code Section 501(d) exempts from federal income taxes certain religious communities. I.R.C. § 501(d), 26 U.S.C. § 501(d). *See* Samuel D. Brunson, *Taxing Utopia*, 47 SETON HALL L. REV. 137 (2016).

[5] I.R.C. § 170(b)(2)(B), 26 U.S.C. § 170(b)(2)(B).

[6] I.R.C. § 170(c)(2)(D), 26 U.S.C. § 170(c)(2)(D).

[7] Edward A. Zelinsky, *Churches and Politics: Why the Johnson Amendment Should Be Modified and Not Repealed*, OUPblog (Oct. 3, 2016), http://blog.oup.com/2016/10/church-politics-johnson-amendment-repealed/.

[8] *See infra* at 188–206.

decisions in *Bob Jones University v. United States*[9] and *Hernandez v. Commissioner of Internal Revenue*.[10]

Bob Jones University,[11] a nonprofit corporation, operates a school from kindergarten through graduate school. Bob Jones University is "dedicated to the teaching and propagation of its fundamentalist Christian religious beliefs."[12] Among these beliefs was the conviction "that the Bible forbids interracial dating and marriage."[13] Students who advocated or engaged in interracial dating or marriage were not admitted to Bob Jones University or, if they undertook such advocacy or engagement after admission, were expelled.[14]

Responding to these policies, the IRS revoked the university's tax-exempt status under Section 501(c)(3). Ultimately, the U.S. Supreme Court upheld this revocation. Underlying the Court's *Bob Jones* decision is the premise that tax-exempt status under Code Section 501(c)(3) requires compliance with "established public policy":

> [U]nderlying all relevant parts of the Code, is the intent that entitlement to tax exemption depends on meeting certain common law standards of charity—namely, that an institution seeking tax-exempt status must serve a public purpose and not be contrary to established public policy.[15]

And, the Court continued, racial nondiscrimination in education is such a public policy:

> [T]here can no longer be any doubt that racial discrimination in education violates deeply and widely accepted views of elementary justice . . . [There is] a firm national policy to prohibit racial segregation and discrimination in public education.[16]

From these premises, it was a short step for the *Bob Jones* Court to conclude that the "compelling" "governmental interest" in racial nondiscrimination in education "substantially outweighs whatever burden denial of tax benefits places on petitioners'

[9] 461 U.S. 574 (1983).

[10] 490 U.S. 680 (1989).

[11] Also involved in the *Bob Jones* decision was Goldsboro Christian Schools. This institution "for the most part accepted only Caucasians." *Bob Jones*, 461 U.S. at 583.

[12] *Id.* at 580.

[13] *Id.*

[14] *Id.* at 580–581. As noted *infra* in note 20, these policies were abandoned in 2000.

[15] *Bob Jones University*, 461 U.S. at 586.

[16] *Id.* at 592–593.

exercise of their religious beliefs."[17] While Bob Jones University admitted students of all races, its policy against interracial dating and marriage discriminated "on the basis of racial affiliation and association."[18]

Both Justice Powell[19] in concurrence and then-Justice Rehnquist in dissent[20] were troubled that the Court's *Bob Jones* opinion unacceptably stretched the language of Code Sections 170 and 501(c)(3). However, in practice, *Bob Jones* has not been applied beyond the particular facts of the case.

In *Hernandez*, Robert L. Hernandez[21] took an income tax deduction under Section 170 for his payments to the Church of Scientology for church-provided "auditing" and "training." The IRS disallowed the deduction, and the Supreme Court agreed with the IRS, holding that Mr. Hernandez's payments were not deductible "contribution[s] or gift[s]" within the meaning of Section 170:[22]

> [T]hese payments were part of a quintessential *quid pro quo* exchange: in return for their money, petitioners received an identifiable benefit, namely, auditing and training sessions.[23]

As a statutory matter, the Supreme Court continued, it does not matter that the benefits obtained through these "quid pro quo" payments were religious in nature.[24] There is no "contribution" or "gift" when something—even something religious—is received in return.[25]

In the face of Mr. Hernandez's claim that the First Amendment mandates an income tax deduction for his payments, the Court responded that the disallowance of such a deduction passed "constitutional muster."[26] Section 170 as construed by the Court applies to all religions, "is neutral both in design and purpose,"[27] "neither . . . advance[s] nor inhibit[s] religion,"[28] and "threatens no excessive entanglement

---

17 *Id.* at 604.

18 *Id.* at 605.

19 *Id.* at 606–612.

20 *Id.* at 612–623. In 2000, Bob Jones University revoked its prohibition on interracial dating and in 2017 again became tax exempt under Section 501(c)(3). Fred Stokeld, *Bob Jones University Is Tax Exempt Again*, Tax Notes Doc. 2017-2460.

21 Three other members of the Church of Scientology were also before the Court in *Hernandez*. *Hernandez*, 490 U.S. at 686 n.3.

22 *Id.* at 691.

23 *Id.*

24 *Id.* at 692–694.

25 *Id.*

26 *Id.* at 695.

27 *Id.* at 696.

28 *Id.*

between church and state."[29] Moreover, citing *Lee*,[30] the Court held that denying a deduction for the church's "auditing" and "training" is justified by the federal government's compelling "public interest in maintaining a sound tax system."[31]

Finally, on procedural grounds, the Court's majority declined to consider the claim (embraced in dissent by Justices O'Connor and Scalia) that, as an administrative matter, the IRS has permitted deductions for similar "*quid pro quo*" payments to other religious groups. In the trial court, the taxpayer had failed to develop the "proper factual record"[32] needed for the Court to assess whether the IRS has permitted deductions for "*quid pro quo*" payments to other churches and synagogues.

In dissent, Justice O'Connor, joined by Justice Scalia, accepted the taxpayer's argument that the IRS, in denying income tax deductions for payments to the Church of Scientology, treated such payments differently from similar payments to other religious entities. Citing a 1919 IRS memorandum,[33] as well as more contemporary revenue rulings,[34] Justice O'Connor argued that the IRS's denial of deductions for payments to the Church of Scientology "involves the differential application of a standard based on constitutionally impermissible differences drawn by the Government among religions."[35] Moreover, Justice O'Connor contended, "there are good reasons why"[36] the IRS permits income tax deductions for payments to these other sectarian entities: It is difficult to value intangible religious benefits which are not traded commercially and therefore have no readily ascertainable fair market value.[37]

Subsequent to the *Hernandez* decision, the Church of Scientology and the IRS entered into a closing agreement, which, under taxpayer privacy rules,[38] remains confidential.[39] A second coda to the *Hernandez* decision was Congress's addition to Code Section 170 of the rule that a taxpayer may deduct a contribution of $250 or more only if "the taxpayer substantiates the contribution by a contemporaneous

---

[29] *Id.*

[30] *Id.* at 699–700 (citing *United States v. Lee*, 452 U.S. 252 (1982)). For discussion of *Lee*, *see supra* at 22–23.

[31] *Hernandez*, 490 U.S. at 699–700 (internal quotations omitted).

[32] *Id.* at 703.

[33] *Id.* at 707 (citing A.R.M. 2, 1 C.B. 150 (1919)).

[34] *Id.* at 708 (citing Rev. Rul. 70-47, 1970-1 C.B. 49 and Rev. Rul. 78-366, 1978-2 C.B. 241).

[35] *Id.* at 712.

[36] *Id.* at 706.

[37] *Id.* at 706–707.

[38] I.R.C. § 6103, 26 U.S.C. § 6103.

[39] Douglas Frantz, *Scientology's Puzzling Journey from Tax Rebel to Tax Exempt*, N.Y. TIMES, Mar. 9, 1997, at A2, http://nyti.ms/1FmTsyP; Peter J. Reilly, *IRS Veteran Weighs in on Deduction for Scientology Auditing in Secret 1993 Agreement*, Forbes.com (July 19, 2012), http://www.forbes.com/sites/peterjreilly/2012/07/19/irs-veteran-weighs-in-on-deduction-for-scientology-auditing-in-secret-1993-agreement/#4cec21d71ecd.

written acknowledgment of the contribution by the donee organization."[40] Such a written substantiation must describe and provide a "good faith estimate of the value of any goods or services" received by the taxpayer for his donation.[41] Adopting Justice O'Connor's argument that intangible religious benefits have no readily ascertainable fair market value, such a written acknowledgment of a contribution need not value any "intangible religious benefit[s]" received by the donor.[42]

Internal Revenue Code Section 511 qualifies the tax-exempt status bestowed by Code Section 501(c)(3). Section 511 (often referred to as the "UBIT"[43]) imposes income taxes on an otherwise tax-exempt entity if such entity earns "unrelated business taxable income,"[44] that is to say, income earned from the conduct of a trade or business unrelated to the purpose for which the entity is granted tax exemption. Prior to the Tax Reform Act of 1969,[45] churches and "conventions[s] or association[s]" of churches were not subject to the UBIT and thus, unlike other 501(c)(3) organizations, could realize unrelated business taxable income without paying tax on such income.[46]

The 1969 act amended the Code to treat churches and conventions and associations of churches like other 501(c)(3) entities, that is, taxable on unrelated business taxable income. The UBIT thus again belies the simple narrative that churches are not taxed. Defenders of the income tax exemption of churches argue that the churches themselves supported the 1969 change to the UBIT to make the federal tax treatment of religious groups more principled and equitable.[47]

A second important qualification to the tax-exempt status bestowed by Code Section 501(c)(3) consists of the regulatory taxes penalizing the misuse of tax-exempt entities or their resources. The Tax Reform Act of 1969[48] divided organizations tax exempt under Section 501(c)(3) into two categories, private foundations and public charities,[49] and subjected the former to a network of penalty taxes for such misfeasance as self-dealing and making investments which jeopardize the purpose for which the private foundation is tax exempt.[50] Congress subsequently

---

40 I.R.C. § 170(f)(8)(A), 26 U.S.C. § 170(f)(8)(A).

41 I.R.C. § 170(f)(8)(B)(iii), 26 U.S.C. § 170(f)(8)(B)(iii).

42 *Id.*

43 For unrelated business income tax.

44 I.R.C. § 511, 26 U.S.C. § 511.

45 Pub. L. No. 91-172, 83 Stat. 487 (1969).

46 *See* I.R.C. § 511(a)(2)(A) prior to amendment by § 121(a)(1) of the Tax Reform Act of 1969, Pub. L. No. 91-172, 83 Stat. 487 (1969).

47 Dean M. Kelley, Why Churches Should Not Pay Taxes 3, 17 (1977).

48 Pub. L. No. 91-172, 83 Stat. 487 (1969). *See* Edward A. Zelinsky, *Why the Buffett-Gates Giving Pledge Requires Limitation of the Estate Tax Charitable Deduction*, 16 Fla. Tax Rev. 393, 397–405 (2014).

49 I.R.C. § 509(a), 26 U.S.C. § 509(a).

50 I.R.C. §§ 4940 through 4948, inclusive; 26 U.S.C. §§ 4940 through 4948, inclusive.

created a second set of regulatory taxes which penalize public charities for making "political expenditures,"[51] undertaking lobbying expenses,[52] or engaging in "excess benefit transactions."[53]

The Code places churches, along with such other tax-exempt institutions as schools and hospitals, in the public charity category[54] and thus subjects them to the second group of regulatory taxes pertaining to public charities. A religious organization which does not constitute a church may trigger private foundation status and thus be covered by the private foundation network of penalty taxes. A nonchurch religious organization might also fall within the public charity category and thus trigger the regulatory taxes pertaining to such charities.

Consider, for example, a private foundation, funded and controlled by a wealthy family, which contributes only to religious causes. This private foundation is subject to the same regulatory taxes as another wealthy family's foundation which encourages secular arts education. If, however, a Section 501(c)(3) entity supporting religious causes has enough public support to be classified as a public charity,[55] this entity is not regulated as a private foundation, but is instead treated as a public charity and is thus subject to the alternative set of penalty taxes governing such public charities.

Like the UBIT on unrelated business incomes, the Code's regulatory taxes contradict the simple narrative that churches are not subject to taxation. A church or other religious institution which triggers these regulatory taxes pays the same tax as a secular 501(c)(3) institution subject to these levies.

In contrast to Code Sections 170 and 501(c)(3), which treat religious entities in the same fashion as secular philanthropic organizations, other features of the income tax narrowly benefit religious organizations and religious actors. Code Section 107,[56] for example, excludes from income taxation housing furnished to a "minister of the gospel," whether such housing is provided through a cash parsonage allowance or is provided in kind.

As a general rule, Code Section 119[57] excludes from a taxpayer's income in-kind housing if an employer-employee relationship exists between the housing recipient and the housing provider, the housing is furnished on the employer's "business premises," the housing is provided "for the convenience of the employer," and the

---

[51] I.R.C. § 4955, 26 U.S.C. § 4955.

[52] I.R.C. §§ 4911 and 4912, 26 U.S.C. §§ 4911 and 4912.

[53] I.R.C. § 4958, 26 U.S.C. § 4958.

[54] I.R.C. §§ 170(b)(1)(A)(i) and 509(a)(1), 26 U.S.C. §§ 170(b)(1)(A)(i) and 509(a)(1).

[55] I.R.C. § 509(a)(2), 26 U.S.C. § 509(a)(2).

[56] I.R.C. § 107, 26 U.S.C. § 107.

[57] I.R.C. § 119, 26 U.S.C. § 119.

employee is required to accept the employer-provided housing "as a condition of his employment." However, under Section 107, none of these requirements need be met to exclude from federal income taxation housing provided to a "minister of the gospel."

The IRS and the courts have been rigorous in their enforcement of Section 119's requirements for excluding from income the value of employer-provided housing. For example, an engineer working on the Trans-Alaska Pipeline could not exclude from his gross income employer-provided housing in Valdez, Alaska, despite the scarcity of housing in that oil-fueled boomtown. The housing in question was not on the "business premises" of the pipeline operator.[58]

Similarly, a college president in Nebraska could not exclude the value of a house provided to him by the college. This house was "approximately four miles away from the College's classroom buildings, administrative offices and other educational facilities" and was thus off the college's business premises.[59] In contrast, under Section 107, a minister of the gospel can exclude from income the value of housing even if the housing is off-site and without having to prove that such housing is required for the employer's convenience.

The more liberal housing exclusion of Code Section 107 is only available to a "minister of the gospel." This requirement raises weighty interpretative issues. For example, for purposes of Section 107, the cantor of a conservative synagogue has been deemed to be a "minister of the gospel" because of

> the ministerial duties required of him in his official position as cantor: he conducted religious worship; he administered sacerdotal functions; he performed marriages and officiated at funerals and services at houses of mourning; and he directed organizations within the congregation.[60]

In contrast, a rabbi working for the American Jewish Committee as its national director of interreligious affairs was not serving as a "minister of the gospel" for purposes of Section 107.[61] According to the court, the rabbi did not perform "a ministerial function within the intendment of the statute [as his] primary function for the American Jewish Committee was in the nature of public relations."[62]

---

[58] *Van Huff v. Commissioner*, 41 T.C.M. 764 (1981).

[59] *Winchell v. United States*, 564 F. Supp. 131, 136 (D. Neb. 1983).

[60] *Silverman v. Commissioner*, 57 T.C. 727, 731 (1972).

[61] *Tanenbaum v. Commissioner*, 58 T.C. 1 (1972).

[62] *Id.* at 9.

As I discuss in chapter six,[63] Code Section 107 has been controversial and will remain so in the future as opponents of that provision attack it as entangling and as subsidizing. While tax-free housing allowances are not completely unknown to the tax law,[64] cash living allowances are generally taxable income.[65] This makes the income tax–free treatment of cash parsonage allowances[66] particularly noteworthy.

To qualify for tax-free treatment, the cash allowance paid to a minister of the gospel must actually be "used by him to rent or provide a home."[67] Thus, if the parsonage allowance paid to a clergyman exceeds his housing-related outlays, the excess is taxable. The tax-free parsonage allowance is further capped at "the fair rental value of the [minister's] home, including furnishings and appurtenances such as a garage, plus the cost of utilities."[68] This limit was added to the Code by Congress in 2002 in response to the *Warren*[69] litigation involving the parsonage allowance received by Reverend Rick Warren. This statutory limit explicitly confirmed the IRS's position that Section 107 implicitly contained such a limit.

As a general rule, a taxpayer forfeits any income tax deduction to the extent such deduction "is allocable" to tax-exempt income.[70] Parsonage allowances receive further favorable tax treatment via relief from this rule.[71] Thus, a minister of the gospel who owns his residence may receive, in colloquial terms, a "double deduction,"[72] first excluding his parsonage allowance from gross income and then deducting the mortgage interest payments and property taxes paid with these tax-free funds. I argue in

---

[63] *See infra* at 163–186.

[64] I.R.C. §§ 911(a)(2) and 911(c), 26 U.S.C. §§ 911(a)(2) and 911(c) (exclusion from gross income of foreign-based "housing cost amount"); *VITA/TCE Training Guide*, IRS Pub. No. 4491 at 163 ("the Basic Allowance for Housing (BAH) can be excluded from gross income as a qualified military benefit" under Code § 134). *See also Armed Forces' Tax Guide*, IRS Pub. No. 3 at 4.

[65] *See, e.g., Commissioner of Internal Revenue v. Kowalski*, 434 U.S. 77 (1977) (employer-provided cash meal allowances are taxable income).

[66] I.R.C. § 107(2), 26 U.S.C. § 107(2). The term "parsonage allowance" does not actually appear in § 107(2), but has become the common label for the tax-free "rental allowance" paid to a minister of the gospel. Section 265(a)(6)(B) explicitly uses the term "parsonage allowance" to describe a payment excluded from gross income under Section 107(2). I.R.C. § 265(a)(6)(B), 26 U.S.C. § 265(a)(6)(B).

[67] I.R.C. § 107(2), 26 U.S.C. § 107(2).

[68] *Id.*

[69] For a discussion of the *Warren* controversy, *see* Edward A. Zelinsky, *Do Religious Tax Exemptions Entangle in Violation of the Establishment Clause? The Constitutionality of the Parsonage Allowance Exclusion and the Religious Exemptions of the Individual Health Care Mandate and the FICA and Self-Employment Taxes*, 33 CARDOZO L. REV. 1633, 1652 (2012); *Warren v. Commissioner*, 114 T.C. 343 (2000).

[70] I.R.C. § 265(a)(1), 26 U.S.C. § 265(a)(1).

[71] I.R.C. § 265(a)(6)(B), 26 U.S.C. § 265(a)(6)(B). Military housing allowances also receive this favorable treatment. I.R.C. § 265(a)(6)(A), 26 U.S.C. § 265(a)(6)(A).

[72] Actually, this minister receives an exclusion from gross income for his parsonage allowance combined with an otherwise impermissible deduction of his mortgage interest and property taxes. However, the common phrase "double deduction" captures the gist of the situation.

chapter six that Section 107 is a constitutionally permissible choice to avoid enforcement entanglement between the IRS and clergy, but that there is no persuasive tax policy justification for Section 107's exclusion from clerical incomes of cash parsonage allowances.

B. THE FEDERAL ESTATE AND GIFT TAXES

The federal estate[73] and gift[74] taxes contain deductions for bequests and gifts to eleemosynary institutions, including charitable, religious, and educational institutions. These deductions largely parallel the income tax deduction of Section 107 and thereby permit a decedent or a living donor to convey wealth to these religious and secular philanthropic institutions free of any federal transfer taxation.[75]

C. THE FICA AND SELF-EMPLOYMENT TAXES

The "payroll taxes" are the most burdensome federal taxes imposed upon churches and other religious institutions. Social Security and Medicare benefits[76] are principally[77] funded[78] through these two taxes, one levied on employees' wages and one assessed on individuals' self-employment incomes. In the case of an employee covered by the Social Security system, the employee[79] and the employer[80] each pay what are commonly denoted as FICA[81] taxes. Specifically, if an individual earns "wages"[82]

---

[73] I.R.C. § 2055, 26 U.S.C. § 2055.

[74] I.R.C. § 2522, 26 U.S.C. § 2522.

[75] *See* Zelinsky, *supra* note 48, at 393, 405–406.

[76] For a summary of the retirement, death, disability, and medical benefits paid by the Social Security system, *see* Jonathan Barry Forman, Making America Work 76–77, 174–175, 186–190, 247–248 (2006).

[77] In addition to the FICA and self-employment taxes imposed on earned income, Internal Revenue Code § 1411 also imposes an additional Medicare tax on certain individuals' net investment incomes. I.R.C. § 1411, 26 U.S.C. § 1411.

[78] This is a controversial assertion today with many commentators arguing that, in practice, FICA and self-employment taxes, borrowed by the federal Treasury, are simply used for general government purposes. *See, e.g., CBO Says Social Security Disability Insurance Insolvent in Eight Years* (Sept. 14, 2010), http://www.verumserum.com/?p=17127 ("Now, I have elsewhere advocated that the 'trust fund' is a bogus way to look at the Social Security issue. I still believe that to be the case. In reality, current benefits like SSDI are coming from current workers. There really is no trust fund but the general fund.").

[79] I.R.C. § 3101, 26 U.S.C. § 3101.

[80] I.R.C. § 3111, 26 U.S.C. § 3111.

[81] For Federal Insurance Contributions Act, the formal name of the Code provisions (I.R.C. § 3101 et seq.) establishing the Social Security taxes paid by employers and employees.

[82] I.R.C. § 3121(a), 26 U.S.C. § 3121(a).

from "employment,"[83] the employer withholds FICA taxes from the individual's pay and remits to the federal government this withheld tax.[84] The employer also makes an equal FICA tax payment.[85]

A self-employed person pays Social Security and Medicare taxes matching the combined FICA payments of an employee and her employer.[86] An individual who conducts a "trade or business"[87] pays tax on her "self-employment income."[88] The statutory rate of this self-employment tax equals the combined FICA rates paid by employers and employees.

In particular, to finance Social Security's retirement, death, and disability benefits, an employee and her employer each pay a tax of 6.2 percent of her wages up to the amount of the employee's wages subject to Social Security coverage.[89] For 2017, this amount is capped at $127,200.[90] To finance the hospital coverage conventionally known as Medicare, an employee and her employer each pay a tax of 1.45 percent on all of the employee's wages without limit.[91] In addition, married couples earning annual wages in excess of $250,000 and single individuals earnings annual wages in excess of $200,000 pay an additional Medicare tax equal to 0.9 percent of such excess.[92]

The tax rates on self-employed income replicate this pattern. A self-employed individual pays a self-employment tax of 12.4 percent on the amount of her self-employment income up to the ceiling amount of such income subject to Social Security coverage.[93] This rate of 12.4 percent equals the total (6.2% + 6.2%) paid by an employee and her employer for Social Security's retirement, disability, and death benefits. In addition, a self-employed individual pays a Medicare tax of 2.9 percent on all of her self-employment income.[94] This rate of 2.9 percent equals the total (1.45% + 1.45%) which an employee and her employer pay for Medicare. Married

---

83 I.R.C. § 3121(b), 26 U.S.C. § 3121(b).

84 I.R.C. § 3102, 26 U.S.C. § 3102.

85 Labor economists generally agree that, for the long run, the economic incidence of the FICA taxes paid by employers falls in significant measure upon employees in the form of lower cash wages and less employment. *See, e.g.*, Ronald G. Ehrenberg & Robert S. Smith, Modern Labor Economics: Theory and Public Policy 86–89 (7th ed. 2000) ("a comprehensive review of these studies led to at least a tentative conclusion that most of a payroll tax is eventually shifted to wages . . .").

86 I.R.C. § 1401 et seq., 26 U.S.C. § 1401 et seq.

87 I.R.C. § 1402(a), 26 U.S.C. § 1402(a).

88 I.R.C. § 1402(b), 26 U.S.C. § 1402(b).

89 I.R.C. §§ 3101(a), 3111(a), and 3121(a)(1); 26 U.S.C. §§ 3101(a), 3111(a), and 3121(a)(1).

90 IRS Publication 15 (Circular E), *Employer's Tax Guide* at 1 (Dec. 19, 2016).

91 I.R.C. §§ 3101(b)(1) and 3111(b), 26 U.S.C. §§ 3101(b)(1) and 3111(b).

92 I.R.C. § 3101(b)(2), 26 U.S.C. §§ 3101(b)(2).

93 I.R.C. §§ 1401(a) and 1402(b)(1); 26 U.S.C. § 1401(a) and 1402(b)(1).

94 I.R.C. § 1401(b)(1), 26 U.S.C. § 1401(b)(1).

couples earning annual self-employment income in excess of $250,000 and single individuals earning annual self-employment income in excess of $200,000 pay an additional Medicare tax of 0.9 percent of such excess.[95]

Churches, other religious employers, and their employees are generally subject to these taxes, which can often be considerable. As to their nonclerical employees, churches and other sectarian institutions are "employers" and, like secular employers, must collect FICA taxes from their employees' wages and then match those withheld taxes with an equal payment.

Suppose, for example, that a church pays its nonclerical executive director $100,000 annually. As the employer, the church must withhold $7,650 in FICA taxes from this employee's salary.[96] In addition, the church matches this withheld tax with an additional payment of $7,650 in FICA taxes.

As to clergy, the term "employment" for FICA purposes excludes "service performed by a duly ordained, commissioned, or licensed minister of a church in the exercise of his ministry."[97] In addition, the term "employment" for FICA purposes excludes services performed "by a member of a religious order in the exercise of duties required by such order" unless the order elects Social Security coverage for its members.[98]

As a result, clergymen generally pay self-employment tax since, as a statutory matter, they are not engaged in "employment" for FICA tax purposes but are instead deemed to be conducting a "trade or business" under the self-employment tax.[99] For these clergymen, self-employment income includes the value of any in-kind housing, as well as cash parsonage allowances they receive.[100]

Like the Internal Revenue Code's taxes on unrelated business incomes and the Code's penalty taxes regulating tax-exempt organizations, the FICA levies contravene the simple narrative that churches and other sectarian institutions pay no taxes. Most churches can avoid the tax on unrelated business income by eschewing such income, just as churches can avoid the Code's regulatory taxes by refraining from the behavior which triggers these penalty taxes. In contrast, the FICA payroll taxes on churches' nonclerical employees' wages and the self-employment taxes paid by clergy cannot be dodged when the church has employees.

The FICA taxes contain limited exemptions for persons who oppose on religious grounds insurance programs like the Social Security system. Internal Revenue

---

95 I.R.C. §§ 1401(b)(2), 26 U.S.C. § 1401(b)(2).

96 6.2% + 1.45% = 7.65%; $100,000 x 7.65% = $7,650.

97 I.R.C. § 3121(b)(8)(A), 26 U.S.C. § 3121(b)(8)(A).

98 *Id. See also* I.R.C. § 3121(r), 26 U.S.C. § 3121(r).

99 I.R.C. § 1402(a)(8), 26 U.S.C. § 1402(a)(8).

100 *Id.*

Code Section 1402(g) grants immunity from the federal self-employment tax to "member[s] of a recognized religious sect" who, by reason of their adherence to the "established tenets or teachings of such sect," are "conscientiously opposed to acceptance of the benefits of any private or public insurance." This exemption was adopted by Congress in 1960[101] and requires the sect member claiming exemption to apply for and prove his eligibility for the exemption. As part of the application process, the individual claiming this exemption from the self-employment tax must waive his eligibility for Social Security benefits.[102]

Section 1402(e) also excuses from the federal self-employment tax "a duly ordained, commissioned, or licensed minister of a church or a member of a religious order" or "a Christian Science practitioner" if such minister, member, or practitioner "is conscientiously opposed to, or because of religious principles [ ]is opposed to, the acceptance of . . . any public insurance" and if he applies for recognition of his status as an opponent of public insurance. Since they contribute no taxes to the Social Security system, ministers and members of orders who oppose "public insurance" on religious grounds do not earn Social Security benefits.[103]

Clergymen religiously opposed to Social Security pay no FICA taxes because, as a statutory matter, they are not engaged in "employment"[104] nor do they pay self-employment taxes because of the Section 1402(e) exemption.

In the wake of *Lee* discussed in chapter one,[105] Congress also exempted from FICA taxation employers and employees who satisfy the terms of Section 1402(g), that is, are "member[s] of a recognized religious sect" who, by reason of their adherence to the "established tenets or teachings of such sect," are "conscientiously opposed to acceptance of the benefits of any private or public insurance."[106] Like the exemption from the self-employment tax under Section 1402(g), this exemption from FICA taxation requires the sect member asserting the exemption to apply for and prove his eligibility for exemption.[107] As part of the application process, the individual claiming this religious exemption from FICA taxation must waive his entitlement to Social Security benefits.[108]

---

[101] Social Security Amendments of 1960, Pub. L. No. 86-778 § 105(c), 74 Stat. 924 (1960).

[102] I.R.C. § 1402(g)(1)(B), 26 U.S.C. § 1402(g)(1)(B).

[103] 42 U.S.C. § 411(c) provides that, for Social Security purposes, a minister or member of an order exempt from self-employment taxes under I.R.C. § 1402(e) does not conduct a "trade or business." Consequently, such minister or member does not have "net earnings from self-employment" for the calculation of Social Security benefits and thus has no "average indexed monthly earnings" to generate Social Security benefits. 42 U.S.C. §§ 411(a), 415(a), and 415(b).

[104] I.R.C. § 3121(b)(8)(A), 26 U.S.C. § 3121(b)(8)(A).

[105] 455 U.S. 252 (1982). *See supra* at 22–23.

[106] I.R.C. § 3127, 26 U.S.C. § 3127.

[107] I.R.C. § 3127(b), 26 U.S.C. § 3127(b).

[108] *Id.*

A church or "church-controlled organization" which "is opposed for religious reasons to the payment of the" employer's FICA tax obligation may elect for its employees' earnings to be treated as self-employment income for FICA purposes.[109] As a result of this election, such church employees are deemed to be conducting a "trade or business"[110] and thus owe self-employment taxes on their earnings and accrue Social Security benefits.[111]

However, these exemptions are not available to most churches or clergy, only to churches and clergy "conscientiously opposed" to Social Security. For most religious institutions and most clergy, FICA taxes on wages and taxes on self-employment incomes are significant burdens, although offset by the Social Security coverage such taxes obtain.

D. THE FEDERAL UNEMPLOYMENT TAX

The eleemosynary organizations described in Code Section 501(c)(3), including educational, charitable, and religious organizations, are exempt from the federal unemployment tax.[112] However, as I discuss in chapter four,[113] eleemosynary and nonchurch religious entities are generally subject to state unemployment tax, though churches are not.

E. THE FEDERAL HEALTH MANDATES FOR INDIVIDUALS AND EMPLOYERS

PPACA and HCERA amended the Internal Revenue Code to require most U.S. residents to carry "minimum essential" health care coverage for themselves and their dependents. This individual health coverage mandate[114] is enforced by a tax penalty. PPACA and HCERA[115] also added to the Code a mandate that "any applicable large employer" must[116] offer medical coverage to its full-time employees. An

[109] I.R.C. §§ 3121(b)(8)(B) and 3121(w), 26 U.S.C. §§ 3121(b)(8)(B) and 3121(w).

[110] I.R.C. § 1402(c)(2)(G), 26 U.S.C. § 1402(c)(2)(G).

[111] 20 C.F.R. §§ 404.1026 and 404.1068(f).

[112] I.R.C. § 3306(c)(8), 26 U.S.C. § 3306(c)(8).

[113] *See infra* at 104–111.

[114] I.R.C. § 5000A, 26 U.S.C. § 5000A, added by PPACA §§ 1501(b) and 10106(b)(1) and HCERA §§ 1002 and 1004. For discussion of the individual mandate, *see* Edward A. Zelinsky, *The Health-Related Tax Provisions of PPACA and HCERA: Contingent, Complex, Incremental and Lacking Cost Controls*, *in* New York University Review of Employee Benefits and Executive Compensation (Alvin D. Lurie ed., 2010).

[115] I.R.C. § 4980H, 26 U.S.C. § 4980H, added by PPACA §§ 1513, 10106, and 10108 and HCERA § 1003.

[116] PPACA § 1513(d).

employer failing to satisfy this statutory mandate owes an excise penalty tax which varies with the nature of the employer's failure. For purposes of the employer health care mandate, an employer is an "applicable large employer"[117] in the current calendar year if, during the prior calendar year, it "employed an average of at least fifty full-time employees" for more than 120 days during such prior year.[118]

The upshot of these rules is that any "large" church or other religious employer with fifty or more full-time employees must maintain medical coverage for its employees or must instead pay a penalty tax to the federal Treasury—just like any secular employer.[119]

By regulation, limited exemption has been extended to churches and religious employers concerning the provision of employer-financed birth control to their employees.[120] These exemptions have proved controversial.[121] However, this controversy should not obscure the fact that, putting the contraception issue aside, churches and other religious employers are subject to the tax-enforced employer health care mandate, just as secular employers are.

The Code's tax-enforced health care mandate for individuals contains two religious exemptions. One religious exemption from the individual mandate incorporates the self-employment tax exemption of Section 1402(g) to excuse from the health care mandate sect members opposed to insurance on religious grounds.[122] The individual health care mandate also exempts from its coverage any "member of a health care sharing ministry" if the members of such ministry "share a common set of ethical or religious beliefs and share medical expenses . . . in accordance with those beliefs."[123]

Other than the contraception-related regulations and the two statutory exemptions for certain religious individuals, the tax-based health care mandates, as added

---

[117] I.R.C. § 4980H(c)(2), 26 U.S.C. § 4980H(c)(2).

[118] I.R.C. §§ 4980H(c)(2)(A) and 4980H(c)(2)(B)(i)(I), 26 U.S.C. §§ 4980H(c)(2)(A) and 4980H(c)(2)(B)(i)(I).

[119] The Internal Revenue Code's rules pertaining to group health plans also apply to church plans, though the potential penalty under these rules is calculated somewhat differently for church employers. I.R.C. § 4980D(b)(3)(C), 26 U.S.C. § 4980D(b)(3)(C).

[120] *See, e.g.*, Edward A. Zelinsky, *The Aftermath of* Hobby Lobby: *HSAs and HRAs as the Least Restrictive Means*, 42 RUTGERS L. RECORD 110 (2015), reprinted in NEW YORK UNIVERSITY REVIEW OF EMPLOYEE BENEFITS AND EXECUTIVE COMPENSATION (Alvin D. Lurie ed., 2015); Edward A. Zelinsky, *The HSA/HRA Response to* Hobby Lobby, OUPblog (Aug. 4, 2014), http://blog.oup.com/2014/08/hobby-lobby-hsa-hra-response-bipartisan/.

[121] *See, e.g.*, Edward A. Zelinsky, Zubik v. Burwell: *The HSA/HRA Alternative*, OUPblog (Apr. 4, 2016), http://blog.oup.com/2016/04/zubik-v-burwell-hsa-hra-alternative/.

[122] I.R.C. § 5000A(d)(2)(A), 26 U.S.C. § 5000A(d)(2)(A). *See* Stephanie Armour, *More People Turn to Faith-Based Groups for Health Coverage*, WALL ST. J., Jan. 4, 2016.

[123] I.R.C. § 5000A(d)(2)(B), 26 U.S.C. § 5000A(d)(2)(B).

to the Internal Revenue Code by PPACA and HCERA, treat churches and their employees in the same fashion as they treat secular employers and their employees.

F. THE CODE'S PROCEDURAL PROVISIONS RELATIVE TO CHURCHES

Entities which are tax exempt under Internal Revenue Code Section 501(c)(3) must generally file annual information returns with the Department of the Treasury.[124] However, "churches, their integrated auxiliaries, and conventions or associations of churches" need not file such annual returns.[125] Moreover, a variety of Section 501(c)(3) organizations with yearly gross receipts of $5,000 or less need not file information returns with the Treasury.[126] "[R]eligious organization[s]" are among these small entities relieved from the obligation to file annual information returns with the IRS.[127]

The Code also requires organizations claiming tax-exempt status to file with the IRS to recognize such status.[128] However, the exempt organizations excused from filing annual information returns also need not file with the IRS for recognition of their tax-exempt status.[129] Thus, churches, associations and conventions of churches, and church auxiliaries, as well as smaller religious groups with gross annual receipts of $5,000 or less, need not obtain IRS recognition of their tax-exempt status.

As we shall see in chapter four,[130] in some states, churches must nevertheless obtain IRS confirmation of their income tax–exempt status to enjoy sales tax exemption. Moreover, some churches obtain IRS confirmation of their tax-exempt status to assure donors of the deductibility of their contributions or because the churches perceive legitimacy from such IRS confirmation.[131] However, as a matter of federal tax law, churches, unlike comparable secular nonprofit organizations, need not apply to the IRS for formal recognition of their tax-exempt status.

The IRS's generally broad ability to enforce[132] the Code is subject to special procedural restrictions in the case of audits of "any organization claiming to be a church,"[133]

124 I.R.C. § 6033(a)(1), 26 U.S.C. § 6033(a)(1).

125 I.R.C. § 6033(a)(3)(A)(i), 26 U.S.C. § 6033(a)(3)(A)(i).

126 I.R.C. § 6033(a)(3)(A)(ii), 26 U.S.C. § 6033(a)(3)(A)(ii).

127 I.R.C. § 6033(a)(3)(C)(i), 26 U.S.C. § 6033(a)(3)(C)(i).

128 I.R.C. § 508(a), 26 U.S.C. § 508(a). *See also* Treas. Reg. § 1.501(a)-1T(a)(2), 26 C.F.R. § 1.501(a)-1T(a)(2).

129 I.R.C. § 508(c)(1), 26 U.S.C. § 508(c)(1).

130 *See infra* at 90–96.

131 Christopher P. Scheitle, Erica J. Dollhopf, & John D. McCarthy, *Exploring Religious Congregations' Registration with the IRS*, 45 NONPROFIT & VOLUNTARY SECTOR Q. 397, 406 (2016).

132 I.R.C. § 7602, 26 U.S.C. § 7602. *See also United States v. Powell*, 379 U.S. 48 (1964).

133 I.R.C. § 7611(h)(1)(A), 26 U.S.C. § 7611(h)(1)(A).

as well as audits of "any convention or association of churches."[134] These restrictions impose higher procedural thresholds and protections for churches being reviewed by the IRS than are extended to other taxpayers being scrutinized by the IRS.

For these purposes, the Code distinguishes between the first step of starting "a church tax inquiry"[135] and the second step of "a church tax examination"[136] advancing that inquiry further. A church tax inquiry is an initial IRS inquest about the status of an entity as a tax-exempt church (or not) or an initial IRS scrutiny about a church's possible conduct of an unrelated trade or business subject to the UBIT under Internal Revenue Code Section 511.[137] A church tax examination is the subsequent review of "church records" or of "the religious activities of any church."[138]

The IRS can begin a church tax inquiry only if three requirements are satisfied. First, such an inquiry must be authorized by "an appropriate high-level Treasury official."[139] That high-level official must be the Regional Commissioner of the IRS or a higher ranking official of the Treasury.[140] Second, that high-level official must "reasonably believe[] on the basis of facts and circumstances recorded in writing" that the church to be audited may not be tax exempt for purposes of Section 501(c)(3) or may be conducting an unrelated trade or business.[141] Third, before the IRS starts such an initial inquiry, the church to be audited must receive a notice which includes a statement of the concerns motivating the inquiry and of the legal and factual background for the proposed audit.[142]

Once a "church tax inquiry" has been commenced, the Code's rules for a "church tax examination" continue to afford the audited church greater procedural protection than extends to nonchurch taxpayers audited by the IRS. While a church examination may be conducted by lower level IRS personnel,[143] prior notice of

---

134 I.R.C. § 7611(h)(1)(B), 26 U.S.C. § 7611(h)(1)(B).

135 I.R.C. §§ 7611(a) and 7611(h)(2), 26 U.S.C. § 7611(a) and 7611(h)(2).

136 I.R.C. §§ 7611(b) and 7611(h)(3), 26 U.S.C. § 7611(b) and 7611(h)(3).

137 I.R.C. § 7611(h)(2), 26 U.S.C. § 7611(h)(2).

138 I.R.C. § 7611(h)(3), 26 U.S.C. § 7611(h)(3).

139 I.R.C. § 7611(a)(2), 26 U.S.C. § 7611(a)(2).

140 Treas. Reg. § 301.7611-1, Q&A(1); 26 C.F.R. § 301.7611-1, Q&A(1). The position of Regional Commissioner no longer exists. *See USA v. Living Word Christian Center*, 2009 U.S. Dist. LEXIS 6902 at *8 (D. Minn.) (confirming judge-magistrate's recommendation that IRS Director of Exempt Organizations, Examinations, does not qualify as an "appropriate high-level Treasury official.").

141 I.R.C. § 7611(a)(2), 26 U.S.C. § 7611(a)(2) (parentheses omitted).

142 I.R.C. § 7611(a)(3), 26 U.S.C. § 7611(a)(3).

143 Such an examination may be conducted by "the Secretary," a term defined statutorily to include regular IRS auditors to whom has been delegated the Secretary's authority under the Code. Code §§ 7611(b)(1) (authorizing "the Secretary" to commence a church tax examination), 7701(a)(11)(B) (defining "the Secretary" as including "his delegate") and 7701(a)(12)(A)(i) (including as the Secretary's delegate "any officer, employee, or agency" who is "duly authorized.").

such examination must be furnished to both the church to be examined and to the regional counsel of the IRS.[144] Upon the receipt of such notice, the church can demand a conference with the IRS "to discuss, and attempt to resolve, concerns relating to such examination."[145] Substantively, the IRS can take no adverse action against a church (such as a declaration that an entity claiming to be a church is not) unless the regional counsel of the IRS confirms the IRS's compliance with Section 7611 and approves the adverse action.[146] While there are exceptions to these rules,[147] the overall import of Internal Revenue Code Section 7611 is to provide churches with unique procedural protection in IRS audits.[148]

G. CHURCH RETIREMENT PLANS

Another narrowly church-favorable feature of the Internal Revenue Code is the Code's lenient treatment of churches' retirement plans for their employees.[149] Qualified pension and profit-sharing plans (including the now ubiquitous 401(k) arrangement[150]) are generally subject to elaborate rules promulgated in the Code and in the Employee Retirement Income Security Act of 1974 (ERISA).[151] These tax- and ERISA-based rules mandate many of the critical features of such plans,

---

144 I.R.C. § 7611(b)(2)(A), 26 U.S.C. § 7611(b)(2)(A).

145 I.R.C. § 7611(b)(3)(A)(iii), 26 U.S.C. § 7611(b)(3)(A)(iii).

146 I.R.C. § 7611(d)(1), 26 U.S.C. § 7611(d)(1).

147 Among the proceedings to which Section 7611 does not apply are criminal investigations, "any inquiry or examination relating to the tax liability of any person other than a church," pursuit of willful tax evasion or a "knowing failure to file a return of tax," and certain routine IRS audits. I.R.C. § 7611(i), 26 U.S.C. § 7611(i); Treas. Reg. § 301.7611-1, Q&A(4); 26 C.F.R. § 301.7611-1, Q&A(4).

148 Code Section 7611 was the subject of amusing, albeit inaccurate, criticism by the comedian John Oliver, who blames the IRS for this Code provision. Congress, not the IRS, passes the Internal Revenue Code. Edward A. Zelinsky, *John Oliver, Televangelists, and the Internal Revenue Service*, OUPblog (Sept. 7, 2015), http://blog.oup.com/2015/09/john-oliver-televangelists/.

149 Rev. Proc. 2011-44, 2011-39 I.R.B. 446, § 2 ("A church plan . . . is ordinarily not subject to various requirements that apply to tax-qualified plans under [Code] § 401(a) and is not covered by the Employee Retirement Income Security Act of 1974 (ERISA)." (parenthesis in original). *See Advocate Health Care Network v. Stapleton*, 2017 U.S. LEXIS 3554.

150 For an introduction to the history and design of 401(k) plans, *see* Edward A. Zelinsky, The Origins of the Ownership Society: How the Defined Contribution Paradigm Changed America 49–52 (2007).

151 ERISA was originally passed as Pub. L. No. 93-406, 88 Stat. 829 (1974). It has subsequently been amended many times. Parts of ERISA are codified in the Internal Revenue Code, Title 26 of the U.S. Code. Other parts of ERISA are codified in Title 29 of the U.S. Code. For an overview of ERISA and the Code provisions governing pension and profit-sharing plans, *see* John H. Langbein, David A. Pratt, Susan J. Stabile, & Andrew W. Stumpff, Pension and Employee Benefit Law (6th ed. 2015); Lawrence A. Frolik & Kathryn L. Moore, Law of Employee Pension and Welfare Benefits (3rd ed. 2012).

including which employees must participate in such plans,[152] such plans' vesting schedules,[153] how such plans must be funded,[154] and how such plans must distribute their benefits when participating employees retire, become disabled, or die.[155]

The Code exempts retirement plans maintained by churches for their employees from much of this federal regulation unless the church elects to be covered by the tighter standards applicable to other employers.[156] For example, most private sector employers[157] maintaining defined benefit pensions for their employees must make distributions in the form of a joint and survivor annuity for the life of the participant with a smaller survivor's annuity continuing after the participant's death for his surviving spouse.[158] However, a church's defined benefit plan need not provide retirees and their spouses with a joint and survivor form of benefit payment.[159]

Similarly, defined benefit pensions maintained by most employers must finance promised benefits in accordance with rigorous funding standards embodied in the Code and ERISA.[160] However, churches' defined benefit plans need not be funded in accordance with these rules unless the church elects to be covered by the same pension regulations as apply to private sector secular employers.[161]

The Code's (and ERISA's) lenient treatment of church retirement plans extends as well to any plan for the employees of "a convention or association of churches."[162]

H. CONCLUSION

The Internal Revenue Code provisions concerning churches and other religious institutions both belie the narrative that churches are not taxed and explain why

[152] I.R.C. § 410, 26 U.S.C. § 410; ERISA § 202, 29 U.S.C. § 1052.

[153] I.R.C. § 411, 26 U.S.C. § 411; ERISA § 203, 29 U.S.C. § 1053.

[154] I.R.C. §§ 412, 430, 431, 432, and 436, 26 U.S.C. §§ 412, 430, 431, 432, and 436; ERISA §§ 302 through 306, inclusive, 29 U.S.C. §§ 1082 through 1085a, inclusive.

[155] I.R.C. §§ 401(a)(11) and 417, 26 U.S.C. § 401(a)(11) and 417; ERISA § 205, 29 U.S.C. § 1055.

[156] I.R.C. § 410(d), 26 U.S.C. § 410 (church election for its retirement plan to be covered by stricter standards); ERISA § 4(b)(2), 29 U.S.C. § 1003(b)(2) (church plan exempt from ERISA absent election to be covered).

[157] Retirement plans for government employees are exempt from many of the requirements of the Code and ERISA. I.R.C. §§ 401(a) (flush language at end of section), 411(e)(1)(A), 414(d), 26 U.S.C. §§ 401(a) (flush language at end of section), 411(e)(1)(A), 414(d); ERISA § 4(b)(1), 29 U.S.C. § 1003(b)(1).

[158] I.R.C. §§ 401(a)(11) and 417, 26 U.S.C. § 401(a)(11) and 417; ERISA § 205, 29 U.S.C. § 1055.

[159] I.R.C. §§ 401(a) (flush language at end of section), 411(e)(1)(B), 26 U.S.C. §§ 401(a) (flush language at end of section), 411(e)(1)(B); ERISA § 4(b)(2), 29 U.S.C. § 1003(b)(2).

[160] I.R.C. §§ 412, 430, 431, 432, and 436, 26 U.S.C. §§ 412, 430, 431, 432, and 436; ERISA §§ 302 through 306, inclusive, 29 U.S.C. §§ 1082 through 1085a, inclusive.

[161] I.R.C. § 412(e)(2)(D), 26 U.S.C. § 412(e)(2)(D); ERISA § 4(b)(2), 29 U.S.C. § 1003(b)(2).

[162] I.R.C. § 414(e)(1), 26 U.S.C. § 414(e)(1); ERISA §3(33)(A), 29 U.S.C. § 1002(33)(A).

that narrative is so prevalent. Churches, along with other religious and eleemosynary institutions, receive major tax advantages under the federal income tax law. These advantages include exemption from the federal income tax as well as income, estate, and gift tax deductions for donors' contributions to such groups. In addition to deductions and exemptions shared with secular philanthropic groups, churches and religious actors also receive more narrowly targeted tax advantages under the Code, including special exclusions from clerical gross incomes of in-kind housing and of cash housing allowances. These targeted tax benefits also include unique procedural protections for churches being audited by the IRS, as well as lenient treatment for church retirement plans.

However, churches and other religious groups also pay significant federal taxes. Like secular employers, churches and other sectarian employers generally pay and withhold FICA payroll taxes for their nonclerical personnel. Churches and religious organizations, like secular eleemosynary entities, pay UBIT on their unrelated business incomes and are subject to the same penalty taxes as their secular counterparts if they misuse their tax-exempt status. Churches and their employees are generally subject to the tax-based federal health care mandates applicable to individuals and employers.

Thus, the Internal Revenue Code's approach to sectarian institutions runs the gamut from taxing churches and religious entities in the same fashion as secular and profit-making entities to favorable treatment for religious organizations along with other eleemosynary organizations to special exemptions limited to churches.

4

STATE TAX STATUTES AND RELIGIOUS EXEMPTIONS

THIS CHAPTER EXPLORES state statutes governing the taxation and exemption of churches and other religious institutions. This exploration reveals that, just as the Internal Revenue Code treats churches and sectarian entities diversely, the states and their various taxes treat churches and other religious institutions diversely. Entanglement concerns help to explain this diversity among taxes and among states.

This chapter first examines property tax exemption statutes in the sixteen states without constitutional property tax exemptions. Like the state constitutional provisions exempting religious property from taxation, the state statutes exempting sectarian property from taxation share a broad common approach. All states relieve from taxation some forms of sectarian property along with secular property used for philanthropic purposes. However, within this broad statutory consensus exempting religious and other eleemosynary properties from taxation, there are notable differences as there are among the state constitutional provisions exempting religious property. Some state statutes, for example, define exempt sectarian property more restrictively ("church") than do other states ("religious"). State statutes also adopt different approaches to the tax status of parsonages. Some states exempt clerical homes from property taxation; others do not. Some states define tax-exempt parsonages more expansively to include homes used by administrative and supervisory clergy. Other states restrict tax-exempt parsonages to the residences of clergy ministering to particular congregations.

The same interpretative issues arise under these state property statutes as occur under the state constitutions' property tax provisions. For example, under these statutes as under the states' constitutions, there is often pressure to broaden the definition of "charitable" exempt property when religious property exemption is defined more narrowly in terms of "churches" or "houses of worship."

The states' sales tax statutes are highly diverse in their respective approaches to religious institutions and belie the narrative that churches are not taxed. Some states treat religious entities like other secular organizations, obligated to pay sales tax on their retail purchases and to collect tax on their retail sales. At the other end of the spectrum, some states extend complete immunity to religious entities, exempting them both from the duty to pay sales tax on their retail purchases and from the duty to collect tax on their retail sales.

Most states fall between these polar positions. Some states require sectarian entities to collect tax on retail sales but not to pay tax on their retail purchases. Conversely, other states compel religious organizations to pay sales tax on their purchases but not to collect tax on their retail sales.

While the states' various approaches to the sales taxation of churches are diverse, the states' income tax statutes all mirror the Internal Revenue Code's income tax exemption of eleemosynary entities including religious entities. Most (though not all) states also mimic the Code's taxation of unrelated business incomes and thus, through their respective unrelated business income taxes (UBITs), tax churches and other religious organizations on unrelated business income.

In revenue terms, property, sales, and income taxes are the "big three" levies of the state and local tax systems. After examining state statutes as they exempt or tax churches and other sectarian entities under these three major taxes, this chapter turns to two other state-imposed taxes which take divergent approaches to churches. Real estate transfer taxes typically apply to sales and purchases by churches and other religious institutions. In contrast, state unemployment taxes generally exempt churches while taxing nonchurch religious entities. The states' taxes on real estate conveyances and unemployment compensation again reflect the diversity of the tax treatment afforded to church and other religious organizations. Entanglement concerns play an important role in understanding that diversity.

A. PROPERTY TAX EXEMPTION STATUTES

Sixteen states have no constitutional mandate to exempt religious property. Nevertheless, each of these states[1] by statute exempts religious property in one form or another, even though there is no constitutional requirement to do so.

Like the state constitutional provisions mandating tax exemptions, the statutory property tax exemptions in these sixteen states have important differences, though they share the broad theme of exempting some religious properties from taxation. These statutes raise the same interpretative and policy issues which arise in the states with constitutional exemptions, for example, the tax treatment of parsonages, the status of camp-style facilities owned by churches, and the courts' extension (or not) of the charitable property tax exemption to cover religious property when sectarian exemption is confined in statutory terms to "churches" or "houses of worship."

Connecticut's statute is among the most detailed of the state laws exempting religious property from taxation. Connecticut exempts from taxation personal property "owned by, or held in trust for, a Connecticut religious organization . . . if the principal or income is used or appropriated for religious or charitable purposes or both."[2] Connecticut also exempts from property taxation "houses of religious worship, the land on which they stand, their pews, furniture and equipment owned by, or held in trust for the use of, any religious organization."[3] The Connecticut statute further exempts from property taxation the land and structure of any parsonage of "any religious organization and actually used by its officiating clergymen."[4] Finally, the Connecticut statute exempts

> real property and its equipment owned by, or held in trust for, any religious organization and exclusively used as a school, a daycare facility, a Connecticut nonprofit camp or recreational facility for religious purposes, a parish house, an orphan asylum, a home for children, a thrift shop, the proceeds of which are used for charitable purposes, a reformatory or an infirmary or for two or more of such purposes.[5]

---

[1] Connecticut, Delaware, Hawaii, Idaho, Iowa, Maine, Maryland, Massachusetts, Mississippi, Nevada, New Hampshire, Oregon, Rhode Island, Vermont, Washington, and Wisconsin.

[2] CONN. GEN. STAT. § 12–81(12).

[3] *Id.* § 12–81(13).

[4] *Id.* § 12–81(15).

[5] *Id.* § 12–81(14).

Similarly detailed is Washington State's statute, which exempts from property taxation "[a]ll churches, personal property, and the ground, not exceeding five acres in area, upon which a church of any nonprofit recognized religious denomination is or will be built, together with a parsonage, convent, and buildings and improvements required for the maintenance and safeguarding of such property."[6] The Washington State statute then elaborates that

> [t]he area exempted in any case includes all ground covered by the church, parsonage, convent, and buildings and improvements required for the maintenance and safeguarding of such property and the structures and ground necessary for street access, parking, light, and ventilation, but the area of unoccupied ground exempted in such cases, in connection with church, parsonage, convent, and buildings and improvements required for the maintenance and safeguarding of such property, does not exceed the equivalent of one hundred twenty by one hundred twenty feet except where additional unoccupied land may be required to conform with state or local codes, zoning, or licensing requirements.[7]

The Washington statute also provides that a tax-exempt "parsonage and convent need not be on land contiguous to the church property."[8] This provision revises an earlier Washington State statute which had been interpreted as requiring a tax-exempt parsonage to be located on the same parcel as the church.[9]

The Washington State statute next declares that "to be exempt the property must be wholly used for church purposes."[10] However, this exclusive use test is qualified by the proviso that exemption is not lost if "otherwise exempt" property is loaned or rented "to a nonprofit organization, association, or corporation, or school to conduct an eleemosynary activity or to conduct activities related to a farmers market."[11] This proviso is in turn conditioned upon the requirement that any rent received must be "reasonable" and cannot "exceed the maintenance and operation expenses attributable to the portion of the property loaned or rented."[12]

---

[6] WASH. REV. CODE § 84.36.020(2)(a).

[7] *Id.*

[8] *Id.*

[9] *Foley v. Oberlin Congregational Church of Steilacoom*, 67 Wash. 280 (1912).

[10] WASH. REV. CODE § 84.36.020(2)(a).

[11] *Id.* § 84.36.020(2)(b)(i). Washington's statutory provision authorizing farmers markets conducted on exempt church property is scheduled to terminate at the end of 2020. *Id.* § 84.36.020 (effective until Dec. 31, 2020).

[12] *Id.* § 84.36.020(2)(b).

Finally, the Washington State statute exempts from taxation camp property which is "owned by any nonprofit church, denomination, group of churches, or an organization or association, the membership of which is comprised solely of churches or their qualified representatives."[13] To be tax exempt, such property must be "utilized as a camp facility . . . used for organized and supervised recreational activities and church purposes."[14] This tax exemption is capped at 200 acres "including buildings and other improvements thereon."[15]

Addressing one of the recurring issues in this area—What is a parsonage?—Washington's supreme court[16] held that the church-owned home occupied by the "ordained district superintendent" of the Pacific Northwest Annual Conference of the United Methodist Church[17] was not a parsonage. This superintendent, the court explained, "ministers to the entire district and not directly to any specific congregation."[18] Thus, the house he uses does not qualify as a "parsonage" for property tax exemption purposes.

Another persistent issue is whether the charitable tax exemption extends to religious property when such property fails to qualify under the particular state's religious exemption. Washington's supreme court held[19] that a church camp (limited to a 200-acre exemption)[20] could not qualify for the unlimited property tax exemption available for nonprofit camps "engaged in character building."[21] If the more general exemption also applies to a religious camp, the court reasoned, the specific and limited 200-acre exemption for religious camps would be "render[ed] . . . superfluous."[22]

In contrast to the detailed statutes of the Nutmeg and Evergreen States, Delaware by statute simply exempts from taxation the property of "any church or religious society, and not held by way of investment."[23] Equally succinct are Mississippi's and Rhode Island's statutes. Mississippi extends exemption to "[a]ll property, real or personal, belonging to any religious society, or ecclesiastical body, or any congregation thereof . . . used exclusively for such society or association and not for profit."[24] Rhode Island exempts from property taxation "buildings for religious worship, and

13 *Id.* § 84.36.030(2).

14 *Id.*

15 *Id.*

16 *Pacific Northwest Annual Conference of the United Methodist Church v. Walla Walla County*, 82 Wash. 2d 138 (1973).

17 *Id.* at 139–140.

18 *Id.* at 142.

19 *Corporation of the Catholic Archbishop of Seattle v. Johnston*, 89 Wash. 2d 505 (1978).

20 Wash. Rev. Code Ann. § 84.36.030(2).

21 *Id.* § 84.36.030(3).

22 89 Wash. 2d at 510.

23 9 Del. Code Ann. § 8105.

24 Miss. Code Ann. § 27-31-1(d).

the land upon which they stand and immediately surrounding them, to an extent not exceeding five (5) acres so far as the buildings and land are occupied and used exclusively for religious . . . purposes."[25]

In a similarly concise fashion, Iowa by statute exempts from property taxation "[a]ll grounds and buildings used or under construction by literary, scientific, charitable, benevolent, agricultural, and religious institutions and societies solely for their appropriate objects . . . not leased or otherwise used or under construction with a view to pecuniary profit."[26] The supreme court of the Hawkeye State decided that this statute did not exempt from property taxation a single-family residence owned by and adjacent to a synagogue since the janitor who lived in this separate structure was "non-ecclesiastical personnel."[27] The Iowa court observed that it might have decided differently had the janitor occupied an apartment in the synagogue or had the occupant of the separate residential structure been a member of the clergy.[28]

Hawaii exempted from taxation "[p]roperty used for church purposes, including incidental activities, parsonages, and church grounds."[29] Idaho exempts from taxation any "property belonging to any religious" organization if such property is "used exclusively for and in connection with any combination of religious, educational, or recreational purposes or activities of such religious" organization.[30] Included in such tax-exempt property are "any and all residences used for or in furtherance of such [religious, educational, or recreational] purposes."[31]

Idaho's previous statute was narrower, exempting from taxation only property "connect[ed] with public worship, and any parsonage."[32] Under this more limited exemption statute, Idaho's supreme court held taxable the home used by the president of the Idaho Boise Mission of the Latter-Day Saints[33] and the residence of the bishop of the Roman Catholic Diocese of Boise and a priest/administrator of that diocese.[34] Like Washington's supreme court,[35] Idaho's supreme court reasoned that

---

[25] R.I. GEN. LAWS § 44-3-3(a)(5).

[26] IOWA CODE § 427.1(8)(a).

[27] *Congregation B'Nai Jeshurun v. Board of Review of the City of Des Moines*, 301 N.W.2d 755, 759 (Iowa 1981).

[28] *Id.* at 757.

[29] HAW. REV. STAT. § 246–32(b)(3) (now repealed). These exemptions are today contained in the county codes governing property taxation in Hawaii. *See, e.g.*, HAWAI'I COUNTY CODE 1983 (2016 Edition, as amended) § 19–77(b)(3) (exempting from taxation "[p]roperty used for church purposes including incidental activities, parsonages, and church grounds . . .").

[30] IDAHO CODE § 63-602B(1).

[31] *Id.*

[32] IDAHO CODE § 63-602B(1) prior to amendment by H.B. 69, 2007 Idaho Sess. Laws 59.

[33] *Corporation of the Presiding Bishop of the Church of Jesus Christ of Latter-Day Saints v. Ada County*, 123 Idaho 410 (1993).

[34] *Ada County Assessor v. Roman Catholic Diocese of Boise*, 123 Idaho 425 (1993).

[35] *Pacific Northwest Annual Conference of the United Methodist Church v. Walla Walla County*, 82 Wash. 2d 138 (1973).

these individuals served in supervisory, rather than pastoral, capacities since they exercised overall administrative responsibility for a large geographical jurisdiction rather than "minister[ing] to a specific localized congregation."[36] Consequently, the homes occupied by these administrators were not "parsonages."

The new Idaho statute overturns these decisions by extending property tax exemption to "any and all residences used for or in furtherance of" religious purposes.[37] The new Idaho statute also liberalizes the tax exemption for property used for "public worship"[38] to exemption for property used for "religious" purposes.[39]

Maine exempts from property taxation "[h]ouses of religious worship, including vestries, and the pews and furniture within them." Maine exempts as well "property owned and used by a religious society as a parsonage up to the value of $20,000, and personal property not exceeding $6,000 in value . . ."[40]

Maryland's statute[41] exempts from taxation "property that is owned by a religious group or organization . . . if the property is actually used exclusively for: (1) public religious worship; (2) a parsonage or convent; or (3) educational purposes." Maryland's courts have grappled with the same interpretative issues as have other state courts construing constitutional and statutory property tax exemptions. For example, the Court of Special Appeals of Maryland held[42] that a church-owned home did not qualify for tax exemption as a parsonage because the main function of the minister living in the house was to organize new congregations, rather than to serve an existing "identifiable parish."[43] The Court of Appeals, Maryland's highest court, held[44] that undeveloped acreage surrounding a church structure was tax exempt as a place of worship as this open space is "actively used by the church for religious worship."[45] On the other hand, Maryland's high court held[46] that caretakers' homes were not tax exempt since they were not used for actual religious worship.[47] However, a Maryland apartment complex housing volunteers who work in

---

36 123 Idaho at 430.

37 IDAHO CODE § 63-602B(1).

38 *Id.* § 63-602B(1) prior to amendment by H.B. 69, 2007 Idaho Sess. Laws 59.

39 *Id.* § 63–602B(1).

40 36 MAINE REV. STAT. § 652(1)G.

41 MD. CODE ANN., TAX-PROP. § 7-204.

42 *East Coast Conference of the Evangelical Covenant Church of America, Inc. v. Supervisor of Assessments of Prince George's County*, 40 Md. App. 213 (Md. Ct. Spec. App. 1978).

43 *Id.* at 218.

44 *Supervisor of Assessments of Baltimore County v. Keeler, Archbishop of Baltimore*, 362 Md. 198 (2001).

45 *Id.* at 222.

46 *Supervisor of Assessments of Baltimore County v. Trustees of Bosley Methodist Church Graveyard*, 293 Md. 208 (1982).

47 *Id.* at 218–219.

the Washington, D.C., temple of the Latter-Day Saints was held[48] to be a tax-exempt convent. "A convent," the Maryland appellate court held

> consists of a community of people who live together, follow strict religious vows, and devote themselves full-time to religious work.[49]

The Massachusetts statute extends property tax exemption to "houses of religious worship" including their "pews," "furniture," and "parsonage[s]."[50] In addition, Massachusetts uniquely grants tax-exempt status to "the official residences" of the "district superintendents" and the "district executives" of several specific churches, including the United Methodist Church and the Baptist General Conference of New England.[51] Consequently, these residences of supervising clergy are tax exempt in the Bay State, though not in other states on the legal theory that supervisors are not "parsons." Moreover, the Massachusetts statute explicitly confers property tax exemption upon "the official residence occupied by a person who has been designated by the congregation of a Hebrew Synagogue or Temple as the rabbi thereof."[52]

Nevada's property tax statute exempts "[c]hurches, chapels . . . and other buildings used for religious worship, with their furniture and equipment, and the lots of ground on which they stand, used therewith and necessary thereto; and owned by some recognized religious society or corporation, and parsonages so owned."[53] Reflecting one of Nevada's local industries, the Silver State's property tax exemption does not extend to "marriage chapels."[54] However, Nevada grants property tax exemption to "[p]arcels of land used exclusively for worship, including, without limitation, both developed and undeveloped portions of a parcel" if such parcels are owned by a "religious society or corporation."[55] In addition, the property of "religious" corporations is tax exempt in Nevada as long as such corporations are substantially supported by "the general public" rather than by "any officer or trustee of the corporation."[56] Under these statutes, Nevada's supreme court upheld a local

---

[48] *Green, Supervisor of Assessments of Montgomery County v. Church of Jesus Christ of Latter-Day Saints*, 430 Md. 119 (2013).

[49] *Id.* at 142.

[50] MASS. GEN. LAWS ch. 59, § 5, cl. 11.

[51] *Id.*

[52] *Id.*

[53] NEV. REV. STAT. ANN. § 361.125(1)(a).

[54] *Id.*

[55] *Id.* § 361.125(1)(b).

[56] *Id.* §§ 361.140(1)(a) and 361.140(2).

assessor's determination that, of a 1,300-acre parcel owned by a church, only 146 acres were used for worship purposes and thus tax exempt.[57]

New Hampshire's statute exempts from taxation

> [h]ouses of public worship, parish houses, church parsonages occupied by their pastors, convents, monasteries, buildings and the lands appertaining to them owned, used and occupied directly for religious training or for other religious purposes by any regularly recognized and constituted denomination, creed or sect, organized, incorporated or legally doing business in this state and the personal property used by them for the purposes for which they are established.[58]

Considering a church which owned a variety of buildings including a chapel, a parsonage, and residential buildings surrounded by "agricultural land, wooded lots, and vacant land,"[59] the Granite State's supreme court held that this camp-like facility did not qualify as a "monastery" because the church's members "do not live in religious retirement or seclusion from the world."[60] Finding this parcel to be tax exempt only in part, the New Hampshire supreme court held that the factual record failed to prove "that the residential living and agricultural work on the [church's] land were essential to its religious purpose."[61]

In another case involving a church-owned camp, New Hampshire's supreme court held that the camp, while not eligible for tax exemption as religious property, qualified for exemption as charitable property.[62] The camp "train[ed] boys and girls in citizenship, character and leadership" including religious-based "self-improvement."[63]

Confronting later yet another camp-style facility owned by a church (this is, after all, New Hampshire), the state's supreme court denied tax exemption as charitable property, but approved limited exemption for the facility as religious property.[64] This church's camp-style facility failed charitable status as it primarily served the church's members rather than "a substantial and indefinite segment of the general public."[65] Parts of the camp, including the chapel, "administrative offices, maintenance center,

---

57 *Simpson v. International Community of Christ*, 106 Nev. 458–459 (1990).

58 N.H. Rev. Stat. Ann. § 72:23(III).

59 *Appeal of Emissaries of Divine Light*, 140 N.H. 552, 554 (1995).

60 *Id.* at 555.

61 *Id.* at 557.

62 *Christian Camps & Conferences, Inc. v. Town of Alton*, 118 N.H. 351 (1978).

63 *Id.* at 355.

64 *East Coast Conference of the Evangelical Covenant Church of America, Inc. v. Town of Swanzey*, 146 N.H. 658 (2001).

65 *Id.* at 662. The Court distinguished its decision in *Christian Camps & Conferences, Inc. v. Town of Alton* by observing that that earlier case did "not address the specific degree to which the organization served the general public or a substantial and indefinite segment of the general public." *Id.*

barn and workshop" were held to be "reasonably related" to religious purposes and thus tax exempt.[66] However, the remainder of the camp, including residential facilities, the "dining hall and other recreational amenities" were held to be taxable.[67]

The evolution of Oregon's property taxation statute illuminates the tensions which can arise when a state defines exempt religious property narrowly and religious groups respond by claiming the charitable tax exemption for their respective holdings. Oregon's statute originally exempted from property taxation "houses of public worship and other additional buildings used solely for entertainment and recreational purposes by religious organizations."[68] This initial property tax exemption extended to "pews, slips and furniture"[69] as well as to parking lots used by "persons going to and from the buildings exempt" on religious grounds.[70] Under this original Oregon statute, "houses of public worship" were property tax exempt only to the extent they were used for "public worship or schools."[71]

Under this limited statutory standard, the Oregon Tax Court[72] held that a religiously oriented "Youth Revival Center" was not exempt as a religious property, but was exempt as a charitable property. While the center had an explicitly religious mission, its property was neither a church nor a church-related recreation center. Rather, the center's buildings were "used primarily as sleeping quarters, workshops, animal barns, storage sheds and a dining hall."[73] While the center's property did not constitute a place of public worship, it did qualify for tax exemption as charitable.[74]

Oregon's Tax Court held similarly[75] with respect to the part of a chancery office owned by the Catholic church and used to publish a Catholic newspaper and "missals" and also used for "general administration and the work of the Canon Law Tribunal."[76] None of this space qualified for religious tax exemption since none of it was used for public worship or schools. However, this space was held exempt as charitable property.[77] Oregon's supreme court affirmed per curiam.[78]

---

[66] 146 N.H. at 663.

[67] *Id.* at 664.

[68] OR. REV. STAT. § 307.140 prior to revision. This earlier version of the Oregon statute is reproduced in a 1960 opinion of Oregon's attorney general, 29 Or. Op. Atty. Gen. 387, 1960 W.L. 66710.

[69] *Id.*

[70] *Id.*

[71] *Id.*

[72] *Parkhurst v. Dept. of Revenue*, 4 Or. Tax 586 (1971).

[73] *Id.* at 591.

[74] *Id.* at 594.

[75] *Archdiocese of Portland v. Dept. of Revenue*, 5 Or. Tax 111 (1972), aff'd per curiam, 266 Or. 419 (1973).

[76] *Id.* at 117.

[77] *Id.* at 124.

[78] 266 Or. 419 (1973).

Oregon's legislature codified and extended the holdings of these cases by granting statutory property tax exemption, not only to "houses of public worship" but as well to all other "buildings and property used solely for administration, education, literary, benevolent, charitable, entertainment and recreational purposes by religious organizations."[79] This version of the Oregon statute remains in effect today.

This broader statute has raised the recurring interpretative issues which have arisen in other states. Thus, under the revised Oregon law, most of a residence owned by a Jehovah's Witnesses congregation[80] was held taxable because "neither church doctrine nor practical necessity require[d the church leader] to live in the residence."[81] In contrast, a parish rectory[82] was held to be fully tax exempt because, as a matter of Roman Catholic doctrine and actual practice, the rectory was "reasonably necessary" to accomplish the church's religious purposes.[83] However, distinguishing this earlier case on its facts, another Catholic rectory in Oregon was subsequently held taxable because the record reflected insufficient use of the rectory for religious as opposed to residential purposes and because the rectory was also adjudged too far from the church to be property tax exempt.[84]

In lieu of the term "religious," Vermont's property tax exemption statute uses the singular term "pious," declaring as tax exempt

> [r]eal and personal estate granted, sequestered or used for public, pious or charitable uses; real property owned by churches or church societies or conferences and used as parsonages and personal property therein used by ministers engaged in full time work in the care of the churches of their fellowship within the State . . .[85]

In the case of "[r]eal estate owned or kept by a religious society," the Vermont tax exemption for "pious" property is then circumscribed to

> a church edifice, a parsonage, the outbuildings of the church edifice or parsonage, a building used as a convent, school, orphanage, home, or hospital, land adjacent to any of the buildings named in this subsection, kept and used as a

---

[79] OR. REV. STAT. § 307.140.

[80] *Washington County Assessor v. West Beaverton Congregation of Jehovah's Witnesses, Inc.*, 18 Or. Tax 409 (2006).

[81] *Id.* at 421.

[82] *Roman Catholic Archdiocese of the Archbishop of Portland v. Dept. of Revenue*, 13 Or. Tax 211 (1995).

[83] *Id.* at 213.

[84] *St. Mary Star of the Sea Catholic Church v. Clatsop County Assessor*, 2015 Or. Tax 49 at *23 (Or. T.C., May 5, 2015).

[85] 32 VT. STAT. ANN. § 3802(4).

> parking lot not used to produce income, lawn, playground, or garden, and the so-called glebe lands.[86]

While Vermont's supreme court has declared that this second statute limits the Green Mountain State's property tax exemption,[87] the statute also provides a safe harbor, describing property which is "pious" and therefore tax exempt. A church summer camp, while "pious," was held to be taxable since it was not one of these enumerated properties.[88]

Wisconsin eschews the concept of "parsonage" for a more inclusive definition of religious "housing." The Wisconsin statute exempts from taxation "[p]roperty owned and used exclusively . . . by churches or religious, educational or benevolent associations."[89] Subject to "a 30-acre limitation," this includes

> property owned and used for housing for pastors and their ordained assistants, members of religious orders and communities, and ordained teachers, whether or not contiguous to and a part of other property owned and used by such associations or churches . . . while such property is not used for profit.[90]

Under this statute, the supreme court of the Badger State[91] declared taxable a church-owned home in which the widow of the church's pastor was allowed to live rent-free after the pastor's death. For two reasons, the court held, the pastor's widow was not a "member of a religious order and community" for purposes of the property tax exemption statute. First, she did not "occupy a position of leadership in her church."[92] Moreover, the widow was "not part of a religious community living apart from the secular community."[93] Hence, the house became taxable on the pastor's demise while his widow continued to live there.

Similarly, the Court of Appeals of Wisconsin[94] held taxable a "church-owned residence of the church custodian"[95] since a custodian does not fall into any of the

---

[86] *Id.* § 3832(2). "In ecclesiastical law, the phrase 'glebe land' refers to 'land possessed as part of the endowment or revenue of a church or ecclesiastical benefice.'" *Weyerhaeuser Co. v. Town of Hancock*, 151 Vt. 279, 280 n.1 (1989) (internal citation omitted).

[87] *Our Lady of Ephesus House of Prayer, Inc. v. Town of Jamaica*, 178 Vt. 35, 41 (2005).

[88] *Brownington Center Church of Brownington, Vermont, Inc. v. Town of Irasburg*, 87 A.3d 502, 506 (2013).

[89] WIS. STAT. § 70.11(4)(a).

[90] *Id.*

[91] *Midtown Church of Christ, Inc. v. City of Racine*, 83 Wis. 2d 72, 75–76 (1978).

[92] *Id.* at 75.

[93] *Id.* at 76.

[94] *Wauwatosa Avenue United Methodist Church v. City of Wauwatosa*, 321 Wis. 2d 796 (2009).

[95] *Id.* at 798.

statutory categories enumerating who may live in tax-exempt religious housing. The custodian was not a pastor, an ordained assistant to a pastor, a member of a religious order and community, or an ordained teacher.[96] Hence, the church-owned custodian's home was subject to property taxation.

In contrast, Wisconsin's supreme court[97] held tax exempt a church-owned house "used for the rest and recreation of the missionaries and employees of the" church.[98] The Wisconsin court similarly upheld[99] the tax-exempt status of a single-family residence occupied by a hospital chaplain.

In sum, the state statutes exempting religious property from taxation reflect a broad consensus under which all states including those without constitutional mandates relieve from taxation some sectarian properties along with secular philanthropic properties. However, within this consensus, there are notable differences as the same interpretative issues arise under these property tax statutes as occur under the state constitutions' property tax exemptions.

Some state statutes exempt all religious housing from property taxation while other state statutes provide more limited property tax immunity for "parsonages." Parsonages are often defined as only the residences of clergy who serve particular, local congregations as pastors. However, some states deem housing occupied by supervising clergy as property tax exempt. Some states interpret tax exemptions for "charitable" property to encompass nonchurch religious property while other states do not construe their charitable property tax exemptions in this broader fashion. These often granular differences occur within a universal agreement among all fifty states that some forms of church and religious property should not be taxed.

B. SALES TAXES: OVERVIEW

The forty-five state statutes which impose sales taxes[100] reflect great diversity in their respective approaches to the sales tax treatment of religious entities. The states' sales taxes, like the federal payroll taxes on wages and self-employment income, belie the simple narrative that churches are not taxed: In some states, churches and other

96 *Id.* at 801–802.

97 *Evangelical Alliance Mission v. Village of Williams Bay*, 54 Wis. 2d 187 (1972).

98 *Id.* at 191.

99 *Sisters of Saint Mary v. City of Madison*, 89 Wis. 2d 372, 382 (1979).

100 The District of Columbia also imposes a general sales tax. Alaska, Delaware, Montana, New Hampshire, and Oregon do not impose general state sales taxes. Walter Hellerstein, Kirk J. Stark, John A. Swain, & Joan M. Youngman, State and Local Taxation: Cases and Materials 651 (10th ed. 2014).

religious institutions both collect and pay sales taxes. In many states, churches and other sectarian entities either collect or pay sales tax.

The various state sales taxes apply to most retail sales of tangible personal property and often apply to sales of specified services.[101] Use taxes back-stop these sales taxes by requiring in-state purchasers of out-of-state goods to pay use tax if these purchasers do not pay sales tax on their out-of-state purchases or if such purchasers pay out-of-state sales tax at a rate lower than the rate imposed in the state in which the purchasers reside.[102] Sales tax is imposed on the retail purchaser and collected and remitted to the state by the seller. Use tax is self-reported by the purchaser of out-of-state goods when he brings these goods in-state for use there.

Religious institutions potentially trigger sales taxes both as retail purchasers and as retail sellers of personal property and of taxed services. For example, a church might buy food for post-service receptions or buy supplies for the church office. In that case, the church potentially confronts sales tax liability as a retail purchaser required to pay sales tax on the food or supplies the church consumes. The church might also operate a gift shop. In that case, the church would potentially have responsibility as a retail seller to collect sales taxes from the buyers and to remit such taxes to the state treasury.

As a logical matter, any state can adopt one of four patterns for the sales tax obligations of religious entities. Sectarian entities can be treated in the same fashion as secular participants in the taxing state's economy, required both to pay sales tax on their retail purchases and to collect taxes on their retail sales. At the other end of the spectrum, a state can provide complete immunity to a religious (or other philanthropic) organization, excusing it both from the obligation to pay sales tax on retail purchases as well as from the duty to collect tax on retail sales. In between these polar positions, a state can require a sectarian entity to collect tax on its retail sales while excusing it from the obligation to pay sales tax on its own retail purchases. Conversely, a state can require a religious organization to pay sales tax as a buyer but not collect sales tax as a seller.

Reflecting pronounced diversity, various states pursue each of these four possible approaches. However, in practice these categories are not airtight since, for example, states which generally require religious sellers to collect sales tax on their sales often excuse that obligation to collect for "casual" "fundraising" sales[103] or for sales of

---

[101] *Id.* at 659, 740.

[102] *Id.* at 785–800.

[103] *See, e.g.*, 830 Mass. Code Regs. 64H.6.1(4)(a) (a Massachusetts entity recognized as tax-exempt by the IRS need not collect sales taxes in its "casual" "fundraising" activity but must collect tax on the sales it makes "in the regular course of business.").

particular types of religious goods such as Bibles or prayer books.[104] Similarly, states which generally require sectarian purchasers to pay sales tax on their retail purchases sometimes relieve them of that obligation when they buy goods for particular religious functions.[105] Moreover, some states (in what can be considered a fifth approach to the tax treatment of churches and sectarian entities) tie sales tax exemption for religious entities to the IRS's formal determination that such entities are income tax exempt under Section 501(c)(3) of the Internal Revenue Code. Among the states which rely in the sales tax context on an IRS determination letter of tax-exempt status, that letter may result in various patterns of sales tax exemption as buyers and sellers.

In sum, there is considerable diversity among the forty-five states which impose sales taxes in their respective approaches to churches and other religious institutions. Even among the states pursuing the same broad policies, for example, generally taxing churches' purchases, there are detailed and sometimes idiosyncratic differences implementing those policies. Most states with sales taxes require churches and other sectarian entities to pay and/or collect sales taxes—contrary to the uncomplicated view that churches are not taxed.

C. STATES SUBJECTING CHURCHES TO SALES TAXES AS BOTH BUYERS AND SELLERS

California exemplifies the first of the possible approaches, that is, subjecting religious groups to the same sales tax liability as secular entities. This was the sales tax sustained by the U.S. Supreme Court in *Jimmy Swaggart Ministries v. Board of Equalization*,[106] discussed in chapter one.[107] "[N]onprofit and religious organizations, in general, are treated just like other California sellers and buyers for sales and use tax purposes."[108] Thus, religious organizations in the Golden State must pay sales tax on their retail purchases and must collect tax on their retail sales such as sales "from a church bookstore."[109]

California provides a limited sales tax exemption for "meals and food products" provided by a religious organization "at a social or other gathering" sponsored by

[104] *See, e.g.*, 45 Ind. Admin. Code 2.2-5-58(c)(2) (an Indiana church need not collect sales tax on "[t]he sale of bibles, choir robes and prayer books" because these items "are primarily intended to further the religious purposes of the organization.").

[105] *See, e.g.*, Idaho Code Ann. § 63-3622J (while Idaho churches must generally collect sales tax, they need not collect sales tax on meals sold to church members "at a church function").

[106] 493 U.S. 378 (1990).

[107] *See supra* at 16–18.

[108] Cal. State Bd. of Equalization, Pub. 18, *Nonprofit Organizations* 5 (Jan. 2016).

[109] *Id.* at 14 ("[T]here is no blanket sales or use tax exemption available for nonprofit religious organizations or churches . . .").

such religious organization.[110] To qualify for this exemption from the obligation to collect sales tax, "the revenue obtained" from selling meals and food must be "actually used in carrying on [the religious] functions and activities" of the selling organization.[111] Religious organizations in California must otherwise collect sales tax on their retail sales, as well as pay sales tax on their retail purchases.

Idaho's law is similar: "Like most other nonprofit organizations, churches and religious organizations must pay sales tax on the goods they buy for their own use and collect sales tax on their sales."[112] The Gem State provides a limited sales tax exemption for meals sold by a church to its members "at a church function."[113] Under a second exemption, if an Idaho religious organization pays sales tax on its purchase of tangible personal property or receives tangible personal property by gift and then resells the property, no further sales tax is due "as long as the proceeds from the sale are used exclusively in the programs of" such organization.[114] Otherwise, an Idaho religious organization's sales to "the general public in the open market in regular competition with commercial enterprise" are subject to Idaho sales tax, as are such organization's retail purchases.[115]

Other states which generally require religious institutions to both pay and collect sales tax on retail sales and purchases are Alabama,[116] Arizona,[117] Georgia,[118]

---

[110] Cal. Rev. & Tax Code § 6363.5.

[111] *Id.*

[112] Idaho Tax Commission, *#50 Nonprofit Groups & Churches* 5 (2006).

[113] Idaho Code § 63-3622J.

[114] *Id.* § 63-3622KK(1).

[115] *Id.*

[116] Ala. Admin. Code r. 810-6-5.16(1) ("[R]eligious organizations and institutions, including churches and church hospitals, are not exempt from the payment of sales or use taxes on their purchases of tangible personal property. Further, these organizations and institutions, when engaging in the business of selling tangible personal property at retail or operating a public place of amusement or entertainment, must comply with the provisions of the sales and use tax laws relative to collecting, reporting, and paying sales or use taxes."). *See also* Alabama Dept. of Revenue, *Sales and Use Tax, Frequently Asked Questions*, http://revenue.alabama.gov/salestax/faq.cfm ("Religious organizations and institutions, including churches, church hospitals, etc., are not exempt from the payment of sales and use taxes.").

[117] Arizona designates its sales tax as the Transaction Privilege Tax. Ariz. Rev. Stat. § 42-5001 et seq. "Generally, sales made to churches, schools and other non-profit organizations are subject to" Arizona sales and use tax. Ariz. Dept. of Rev., Pub. 501, *Non-Profit Organizations* 1 (Sept. 2009). Arizona churches need not collect tax on food or drink they sell as long as such churches "do not regularly engage or continue in the restaurant business for the purpose of fund-raising." Ariz. Rev. Stat. § 42-5074(B)(3). There is no other relief from sales tax liability for products sold by religious entities, unlike charitable organizations in Arizona, which need not collect tax on the products they sell. *Id.* § 42-5061(A)(4).

[118] Ga. Comp. R. & Regs. 560-12-2.22 ("No exemption is granted to churches, religious, charitable, civic and other non-profit organizations. They are required to pay the tax on all purchases of tangible personal property. Further, when such organizations engage in selling tangible personal property at retail, they are required to comply with provisions of the Act relating to collection and remittance of the tax."). There is sales tax

Mississippi,[119] North Carolina,[120] North Dakota,[121] South Dakota,[122] and Washington.[123]

D. STATES EXEMPTING CHURCHES ON SALES TAXES AS BOTH BUYERS AND SELLERS

In contrast to these ten states which subject religious entities to sales and use tax obligations both as purchasers and as sellers, five states relieve sectarian organizations

immunity for the sale of religious newspapers and for religious fundraising of 30 or fewer days in any calendar year. GA. CODE ANN. § 48-8-3(15).

[119] In Mississippi, "churches must pay sales tax." Dept. of Rev., State of Miss., *Sales Tax Frequently Asked Questions*, http://www.dor.ms.gov/Pages/SalesTax-FAQs.aspx. Religious institutions in the Magnolia State can qualify for certain sales tax exemptions which apply to secular institutions as well. For example, nonprofit orphanages in Mississippi pay no sales tax, whether such orphanages are religiously sponsored or are operated by a secular nonprofit organization. MISS. CODE ANN. § 27-65-111(e). Moreover, Mississippi extends to "religious institutions" a use tax exemption for "literature, video tapes, photographic slides or specified digital products" used in their religious missions as well as previously used "tangible personal property or specified digital products." *Id.* § 27-67-7(i). However, churches and religious entities as such do not enjoy sales tax immunity in Mississippi.

[120] Retail purchases of tangible personal property for consumption by North Carolina nonprofit organizations, including churches and other religious institutions, are subject to sales and use tax. North Carolina Dept. of Revenue, *Sales and Use Tax Technical Bulletins*, § 17-1C(1) (Jan. 15, 2009). Retail sales by North Carolina nonprofit organizations are subject to sales tax. *Id.* at § 17-1B. There is, however, a limited North Carolina sales tax exemption for sales of food when a church or other religious organization uses "the proceeds of the sales . . . for religious activities. *Id.* at § 17-1A(3). *See also* N. CAR. GEN. STAT. § 105-164.13(31a).

[121] N.D. CENT. CODE § 57-39.2-04(25) (only tax-exempt purchases by sectarian entities are "the sale of Bibles, hymnals, textbooks, and prayerbooks sold to nonprofit religious organizations"); *id.* § 57-39.2-04(4)(b) (tax-free status of sales by "educational, religious, or charitable" seller does not apply "if the seller competes with retailers by maintaining inventory, conducting retail sales on a regular basis from a permanent or seasonal location, or soliciting sales from a website prepared for or maintained by the seller" or if the religious seller has gross receipts "in excess of ten thousand dollars for an event if the activities are held in a publicly owned facility").

[122] S.D. CODIFIED LAWS § 10-45-13(5) (As to "[r]eligious . . . activities . . . receipts from tangible personal property, any product transferred electronically, or services purchased for use in the activity are included in the measure of sales tax."); S.D. Admin. R. 64:06:01:21 ("Fraternal, religious, benevolent, and charitable organizations are not exempt from payment of sales tax or use tax when the organization is the purchaser at retail of merchandise which it will consume or use."); South Dakota Dept. of Rev., *Sales and Use Tax Guide* 10 (July 2016), http://dor.sd.gov/Taxes/Business_Taxes/Publications/PDFs/STGuide.pdf ("The following are examples of taxable transactions. Sales to: Churches."); South Dakota Dept. of Rev., *Exempt Entities* 1 (March 2011), http://dor.sd.gov/Taxes/Business_Taxes/Publications/PDFs/exempt.pdf ("Churches are not exempt organizations; therefore, they are subject to sales tax on all purchases made for use by the church, its clergy and members."). South Dakota does extend sales tax exemption to "religious" and "private educational institutions." S.D. CODIFIED LAWS §10-45-14.

[123] WASH. REV. CODE § 82.08.02573 (no sales tax on qualifying fundraising sales of 501(c)(3) organizations); *id.* § 82.04.3651(3) (Sales tax–exempt fundraising "does not include the operation of a regular place of business in which sales are made during regular hours such as a bookstore, thrift shop, restaurant, or similar

from both the obligation to pay tax on their retail purchases and from the responsibility to collect tax on their retail sales. Florida exemplifies this no-tax approach. In the Sunshine State, no sales tax is due on purchases by "churches, synagogues, and established physical places for worship at which nonprofit religious services and activities are regularly conducted and carried on."[124] Moreover, no Florida sales tax is collected if such institutions sell tangible personal property.[125] This complete sales tax immunity also extends to entities which broadcast or record religious programming or assist places of worship.[126]

Embracing another variant of the no-tax approach, Missouri generally exempts from sales tax "[a]ll sales made by or to religious and charitable organizations and institutions in their religious, charitable or educational functions."[127] Under this statute, a church in the Show Me State does not collect sales tax on "its coffee services within its church" because this is a religious activity.[128] However, a church's catering activities, both within the church and at outside locations, are subject to sales tax because the church "is in competition with other businesses in providing these services."[129]

Nevada's law is particularly sweeping, exempting from the Silver State's sales tax "any tangible personal property sold by or to a nonprofit organization created for religious, charitable or educational purposes."[130]

In a similar vein, Vermont generally exempts from tax both sales "by or to"[131] all "[o]rganizations which qualify for exempt status under the provisions of

business."); Wash. State Dept. of Rev., *Nonprofit Organizations* 1 (Oct. 2013), http://dor.wa.gov/docs/pubs/industspecific/nonprofit.pdf ("Generally, nonprofit organizations are required to pay the sales or use tax on items of tangible personal property they purchase for their own use . . ."); Wash. State Dept. of Rev., *Schools, Government, Churches, and Other Organizations—Sales Tax*, http://dor.wa.gov/content/doingbusiness/businesstypes/industry/NonProfit/default.aspx ("Churches must pay sales tax on goods and retail services they purchase as consumers, unless a specific exemption applies."); Wash. State Dept. of Rev., *Fundraising*, http://www.dor.wa.gov/content/doingbusiness/businesstypes/industry/nonProfit/default.aspx ("Nonprofit organizations are generally required to collect and remit retail sales tax . . . on their sales of goods and retail services.").

[124] Fla. Stat. § 212.08(7)(m)(2).

[125] *Id.*

[126] *Id.* As noted *infra*, under Fla. Stat. § 212.08(7)(p), Florida also extends sales tax immunity on purchases to religious institutions which do not qualify for dual immunity because they are not places of worship.

[127] Mo. Rev. Stat. § 144.030.2(20).

[128] Missouri Dept. of Revenue, *Taxability of Coffee Sold at Church & Taxability of Catering Services*, Letter Ruling 7329 (Dec. 20, 2013).

[129] *Id.*

[130] Nev. Rev. Stat. Ann. § 372.326. *See also id.* §§ 372.3261(2) and 372.3261(5) (defining a religious organization for purposes of sales tax exemption, *inter alia*, as "a church, synagogue or other place of religious worship at which nonprofit religious services and activities are regularly conducted.").

[131] 32 Vt. Stat. Ann. § 9743.

26 U.S.C. § 501(c)(3)."[132] However, a 501(c)(3) entity in the Green Mountain State can only sell tax free $20,000 per year.[133] This $20,000 annual limit does not apply to "[f]ood or beverage . . . served or furnished on the premises of a nonprofit corporation or association organized and operated exclusively for religious or charitable purposes, in furtherance of any of the purposes for which it was organized; with the net proceeds of the food or beverage to be used exclusively for the purposes of the corporation or association."[134] There is no equivalent limit on the tax-free purchases of a Vermont 501(c)(3) entity.[135]

Oklahoma generally taxes neither sales to nor purchases by churches.[136] However, a church must collect tax on its sales if such sales are "made in the course of business for profit or savings, competing with other persons engaged in the same or a similar business."[137] Whether a church's sales are "competitive with business establishments" and thus subject to sales tax collection depends, *inter alia*, upon a variety of factors.[138] These "tests" for taxability include whether such sales by a church are "continuing" or are instead conducted "annually or a reasonably small number of times within a year."[139]

---

[132] *Id.* § 9743(3). As discussed *infra*, under Vermont law, an organization holding an IRS determination of tax-exempt status automatically qualifies for sales tax immunity in the Green Mountain State. However, an organization which could receive such a determination but does not possess it can be certified for sales tax exemption by Vermont's Commissioner of Taxes.

[133] *Id.* § 9743(3)(C). In addition, "[s]ales of fresh cut flowers only, by a qualified Section 501(c)(3) organization, during a single annual sales event not to exceed seven days, shall be exempt" from Vermont sales tax. *Id.* § 9743(3)(D).

[134] *Id.* § 9202(10)(D)(ii)(I). Chapter 225 of the Vermont Statutes, 32 VT. STAT. ANN. § 9201 et seq., creates a separate meals and room tax which operates independently of the general Vermont sales tax established by Chapter 233 of the Vermont Statutes, 32 VT. STAT. ANN. § 9701 et seq. Vermont's general sales tax does not apply to food and beverage subject to the separate meals and room tax. *Id.* § 9741(10). The $20,000 annual limit only applies to sales that would otherwise be taxable "under this chapter," that is, Vermont's general sales tax. *Id.* § 9743(3)(C). Since sales of food and beverage would be taxable under the separate meals and room tax of Chapter 225, such sales do not count against the $20,000 limit. That limit also does not apply as to otherwise taxable "entertainment charges." *Id. See also* State of Vermont, Dept. of Taxes, *Technical Bulletin 19*, 2000 Vt. Tax LEXIS 4 ("Sales of meals are not considered in determining the $20,000 threshold.").

[135] State of Vermont, Dept. of Taxes, *Technical Bulletin 2*, 1995 Vt. Tax LEXIS 20 at *3 ("Purchases made by the 501(c)(3) organization are exempt from Vermont sales and use tax.").

[136] 68 OKLA. ST. § 1356(7).

[137] *Id.*

[138] Okla. Admin. Code § 710:65-13-40(a).

[139] *Id.* § 710:65-13-40(a)(1)(C). Oklahoma provides a limited tax exemption for sales by a 501(c)(3) organization supporting a church if such sales are "conducted not more than once each calendar year for a period not to exceed three (3) days . . ." 68 OKLA. ST. § 1356(7). In addition, a nonprofit religious organization "operate[d] under what is commonly termed the lodge plan or system" need not collect sales taxes on the dues paid by its members. *Id.* § 1356(6).

E. STATES EXEMPTING CHURCHES AS BUYERS BUT NOT AS SELLERS

In between these two polar positions (religious organizations are subject to sales tax liability both as buyers and as sellers, such organizations are immune from sales tax obligations as both buyers and sellers), sixteen states exempt religious entities when they purchase tangible personal property at retail but require such organizations to collect tax on their retail sales. These states often provide limited exemptions to sectarian organizations when they sell tangible personal property for "casual" "fundraising" or similar purposes. However, the default position of these states is that religious sellers collect tax on their retail sales, particularly sales conducted in a business-like fashion—even though these sectarian entities need not pay sales tax on their retail purchases.

Just as there is diversity among the states in terms of fundamental sales tax policies, there is diversity in the details with which these states exempt the purchases of churches and other religious institutions while requiring these entities to collect tax on their respective retail sales.

For example, Illinois exempts from its sales tax the purchases of personal property by a "corporation, society, association, foundation, or institution organized and operated exclusively for charitable, religious or educational purposes."[140] However, subject to three exemptions, Illinois religious organizations (along with charitable and educational entities)[141] must collect sales tax on their sales of tangible personal property.[142] First, a religious organization need not collect Illinois sales tax on its sales of tangible personal property to its members.[143] Second, an Illinois religious organization need not collect sales tax on "occasional dinners, socials or similar activities" even if "such activities are open to the public."[144]

Third, an Illinois religious entity need not collect tax on its sales of tangible personal property which are not "competitive with business establishments."[145] Compliance with this exception depends upon the particular facts and circumstances of the sale, including the frequency with which the religious organization conducts such sales[146] and "[t]he nature of the particular item sold."[147] For a sale by a religious institution to be noncompetitive with business establishments and therefore tax free, "[t]he

---

[140] 35 ILL. COMP. STAT. 120/2-5(11). There is an identical exemption for purposes of the Illinois use tax. *Id.* 105/3-5(4).

[141] 86 Ill. Admin. Code § 130.2005(a)(1)(E).

[142] 35 ILL. COMP. STAT. 120/1 (seventh paragraph, defining "sale at retail").

[143] *Id.* at subparagraph (1).

[144] *Id.* at 120/1 (seventh paragraph, last sentence).

[145] 86 Ill. Admin. Code § 130.2005(a)(3)(A). The statutory basis for this exemption is 35 ILL. COMP. STAT. 120/1 (seventh paragraph, subparagraph (2)).

[146] 86 Ill. Admin. Code §§ 130.2005(a)(3)(B)(iii) and 130.2005(a)(3)(D).

[147] *Id.* § 130.2005(a)(3)(C)(i).

reasonably ascertainable dominant motive of most transferees of the items sold must be the making of a charitable contribution, with the transfer of property being merely incidental and secondary to the dominant purpose of making a gift to the charity."[148] Examples of the kind of noncompetitive sales on which Illinois religious (and charitable and educational) institutions need not collect sales tax "are infrequent sales of cookies, doughnuts, candy, calendars or Christmas trees" by such institutions.[149]

Except for these three exemptions, an Illinois religious organization (like a secular charitable or educational entity) must collect sales tax on its sales of tangible personal property, though it need not pay sales tax on its purchases.[150] Thus, for example, a Illinois church gift shop must collect Illinois sales tax if it sells Bibles to nonmembers.[151]

Similarly, in Indiana, eleemosynary institutions including religious groups, churches, monasteries, and convents[152] need not pay sales tax on their purchases implementing their respective purposes.[153] However, when such institutions sell, they must collect sales taxes unless the sale arises in any of three contexts. The first of these sales tax–exempt contexts is a "Meals on Wheels" program or a food sale in a hospital: If a sectarian entity in Indiana sells food to a person confined to her "home because of age, sickness, or infirmity"[154] or to a person in a hospital run by such entity, no sales tax is collected.[155] Second, a religious seller (along with other nonprofit institutions) collects no sales tax in Indiana if such sales are made for thirty or fewer days in any calendar year.[156]

Third, a religious seller need not collect Indiana sales tax if "the property sold is designed and intended primarily . . . for . . . religious purposes."[157] Under this exemption, a church need not collect sales tax on "[t]he sale of bibles, choir robes and prayer books" because these items "are primarily intended to further the religious purposes of the organization."[158]

Except for these three exemptions, a religious seller in the Hoosier State (along with secular eleemosynary institutions) must collect sales tax on its sales.[159] For example, a church bookstore must collect sales tax if it sells "greeting cards" since these cards do not serve a religious purpose.[160]

---

[148] *Id.* § 130.2005(a)(3)(B)(iv).
[149] *Id.* § 130.2005(a)(3)(D).
[150] *Id.* § 130.2005(a)(1)(E).
[151] *Id.* §§ 130.2005(a)(2)(B) and 130.2005(b)(2).
[152] Ind. Code Ann. §§ 6-2.5-5-21(b)(1)(B) and 6-2.5-5-21(b)(1)(D).
[153] *Id.* § 6-2.5-5-25(a).
[154] *Id.* § 6-2.5-5-21(b)(2).
[155] *Id.* §§ 6-2.5-5-21(b) and 6-2.5-5-21(c).
[156] *Id.* § 6-2.5-5-26(a).
[157] *Id.* § 6-2.5-5-26(b)(3).
[158] 45 Ind. Admin. Code 2.2-5-58(c)(2).
[159] Indiana Dept. of Revenue, Information Bulletin #10, *Sales Tax* (April 2012) at 2.
[160] 45 Ind. Admin. Code 2.2-5-58(c)(5).

Other states implementing this third approach—sales tax exemption for religious entities as purchasers, no (or limited) sales tax exemption for such entities as sellers—are Colorado,[161] Minnesota,[162] Maine,[163] Nebraska,[164] New Jersey,[165] New York,[166] Ohio,[167] Pennsylvania,[168] Tennessee,[169] Texas,[170] Virginia,[171] West Virginia,[172] Wisconsin,[173] and Wyoming.[174]

---

[161] COLO. REV. STAT. 39-26-102(2.5) (for Colorado sales and use tax purposes, "charitable organization" includes "religious" entities); *id.* 39-26-718(1)(a) (no sales tax on "[a]ll sales made to charitable organizations, in the conduct of their regular charitable functions and activities . . ."); *id.* 39-26-718(1)(b) (no sales tax on "occasional sales by a charitable organization").

[162] MINN. STAT. § 297A.70, subd. 4(a)(1) (sales to a nonprofit "corporation, society, association, foundation, or institution organized and operated exclusively for charitable, religious, or educational purposes" is tax exempt "if the item purchased is used in the performance of charitable, religious, or educational functions"); *id.* § 297A.70, subd. 9 (no sales tax on purchases of "[w]ine for sacramental purposes in religious ceremonies . . . if the wine is purchased from a nonprofit religious organization"); *id.* § 297A.70, subd. 14 (limited exemption for sales by nonprofit groups' "fund-raising events"; Minn. R. 8130.6200, Subpara. 3 (defining "religious organization" for sales and use tax purposes).

[163] 36 ME. REV. STAT. § 1760(16)(M) (no sales tax on "[s]ales to . . . [r]egularly organized churches or houses of religious worship."); *id.* § 1752(1-D) (casual sales, immune from Maine sales tax, include "transactions at a bazaar, fair, rummage sale, picnic or similar event by a civic, religious or fraternal organization that is not a registered retailer").

[164] NEB. REV. STAT. § 77-2704.12(1) ("Sales and use taxes shall not be imposed on the gross receipts from the sale, lease, or rental of and the storage, use, or other consumption in this state of purchases by (a) any nonprofit organization created exclusively for religious purposes . . ."); *id.* § 77-2704.10(2) (no sales or use tax on "[p]repared food and food and food ingredients sold by a church at a function of such church . . .").

[165] N.J. STAT. § 54:32B-9(b) (no sales tax on sales "by or to" entities "organized and operated exclusively (1) for religious, charitable, scientific, testing for public safety, literary or educational purposes"); *id.* § 54:32B-9(c)(2) (sales tax is due on "retail sales . . . by any shop or store operated by" any such entity unless inventory is contributed by gift and shop or store is operated by volunteers "without compensation"); New Jersey Division of Taxation, *Tax Treatment of Nonprofit Organizations and Government Entities, Bulletin MISC-3* (rev. 6/13), at 5 ("An exempt organization must collect sales tax if it operates a retail business (except a qualifying 'thrift' store) or if it maintains a business operation selling taxable services or merchandise more than occasionally. However, an exempt organization is not required to collect sales tax if it makes only occasional fundraising sales that are relatively short in duration, and all of the proceeds go to the exempt organization.") (parentheses in original).

[166] NY CLS TAX § 1116(a)(4) (no tax on sales "by or to" an entity "organized and operated exclusively for religious, charitable, scientific, testing for public safety, literary or educational purpose . . ."); *id.* § 1116(b)(1)(i) (sales tax due on "retail sales of tangible personal property by any shop or store operated by" such an entity); *id.* § 1116(b)(2) (sales tax due on "sales of food or drink in or by a restaurant, tavern, or other establishment operated by" such an entity). *See also* 20 N.Y. Comp. Codes R. & Regs § 529.7(i)(2)(i), Example 2 ("An exempt organization operates a gift shop and book store. Sales made by such shop or store are taxable."); *id.* § 529.7(i)(2)(i), Example 3 (counter in back of church is "a shop or store" making taxable sales); *id.* § 529.7(i)(3), Example 11 ("An exempt organization caters weddings and other banquet. Such catering is subject to tax."); and *id.* § 529.7(i)(3), Example 12 ("An exempt organization holds a monthly supper. The suppers are subject to tax.").

[167] OHIO REV. CODE ANN. § 5739.02(B)(12) ("Sales of tangible personal property or services to churches" are sales tax free); *id.* § 5739.02(B)(9)(a) (churches may sell tangible personal property sales tax free for six or fewer days "in any calendar year.").

[168] 72 PA. CONS. STAT. § 7204(10) (No tax on "[t]he sale at retail to or use by . . . (ii) a religious organization for religious purposes of tangible personal property or services." However, there is sales tax "with respect to any tangible personal property or services used in any unrelated trade or business" or for nonroutine "maintenance and repair" of real estate). Pennsylvania characterizes its sales tax as a "Tax for Education." *See id.* § 7201 et seq.

See also 61 PA. CODE § 32.21(a)(2)(ii)(A)(I) ("A church's purchase of a furnace which will be installed by its membership" is taxable since it is not routine maintenance or repair); *id.* § 32.21(c)(1) ("An exempt organization making sales of tangible personal property or services has the same responsibility as another vendor under the sales tax law . . ."); *id.* § 32.21(c)(2) (no obligation to collect sales tax on "an isolated sale"); *id.* § 32.21(c)(3)(ii) (no need to collect tax on sales of food and beverage "made on the premises of a school or church in the ordinary course of its activities.").

169 TENN. CODE ANN. § 67-6-322(a)(1) (no tax on sales to a "[c]hurch, temple, synagogue or mosque"); Tenn. Comp. R. & Regs. 1320-5-1-.51(2) (If "any church or other similar institution is regularly engaged in the business of selling tangible personal property or furnishing any taxable service, it shall qualify with the Department as a dealer and be liable for any tax due on such sales").

170 TEX. TAX CODE § 151.310(a)(1) (sales tax exemption for purchases of "an organization created for religious, educational, or charitable purposes if no part of the net earnings of the organization benefits a private shareholder or individual and the items purchased, leased, or rented are related to the purpose of the organization"); *id.* § 151.310(c) (permitting "two tax-free sales or auctions . . . during a calendar year . . . for one day only"). 34 Tex. Admin. Code § 3.322(b)(3) (defining a "nonprofit religious organization" for purposes of sales tax exemption as "an organized group of people who regularly meet for the primary purpose of holding, conducting, and sponsoring religious worship services according to the rites of their sect."); *id.* § 3.322(h)(1) ("An exempt organization that sells taxable items must obtain a sales tax permit and is responsible for collection and remittance of tax on all sales of taxable items that the organization makes . . ."); *id.* § 3.322(h)(2) (permitting "two one-day tax-free sales or auctions each calendar year.").

171 Virginia's statutory and regulatory scheme is the most elaborate among the states implementing this third approach, namely, general sales tax exemption for religious entities as purchasers, no (or limited) sales tax exemption for such sectarian entities as sellers. The Old Dominion's sales tax exemption for church purchasers contains particularly detailed definitions of a "nonprofit church" and of the church purchases of tangible personal property which enjoy sales tax exemption. VA. CODE ANN. § 58.1-609.10(16). To enjoy sales tax exemption, a Virginia church must qualify as income tax exempt under Internal Revenue Code Section 501(c)(3) or as property tax exempt under Virginia law. *Id.* In addition, for a Virginia church's purchases of tangible personal property to be sales tax exempt, the church's use of the property must meet one of several statutory tests. A qualifying Virginia church purchases property sales tax free if such purchased property is used "in religious worship services by a congregation or church membership while meeting together in a single location." *Id.* § 58.1-609.10(16)(i). Alternatively, a church in the Old Dominion buys property free of sales tax if the property is used "in the libraries, offices, meeting or counseling rooms or other rooms in the public church buildings used in carrying out the work of the church and its related ministries, including kindergarten, elementary and secondary schools." *Id.* § 58.1-609.10(16)(ii). The Virginia sales tax exemption for churches' purchases of tangible personal property shall also include baptistries; bulletins, programs, newspapers, and newsletters that do not contain paid advertising and are used in carrying out the work of the church; gifts including food for distribution outside the public church building; food, disposable serving items, cleaning supplies, and teaching materials used in the operation of camps or conference centers by the church or an organization composed of churches that are exempt under this subdivision and which are used in carrying out the work of the church or churches; property used in caring for or maintaining property owned by the church including, but not limited to, mowing equipment; and building materials installed by the church and for which the church does not contract with a person or entity to have installed, in the public church buildings used in carrying out the work of the church and its related ministries, including, but not limited to, worship services; administrative rooms; and kindergarten, elementary, and secondary schools. *Id.* § 58.1-609.10(16).

Virginia's regulations further provide an exhaustive list of particular items which, pursuant to the statutory exemption, may be purchased by qualifying churches sales tax free. *See* 23 Va. Admin. Code § 10-210-310(D). Among these sales tax–exempt items are acolyte and choir robes, administrative supplies, prayer books, torahs, television broadcasting cameras, mops, brooms, and telephone wires and windows if they are installed by the church itself rather than by a contractor. *Id.* Virginia's regulations then characterize churches' purchases of tangible personal property as subject to sales tax unless such purchased property is "used in religious worship services" or is used "in the public church buildings . . . in carrying out the work of the church and its related ministries." *Id.* § 10-210-310(E)(1). A Virginia church's purchase of tangible personal property is also taxable if such property is "used by separate legal or business entities that may be associated with the church." *Id.*

The regulations then advise, by way of example, that property purchased by a church is subject to Virginia sales tax if the property is "used on church trips, picnics, or similar outings outside a public church building." *Id.* § 10-210-310(E)(3)(a). On the other hand, supplies for a church camp can be purchased sales tax free. *Id.* § 10-210-310(F)(1)(a).

In contrast to these detailed rules governing the tax-free purchases of qualifying Virginia churches, the tax rules pertaining to the retail sales of Virginia churches are straightforward: Like all other sellers of tangible personal property in the Old Dominion, Virginia churches "are required to register as dealers, collect the tax from customers (who may include church members, visitors, or other persons outside the church membership) and remit the" sales tax to the state. *Id.* § 10-210-310(I)(1). A Virginia church's obligation to collect tax on its retail sales is subject to the normal exceptions for other sellers of tangible personal property such as Virginia's sales tax exemption for occasional sales. *Id.* § 10-210-310(I)(4).

In addition to Virginia's detailed exemptions for churches' purchases of tangible personal property, Virginia also provides a separate sales tax exemption for the purchases of 501(c)(3) organizations. VA. CODE ANN. § 58.1-609.11. A church may elect to use this alternative sales tax exemption for its purchases rather than the church sales tax exemption. 23 Va. Admin. Code § 10-210-310(B). Religious, but nonchurch entities, seeking sales tax exemption in the Old Dominion must use this sales tax exemption for 501(c)(3) purchasers. Organizations enjoying the 501(c)(3)-based sales tax exemption on their purchases need not collect sales tax on their "occasional" retail sales, defined as "sales on three or fewer separate occasions within the calendar year." *Id.* § 10-210-1072(C). However, for these purposes, "sales made at fairs, flea markets, festivals and carnivals are not considered occasional sales." *Id.*

172 W. VA. CODE § 11-15-9(a)(5) (no sales tax on "[s]ales of property or services to churches which make no charge whatsoever for the services they render" as long as purchases are "directly used or consumed by" such churches); *id.* § 11-15-9(a)(6)(A) (no sales tax on "[s]ales of tangible personal property or services to a corporation or organization . . . which is exempt from federal income taxes under Section 501(c)(3) . . . [and is a] church or a convention or association of churches . . ."); *id.* § 11-15-9(a)(14) (no sales tax on "[c]asual and occasional sales of property or services" by such a church corporation or organization); and *id.* § 11-15-9(a)(24)(F) (no sales tax on sales "by any religious organization at a social or other gathering conducted by it or under its auspices, if the purpose in selling the food is to obtain revenue for the functions and activities of the organization and the revenue obtained from selling the food is actually used in carrying out those functions and activities . . ."). *See also* West Virginia State Tax Dept., *Special Sales and Use Tax Rules for Nonprofit Organizations* (Publication TSD-320) (Rev. Nov., 2011), at 1 (501(c)(3) organization without an IRS determination letter instead "must receive a prior written ruling from the [West Virginia] Tax Commissioner.") and at 2 (outside of statutory exemptions, exempt organizations "must collect sales tax on all of their sales.").

173 WIS. STAT. § 77.54(9a)(f)(no sales tax on "sales to . . . [a]ny corporation, community chest fund, foundation or association organized and operated exclusively for religious, charitable, scientific or educational purposes . . .") and *id.* § 77.54(7m) (no sales tax on "[o]ccasional sales of tangible personal property . . . by a neighborhood association, church, civic group, garden club, social club or similar nonprofit organization . . ."). *See also* State of Wisconsin, Dept. of Revenue, *Wisconsin Sales and Use Tax Information* (Publication 201; April 2012), at 60 ("most *sales by* these organizations of taxable property and services are subject to sales tax unless the occasional sale exemption applies.") (emphasis in original).

174 WYO. STAT. § 39-15-105(a)(iv)(B) (no tax on "[s]ales made to religious or charitable organizations . . . in or for the conduct of the regular religious [or] charitable . . . functions and activities"); *id.* § 39-15-105(a)(iv)(C) (no sales tax on "[o]ccasional sales made by religious or charitable organizations for fund raising purposes for the conduct of regular religious or charitable functions and activities, and not in the course of any regular business"); Wyoming Depart. of Revenue, *Rules and Regulations*, Chap. 2 (doc. #9586) § 7(c)(iv) ("Occasional sales of tangible personal property or services by religious or charitable organizations for fund raising purposes for the conduct of their regular religious or charitable functions and activities shall be exempt from the sales tax."); *id.* § 7(c)(v) ("Purchases made by religious or charitable organizations in or for their regular religious or charitable functions and activities shall be exempt from the sales and use tax.").

F. STATES EXEMPTING CHURCHES AS SELLERS BUT NOT AS BUYERS

South Carolina exemplifies the fourth pattern: Churches and other religious institutions in the Palmetto State pay sales taxes on their retail purchases,[175] but do not collect tax on their retail sales "if the net proceeds are used exclusively for exempt purposes and no benefit inures to any individual."[176] For example, a South Carolina church does not collect sales tax on its charges for its weekly fellowship dinner.[177] On the other hand, if a South Carolina church buys food or prepared meals, not for resale by the church but for consumption by its members, the church owes sales tax on its purchase.[178]

Iowa's sales tax treatment of sectarian entities is similar. Religious institutions in the Hawkeye State must pay sales tax on their retail purchases.[179] However, nonprofit religious entities need not collect Iowa sales tax on their retail sales as long as the proceeds of such sales are used for religious purposes.[180] Thus, an Iowa church need not collect sales tax on a bake sale if "the net proceeds are returned to the church for religious purposes."[181] "However, any purchases made by the church that are not for resale are subject to sales tax."[182]

Likewise, in Arkansas[183] retail sales to churches are taxable[184] but retail sales by churches are tax exempt as long as such churches are not "engaged in business for profit."[185]

Hawaii's sales tax law is comparable.[186] Purchases by nonprofit eleemosynary organizations in the Aloha State, including religious purchasers, are taxable.[187] The

---

175 South Carolina Dept. of Revenue, S.C. Revenue Procedure #03-6 at 3 (Nov. 20, 2003) ("Items purchased for an organization's use are subject to the sales and use tax. For example, a computer and office supplies purchased to keep track of sales are subject to the tax.").

176 S.C. CODE ANN. § 12-36-2120(41) ("items sold by" enumerated organizations are exempt from sales tax "if the net proceeds are used exclusively for exempt purposes and no benefit inures to any individual"); *id.* § 12-37-220(A)(3) ("churches"); *id.* § 12-37-220(B)(16)(b) ("religious, charitable, or eleemosynary society, corporation, trust or other association . . .").

177 South Carolina Dept. of Revenue, S.C. Revenue Ruling #12-3 at 11–12 (June 12, 2012) (example 2).

178 *Id.* at 13 (example 5).

179 Iowa Admin. Code r. 701-17.1(3) ("Purchases by educational, religious, or charitable organizations which are not for resale, cannot be purchased free of sales tax."); *id.* 701-17.1(4)(c) ("Nonprofit corporations and educational, religious, or charitable organizations can be held responsible for the payment of sales and use taxes as would any other individual, retailer, or corporation.").

180 IOWA CODE § 423.3(78)(a).

181 Iowa Admin. Code r. 701-17.1(1)(b), example 1.

182 *Id.*

183 Arkansas designates its sales tax as a "gross receipts" tax. ARK. CODE ANN. § 26-52-101.

184 Arkansas Dept. of Finance and Administration, *Gross Receipts Tax Rules* GR-39B (2008).

185 ARK. CODE ANN. § 26-52-401(1).

186 Hawaii's sales tax is denoted as the General Excise Tax (GET). HAW. REV. STAT. § 237-1 et seq.

187 *Id.* § 237-23(a)(4) and § 237-23(b). State of Hawaii, Dept. of Taxation, Tax Facts, 93-3, *Tax Issues for Hawaii Nonprofit Organizations* (Nov. 1998), at 2, question 10 ("businesses still are subject to the GET on their sales

sales-based income earned by such institutions through fundraising activity is taxable though other income is not.[188] The distinction between sales which are not subject to Hawaii sales taxation and taxable fundraising is determined "on a case-by-case basis taking into account all of the facts involved."[189]

G. CHURCH SALES TAX EXEMPTION TIED TO IRS CONFIRMATION OF INCOME TAX EXEMPTION

What can be considered a fifth approach conditions state sales tax exemption upon an organization obtaining a written determination from the IRS, confirming the organization's tax-exempt status for federal income tax purposes. States which tie sales tax immunity to formal IRS confirmation of 501(c)(3) status differ among themselves as to the breadth of the resulting immunity, that is, whether sales tax exemption is for the religious entities' purchases or sales, or both; whether the requirement to obtain an IRS determination letter confirming tax-exempt status applies to all religious organizations including churches or just applies to nonchurch religious entities.

As we saw earlier,[190] the Internal Revenue Code grants churches the unique right to tax-exempt status under Code § 501(c)(3)[191] without obtaining IRS confirmation of that status.[192] This fifth approach to sales tax exemption requires a church to surrender this right and obtain a written IRS determination of income tax exemption. Absent such a written determination, a church in a state embracing this approach is subject to sales tax responsibility. In some states, a church need not obtain an IRS determination letter to enjoy sales tax immunity, but a nonchurch sectarian entity must obtain such a letter to be relieved of sales tax liability.

Of the states which condition sales tax exemption on IRS confirmation of 501(c)(3) status, Utah provides the broadest exemption, namely, complete immunity

---

to tax-exempt organizations. The business is not tax-exempt, even if the customer is. Therefore, tax-exempt organizations may have the GET visibly passed on to them when they buy goods and services.").

[188] State of Hawaii, Depart. of Taxation, Tax Facts, 98-3, *Tax Issues for Hawaii Nonprofit Organizations* (Nov. 1998), at 2, question 8 ("gross income received from the conduct of any fundraising activity is subject to the GET."); *id.* at 3, question 14 ("The sale (including sales by auction) by a tax-exempt organization of donated items for fundraising purposes is an 'activity the primary purpose of which is to produce income'; consequently, the gross proceeds derived from the activity is subject to the GET.").

[189] State of Hawaii, Dept. of Taxation, *Tax Advisory on the Application of the General Excise Tax to Tourist Wedding Activities of Churches* at 1 (Apr. 21, 1997), http://files.hawaii.gov/tax/legal/info/wedding.pdf.

[190] *See supra* at 59.

[191] I.R.C. § 501(c)(3), 26 U.S.C. § 501(c)(3).

[192] I.R.C. § 508(c)(1), 26 U.S.C. § 508(c)(1).

from tax on both the purchases of and sales by entities holding IRS determination letters.[193] Thus, in Utah a church as well as a nonchurch religious group obtaining IRS confirmation of its tax-exempt status under the Internal Revenue Code receives exemption under the Utah sales tax both for purchases and sales.

Among the states which tie sales tax exemption to formal IRS recognition of 501(c)(3) status, Louisiana provides the most limited exemption. Under Louisiana law, "a church or synagogue that is recognized by the United States Internal Revenue Service as entitled to exemption under Section 501(c)(3) of the United States Internal Revenue Code"[194] need not pay sales tax on "purchases of bibles, song books, or literature used for religious instruction classes."[195] Religious organizations (including churches and synagogues) must otherwise pay the sales or use taxes "required by law to be made on purchases made by these organizations."[196] Thus, a church or synagogue in Louisiana which obtains an IRS determination letter confirming its tax-exempt status under the Internal Revenue Code receives very limited sales tax exemption on its purchases as a result of that letter.

When religious organizations sell in the Pelican State, tax is imposed on their sales in their "regular commercial ventures of any type such as bookstores, restaurants, gift shops, commercial flea markets, and similar activities that are . . . in competition with retail merchants."[197] However, religious groups (as well as other nonprofit entities) with IRS determination letters need not collect sales tax at their other fundraising events as long as the proceeds from such events are used for religious purposes.[198]

While Utah provides broad sales tax immunity to a religious group with an IRS determination letter confirming its 501(c)(3) status and Louisiana grants limited sales tax exemption to a church or synagogue with such a letter, Connecticut's sales tax statute places the Nutmeg State between these two polar patterns. Connecticut excuses purchases by recognized 501(c)(3) organizations from sales tax but requires

---

[193] Utah Admin. Code R865-19S-43(A) ("In order to qualify for an exemption from sales tax as a religious or charitable institution, an organization must be recognized by the Internal Revenue Service as exempt from tax under Section 501(c)(3) of the Internal Revenue Code."); UTAH CODE ANN. § 59-12-104.1(1) ("sales made by religious or charitable institutions" in Utah are tax exempt "if the sale is made in the conduct of the institution's or organization's regular religious or charitable functions or activities."); *id.* § 59-12-104.1(2)(a) ("sales made to" such 501(c)(3) organizations are tax free if such sales are "made in the conduct of the institution's or organization's regular religious or charitable functions and activities.").

[194] LA. STAT. ANN. § 47:301(8)(d)(i).

[195] *Id.* § 47:301(8)(d)(iv).

[196] *Id.* § 47:305.14A(3). *See also* La. Atty. Gen. Op. No. 1983-618, 1983 La. AG LEXIS 303 at *3 ("sales tax is due on normal purchases of tangible personal property made by charitable or religious organizations.").

[197] LA. STAT. ANN. § 47:305.14A(4).

[198] *Id.* § 47:305.14A(1)(a). In addition, IRS-confirmed religious organizations in Louisiana need not collect sales tax on the newspapers they publish as long as they charge for such newspapers no more than the cost of publication. *Id.*

such organizations to collect tax on their retail sales. In particular, the Nutmeg State waives sales and use tax on

> [s]ales of tangible personal property or services to any organization that is exempt from federal income tax under Section 501(a) of the Internal Revenue Code of 1986, or any subsequent corresponding internal revenue code of the United States, as from time to time amended, and that the United States Treasury Department has expressly determined, by letter, to be an organization that is described in Section 501(c)(3) or (13) of said internal revenue code . . . The organization shall be liable for the tax otherwise imposed if such tangible personal property or services are not used or consumed exclusively for the purposes for which the organization was established.[199]

Thus, a Connecticut church must obtain an IRS determination letter of its 501(c)(3) status to enjoy sales tax immunity on its purchases—even though such church is not required by the Code to obtain this letter to confirm its federal income tax exemption.

While Connecticut organizations recognized by the IRS as tax exempt under Code Section 501(c)(3) need not pay sales or use tax on their purchases of tangible personal property "used or consumed exclusively for the purposes for which the organization was established," such organizations must collect sales tax when they sell tangible personal property.[200] A statutory exemption relieves Connecticut nonprofit organizations of their obligations to collect sales taxes on their sales of tangible personal property "at bazaars, fairs, picnics, tag sales or similar events to the extent of five such events of a day's duration held during any calendar year."[201] For example, a Connecticut church need not collect sales tax if it holds a special, one day "tag sale" at which it sells tangible personal property.[202] However, a regularly operated church gift shop in Connecticut must collect sales tax on its ongoing sales of tangible personal property.[203]

Kentucky's sales tax law is similar: If a religious (or educational or charitable) institution has received IRS confirmation of its status as income tax exempt under Code Section 501(c)(3),[204] the institution need not pay Kentucky sales tax on its

---

199 CONN. GEN. STAT. § 12-412(8).

200 *Id.*

201 *Id.* § 12-412(94).

202 *Id.*

203 Connecticut Dept. of Revenue Services, *Exemption from Sales and Use Taxes of Sales by Nonprofit Organizations at Fundraising or Social Events*, SN 98(11) (Aug. 17, 1998).

204 Dept. of Revenue, Commonwealth of Kentucky, *Application for Purchase Exemption Sales and Use Tax*, 51A125(12-09), at 2 ("The letter from the Internal Revenue Service which determines that your organization

retail purchases "used solely" within the institution's "religious function."[205] On the other hand, a religious institution in the Bluegrass State must collect tax on its retail sales.[206]

The rules of Massachusetts[207] and New Mexico[208] are comparable. In these two states, IRS confirmation of a religious group's tax-exempt status under Code Section 501(c)(3) relieves the group of the obligation to pay sales tax on its retail purchases. However, an IRS-recognized sectarian entity must collect sales tax on its retail sales, subject to some exceptions such as the right of a church to sell tax free if the church's sales do not compete commercially with business establishments.

Florida reflects yet another variant. Florida, as we saw above,[209] extends broad sales tax immunity to "religious institutions," defined as "churches, synagogues, and established physical places for worship."[210] Institutions meeting this narrow definition need not collect taxes on their retail sales, need not pay taxes on their retail

---

is exempt from income taxation under Section 501(c)(3) of the Internal Revenue Code must be attached to this application.").

205 Ky. Rev. Stat. Ann. § 139.495(2).

206 *Id.* § 139.495(8).

207 Purchases by an IRS-certified tax-exempt organization are relieved of the Bay State's sales tax as long as the property purchased is used for the organization's exempt purpose. Mass. Gen. Laws Ann. ch. 64H, § 6(e). While such an organization need not collect sales tax on its "casual" "fundraising" activity, such 501(c)(3) organization must collect tax on the sales it makes "in the regular course of business." 830 Mass. Code Reg. 64H.6.1(4); *id.* 64H.6.1(5). *See also* Massachusetts Dept. of Revenue, *A Guide to Sales and Use Tax*, http://www.mass.gov/dor/individuals/taxpayer-help-and-resources/tax-guides/salesuse-tax-guide.html#questions.

("Tax-exempt organizations that sell tangible personal property or telecommunication services in the regular course of business are considered vendors and are required to collect sales/use tax."). Thus, for example, a regularly operated church gift shop in Massachusetts must collect sales tax on the inventory it sells, even though the church need not pay sales tax on its purchases provided that its tax-exempt status has been formally confirmed by the IRS. 830 Mass. Code Reg. 64H.6.1(7)(b)(7) ("Sales by a museum shop of postcards, books, jewelry, games, chinaware, etc." are subject to sales tax.).

208 New Mexico fashions its sales tax as a "gross receipts" tax. When an organization (including a religious organization) recognized in writing by the IRS as tax exempt under Section 501(c)(3) purchases tangible personal property, no gross receipts tax is due from such purchase as long as the purchased property is used for the organization's exempt function and not for an "unrelated trade or business" as defined by the Internal Revenue Code. There is no exemption from the New Mexico gross receipts tax if a 501(c)(3) organization makes another kind of taxable purchase, such as a purchase of a taxable service. There is, moreover, no exemption if a 501(c) organization sells taxable property or services. *See* N.M. Stat. Ann. §§ 7-9-1, 7-9-15 (use tax exemption for 501(c)(3) organization), 7-9-29, and 7-9-41 (exemption from gross receipts tax of minister of a 501(c)(3) religious organization for providing religious services). *See also* New Mexico Taxation & Revenue, Type 9 NTTC, http://www.tax.newmexico.gov/Government/type-9-nttc.aspx and *In the Matter of the Protest of Kids Love to Dance* (98-26 Hearing Office of the Taxation and Revenue Department of the State of New Mexico) (Apr. 27, 1998), 1998 WL 3507572 at *3 (confirming that the gross receipts tax exemption is only for purchases of tangible personal property by 501(c)(entities)).

209 *See supra* at 82.

210 Fla. Stat. § 212.08(7)(m).

purchases, and need not obtain an IRS confirmation of tax-exempt status under the Internal Revenue Code to enjoy this complete sales tax immunity.[211]

However, nonchurch religious entities in Florida, like other nonprofit eleemosynary organizations in the Sunshine State, must receive IRS confirmation of their 501(c)(3) status to receive sales tax exemption.[212] That exemption is limited to the purchases of such entities "used in carrying on their customary nonprofit activities."[213] The Texas sales tax statute is similar.[214]

Vermont's sales tax statute represents yet another variation on this theme: Vermont automatically bestows sales tax–free status on an organization holding an IRS determination letter confirming that the organization is tax exempt under Section 501(c)(3) of the Internal Revenue Code.[215] However, Vermont's Commissioner of Taxes "may" recognize a nonprofit entity as qualifying for sales tax exemption even if such entity lacks a determination letter from the IRS.[216] Consequently, a Vermont church which eschews the IRS determination letter process can apply to the commissioner to recognize the church's exemption from the sales and use taxes of the Green Mountain State.[217]

In a similar vein, Michigan distinguishes between churches and other 501(c)(3) organizations, including religious organizations. As purchasers, Michigan churches benefit from three overlapping sales tax exemptions on such churches' purchases. As a result of these three exemptions, purchases by religious organizations in Michigan are largely sales tax free while retail sales by such groups are generally taxable.

One of these exemptions is limited to retail purchases by both churches and other nonprofit entities which are tax exempt under Section 501(c)(3).[218] To qualify for this sales tax exemption, most buyers other than churches must have received

---

211 *Id.*

212 *Id.* § 212.08(7)(p).

213 *Id.*

214 In the Lone Star State, churches are sales tax exempt on their purchases, need not obtain IRS determination letters to enjoy this exemption, and must generally collect tax on their retail sales. While the Texas sales statute extends automatic exemption to "religious" entities, the regulations limit this exemption to church-like groups. Compare TEX. TAX CODE § 151.310(a)(1) with 34 Tex. Admin. Code § 3.322(b)(3). However, other 501(c)(3) organizations in Texas (including nonchurch religious groups) must obtain IRS confirmation of 501(c)(3) status to enjoy sales tax exemption on their purchases. TEX. TAX CODE § 151.310(a)(2); 34 Tex. Admin. Code § 3.322(b)(5).

215 32 VT. STAT. ANN. § 9743(3)(A).

216 *Id.*

217 State of Vermont, Dept. of Taxes, *Technical Bulletin TB-2*, 1995 Vt. Tax LEXIS 20 ("Qualified organizations" include "organizations excused from making application for 501(c)(3) status under the provisions of section 508(c) of the United States Internal Revenue Code.").

218 MICH. COMP. LAW SERV. § 205.54q(1)(b).

written confirmation from the IRS of their tax-exempt status under the Internal Revenue Code.[219]

This Michigan sales tax exemption is conditioned upon the tangible personal property purchased tax free being "used to carry out the purposes of the organization or to raise funds or obtain resources necessary to carry out the purposes of the organization as stated in the organization's bylaws or articles of incorporation."[220] Under this statute, a Michigan church need not choose between sales tax exemption on its purchases and waiving its entitlement to 501(c)(3) status without IRS confirmation of that status. However, a nonchurch religious group must obtain IRS confirmation to benefit from this sales tax exemption on its purchases.[221]

When Michigan churches sell tangible personal property at retail "for fund-raising purposes," their sales are subject to sales tax unless they sell "less than $5,000" in any calendar year.[222] This exemption limited to organizations selling less than $5,000 annually is also available to other nonprofit groups (including nonchurch religious groups) which are recognized as tax exempt under Code Section 501(c)(3).[223]

Ohio law also distinguishes between churches and other 501(c)(3) organizations, including nonchurch religious entities. As we saw above,[224] churches in the Buckeye State can buy sales tax free but are allowed to sell tax free for only six or fewer days each year.[225] Other 501(c)(3) groups (including nonchurch religious groups) receive this treatment—tax-free purchases, up to six days of tax-free sales—only if their

---

[219] *Id.* § 205.54q(3)(b). ("The transferee shall also provide to the transferor a copy of the federal exemption letter. However, a copy of the federal exemption letter is not required if the organization is exempt from filing an application for exempt status with the internal revenue service."). As noted above, churches, associations, and conventions of churches, church auxiliaries, and smaller religious groups with gross annual receipts of $5,000 or less need not apply to the IRS for confirmation of their tax-exempt status under Code Section 501(c)(3).

[220] MICH. COMP. LAW SERV. § 205.54q(5).

[221] Under Michigan's first exemption, a retail sale of tangible personal property to "a regularly organized church, religious, or fraternal" organization is tax exempt if three conditions are met. *Id.* § 205.54a(1)(a). To qualify for this first sales tax exemption, the purchaser cannot benefit or distribute income "in whole or in part, to an individual or private shareholder, directly or indirectly"; the purchaser's activities must be "for the benefit of the public at large" rather than for the benefit of the purchaser's "members or any restricted group," *id.*; and the purchased property must be "used for the [purchaser's] exempt purpose." *Id.* § 205.54a(2).

A second Michigan sales tax exemption is available only to "regularly organized church[es and] house[s] of religious worship." *Id.* § 205.54a(1)(b). To qualify for this alternative sales tax exemption for churches' retail purchases, churches' purchases may not be made "in activities that are mainly commercial enterprise," *id.*, the purchases cannot be of "vehicles licensed for use on public highways other than a passenger van or bus," *id.*, and the purchased property must be "used for the [church's] exempt purpose." *Id.* § 205.54a(2).

[222] *Id.* § 205.540(1).

[223] *Id.*

[224] *See supra* note 167.

[225] OHIO REV. CODE ANN. § 5739.02(12) ("Sales of tangible personal property or services to churches" are sales tax free); *id.* § 5739.02(9)(a) (churches may sell tangible personal property sales tax free for six or fewer days "in any calendar year.").

tax-exempt status has been confirmed in writing by the IRS.[226] Tennessee's law follows this pattern as well.[227]

Virginia allows churches to elect to secure IRS confirmation of 501(c)(3) status and thus use the same sales tax exemption which applies to other eleemosynary institutions.[228] Alternatively, churches can qualify under a separate sales tax exemption for their purchases.[229] A nonchurch religious group in the Old Dominion can only use the same sales tax exemption which applies to other secular 501(c)(3) groups.[230]

H. SALES TAX: SUMMARY

In light of this welter of state sales tax laws, there is no single approach qualifying as a majority, or even a plurality, rule for the sales tax treatment of churches. The states' sales taxes run the gamut from taxing churches and religious institutions on their purchases and sales to broad sales tax immunity for sectarian institutions, both as sellers and buyers. Many states fall in between, often with detailed and idiosyncratic approaches.

The various state sales tax statutes raise a variety of interpretive issues as these statutes are applied to modern technology. Some states, for example, limit the number of days in a year during which a church or other religious organization may sell tax free. In Connecticut, for instance, a 501(c)(3) organization may sell sales tax free for five days.[231] Suppose that, for six days, a church in the Nutmeg State displays on the Internet the items it is selling at a one-night tag sale. Has this church, by virtue of this six-day Internet display, forfeited the right to sell tax free? Or is this Internet advertising disregarded in the application of Connecticut's five-day limit?

Noteworthy in this context is the concern evident in many of these statutes to establish a level sales tax playing field between eleemosynary institutions

---

[226] *See id. See also* Ohio Dept. of Taxation, *Frequently Asked Questions*, http://www.tax.ohio.gov/faq/tabid/6315/Default.aspx?QuestionID=433&AFMID=11354 ("633. What sales are exempt/excepted from sales tax . . . Sales to organizations that have been granted and have maintained 501(c)(3) status by the Internal Revenue Service.").

[227] In the Volunteer State, no tax is due on any sale "to any . . . [c]hurch, temple, synagogue or mosque." TENN. CODE ANN. § 67-6-322(a)(1). No IRS determination letter is required for this sales tax exemption on purchases by church-type institutions. However, other nonprofit eleemosynary entities (including nonchurch religious groups) only receive sales tax exemption on their purchases if they possess an IRS determination letter, recognizing their tax-exempt status under the Internal Revenue Code. *Id.* §§ 67-6-322(b) and 67-6-322(d). All of these institutions must collect Tennessee sales tax if they are "regularly engaged in the business of selling tangible personal property or furnishing any taxable service . . ." Tennessee Dept. of Revenue, State Sales and Use Tax Rules, Rule 1320-05-01-.51(2).

[228] 23 Va. Admin. Code 10-210-310(D) ("Churches also have the option of using the general nonprofit entity sales tax exemption provided for under § 58.1-609.11 of the Code of Virginia.").

[229] VA. CODE ANN. § 58.1-609.10(16).

[230] *Id.* § 58.1-609.11.

[231] CONN. GEN. STAT. § 12-412(94).

(including churches and other religious organizations) and commercial enterprises. One theme articulated in many state statutes is the denial of sales tax immunity when the seller's activities become "regular commercial ventures . . . in competition with retail merchants."[232] Under these statutes, when a church or other religious institutions crosses the (often indistinct) line into commercial enterprise, it must collect sales tax like any other seller.

In sum, on the issue of religion, the states' sales tax statutes are diverse, both in the fundamental policies the states pursue and in the details by which they implement such policies. The states' sales taxes belie the simple narrative that churches pay no tax. Churches in many states must pay sales tax on purchases, must collect sales tax on retail sales, or must do both. It is a strength of our federal system that the states can pursue different approaches in this important area—though, as I discuss in chapter seven,[233] many states could expand the sales tax liabilities of churches and other religious institutions.

I. STATE INCOME TAXES

As we have just seen, the states take fundamentally different approaches to the sales tax treatment of religious entities while there is more limited diversity in the states' respective property tax exemptions for sectarian properties. In contrast, the states' income tax statutes uniformly take the same tack toward religious entities. In strikingly homogeneous fashion, virtually every state with an income tax either incorporates[234] into its law or largely tracks[235] the income tax exemption

[232] LA. STAT. ANN. § 47:305.14(A)(b)(4).

[233] *See infra* at 206–211.

[234] ALA. CODE § 40-18-32; ALASKA STAT. §43.20.021(a); ARIZ. REV. STAT. ANN. §§ 43-1201(A) and 43-1231; COLO. REV. STAT. § 39-22-112; CONN. GEN. STAT. §§ 12-214(a)(2)(B), 12-242aa, and 12-242bb; FLA. STAT. §220.13(2)(h); GA. CODE ANN. §§ 48-7-25(a)(1) and 48-7-25(c)(1); IDAHO CODE §§ 63-3025B(1) and 63-3025B(4); 35 ILL. COMP. STAT. 5/205(a); BURNS IND. CODE ANN. §§ 6-3-2-2.8(1) and 6-3-2-3.1(a); IOWA CODE §§ 422.33(1A) and 422.34(2)(a); KAN. STAT. ANN. §§ 79-32,113(a) and 79-32,113(b); LA. REV. STAT. § 47:608(5); 36 MAINE REV. STAT. ANN. §§ 5102(6), 5162(2), and 5200(5); MD. TAX-GENERAL CODE ANN. §§ 10-101(e)(3), 10-104(2), and 10-304(2); MASS. ANN. LAWS. CH. 63, §§ 30(4) and 38Y; MINN. STAT. §§ 290.05, subd. 2 and 290.05, subd. 3(a)(iii); MO. REV. STAT. § 143.441(2)(1); MONT. CODE ANN. §§ 15-31-102(1)(d) and 15-31-102(3); NEB. REV. STAT. ANN. § 77-2714; N.M. STAT. ANN. §7-2A-4C; N.Y. CLS TAX LAW § 290 and 20 N.Y. Comp. Codes R. & Regs. § 1-3.4(b)(6); N.C. GEN. STAT. §§ 105-130.11(a) and 105-130.11(b); N.D. CENT. CODE § 57-38-09; 68 OKLA. STAT. §§ 2359(A) and 2359(B); ORE. REV. STAT. §§ 317.080(1), 317.920(1), and 318.040; 72 PA. CON. STAT. §§ 7401(1)(3) and 7401(1)(4); S.C. CODE ANN. § 12-6-540; TENN. CODE ANN. §§ 67-4-2007(a) and 67-4-2105(a); TEX. TAX CODE ANN. §§ 171.058 and 171.063(a)(1); UTAH CODE ANN. §§ 59-7-102(1)(a) and 59-7-801 et seq.; 32 VT. STAT. ANN. § 5811(18)(D); VA. CODE ANN. § 58.1-401(5); and W. VA. CODE §§ 11-23-7(b) and 11-24-5(a).

[235] ARK. CODE ANN. §§ 26-51-303(a)(9) and 26-51-206(a); CAL. REV. & TAX CODE §§ 23701, 23701d(a), 23731, and 23732; 30 DEL. CODE ANN. § 1902(b)(2); KAN. REV. STAT. ANN. § 141.040(1)(g); MISS. CODE

of Section 501(c)(3) of the Internal Revenue Code, applicable to religious and secular eleemosynary corporations. Thirty-eight[236] states simultaneously apply or copy the Code's UBIT tax on the unrelated business income of exempt institutions. Thus, states' income taxes uniformly relieve religious organizations and other philanthropic entities from basic income taxation while generally taxing them on the earnings of their unrelated businesses.

The states' universal adoption of the federal approach to the income tax exemption of religious and other eleemosynary institutions implicitly acknowledges the Internal Revenue Code as a dominant statement of income tax policy. That statement establishes the national norms that churches and other 501(c)(3) organizations should not be taxed on their basic incomes but should be taxed on their unrelated business incomes. In chapter eight,[237] I discuss the legal and tax policy merits of these norms.

As a political matter, these national norms constrain governors and state legislators who might contemplate taxing the basic incomes of religious and other eleemosynary institutions. It would be politically awkward for governors and legislators to justify such taxation while the federal government exempts such income from taxation. By the same token, the federal UBIT provides political cover for the states' respective UBITs. If challenged, governors and legislators can readily reply that their state's UBIT simply follows the lead of the federal government.

In contrast, there is no federal property or sales tax statute to serve as a national standard for the states to follow. Thus, the states have greater political latitude to tax or not religious sales and property since, in these cases, there is no nationwide norm established by federal law.

Moreover, the Code's policy—exempt from taxation 501(c)(3) organizations' basic incomes, tax their unrelated business income—implements a theme expressed in many state sales tax statutes: Level the tax playing field when otherwise exempt institutions start to compete with commercial businesses. The states' sales tax statutes often provide immunity from the sales tax until the church or other nonprofit seller starts to behave commercially.[238] The Internal Revenue Code, incorporated

---

ANN. §§ 27-7-29(a)(3) and 27-7-29(b); N.H. REV. STAT. ANN. 77:8, 77-A:1(I), and 77-E:1(III); N.J. STAT. ANN. § 54:10A-3(e); OHIO REV. CODE ANN. § 5751.01(E)(8); R.I. GEN. LAWS §§ 7-6-4(1) and 44-11-1(4)(iv); and WIS. STAT. § 71.26(1)(a).

[236] The states which do not tax unrelated business income of churches and other nonprofit institutions are Delaware, Kentucky, Nevada, New Jersey, Ohio, Pennsylvania, South Dakota, Texas, and Wyoming. Nevada, South Dakota, and Wyoming do not tax any corporate income.

[237] *See infra* at 235–243.

[238] *See, e.g.*, LA. STAT. ANN. § 47:305.14.A(4) ("regular commercial ventures . . . in competition with retail merchants."); 86 Ill. Admin. Code § 130.2005(a)(3)(A) ("competitive with business establishments.").

or tracked by the state income tax statutes, reflects the same policy: Eleemosynary institutions are not subject to income tax unless they engage in businesses "unrelated" to their tax-exempt purposes and thereby compete with for-profit enterprise.

In chapter eight,[239] I discuss the commentators who favor and criticize this pattern of income taxation. The UBIT contravenes the uncomplicated notion that churches are not taxed. As I observe in chapter five,[240] the UBIT also challenges my thesis that the states tend to impose upon churches those taxes which entail relatively less enforcement entanglement. The UBIT is highly entangling.

For now, however, I emphasize that the states' income taxes do not reflect the same degree of diversity manifested in the states' sales and property tax treatment of churches and other religious entities. Rather, the states embrace with minor variation the federal income tax pattern—no general income taxation of churches and other religious and secular philanthropic entities; taxation of such entities' unrelated business income.

J. REAL ESTATE TRANSFER TAXES

Thirty-five states levy taxes on the transfer of real estate. These taxes, which replace a now-repealed federal documentary stamp tax,[241] have different names: real estate conveyance taxes, deed taxes, documentary transfer taxes, realty transfer fees, recordation taxes, mortgage taxes, excise taxes on real estate conveyances, real estate transfer taxes. Sometimes, the revenue from these levies goes into the state's treasury. In other cases, the revenue generated by these taxes is retained, in part or in whole, by the localities in which the transferred real estate is located. Despite the differing nomenclature and details, the basic policy of these taxes is the same: When an interest in real estate passes from one owner to another, the seller or the buyer (or both) pays a tax based on the price of the transferred property.[242] Typically, the tax is

---

239 *See infra* at 235–238, 241–242.

240 *See infra* at 140–143.

241 *See* Sections 4361 and 4382 of the original Internal Revenue Code of 1954. These provisions were repealed by Section 401(a) of the Excise Tax Reduction Act of 1965, PL 89-44.

242 Some states backstop their respective real estate transfer taxes by also imposing tax upon the sale of a controlling interest in an entity which owns real estate. These controlling interest taxes are designed to prevent avoidance of the real estate conveyance tax by putting real estate into an LLC, partnership, corporation, or other entity and then selling the partnership interests, membership interests, or stock rather than the underlying real estate. To preclude such avoidance techniques, these controlling interest taxes apply when a majority interest is transferred in an entity which owns real property. A controlling interest tax is intended to impose the same burden as would a direct sale of the real property owned by the entity. *See, e.g.*, CONN. GEN. STAT. § 12-638a et seq.; FLA. STAT. § 201.02(1)(b) ("conduit entity" tax); 36 MAINE REV. STAT. § 4641-A.2; N.J. STAT. § 54:15C-1; NY CLS TAX LAW §§ 1401(b) and 1401(e); WASH. REV. CODE §§ 82.45.033 and 82.45.010(2). *See* Sean

calculated as a percentage of such price. If consideration for the transfer takes a form other than cash, the tax is calculated as a percentage of the fair market value of such noncash consideration.

Most states with real estate transfer taxes apply those taxes to sales and purchases by churches and other nonprofit institutions, just as the now-repealed federal documentary stamp tax applied to such sales and purchases. In particular, twenty-seven states subject churches or other religious entities to their respective real estate conveyance taxes: Arkansas,[243] California,[244] Colorado,[245] Florida,[246] Georgia,[247] Hawaii,[248] Iowa,[249] Kansas,[250] Maine,[251] Maryland,[252] Massachusetts,[253] Minnesota,[254] Nevada,[255] New Hampshire,[256] New Jersey,[257]

Kanousis, Sam Melehani, & Reed Schreiter, *Losing Control: How Varying Real Estate Transfer Tax Treatment of Entity Interest Transfers Creates Confusion for Taxpayers*, BNA DAILY TAX REPORT (Nov. 12, 2014).

[243] ARK. CODE ANN. § 26-60-102 (exemptions from the Arkansas real property transfer tax do not include an exemption applicable to churches or other religious groups).

[244] California's "documentary transfer tax," imposed by localities in the Golden State, has no generally applicable exemption for churches, religious institutions, or nonprofit entities. The tax does contain a narrow exemption for certain transfers of real estate from the state, any locality, or any "agency or instrumentality" of the state or a locality to "nonprofit corporation[s]." CAL. REV. & TAX CODE § 11929.

[245] Colorado's "documentary fee on conveyances of real property" has no generally applicable exemption for church, religious, or eleemosynary entities. COLO. REV. STAT. § 39-13-104.

[246] Florida's tax on real estate deeds has no generally applicable exemption for churches, religious institutions, or nonprofit entities. The tax does contain a narrow exemption for transfers of real estate from nonprofit organizations to local governments, state agencies, water management districts, or the trustees of an Internal Improvement Trust Fund. FLA. STAT. § 201.02(6).

[247] Georgia's real estate transfer tax does not exempt churches, religious institutions, or private nonprofit entities. GA. CODE ANN. § 48-6-2.

[248] Hawaii's real estate conveyance tax does not exempt churches, religious institutions, or private nonprofit entities. HAW. REV. STAT. § 247-3.

[249] Iowa's real estate transfer tax does not exempt churches, religious institutions, or nonprofit entities. IOWA CODE § 428A.2.

[250] Kansas imposes upon mortgages a fee payable "to the register of deeds of the county in which" the mortgaged property is located. There is no exemption for mortgages of property held by religious, church, or nonprofit entities. KAN. STAT. ANN. § 79-3102(a).

[251] Maine's real estate transfer tax does not exempt properties purchased or sold by religious, church, or nonprofit entities. 36 MAINE REV. STAT. § 4641-C.

[252] Maryland's recordation tax does not exempt properties purchased or sold by religious, church, or nonprofit entities. MD. TAX-PROPERTY CODE ANN. § 12-108.

[253] Massachusetts imposes a tax on "deeds, instruments and writings" with no exemption for religious, church, or nonprofit entities. MASS. GEN. LAWS ANN. ch. 64D, §1.

[254] Minnesota imposes a tax on the recording of mortgages and a parallel tax on real estate deeds. Neither tax exempts religious, church, or nonprofit entities. MINN. STAT. §§ 287.04 and 287.22.

[255] Nevada's real estate transfer taxes do not exempt religious institutions or churches. NEV. REV. STAT. ANN. § 375.090.

[256] New Hampshire's real estate transfer tax does not exempt religious institutions or churches. N.H. REV. STAT. § 78-B:2.

[257] New Jersey's realty transfer fee does not exempt churches or other religious institutions. N.J. STAT. § 46:15-10.

New York,[258] North Carolina,[259] Ohio,[260] Oklahoma,[261] Rhode Island,[262] South Carolina,[263] South Dakota,[264] Tennessee,[265] Vermont,[266] Washington,[267] West Virginia,[268] and Wisconsin.[269] Thus, in these twenty-seven states, a sale or purchase of real estate by a religious organization is taxed in the same fashion as a sale or purchase of real property by any other seller or buyer, namely, an amount equal to a statutorily fixed percentage of the total purchase price is remitted to the state and/or the municipality in which the purchased property is located.

The remaining eight states with real estate transfer taxes each exempt some real estate transactions involving churches and other religious institutions. For example, Alabama's limited exemption from its "recordation tax"[270] only applies if religious congregations split or merge. If an Alabama religious organization divides into two

---

258 New York State does not exempt from its real estate transfer tax religious, church, or other eleemosynary entities. N.Y. CLS Tax Law § 1405. *See also In the Matter of the Petition of Hebrew Academy of Long Beach*, DTA No. 818273, 2001 W.L. 811645 (N.Y. Div. Tax. App.), at *3 ("petitioner has not shown that the conveyance at issue was eligible for any of the exemptions from the imposition of real estate transfer taxes . . ."). However, New York City exempts from its real property tax deeds executed by or to "religious, charitable, or educational" organizations. NYC Admin. Code § 11-2106(b)(2).

259 North Carolina's tax on conveyances of real property does not exempt religious, church, or other eleemosynary organizations. N.C. Gen. Stat. § 105-228.29.

260 Ohio authorizes its counties to tax real estate transfers. The transfer tax statutes of the Buckeye State provide no general exemption for churches or religious institutions. There is a limited exemption from transfer taxation when the transferor or transferee is a 501(c)(3) organization and the transfer occurs for no consideration. Ohio Rev. Code §§ 322.01(D) and 319.54(G)(3)(r).

261 Oklahoma imposes both a real estate mortgage tax and a documentary stamp tax on real estate sold in the Sooner State. Neither tax has an exemption for church, religious, or eleemosynary entities. 68 Okla. St. §§ 1903 and 3202.

262 Rhode Island's real estate conveyance tax does not exempt religious, church, or other eleemosynary entities. R.I. Gen. Laws § 44-25-2.

263 South Carolina's deed recording fee has no exemption for church, religious, or eleemosynary organizations, though there is a limited exemption from the fee for "transfers from a trust established for the benefit of a religious organization to the religious organization." S.C. Code Ann. §12-24-40(8).

264 South Dakota's fee on the transfer of real property has no exemption for church, religious, or eleemosynary institutions. S.D. Codified Laws § 43-4-22.

265 Tennessee's recordation tax has no exemption for church, religious, or eleemosynary institutions. Tenn. Code Ann. § 67-4-409(3).

266 Vermont's property transfer tax has no general exemption for church, religious, or eleemosynary institutions. 32 Vt. Stat. Ann. § 9603.

267 Washington's excise tax on real estate sales has no general exemption for church, religious, or eleemosynary institutions. Wash. Rev. Code §§ 82.45.010(3), 82.45.190, 82.45.195, and 82.45.197.

268 West Virginia's excise tax on the privilege of transferring real property has no exemption for churches or other religious institutions. W. Va. Code § 11-22-1(4); 58 Op. Atty. Gen. W. Va. 205 (1980), at *6, WL 119406 ("since Code 11-22-1 contains no express exception provision for property used for divine worship or other church owned property, its transfer is subject to the excise tax levied on property transfers by Code 11-22-2.").

269 Wisconsin's real estate transfer fee has no general exemption for church, religious, or other eleemosynary institutions. Wis. Stat. § 77.25.

270 Ala. Code § 40-22-1 et seq.

or more entities or if two or more sectarian organizations combine into a single entity, no recordation tax is levied on any deeds which implement this division or combination.[271] Otherwise, the Alabama real estate conveyance tax applies to religious bodies. For example, if an Alabama church sells its building to or acquires a new location from a third party, the Alabama real estate conveyance tax applies.

Michigan's real estate transfer tax contains a similarly narrow exemption for religious entities. In the Wolverine State, there is no transfer tax on "[a] written instrument conveying an interest from a religious society in property exempt" from property taxation to another "religious society if that property continues to be exempt" from property taxation.[272] Thus, if a Michigan church sells its church building to another denomination which will also operate that building as a church, no transfer tax is due. However, if a Michigan church buys real estate from a commercial developer or sells its parcel to such a developer, the transfer tax applies.

Pennsylvania's realty transfer tax has two exemptions similar to those of Alabama and Michigan. The Keystone State's transfer tax does not apply if one religious organization conveys noncommercial real estate to another religious entity.[273] The Pennsylvania tax also exempts any real estate transfer made pursuant to the merger, consolidation, or division "of a nonprofit corporation" unless such merger, consolidation, or division is primarily intended to avoid the transfer tax.[274]

A few other states exempt more broadly. Connecticut, for example, exempts from its real estate conveyance tax all deeds granted by a 501(c)(3) nonprofit organization.[275] In addition, deeds between 501(c)(3) organizations are exempt if they are "affiliated" organizations.[276] Thus, if a homeowner in the Nutmeg State sells her house to a church to be a parsonage for the church's minister, conveyance tax is due since no exemption applies to a transfer of real estate to a Connecticut church. On the other hand, if a church sells its parsonage to a Connecticut developer, the sale of this house is exempt from conveyance tax because the deed goes from a 501(c)(3) religious organization to an unaffiliated third party.

Kentucky similarly exempts sales by religious entities from real estate conveyance tax.[277]

---

[271] *Id.* § 40-22-5.1.

[272] MICH. COMP. LAW SERV. § 207.526(w).

[273] 72 PA. STAT. § 8102-C.3(17).

[274] *Id.* § 8102-C.3(12).

[275] CONN. GEN. STAT. § 12-498(a)(12).

[276] *Id.* § 12-498(a)(11).

[277] On its face, Kentucky's real property transfer tax has no exemption for churches or other eleemosynary institutions. KY. REV. STAT. § 142.050(7). The Kentucky tax is paid by the seller and is remitted to the county in which the property sold is located. *Id.* § 142.050(4). However, the Attorney General of Kentucky has opined that § 170 of Kentucky's state constitution prohibits the application of that state's real property transfer tax to

Delaware's exemption is the opposite of Connecticut's and Kentucky's exemptions on sales by religious sellers: Delaware exempts from its real estate transfer tax a religious institution's purchase of real property as long as the purchased property will not be used for "any commercial purpose."[278] Thus, if a Delaware church buys a building from a developer, the transfer is not taxed as long as the church does not use the building commercially. On the other hand, real estate sold by a Delaware church is subject to transfer taxation.

Illinois's particularly liberal exemption applies when any Illinois eleemosynary entity is a buyer or a seller of real property. In particular, Illinois exempts from its real estate transfer tax any "property acquired by or from any corporation, society, association, foundation or institution organized and operated exclusively for charitable, religious or educational purposes."[279] Thus, churches' sales and purchases of Illinois real property are exempt from transfer taxation as are sales and purchases by secular groups dedicated to charity and education.

Virginia's recordation tax statute imposes several levies, including a general tax on deeds,[280] an additional tax,[281] a tax on "deeds of trust or mortgages,"[282] and a tax on contracts including leases.[283] The Virginia statute contains religious exemptions from these taxes. The general tax on deeds and the tax on contracts and leases does not apply to any transfer to a church or other religious entity for real estate "to be used exclusively for religious purposes" or to be used as a residence for a minister of such church or other religious entity.[284] The Virginia tax on deeds of trust and mortgages exempts any trust deed or mortgage issued by a church or by a religious entity.[285] The additional tax does not apply to any deed from a church or from any other religious organization of the Old Dominion.[286]

The states' real estate transfer taxes, like the states' sales taxes and their taxes on unrelated business income, contravene the simple narrative that churches pay no

---

sales by public charities. 1982 Ky. Op. Atty. Gen. 2-509, Ky. OAG 82-484 (Sept. 10, 1982), 1982 Ky. AG LEXIS 155, 1982 WL 176971. That opinion implies that sales of real property by "institutions of religion" are also constitutionally exempted from the transfer tax of the Bluegrass State. KY. CONST. § 170.

[278] 30 DEL. C. § 5401(1)q. In addition, Delaware exempts from its realty transfer tax any conveyance without consideration to a 501(c)(3) nonprofit organization. *Id.* § 5401(1)(t).

[279] 35 ILL. COMP. STAT. 200/31-45(b)(3). In a similar fashion, New York City exempts from its real property tax deeds executed by or to "religious, charitable, or educational" organizations. N.Y.C. Admin. Code § 11-2106(b)(2).

[280] VA. CODE ANN. § 58.1-801.

[281] *Id.* § 58.1-802.

[282] *Id.* § 58.1-803.

[283] *Id.* § 58.1-807.

[284] *Id.* § 58.1-811A2.

[285] *Id.* § 58.1-811B2.

[286] *Id.* § 58.1-811C6.

taxes. In most states with real estate transfer taxes, those taxes reach transactions involving churches and religious entities in the same manner as these taxes apply to secular sellers and buyers of real estate. Even in the eight states which exempt some sectarian purchasers and sellers of real estate, those exemptions are usually narrow and leave subject to transfer taxation important categories of real estate transactions involving churches.

As I discuss in chapter five,[287] the widespread transfer taxation of real estate sales by and to churches, even as church buildings are exempt from annual property taxation, can be understood in terms of the trade-off between borderline and enforcement entanglement: In light of valuation and liquidity concerns, annual ad valorem property taxation entails more enforcement entanglement than does the taxation of episodic real estate sales, sales which typically are self-valuing cash transactions.

K. STATE UNEMPLOYMENT TAXES

Manifesting what is sometimes called "cooperative federalism,"[288] the nation's system of unemployment compensation is run jointly by the federal and state governments. The Federal Unemployment Tax Act (FUTA)[289] establishes detailed standards for state unemployment compensation programs. The federal government also subsidizes the states' costs of administering the states' respective programs of unemployment compensation.[290] The states, through their statutes and programs, undertake much of the tax-based financing of the unemployment compensation system and pay the unemployment compensation benefits due to eligible individuals.

FUTA imposes a 6 percent federal tax on the first $7,000 in annual compensation a covered employer pays to each of its employees.[291] If a state's unemployment compensation law meets the standards outlined in FUTA, employers credit the state unemployment taxes they pay against the employers' FUTA tax obligations to the

[287] *See infra* at 138–139.

[288] *General Motors Corporation v. Unemployment Compensation Board of Review*, 948 A.2d 256, 262 n.9 (2007) ("Unemployment insurance has been described as a system of 'cooperative federalism' . . ."); Frank James Singer III, *Health and Welfare: Providing the General Welfare? Compelling Indian Tribes to Participate in State Unemployment Programs*, 33 McGeorge L. Rev. 323, 328 (2002) ("FUTA represents 'cooperative federalism'. . .").

[289] I.R.C. §§ 3301 et seq., 26 U.S.C. §§ 3301 et. seq.

[290] 42 U.S.C. § 501 et seq.

[291] I.R.C. § 3301, 26 U.S.C. § 3301 (federal unemployment tax imposed on "wages") and I.R.C. § 3306(b)(1), 26 U.S.C. § 3306(b)(1) ("wages" for FUTA purposes limited to first $7,000 of annual compensation to each employee).

federal government.[292] This crediting of state taxes eliminates most of employers' liability for federal unemployment taxes.

Among the standards promulgated by FUTA for the states' unemployment compensation statutes, a state law cannot deny compensation to an employee fired for cause unless the employee was "discharge[d] for misconduct connected with his work."[293] As we shall see in chapter five,[294] this "misconduct" standard raises significant issues of enforcement entanglement if terminated employees of churches and other religious employers can claim unemployment compensation benefits.

As observed earlier,[295] FUTA exempts from the 6 percent federal unemployment tax any "religious, charitable, educational, or other organization described in" Code Section 501(c)(3).[296] Thus, these entities which pay no federal income taxes[297] pay no federal unemployment taxes either. However, with several notable exceptions, eleemosynary organizations do pay state unemployment taxes, as FUTA declares that state unemployment compensation laws must cover 501(c)(3) organizations and their respective employees.[298] Consequently, with important qualifications, eleemosynary organizations pay state unemployment taxes, though they do not pay federal unemployment taxes.

One important qualification is that FUTA permits the states to offer nonprofit organizations an alternative to paying the state's regular unemployment tax rate.[299] A state can give each 501(c)(3) organization the option, in lieu of making regular state unemployment tax payments, to instead reimburse the state's unemployment system for the amount of the unemployment compensation actually paid to the organization's terminated employees.[300] For example, in lieu of paying regular state unemployment taxes on all its employees' salaries, a nonprofit hospital can instead

---

292 I.R.C. § 3302, 26 U.S.C. § 3302 (credit against FUTA tax if state unemployment law meets federal standards), I.R.C. § 3303, 26 U.S.C. § 3303 (federal standards which state unemployment law must satisfy for state taxes to be creditable against FUTA tax), and I.R.C. § 3304, 26 U.S.C. § 3304 (same).

293 I.R.C. § 3304(a)(10), 26 U.S.C. § 3304(a)(10).

294 *See infra* at 143–147.

295 *See supra* at 57.

296 I.R.C. § 3306(c)(8), 26 U.S.C. § 3306(c)(8). *See also* http://www.irs.gov/Charities-&-Non-Profits/Exempt-Organizations:-What-Are-Employment-Taxes%3F ("organization that is exempt from income tax under section 501(c)(3) of the Internal Revenue Code is also exempt from FUTA. This exemption cannot be waived.").

297 These groups can pay tax on unrelated business income per I.R.C. §§ 511 et seq., 26 U.S.C. §§ 511 et seq.

298 I.R.C. § 3304(a)(6)(A), 26 U.S.C. § 3304(a)(6)(A) (state unemployment compensation law will be certified as FUTA-compliant if unemployment "compensation is payable" to employees of nonprofit employers "in the same amount, on the same terms, and subject to the same conditions as compensation payable" to employees of other employers).

299 I.R.C. § 3303(e), 26 U.S.C. § 3303(e). While § 3303(e) is permissive, § 3309(a)(2) describes this option as an alternative that the states "shall" furnish to nonprofit employers. I.R.C. § 3309(a)(2), 26 U.S.C. § 3309(a)(2).

300 *Id.*

reimburse the state for the amount of unemployment compensation paid to the hospital's former employees.[301]

Electing this option can save a nonprofit employer money when few of its former employees claim unemployment compensation. However, this election can also cause a nonprofit employer to pay more than the state's regular unemployment tax if the employer's former employees are paid large amounts of unemployment compensation which the nonprofit employer is obligated to reimburse to the state.[302]

Consequently, while an eleemosynary employer pays no federal unemployment taxes, as a general rule, such an employer typically either pays regular state unemployment taxes or reimburses the state unemployment fund for the actual amounts paid to the employer's former employees. However, FUTA permits the states to enact three exemptions which are of particular import to churches and other religious organizations. First, a state need not subject 501(c)(3) nonprofits with less than four employees to state unemployment compensation laws.[303] As a result, many small nonprofit employers (including small religious employers) do not pay any federal or state unemployment taxes nor do the employees of such small nonprofit organizations receive unemployment compensation if their employment is terminated.

Second, state unemployment laws need not apply to "a duly ordained, commissioned or licensed minister of a church in the exercise of his ministry, or by a member of a religious order in the exercise of duties required by such order."[304]

Third, state unemployment laws need not apply to specified religious organizations. These potentially exempted sectarian organizations include any "church or convention or association of churches."[305] These sectarian organizations potentially exempted from state (as well as federal) unemployment taxation also include any "organization which is operated primarily for religious purposes and which is operated, supervised, controlled, or principally supported" by any such church, convention, or association.[306] Moreover, state unemployment laws need not cover any nonprofit "elementary or secondary school which is operated primarily for religious purposes."[307]

---

[301] *Wilmington Medical Center v. Unemployment Insurance Appeal Board*, 346 A.2d 181 (Del. Super. Ct. 1975), aff'd per curiam, 373 A.2d 204 (Del. 1977).

[302] *See* Cynthia Koral, GuideStar, *Alternatives to Unemployment Taxes for 501(c)(3)s* (Apr. 1, 2005), http://www.guidestar.org/rxa/news/articles/2005/alternatives-to-unemployment-taxes-for-501c3.aspx.

[303] I.R.C. § 3309(c), 26 U.S.C. § 3309(c).

[304] I.R.C. § 3309(b)(2), 26 U.S.C. § 3303(b)(2).

[305] I.R.C. § 3309(b)(1)(A), 26 U.S.C. § 3303(b)(1)(A).

[306] I.R.C. § 3309(b)(1)(B), 26 U.S.C. § 3303(b)(1)(B).

[307] I.R.C. § 3309(b)(1)(C), 26 U.S.C. § 3303(b)(1)(C). In *St. Martin Evangelical Lutheran Church v. South Dakota*, 451 U.S. 772 (1981), the U.S. Supreme Court distinguished between a "church-run school" and "a separately incorporated church school." The former was exempt from state unemployment compensation because it had "no legal identity separate from a church." The latter was subject to state unemployment compensation

The states' respective unemployment compensation laws track closely FUTA's statutory standards for such laws, including these permitted exemptions for religious entities and actors. The states want their unemployment compensation statutes to satisfy FUTA's standards so that the state unemployment taxes employers pay will be creditable against such employers' federal unemployment tax obligations.

Alabama's unemployment compensation statute is typical of these FUTA-compliant state laws. Mirroring FUTA's standards for a state unemployment compensation law,[308] Alabama requires a 501(c)(3) nonprofit organization to pay state unemployment tax if the organization has four or more employees.[309] However, Alabama churches, conventions of churches, and associations of churches do not pay state unemployment compensation tax.[310] Similarly, an Alabama "organization that is operated primarily for religious purposes and which is either operated, supervised, controlled, or principally supported by a church or convention or association of churches" is also exempt from Alabama unemployment tax.[311] Likewise, in Alabama, the service of "a duly ordained, commissioned or licensed minister of a church in the exercise of his or her ministry or by a member of a religious order in the exercise of duties required by such order" is not subject to unemployment compensation taxation.[312]

Also reflecting the provisions of FUTA,[313] a 501(c)(3) organization subject in Alabama to unemployment compensation taxation may elect, in lieu of paying the regular state tax rate, to instead reimburse the state unemployment compensation fund for the actual benefits paid to such organization's former employees.[314] A terminated employee is not eligible to receive unemployment compensation in Alabama if he leaves employment "voluntarily without good cause"[315] or if he is fired for "actual or threatened misconduct."[316]

because it had "a separate legal existence" and was not "integrated into a church's structure." I.R.C. § 3309(b)(1)(C), adopted in 1997 by § 5407 of P.L. 105-33, authorized exemption from state unemployment compensation for such separately incorporated religious schools.

308 I.R.C. §§ 3304(a)(6) and 3309(c), 26 U.S.C. §§ 3304(a)(6) and 3309(c).

309 Ala. Code §§ 25-4-10(a)(3) and 25-4-10(b)(8). *See also* State of Alabama, Dept. of Labor, Unemployment Compensation Division, *Employer Handbook* 60 (2014) (hereinafter *Alabama Handbook*).

310 Ala. Code § 25-4-10(b)(21)(a)(1).

311 *Id.* § 25-4-10(b)(21)(a)(2).

312 *Id.* § 25-4-10(b)(21)(b).

313 I.R.C. §§ 3303(e) and 3309(a)(2), 26 U.S.C. §§ 3303(e) and 3309(a)(2).

314 Ala. Code § 25-4-51(a)(3); *Alabama Handbook* at 60–62.

315 *Id.* § 24-5-78(2).

316 Id. § 24-5-78(3)(b).

The unemployment compensation laws of the other states[317] follow this same pattern, complying with FUTA's standards so that employers' state tax payments will be creditable against federal unemployment taxes.[318]

---

[317] Oregon is an outlier in that it does not utilize the religious-based exemptions authorized by FUTA and embraced by the other states.

[318] *See* ALASKA STAT. §§ 23.20.276, 23.20.379(a), 23.20.525(a)(4), 23.20.526(d)(1), and 23.20.526(d)(9); ARIZ. REV. STAT. §§ 23-615.A.7, 23-615.B.1, 23-615.B.2, 23-750, 23-775.1, and 23-775.2; ARK. CODE ANN. §§ 11-10-210(a)(3), 11-10-210(a)(4)(A), 11-10-210(a)(4)(B), 11-10-513(a)(1), 11-10-514(a)(1), and 11-10-713; CAL. UNEMP. INS CODE §§ 608, 634.5(a), 634.5(b), 801 and 1256; COLO. REV. STAT. §§ 8-70-118, 8-70-140(1)(a), 8-70-140(1)(b), 8-73-108(5)(e), and 8-76-110; CONN. GEN. STAT. §§ 31-222(a)(1)(D), 31-222(a)(1)(E), 31-225(g), and 31-236(a)(2); 19 DEL. C. §§ 3302(10)(C), 3302(10)(D)(i), 3302(10)(D)(ii), 3314(1), 3314(2), and 3345(b)(3); FLA. STAT. §§ 443.101(1), 443.1216(3), 443.1216(4)(a), 443.1216(4)(b), and 443.1312; GA. CODE ANN. §§ 34-8-33(a)(4), 34-8-35(j)(1), 34-8-(j)(2), 34-8-158, 34-8-194(1), and 34-8-194(2); HAW. REV. STAT. §§ 383-7(a)(9)(A), 383-30(1), 383-30(2), and 383-62(d); IDAHO CODE §§ 72-1315(10), 72-1316A(7), 72-1322D, 72-1349A, and 72-1366(5); 820 ILL. COMP. STAT. ANN. §§ 405/205(B)(4), 405/211.2, 405/211.3(A), 405/211.3(B), 405/601(A), 405/602, and 405/1404; BURNS IND. CODE ANN. §§ 22-4-7-2(h), 22-4-8-2(j), 22-4-10-1(b), 22-4-15-1(a), and 22-4-15-6.1; IOWA CODE §§ 96.5(1), 96.5(2), 96.7(8), 96.19(18)(a)(5), 96.19(18)(a)(6)(a), and 96.19(18)(a)(6)(b); KAN. STAT. ANN. §§ 44-703(i)(3)(F), 44-703(i)(4)(I), 44-703(i)(4)(J), 44-706(a), 44-706(b), and 44-710(e); KY. REV. STAT. ANN. §§ 341.050(e), 341.055(19), 341.070(4), 341.275, 341.370(1)(b), and 341.370(1)(c); LA. REV. STAT. §§ 23:1472(12)F.II, 23:1472(12)F.III(a), 23:1472(12)F.III(b), 23:1472(12)H.VIII, 23:1552, 23:1601(1)(a), and 23:1601(2)(a); 26 MAINE REV. STAT. § 1043(11)(A-1)(3), 1043(11)(F)(17)(a), 1043(11)(F)(17)(b), 1193(1)(A), 1193(2), and 1221(10); MD. LAB. & EMPLOY. CODE ANN. §§ 8-208, 8-616, 8-1001(a)(1), 8-1002, 8-1002.1, and 8-1003; MASS. GEN. LAWS ANN. ch. 151A §§ 6(r), 6(s), 14A, and 25(e); MICH. COMP. LAW SERV. §§ 421.13a, 421.29(1)(a), 421.29(1)(b), 421.42(10), 421.43(o)(i), and 421.43(o)(ii); MINN. STAT. §§ 268.035 subd. 20(7), 268.035 subd. 20(8), 268.035 subd. 21(1), 268.053, and 268.095; MISS. CODE ANN. §§ 71-5-11.H(3), 71-5-11.I(4), 71-5-11.I(5)(a), 71-5-11.I(5)(b), 71-5-357, and 71-5-513.A(1); MO. STAT. ANN. §§ 288.032.1(4), 288.034.8, 288.034.9(1), 288.034.9(2), 288.050.1(1), 288.050.2, and 288.090.3; MONT. CODE ANN. §§ 39-51-201(19), 39-51-203(6), 39-51-204(2)(a), 39-51-204(4), 39-51-1103(4), 39-51-2302(1), and 39-51-2303; NEB. REV. STAT. §§ 48-603(10), 48-604(4)(b), 48-604(6)(g)(i), 48-604(6)(g)(ii), 48-628(1)(a), 48-628(2), 48-628.01, and 48-660.01; NEV. REV. STAT. ANN. § 612.120, 612.121, 612.380.1(a), 612.383, 612.385, and 612.553; N.H. REV STAT. ANN. §§ 282-A:9.IV(p)(1), 282-A:9.IV(p)(2), 282-A:32.I(a)(1), 282-A:32.I(b), 282-A:34, 282-A:35, and 282-A:69.I; N.J. STAT. §§ 43:21-5(a), 43:21-5(b), 43:21-7.2, 43:21-19(h)(6), 43:21-19(i)(1)(C), 43:21-19(i)(1)(D)(i), and 43:21-19(i)(1)(D)(ii); N.M. STAT. ANN. §§ 51-1-7.A(1), 51-1-7.A(2), 51-1-13, 51-1-42.F(8), 51-1-42.F(12)(a), and 51-1-42.F(12)(b); NY CLS LABOR LAW §§ 563, 593.1, 593.3, and 593.4; N.C. GEN. STAT. §§ 96-1(b)(11)(c), 96-1(b)(12)(a), 96-1(b)(12)(b)(2), 96-9.6, 96-14.5(a), and 96-14.6; N.D. CENT. CODE §§ 52-01-01.15.i, 52-01-01.17.g, 52-01-01.17.h(1), 52-01-01.17.h(2), 52-04-18, 52-06-02.1.a, and 52-06-02.2; OHIO REV. CODE ANN. §§ 4141.01(A)(1)(a), 4141.01(A)(1)(b), 4141.01(B)(2)(b), 4141.01(B)(3)(h)(i), 4141.01(B)(3)(h)(ii), 4141.241, 4141.29(D)(1)(b), and 4141.29(D)(2)(a); 40 OKLA. STAT. §§ 1-208.8, 1-210(4), 1-210(7)(a), 1-210(7)(b), 2-404.A, 2-405, 2-406, and 3-803; 43 PA. CON. STAT. §§ 753(l)(4)(8)(a), 753(l)(4)(8)(b), 802(b), 802(e), 901, 902, and 904; R.I. GEN. LAWS §§ 28-42-3(18)(i), 28-42-3(25), 28-42-8(4)(i), 28-42-8(4)(ii), 28-43-29, 28-44-17, and 28-44-18; S.C. CODE ANN. §§ 41-27-210(6), 41-27-230(3), 41-27-230(4),41-27-260(10)(a), 41-27-260(10)(b), 41-31-610, 41-35-120(1), and 41-35-120(2)(a); S.D. CODIFIED LAWS §§ 61-1-4(3), 61-1-15, 61-1-36(1), 61-1-36(2), 61-5A-6, 61-6-9, 61-6-14, and 61-6-14.1; TENN. CODE ANN. §§ 50-7-205(5), 50-7-207(b)(4), 50-7-207(c)(5)(A), 50-7-207(c)(5)(B), 50-7-207(c)(5)(C), 50-7-303(a)(1), 50-7-303(a)(2), and 50-7-403(h); TEX. LAB. CODE §§ 201.012, 201.023, 201.066, 205.002, 207.044, and 207.045(a); UTAH CODE ANN. §§ 35A-4-204(2)(e), 35A-4-205(1)(g)(i), 35A-4-205(1)(g)(ii), 35A-4-309, 35A-4-405(1), and 35A-4-405(2); 21 VT. STAT. ANN. §§ 1301(5)(B)(i), 1301(6)(C)(vii)(I), 1301(6)(C)(vii)(II), 1321(c), 1344(a)(1), and 1344(a)(2); VA. CODE ANN. §§ 60.2-210.B.8, 60.2-213.A.4, 60.2-213.B.1, 60.2-213.B.2, 60.2-501, 60.2-618.1, and 60.2-618.2; WASH. REV. CODE §§ 50.20.050, 50.20.060, 50.44.010, 50.44.040(1), 50.44.040(2), 50.44.045, and 50.44.060; W. VA. CODE §§ 21A-1A-15(6), 21A-1A-16(10), 21A-1A-17(9)

Within this general pattern of state statutes complying with FUTA's federal standards, some states elect for their unemployment compensation laws and taxes to cover all nonprofit employers, not just nonprofit employers with four or more employees. Connecticut, for example, explicitly extends unemployment compensation coverage to the employees of any 501(c)(3) organization which has "one or more employees."[319] Minnesota reaches the same result by subjecting to that state's unemployment compensation law any "nonprofit" employer without regard to the number of the nonprofit employer's employees.[320]

Many states' unemployment compensation statutes elaborate the FUTA "misconduct" standard which disqualifies a former employee from receiving unemployment compensation if he was fired for misconduct. Maryland's unemployment compensation statute, for example, distinguishes among "gross misconduct,"[321] "aggravated misconduct,"[322] and simple "misconduct"[323] and imposes different periods of benefit ineligibility depending upon which of these standards the former employee's misbehavior triggered.[324]

Similarly, Georgia's unemployment compensation statute denies benefits to an employee "discharged or suspended from work with the most recent employer for failure to obey orders, rules, or instructions or for failure to discharge the duties for

---

(A), 21A-1A-17(9)(B), 21A-5-3a, 21A-6-3(1), and 21A-6-3(2); Wis. Stat. §§ 108.02(13)(b), 108.02(15)(h), 108.02(19), 108.04(5), 108.04(5g), 108.04(7)(b), and 108.151; Wyo. Stat. §§ 27-3-102(a)(xxiv), 27-3-103(a)(vii), 27-3-105(a)(ii), 27-3-105(b)(i), 27-3-105(b)(ii), 27-3-105(b)(iii), 27-3-105(b)(iv), 27-3-311(a), 27-3-311(f), 27-3-501(a)(v), and 27-3-509.

319 Conn. Gen. Stat. § 31-222(a)(1)(D).

320 Minn. Stat. § 268.035 subd. 21(1). *See also* Minnesota Unemployment Insurance, *Unemployment Insurance (UI) Employer Handbook*, "Special Provisions Relating to Governmental, Indian Tribal, and Nonprofit Organizations," http://www.uimn.org/employers/publications/emp-hbook/special-provisions-government.jsp ("Nonprofit organizations must ... [r]egister with the Minnesota Unemployment Insurance (UI) Program as soon as possible after *an* employee is paid covered wages for services performed in Minnesota.") (emphasis added).

321 Md. Lab. and Employ. Code Ann. § 8-1002.

322 *Id.* § 8-1002.1.

323 *Id.* § 8-1003.

324 Compare *id.* § 8-1002(c)(2) with § 8-1002.1(c)(2) with § 8-1003(b)(2). The Maryland law defines "gross misconduct" as employee conduct that constitutes "deliberate and willful disregard of standards of behavior that an employing unit rightfully expects and that shows gross indifference to the interests of the employing unit" or "repeated violation of employment rules that prove a regular and wanton disregard of the employee's obligations." *Id.* § 8-1002(a)(1). Maryland defines "aggravated misconduct" as "behavior committed with actual malice and deliberate disregard for the property, safety, or life of others that: (i) affects the employer, fellow employees, subcontractors, invitees of the employer, members of the public, or the ultimate consumer of the employer's product or services; and (ii) consists of either physical assault or property loss or damage so serious that the penalties of misconduct or gross misconduct are not sufficient." *Id.* § 8-1002.1(a)(1). Finally, Maryland's unemployment compensation law delineates simple "misconduct" residually, as misconduct that is neither gross nor aggravated. *Id.* § 8-1003(a).

which the individual was employed . . ."[325] Georgia also imposes longer periods of benefit ineligibility if an employee engages in a variety of forms of "[i]ntentional conduct" including "physical assault,"[326] "theft,"[327] "property loss,"[328] "sabotage,"[329] or "embezzlement."[330]

Some states likewise elaborate the "good cause" standard governing when an employee can quit work and still collect unemployment compensation benefits. For example, Oklahoma's unemployment compensation statute specifies that "good cause" "may include, among other factors" changes in an employee's "working condition" which make continuation of the job "so harmful, detrimental, or adverse to the individual's health, safety, or morals, that leaving the work was justified."[331] Oklahoma's statute also states that "good cause" may encompass "[s]ubstantially unfair treatment of the employee or the creating of substantially difficult working conditions by the employer."[332] Virginia's unemployment compensation statute specifies that "good cause" does not exist if an employee quits "to become self-employed"[333] or to follow a spouse to "a new locality" unless the spouse's relocation is related to military duty.[334]

Utah's unemployment compensation law provides that an employee has "good cause" for voluntarily quitting employment if there are "circumstances where it would be contrary to equity and good conscience" to deny unemployment benefits.[335] In assessing whether such equity and good conscience are present, the "reasonableness" of the Utah employee's actions shall be considered.[336] Quitting work "to accompany or follow the claimant's spouse to a new locality" qualifies as good cause only if the spouse has relocated for qualifying military service.[337]

A final notable feature of most states' unemployment compensation statutes is that these statutes allow otherwise exempted employers to waive exemption and thereby cover themselves and their employees within the state's unemployment

---

325 GA. CODE ANN. § 34-8-194(2)(A).

326 *Id.* § 34-8-194(2)(A)(i)(I).

327 *Id.* § 34-8-194(2)(A)(i)(II).

328 *Id.* § 34-8-194(2)(A)(ii)(I).

329 *Id.* § 34-8-194(2)(A)(ii)(II).

330 *Id.*

331 40 OKLA. ST. § 2-405(1).

332 *Id.* § 2-405(2).

333 VA. CODE ANN. § 60.2-618.1(1).

334 *Id.* § 60.2-618.1(2).

335 UTAH CODE ANN. § 35A-4-405(1)(b).

336 *Id.* § 35A-4-405(c).

337 *Id.* §§ 35A-4-405(d) and § 35A-4-405(e).

compensation program.[338] If, for example, a church elects coverage under a state's unemployment compensation law, the church, as employer, and its workforce are treated like any other nonprofit employer and employees.[339] This electing church must either pay regular unemployment taxes or instead reimburse the state fund for the actual unemployment benefits paid to the church's former employees. Correspondingly, the terminated employees of this electing church have the same rights to collect benefits under the state unemployment statute as do the former employees of other covered employers.

As I discuss further in chapter five,[340] the best understanding of the federal and state unemployment compensation statutes is that they accept the problems of church-state entanglement at the borders of exemption to avoid the church-state enforcement entanglement which would result if terminated church employees could claim unemployment compensation benefits.

L. CONCLUSION

Under the states' property, income, sales, real estate conveyance, and unemployment taxes, churches and religious institutions pay more taxes than many believe. In tax terms, churches and other sectarian entities are treated quite diversely by different states and by different taxes. As is now explored in chapter five, entanglement concerns play an important role in explaining this diversity.

---

338 Alabama, for example, is one of the few states which forbids a church from waiving its exemption to elect coverage of that state's unemployment compensation law. ALA. CODE § 25-4-131(a) (election for unemployment coverage not available if "employment is specifically exempt under the provisions of subsection (b) of Section 25-4-10)"); *id.* § 25-4-10(b)(21) (exemption for churches, religious organizations controlled by churches, and clergy).

339 *Cf. Mitchell v. Administrator, Unemployment Compensation Act*, 2005 Conn. Super. LEXIS 2241 (terminated church employee not entitled to unemployment compensation benefit when church "did not elect to be covered by the Connecticut Unemployment Compensation Act.").

340 *See infra* at 143–147.

5

UNTANGLING ENTANGLEMENT

THE FIRST FOUR chapters document this book's empirical themes: Churches and religious institutions pay more taxes than many believe. From a tax perspective, churches and other sectarian entities are treated diversely by different states and by different taxes. The taxes paid by churches, other religious institutions, and clerical personnel include the federal FICA and self-employment payroll taxes, which finance Social Security and Medicare benefits and federal taxes on unrelated business income. These taxes include as well numerous states' taxes on unrelated business income, sales taxes in many states, and the real estate conveyance taxes typically paid by churches and other sectarian entities when they buy or sell real property. Even though all churches are exempt from annual ad valorem property taxation, in certain states, properties owned by religious entities (such as residences used as parsonages and summer camps) are subject to such taxation.

In their discussions about churches and taxes, courts often focus upon the possibilities of church-state entanglement. Enforcement entanglement arises when the government implements the tax obligations of a church (or other religious institution) and the church satisfies its tax liability. Borderline entanglement occurs when sectarian entities are exempted from taxation, the tax collector polices the boundaries of exemption, and claimants assert their entitlement to exemption. The courts are more receptive to tax exemptions for churches and other religious actors when sectarian exemptions are embedded within broader tax exemptions covering secular philanthropic agencies and activities as well. Similarly, the constitutions of the states as well as federal and state tax statutes often grant tax exemptions to broad classes of secular and religious institutions—though such statutes also sometimes grant exemptions narrowly only to churches and religious actors. Many commentators reflexively equate exemption with subsidy.

This fifth chapter evaluates and explains this diverse empirical reality by exploring five more themes of this book: First, either taxing or exempting churches and other sectarian entities involves entanglement between church and state. In the tax context, there are no disentangling alternatives. The trade-off between enforcement entanglement and borderline entanglement is central to the decision to tax or exempt churches and other religious entities. Taxing the church engenders enforcement-related entanglement when the tax collector collects revenue from religious taxpayers, often by intrusive means. Exempting the church entails borderline entanglement, as churches and other sectarian actors claim exemption from taxation while tax collectors police the boundaries of exemption and sometimes reject those claims. This policing intertwines church and state at the borders of exemption as they contest such definitions as "church" and "religion" to determine whether exemption applies or not.

Some taxes entail more church-state entanglement than do other taxes. Moreover, different tax provisions entail different types of entanglement risk. Tax policy invariably involves trade-offs among conflicting goals, none of which can ever be achieved in toto. These goals include revenue, administrability, the proper valuation of tax liability, liquidity concerns, public acceptability, and economic neutrality. When tax laws impact churches and other sectarian entities, the minimization of church-state entanglement should also be an important, often controlling, goal. Much of current law is best understood in terms of minimizing church-state entanglement. However, church-state entanglement can never be eliminated in its entirety, any more than any other legitimate objective of tax policy can ever be obtained perfectly.

On balance, our federal system of decentralized lawmaking minimizes tax-related entanglement of church and state reasonably well, though there is room for improvement in important cases. The taxes to which churches and other religious institutions are subject—FICA payroll taxes, sales taxes, real estate conveyance taxes—engender less enforcement entanglement between church and state. The taxes from which sectarian entities are exempt—general corporate income taxes, ad valorem property taxes, unemployment compensation taxes—would engender greater enforcement entanglement if they applied to sectarian actors. The taxes generating the greatest enforcement entanglement are those, like ad valorem property taxation, where the amount of the taxpayer's liability may be difficult to determine and where the taxpayer may lack the cash to pay the tax.

The reflexive equation of exemption with subsidization is unpersuasive. It is only persuasive to label a tax exemption, exclusion, or deduction as a "subsidy" when there is agreement on a normative baseline from which such exemption, exclusion, or deduction departs. There are many things we refrain from taxing, not to subsidize them but because they are properly excluded from the normative tax base. Exemptions for religious actors and institutions can be legitimate, nonsubsidizing features of a tax base when such exemptions minimize enforcement entanglement between church and state. In a world of imperfect choices between entangling alternatives, it is often a plausible and nonsubsidizing choice to exempt sectarian actors and institutions and thereby incur the problems of borderline entanglement rather than enmesh church and state in the difficulties of enforcement entanglement.

An important task of this chapter is to identify those taxes which present the greatest (and the least) threats of church-state entanglement. The possibilities of borderline entanglement between tax collectors and sectarian actors are greatest when exemption is granted narrowly to churches or to religious actors, rather than to a broad range of eleemosynary institutions. A narrow category for exemption, such as "church" or "houses of worship," forces the tax collector and the entity claiming exemption to fight over limited territory to dispute the nature of churches or of religious worship.

In contrast, a broader tax exemption, such as one covering religious, educational, and charitable organizations, creates more space for any entity to qualify for exemption and thus reduces the instances in which sectarian actors and the tax collector dispute the borders of exemption by contesting the nature of religion. This was Justice Harlan's rationale for upholding New York's property tax exemption in *Walz* and, more generally, helps to explain the greater judicial acceptance of religious tax exemptions when they are coupled with secular exemptions for charity and education: There is less opportunity for borderline entanglement when sectarian institutions might qualify for exemption under alternative secular headings.

Conversely, the absence of exemption eliminates borderline entanglement between church and state since, in this context, there is no border for the church and state to contest. However, taxing, rather than exempting, churches and other religious entities increases enforcement entanglement as churches and sectarian institutions comply with the tax laws and as the collector implements those laws against religious actors.

The likelihood of enforcement entanglement is greatest when taxes are levied on hard-to-value phenomena and when taxes are imposed on a taxpayer without regard to the taxpayer's liquidity to pay the tax. Valuation disputes and taxpayer illiquidity present classic situations in which the tax collector must take intrusive administrative action such as foreclosure to enforce the tax and litigation to defend the fisc.

This chapter also discusses why entanglement should be an important, often controlling, consideration when deciding to tax or exempt religious institutions. The courts have expressed concern about church-state entanglement in terms of respect for the autonomy of religious institutions and the peculiar divisiveness of political fights along religious lines. This chapter further elaborates entanglement concerns in terms of the institutional competences of courts and tax collectors, and the collector's ability to impose costs and grant favors in his administration of the tax law.

Certain taxes can enmesh judges and tax administrators in doctrinal issues beyond their institutional competence. Moreover, if the power to tax is not always the power to destroy, it is often the power to hamper. The prospect of tax collectors hampering religious activity through the exercise of administrative discretion is unsettling for a society which cherishes the free exercise of religion.

In light of these considerations, tax exemption in particular cases can have the secular, rather than the subsidizing, purpose of minimizing church-state entanglement when the challenges of enforcement entanglement are deemed greater than the risks of borderline entanglement. On the other hand, taxes imposed on easily valued cash transactions are less pregnant with the possibilities of enforcement entanglement since the amount of tax owed is easily determined and the taxpayer has cash readily available to pay the tax. The existing pattern of taxing and exempting the church largely reflects the reality that taxes imposed on cash transactions entail less church-state entanglement than do levies imposed on illiquid, difficult to value events.

Tax exemption can clash with important values. For example, when the state taxes some persons and not others, the values of economic neutrality and equality are jettisoned. Revenue considerations re-enforce the propriety of taxing religious actors and institutions when the resulting church-state entanglement is deemed manageable. Churches and other sectarian institutions utilize public services, sometimes quite heavily. Such institutions are often wealthy and engage in economically significant transactions including the purchase and sale of real estate. Such wealth and transactions reflect capacity to pay tax. Exemption, even when motivated by the desire to avoid enforcement entanglement, has a revenue cost.

There are, in the final analysis, no perfect answers to the quandaries of taxing or exempting the church. Whether to tax or exempt the church or other religious institutions and actors involves trades-off among competing values, for example, borderline entanglement versus enforcement entanglement; entanglement avoidance versus formal neutrality; entanglement avoidance versus revenue concerns. By the end of this chapter, I hope to convince the reader that, on balance, our decentralized federal and state tax systems make these trade-offs diversely and reasonably, though not perfectly, and are thus an important exemplar of productive federalism.

A. THE INEVITABILITY OF TAX-RELATED ENTANGLEMENT: BORDERLINE ENTANGLEMENT AND ENFORCEMENT ENTANGLEMENT IN THE COURTS

Let us begin by revisiting U.S. Supreme Court cases which highlight the issue of entanglement. The Court's decision in *Walz v. Tax Commission*,[1] introduced in chapter one,[2] is a useful departure point from which to explore the inevitability of church-state entanglement in the context of taxing or exempting the church. Among its other important features, *Walz* highlights the distinction between enforcement entanglement and borderline entanglement as well as the trade-off between them.

Chief Justice Burger's majority opinion in *Walz* focused upon what I call "enforcement entanglement," the intrusion into internal church operations which results when the church is taxed. The autonomy of religious institutions is protected by excluding those institutions from the tax base. Justice Harlan's concurrence in *Walz* highlights what I denote as the "borderline entanglement" stemming from religious exemptions, the entanglement which flows from the need to define and police the boundaries of such exemptions. These two opinions—the first highlighting sectarian autonomy in the context of tax enforcement, the second concentrating on borderline enforcement—illustrate the entanglement concerns at play when deciding whether to tax or to exempt the church and other religious institutions and actors.

In *Walz*, an owner of taxable real property mounted a First Amendment challenge to New York's property tax exemption for "real or personal property used exclusively for religious . . . purposes."[3] Chief Justice Burger's *Walz* opinion succinctly summarizes the problem of enforcement entanglement, the enmeshing of church-state when the tax collector is required to apply the tax law against the church. While tax exemption yields "an indirect economic benefit" to the exempted religious institutions, such exemption also minimizes "entanglement" between the government and those institutions.[4] The tax exemption of church property, wrote Chief Justice Burger, recognizes "the autonomy and freedom of religious bodies"[5] and

> creates only a minimal and remote involvement between church and state and far less than taxation of churches. It restricts the fiscal relationship between

---

[1] 397 U.S. 664 (1970). For more on *Walz, see* Edward A. Zelinsky, *Are Tax "Benefits" Constitutionally Equivalent to Direct Expenditures?*, 112 HARV. L. REV. 379, 392–395 (1998).

[2] *See supra* at 410.

[3] 397 U.S. at 666–667 (quoting Article 16, Section 1 of the New York Constitution).

[4] *Id.* at 674–676.

[5] *Id.* at 672.

> church and state, and tends to complement and reinforce the desired separation insulating each from the other.[6]

In contrast, taxing church properties

> would tend to expand the involvement of government by giving rise to tax valuation of church property, tax liens, tax foreclosures, and the direct confrontations and conflicts that follow in the train of those legal processes.[7]

Taxation is inherently intrusive, as anyone who has undergone a tax audit understands.[8] Exempting religious institutions and their personnel from taxation "separat[es]" and "insulat[es]" government and sectarian institutions from each other, thereby respecting the internal autonomy of such institutions by protecting them from the need to comply with tax laws. Exemption likewise protects churches from the enforcement activities of the tax collector, including valuation, lien, and foreclosure disputes.[9]

Justice Harlan's *Walz* concurrence emphasizes the problem of borderline entanglement. Justice Harlan, like his colleagues, noted the "broad and divergent groups"[10] covered by New York's property tax exemption. Since that exemption is "so sweeping," Justice Harlan wrote, the exemption's "administration need not entangle government in difficult classifications of what is or is not religious."[11] Justice Harlan's analysis suggests that narrower tax exemptions than New York's might fail First Amendment scrutiny since they require more intrusive activity to police the exemptions' boundaries by determining what is and is not religious. This is precisely what happened in *Texas Monthly* two decades later.[12]

One year after *Walz*, that decision's concern about "excessive entanglement"[13] became one of the three components[14] of the famous and controversial *Lemon*

---

[6] *Id.* at 675.

[7] *Id.* at 674.

[8] Professors Crimm and Winer agree. NINA J. CRIMM & LAWRENCE H. WINER, POLITICS, TAXES, AND THE PULPIT: PROVOCATIVE FIRST AMENDMENT CONFLICTS (2011), at 176 ("Anyone who has been subject to an IRS audit appreciates how intrusive it can be.")

[9] *Walz*, 397 U.S. at 674.

[10] *Id.* at 696.

[11] *Id.* at 698.

[12] *See infra* at 119–122.

[13] *Walz*, 397 U.S. at 669–670.

[14] The other two elements of the *Lemon* test are intent and effect. *See* ERWIN CHEMERINSKY, CONSTITUTIONAL LAW: PRINCIPLES AND POLICIES § 12.2.3 (3rd ed. 2006); RONALD D. ROTUNDA & JOHN E. NOWAK, TREATISE ON CONSTITUTIONAL LAW: SUBSTANCE AND PROCEDURE § 21.4(a)(v) (6th ed. Supp. 2016).

test. In *Lemon v. Kurtzman*,[15] the Supreme Court, in another opinion by Chief Justice Burger, struck on First Amendment grounds Pennsylvania and Rhode Island statutes channeling financial assistance to nonpublic education. In particular, the Court declared that the challenged statutes "involve[d] excessive entanglement between government and religion."[16] While the funds given by these states to religious schools were restricted to secular subjects, "[a] comprehensive, discriminating, and continuing state surveillance will inevitably be required to ensure that these restrictions are obeyed . . . These prophylactic contacts will involve excessive and enduring entanglement between state and church."[17]

This is the same entanglement concern that the Chief Justice expressed in *Walz*, namely, the enforcement-related intrusion of the government into internal church autonomy as the government administers the law. In *Lemon*, the challenged laws unconstitutionally impaired sectarian autonomy by requiring the states to audit religious schools to determine such schools' compliance with the restrictions on the government funds the religious schools received.

Lemon also identified as an entanglement problem the possibility of political divisiveness along sectarian lines: "Here we are confronted with successive and very likely permanent annual appropriations that benefit relatively few religious groups. Political fragmentation and divisiveness on religious lines are thus likely to be intensified."[18]

Chief Justice Burger distinguished in two ways the Rhode Island and Pennsylvania statutes stricken in *Lemon* from the New York property tax exemption upheld against First Amendment challenge in *Walz*. The former required regular, annual appropriations of public monies and thus, as a procedural matter, heightened the danger of sectarian political conflict. Moreover, the property tax exemption for churches has a long tradition. This history indicated to the Chief Justice that such exemption entails less potential for sectarian political division than the new statutes which had recently been adopted by the Ocean and Keystone States. *Lemon*'s concern about ongoing administrative entanglement between church and state cautions against taxing religious institutions since taxation invariably involves continuing enforcement activity by the tax collector and continuing compliance efforts by the religious taxpayer.

In contrast, the plurality opinion in *Texas Monthly, Inc. v. Bullock*[19] focuses upon borderline entanglement. Justice Brennan, writing for a three-justice plurality,

---

[15] 403 U.S. 602 (1971).

[16] *Id.* at 614.

[17] *Id.* at 619.

[18] *Id.* at 623.

[19] 489 U.S. 1 (1989).

struck a Texas sales tax exemption because it was limited to sales of religious publications. The facts in *Texas Monthly* were as straightforward as they were in *Walz*: As observed in chapter one,[20] for three years Texas imposed sales and use taxes on the sale of secular publications like *Texas Monthly* magazine while exempting from such taxes the sale of religious periodicals and books.[21] Texas Monthly, Inc., the publisher of *Texas Monthly*, collected and paid the sales taxes to the Lone Star State and then sued for a refund, claiming that the exemption for sales of religious publications violated the Establishment Clause of the First Amendment.

For himself, as well as Justices Marshall and Stevens, Justice Brennan interpreted *Walz* as upholding the New York property tax exemption for churches only because the benefits of such exemption "flowed to a large number of nonreligious groups as well."[22] Equally critical for Justice Brennan was the proposition that "[e]very tax exemption constitutes a subsidy."[23] Since exemption is subsidization, Justice Brennan concluded, such subsidization cannot, consistent with the Establishment Clause, be directed "exclusively to religious organizations."[24]

As to the entanglement considerations so prominent in *Walz*, Justice Brennan opined in *Texas Monthly* that the Texas sales tax exemption for religious periodicals "produce[s] greater state entanglement with religion than the denial of an exemption"[25] since Texas must determine which publications are religious and thus qualify for exemption. This is the borderline version of entanglement, the concern that a narrowly drawn exemption restricted to religious institutions engenders conflict as institutions seek to qualify for the exemption and the state must police the boundaries of the religious exemption. This requires the tax collector and the entity claiming exemption to joust over the definition of religion.

In a blistering dissent joined by Chief Justice Rehnquist and Justice Kennedy, Justice Scalia found *Walz* "utterly dispositive" of *Texas Monthly* magazine's First Amendment challenge to the Texas sales tax exemption for sales of religious literature.[26] Effectively dismissing as *dicta Walz*'s discussion of the exemption New York simultaneously extends to secular eleemosynary institutions,[27] Justice Scalia opined that "[t]he *Walz* Court did not approve an exemption for charities that happened to benefit religion; it approved an exemption for religion *as* an exemption for religion."[28]

---

[20] *See supra* at 10–16.
[21] *Texas Monthly*, 489 U.S. at 5–6.
[22] *Id.* at 11.
[23] *Id.* at 14.
[24] *Id.* at 15.
[25] *Id.* at 20.
[26] *Id.* at 36.
[27] *Id.*
[28] *Id.* at 38.

The First Amendment "principle of permissible accommodation,"[29] Justice Scalia wrote, allows exemptions limited to religious actors so as to preclude enforcement-related entanglement of church and state:

> [I]t is a permissible legislative purpose to alleviate significant governmental interference with the ability of religious organizations to define and carry out their religious missions.[30]

Such entanglement-avoiding exemptions, Justice Scalia argued, may "single . . . out religious entities for a benefit, rather than benefiting a broad grouping of which religious organizations are only a part."[31]

In *Texas Monthly*, Justice Brennan declared that the Texas sales tax exemption "appears, on its face, to produce greater state entanglement with religion than the denial of an exemption."[32] In *Walz*, Chief Justice Burger advanced the opposite claim, that tax exemption "creates only a minimal and remote involvement between church and state and far less than taxation of churches."[33]

The tension between Chief Justice Burger's *Walz* opinion and Justice Brennan's opinion in *Texas Monthly* highlights the reality that, in the interactions of tax systems with religious institutions and actors, there are no disentangling alternatives. There is only the trade-off between borderline and enforcement entanglement. If churches and religious actors are exempt from taxation, church-state conflict occurs at the boundaries of exemption as institutions and individuals claim religious exemption and the tax collector protects the fisc by policing the boundaries of such exemption. If churches and religious actors are taxed, church-state entanglement arises as the tax collector enforces the tax obligations of sectarian institutions and personnel and as such institutions and personnel comply with those obligations.

The decision to tax or exempt thus invariably involves trade-offs between borderline entanglement and enforcement entanglement. Different taxes present different trade-offs because they present more or fewer opportunities for such entanglement. Because of valuation disputes[34] and liquidity concerns, the annual ad valorem property taxation at issue in *Walz* is more entangling than is the sales taxation involved in

---

[29] *Id.* at 39.

[30] *Id.* (quoting *Corporation of the Presiding Bishop of the Church of Jesus Christ of Latter-Day Saints v. Amos*, 483 U.S. 327, 335 (1987)).

[31] *Id.* (quoting *Corporation of the Presiding Bishop*, 483 U.S. at 333).

[32] *Texas Monthly*, 489 U.S. at 20.

[33] *Walz*, 397 U.S. at 675.

[34] On the myriad valuation disputes which arise under systems of ad valorem property taxation, *see* Walter Hellerstein, Kirk J. Stark, John A. Swain, & Joan M. Youngman, State and Local

Texas Monthly. Such sales taxation is aimed at self-valuing cash transactions which generate the cash to pay tax.

The Court has acknowledged the impossibility of completely disentangling the modern state from the modern church.[35] In the tax context, we can and should go beyond this initial observation to systematize our understanding of the entanglement problem: In the tax context, enforcement entanglement is different from borderline entanglement. Different taxes create different kinds and different levels of entanglement.

B. REDUCING BORDERLINE ENTANGLEMENT THROUGH BROADER EXEMPTIONS OR NO EXEMPTIONS

In the tax context, borderline entanglement between church and state can be abated by either of two opposite strategies: broadening tax exemption or eliminating exemption altogether. Borderline entanglement is reduced when tax exemption extends to charitable and educational groups as well as to churches and religious institutions. Borderline entanglement is eliminated when all religious entities are taxed, leaving no borderline of exemption for church and state to contest.

Broader categories create more space for any entity to qualify for tax exemption and thus decrease the instances in which sectarian actors and the tax collector dispute the borders of exemption by contesting the nature of religion. In contrast, narrow categories, such as "churches" and "houses of worship," force the tax collector and the entity claiming exemption to joust over more limited territory and thus increase the possibilities that the church and state will clash at the borders of exemption as each seeks to advance its respective definition of "church" or "worship" or "religion."

Conversely, borderline entanglement is eliminated altogether when there is no exemption for the church to claim or for the tax collector to police. However, taxing, rather than exempting, religious institutions and actors enhances enforcement entanglement as those institutions and actors comply with the tax laws and as the collector enforces the tax laws against these entities and individuals.

TAXATION: CASES AND MATERIALS 919 (10th ed. 2014); JOAN YOUNGMAN, LEGAL ISSUES IN PROPERTY VALUATION AND TAXATION: CASES AND MATERIALS 33 (2006). *See also infra* at 128–134.

[35] *Agostini v. Felton*, 521 U.S. 203, 233 (1997) ("Interaction between church and state is inevitable and we have always tolerated some level of involvement between the two. Entanglement must be 'excessive' before it runs afoul of the Establishment Clause.") (internal citation omitted).

Consider initially the paradigmatic version of a broad tax exemption, Internal Revenue Code Section 501(c)(3). Section 501(c)(3) grants immunity from the federal income tax to nonprofit entities "organized and operated exclusively for religious, charitable, . . . or educational purposes."[36] Under this generous standard for federal income tax exemption, an entity which might not qualify as a "church" may nevertheless qualify as a "religious" organization. Such entity may also qualify as a "charitable" or "educational" institution, making it unnecessary for the IRS and the entity to dispute whether or not the entity is "religious." There is accordingly less borderline entanglement under this kind of broad exemption standard than under a narrower exemption just for "religion" or just for "churches." A more expansive exemption standard reduces the possibility that the IRS and the sectarian entity claiming exempt status will dispute whether the entity is a "church" or is "religious" as the entity may qualify under the alternative secular hearings of charity or education.

The kind of property tax exemption at issue in *Walz* is similarly expansive and thus reduces the possibility that the tax collector and the organization claiming exemption will dispute the nature of religion at the boundary of the exemption. New York's constitution guarantees tax exemption for

> real or personal property used exclusively for religious, educational or charitable purposes as defined by law and owned by any corporation or association organized or conducted exclusively for one or more of such purposes and not operating for profit.[37]

As Justice Harlan wrote in *Walz*, because of its breadth, the administration of the Empire State's exemption "need not entangle government in difficult classifications of what is or is not religious."[38] There is less opportunity for church and state to fight over the definition of religion (or of a "house of worship") when tax exemption may be available under alternate secular headings such as education or charity.

As we saw in chapter two,[39] many states' constitutions are similar to New York's and exempt from taxation "religious" property along with other eleemosynary properties. As we saw in chapter four,[40] other states, though not required by their respective constitutions, by statute relieve from property taxation churches or religious holdings along with educational and charitable properties. In these instances, there is less potential for church-state entanglement at the borderlines of exemption since

---

36 I.R.C. § 501(c)(3), 26 U.S.C. § 501(c)(3).

37 McKinney's Const. Art. 16, § 1.

38 *Walz*, 397 U.S. at 698.

39 *See supra* at 26–30.

40 *See supra* at 67–77.

there is greater room for an entity to obtain exemption for its property as educational or charitable property. Even broad exemptions will entangle church and state in particular cases: Some groups claiming religious status cannot credibly claim exemption under the alternative rubrics of charity or education. Borderline entanglement arises in such cases since the tax collector must determine whether the entity claiming to be religious is indeed religious. However, broad exemptions entail less possibilities for church-state borderline entanglement since there is greater room for any particular sectarian institution to qualify as tax exempt under the alternative secular rubrics of education or charity.

Particularly instructive in this context are those states which exempt a relatively narrow category of sectarian properties (e.g., "houses of worship") while simultaneously exempting charitable and educational properties. As we saw in chapters two[41] and four,[42] courts in these states often extend tax-exempt status to religious publishing houses, sectarian camps, and similar facilities under these alternative secular headings. Though such religious facilities are not churches or houses of worship and though these states do not extend exemption to "religious" properties as such, the courts often deem sectarian institutions tax exempt as charitable or educational entities.

Judicial decisions such as *Hubbard Press*[43] might be criticized as improperly exempting from taxation nonchurch religious property where the legislature has not granted such exemption. A competing perspective on these cases is that the broad application of exemptions for educational and charitable properties minimizes borderline entanglement over the nature of religion. Decisions like *Hubbard Press* lessen the instances in which tax collectors fight with institutions claiming to be "houses of worship" by bestowing property tax exemption under the alternative secular headings of charity or education.

The expansive exemptions exemplified by Code Section 501(c)(3) and the New York property tax exemption upheld in *Walz* contrast with the kind of narrow exemption at issue in *Texas Monthly*. While Justice Brennan supported the New York property exemption in *Walz*, his plurality opinion in *Texas Monthly* rejected the Texas sales tax exemption for religious publications. One characterization of Justice Brennan's position is that he (like Justice Harlan) approved the broad New York exemption because the availability of alternative exemption categories (such as education and charity) implies less borderline entanglement as to the definition of "religion." In contrast, the narrow Texas sales tax exemption, restricted solely to religious

---

[41] *See supra* at 30–33.

[42] *See supra* at 69, 73–74.

[43] *Hubbard Press v. Glander, Tax Commissioner*, 156 Ohio St. 170 (1951). I discuss *Hubbard Press, supra* at 30–31.

publications, generated more borderline entanglement as church and state battled over eligibility for that exclusively religious-based category for sales tax exemption.

Consider as well the many state unemployment statutes which exempt from taxation churches as well as conventions and associations of churches.[44] Like the limited sales tax exemption challenged in *Texas Monthly*, these narrow exemptions create heightened possibilities for borderline entanglement since the state must assess whether an entity claiming exemption is a "church." Some states also exempt eleemosynary employers with less than four employees.[45] When this small-employer exemption is unavailable (if, for example, a church has four or more employees), the government and the sectarian actors claiming exemption from the unemployment tax may dispute what constitutes a "church," eligible for such exemption.

Thus, narrowly exempting churches from the unemployment tax engenders significant possibilities for borderline entanglement over the definition of a "church." However, as I discuss below,[46] such exemption for churches obviates enforcement entanglement when terminated church employees might otherwise claim unemployment benefits. This again illustrates the inherent trade-off between borderline entanglement and enforcement entanglement.

The greater judicial acceptance of broader exemptions like New York's property tax exemption may in part be optical: It looks better when religious exemptions are coupled with charitable and educational educations. A more rigorous assessment is that, as Justice Harlan stated, there is less scope for church-state entanglement when tax exemption is extended more expansively to secular eleemosynary actors and entities. When exemption applies more broadly, sectarian entities may qualify under secular headings, obviating the need for the tax collector and the institution claiming exemption to dispute the definition of "religion" or "church" at the borderline of exemption.

Just as broader exemptions reduce borderline church-state entanglement by creating opportunities for institutions to claim tax exemption under such secular headings as charity or education, the opposite approach—no exemptions at all—eliminates borderline entanglement altogether since there is no boundary to dispute when there is no exemption to claim. However, the no-exemptions approach increases enforcement entanglement since all eleemosynary entities, including churches, are subject to taxation across the board if there are no exemptions.

Consider again in this context the state sales taxes as they apply to purchases and sales of tangible personal property by churches and other religious institutions. As we

[44] *See supra* at 106.

[45] *See supra* at 106.

[46] *See infra* at 143–147.

saw, ten states tax both purchases and sales by churches.[47] Other states tax churches' sales of tangible personal property but exempt from sales taxation churches' purchases of such property.[48] Yet other states take the opposite tack, taxing churches' purchases of tangible personalty but exempting their sales of such personalty.[49]

The state statutes which tax churches' purchases or sales obviate borderline entanglement since, under these statutes, there is no religious exemption with boundaries requiring demarcation. In this context, the U.S. Supreme Court's decision in *Swaggart Ministries*[50] is instructive. California is one of the ten states which impose sales tax both when churches buy tangible personal property and when they sell such property.[51] Swaggart Ministries, a religious enterprise, cited *Follett*[52] and *Murdock*[53] to oppose on First Amendment grounds the application to that enterprise of the Golden State's sales tax. All nine justices rejected this claim.

There is no danger of borderline entanglement when everyone is taxed across the board and thus there are no boundaries of exemption for the church and state to dispute. As Justice O'Connor stated for the *Swaggart Ministries* Court:

> Most significantly, the imposition of the sales and use tax without an exemption for appellant does not require the State to inquire into the religious content of the items sold or the religious motivation for selling or purchasing the items, because the materials are subject to the tax regardless of content or motive. From the State's point of view, the critical question is not whether the materials are religious, but whether there is a sale or a use, a question which only involves a secular determination.[54]

A sales tax like California's also presents minimal possibilities for church-state enforcement entanglement since cash sales of tangible personal property are self-valuing and impose liability when there is cash to pay the sales tax.

Similar observations are to be made about the states' real estate conveyance taxes. These taxes generally apply to transfers of church and other religious properties.[55] There is thus no borderline entanglement between church and state since there is no

---

47 *See supra* at 79–81.

48 *See supra* at 84–88.

49 *See supra* at 89–90.

50 *Jimmy Swaggart Ministries v. Board of Equalization*, 493 U.S. 387 (1990). *See supra* at 16–18.

51 Cal. State Bd. of Equalization, *Nonprofit Organizations: Publication 18*, at 5 (2016), http://www.boe.ca.gov/pdf/pub18.pdf.

52 319 U.S. 105 (1943).

53 321 U.S. 573 (1944).

54 *Jimmy Swaggart Ministries*, 493 U.S. at 396.

55 *See supra* at 99–104.

religious exemption borderline to dispute. Moreover, when real estate is purchased for cash, real estate conveyance taxes entail minimal enforcement entanglement since cash conveyances of real estate are easily taxed, both in terms of valuing the conveyance and of obtaining cash payments of the tax.

A statute like Alabama's recordation tax law[56] buttresses this analysis. Under that law, a church's purchase or sale of real estate from or to a third party is a taxable event, like an equivalent taxable sale to or purchase by a secular person. Considering the minimal possibilities of enforcement-related entanglement, Alabama imposes transfer taxation on most real estate transactions between churches and third parties. Such transactions will typically involve cash consideration, which obviates both valuation challenges and liquidity problems.

On the other hand, cash consideration will rarely accompany a merger- or division-related transfer of a church property when a congregation splits or two congregations combine. In such circumstances, levying a tax on a noncash real estate transfer by a church or other religious institution entangles church and state in the same kinds of valuation and liquidity questions as arise in the context of annual property taxation: What is the transferred property worth? How does a church pay tax when it lacks cash? When churches merge or divide, the likely absence of cash consideration creates enhanced possibilities for enforcement entanglement in terms of valuation controversies and liquidity problems paying tax. It is thus plausible for Alabama to avoid enforcement-related entanglement by eschewing recordation taxation in the contexts of congregational mergers and splits. The trade-off is that Alabama's recordation tax exemption potentially engenders borderline entanglement in some cases. Alabama (like Pennsylvania[57] and Michigan[58]) must determine if a group merging or dividing is religious and therefore qualifies for real estate transfer tax exemption. Alabama's statute avoids enforcement entanglement when a church merger or division occasions a noncash transfer of real estate with consequent problems of valuation and liquidity. Implicit in this choice is the acceptance of borderline entanglement when the state must determine whether an institution claiming transfer tax exemption is "religious."

In contrast to Alabama (as well as Pennsylvania and Michigan), the twenty-seven states without religious exemptions in their respective transfer taxes accept enforcement entanglement when religious institutions convey and acquire real estate for noncash consideration. In return, these twenty-seven states avoid borderline entanglement under their respective transfer taxes since there is no religious exemption

---

56 Code of Ala. § 40-22-1 et seq., discussed *supra* at 210–211.

57 72 P.S. §§ 8102-C.3(12) and 8102-C.3(17).

58 Mich. Comp. Law Serv. § 207.526(w).

with boundaries to police when taxation applies across the board to all real estate transfers.

Unlike the narrow exemptions of Alabama, Michigan, and Pennsylvania, Illinois[59] broadly exempts from its transfer tax any kind of real estate conveyance to or by a religious, charitable, or educational institution. Such a broad exemption mitigates borderline entanglement: Institutions otherwise claiming religious status may qualify for transfer tax exemption as charitable or educational. This reduces the number of church-state controversies over the meaning of "religion."

On the other hand, Illinois loses revenue by exempting so broadly. When a church, charity, or school buys real estate for cash, no transfer tax is collected even though there is no valuation controversy or liquidity problem enforcing such a tax. Tax policy choices are never costless.

C. ENFORCEMENT ENTANGLEMENT, PROPERTY TAXES, AND GENERAL INCOME TAXES

As we saw in chapters two[60] and four,[61] every state, constitutionally or by statute, exempts churches from property taxation. Many states also exempt from taxation some forms of nonchurch religious property. The universal practice of exempting church and other sectarian property reflects deeply rooted historic practice. The historical lineage of the tax exemption was important to the *Lemon* Court when it distinguished that venerable exemption from the then recently adopted financial assistance to parochial schools invalidated in *Lemon*.[62]

Reinforcing the weight of history, issues of valuation and taxpayer liquidity counsel that ad valorem property taxes can give rise to severe enforcement entanglement. As *Walz* held, churches and other religious properties are plausibly exempted from property taxation to avoid such enforcement-related entanglement.

Central to ad valorem property taxation is the periodic determination of each property's fair market value to be taxed. The valuation of nonfungible properties often leads to difficult controversies, as the tax collector asserts higher values to generate greater property tax liabilities while taxpayers seek lower valuations to minimize their obligations to the fisc. Valuation can be particularly contentious in the case of specialized, single-purpose buildings such as churches, buildings which are not sold frequently and often are not readily adaptable to other uses. Were churches

[59] 35 Ill. Comp. Stat. Ann. 200/31-45(b)(3).

[60] *See supra* at 26–30.

[61] *See supra* at 67–77.

[62] 403 U.S. 602 (1971).

subject to annual property taxation, those churches would routinely entangle with tax collectors, who would often enforce the tax by pressing for higher assessments of church property.

Moreover, annual property taxation is levied on the value of real estate irrespective of the taxpayer's liquidity. A property owner without cash still owes ad valorem property taxation. When a property owner lacks cash to pay property taxes, the tax collector enforces the tax through liens and foreclosures, thereby entangling church and state in often bitter enforcement proceedings.

In the context of churches and other religious properties, these valuation- and liquidity-related enforcement problems indicate that, as the *Walz* Court concluded, exemption is permitted to avoid the entanglement which would result from enforcement of the property tax against churches and other sectarian entities.

For property tax purposes, the fair market value of any particular piece of real estate is generally assessed by one of three methods: comparable sales, income-capitalization, or replacement cost.[63] The comparable sales method of valuing real estate examines recent sales of similar properties to determine the fair market value of the property in question. When a residential home is assessed for ad valorem property taxation, recent sales of similar properties in an active market typically guide the valuation inquiry. These sales of comparable properties indicate the market value of the home in question since comparable sales indicate the price upon which willing buyers and willing sellers have agreed for analogous homes.

Comparable sales data is often also available for commercial and investment properties so that the value of any particular building can be assessed by looking at the recent prices fetched in the market for similar properties. The comparable sales method works well for standardized, fungible forms of property for which there is ample evidence of value through market sales of analogous properties.

When comparable sales data is not available or is sparse, a second method of valuing a property determines the income generated by the property and then capitalizes that income to its present value. The income-capitalization approach postulates that a potential buyer of a property would pay for it no more than the discounted income stream anticipated from the property. At the same time, the property's owner would sell it for no less than the discounted present value of that income stream.

Thus, absent comparable sales of similar properties in an active market, the best indicator of a property's worth is the discounted present value of the income that property will generate. This income-based value is the price which would be determined through arm's-length negotiation between a willing buyer and a willing seller. The income-capitalization approach is particularly appropriate for valuing

[63] *See, e.g.*, 26 Pa. C.S. § 1105(2); Hellerstein et al., *supra* note 34, at 920; Youngman, *supra* note 34, at 34.

investment and commercial buildings which can be expected to generate rental income or which can easily be converted to rent-producing activity.

When neither the comparable sales nor the income capitalization method is available—because there are no or few sales of similar properties and because the property being appraised is not income-producing or easily adaptable to income-producing activity—property is valued based on its replacement cost. This third valuation method postulates that a potential buyer of a unique structure would pay no more for it than the cost of reproducing that structure. If a potential seller insists on receiving more for a property than the property's replacement cost, the potential buyer would instead reproduce the property from scratch rather than buy it for more than its replacement cost.

Likewise, a would-be seller of an unusual structure would not sell it for less than it would cost to replicate the structure. A price lower than replacement cost would bestow a windfall on the buyer who must pay the higher replacement cost to build a similar structure from the ground up. Thus, replacement cost is the best indicator of the price upon which a willing buyer and a willing seller would agree for a unique property when neither comparable sales nor capitalized income are available to guide the valuation process.

Churches are typically specialized, single-use structures which, if they must be valued, must be valued using the replacement cost method.[64] Since they are rarely sold and are often not adaptable to other uses, there is no active market for church buildings and thus no comparable sales to determine market values. Since a church is conventionally understood as not producing income,[65] there is no income stream to capitalize to determine the church's value. Hence, if the value of a church is to be determined, the replacement cost method is, by default, the approach which must be used. That approach can be very entangling, enmeshing the church and the tax assessor in contentious disputes about replacement costs.

---

[64] 4-12C NICHOLS ON EMINENT DOMAIN § 12C.01[4][b] ("In some cases, the cost approach method has been used. . . ."); MD. REAL PROPERTY CODE ANN. § 12-104(d) ("The damages to be awarded for the taking of a structure, such as a church or place of religious worship, held in fee simple, or under a lease renewable forever, by or for the benefit of a religious body and regularly used by the religious body, are the cost of reproducing or replacing the improvements, adjusted for physical and functional depreciation, to which shall be added the fair market value of the land."); *United States v. Two Acres of Land*, 144 F.2d 207, 209 (7th cir. 1944) ("In the case of nonprofit, religious or service properties, cost of replacement is regarded as cogent evidence of value although not in itself the only standard of compensation. But people do not go about buying and selling country churches. Such buildings have no established market values."); *Department of Transportation v. Marston Baptist Church, Inc.*, 196 N.C. App. 756, 759 (Ct. of App., N. Car. 2009) ("the trial court property allowed testimony on the cost of reproduction for a replacement church building.").

[65] This assumption is discussed further in chapter 8. *See infra* at 235–241.

While church buildings are not taxed, they are sometimes acquired by the state through eminent domain for highways or for other public projects. When that happens, the value of the church building must be determined to establish the compensation to be paid for the property the state is taking. This valuation process can enmesh the church and the state in complex and often bitter valuation controversies over replacement costs.

Instructive in this context is the decision of the Court of Appeal of California in *Redevelopment Agency of the City of Long Beach v. First Christian Church of Long Beach*,[66] a case involving an eminent domain controversy about a church taken for an urban renewal project. The local redevelopment agency condemned the church building and its land. The church's "main sanctuary [was] . . . richly decorated with molded plaster, stained glass windows, carved and curved pews, and other ornamental detail."[67] Adopting a tone of wearied resignation, the appellate court observed that, in the trial court,

> [a]s might be expected witnesses for both the parties varied widely as to the value of the property. [The agency's] appraiser fixed the total value of the property at $1,096,100, of which $315,000 was attributed to the land. [The church's] appraiser fixed the total value at $4.6 million, of which $765,000 was attributable to the land.[68]

In the face of "the complicated testimony,"[69] the jury valued the church at $3,027,291. The jury also awarded the church over a quarter of a million dollars "in litigation expenses, including attorney's fees."[70]

Since, the court observed, "certain types of buildings such as churches are not, as such, regularly bought and sold in the commercial market,"[71] determining "reproduction or replacement costs less depreciation or obsolescence . . . provide[s] a more just and equitable approach in evaluating special use buildings such as churches."[72] After reviewing the "complicated" evidence presented to the jury in a contentious trial,[73] the appeals court affirmed the lower court, thus bringing to an end a querulous dispute between church and state.

---

66 140 Cal. App. 3d 690 (1983, 2d App. Dist., Div. Two).

67 *Id.* at 696.

68 *Id.*

69 *Id.*

70 *Id.*

71 *Id.* at 698.

72 *Id.*

73 *Id.* at 699–703

Church-related eminent domain controversies, since they are one-time affairs involving a single congregation, are infrequent. Thus, the resulting church-state entanglement can be deemed tolerable. In contrast, the periodic ad valorem property taxation of all church properties would routinely entangle every church in the taxing jurisdiction with the tax collector, who continually enforces the tax by insisting on higher valuations. Property tax exemption is, as *Walz* observes, an acceptable response to the prospect of such ongoing church-state enforcement entanglement over the periodic valuation required by annual ad valorem property taxation.

In contrast to single-purpose church buildings, the land on which churches sit is not unique or specialized; it's just land. Moreover, some churches operate in storefronts[74] or in locations such as "abandoned shopping centers."[75] These commonplace structures pose no unique valuation issues since they are comparable to other storefronts and shopping centers and are readily usable for nonreligious purposes. As to these fungible structures, the comparable sales method of valuation is typically available, just as that method is usually used to assess any other standardized commercial structure. When property taxation is based on the historic price originally paid for a property, rather than the property's current fair market value, that historic acquisition cost is easily determined and does not give rise to enforcement entanglement.[76]

Based on these considerations, one could envision property tax systems which treat churches differently from prevailing patterns. For example, a property tax system could exempt specialized use church buildings to avoid the enforcement entanglement inherent in valuing single-use structures through the replacement cost method. However, that system could simultaneously tax fungible buildings, such as storefronts or other commercially adaptable buildings, serving as churches. One could also envision systems which exempt church structures from property taxation (because they are difficult to value, special use structures) but which tax church land (because land is fungible and thus more easily valued).

One could also visualize a property tax assessed on the original cost of constructing or purchasing church buildings, thereby forgoing subsequent valuation increases or decreases premised on current market values. An acquisition cost approach to the property taxation of churches would avoid the kind of valuation-related entanglement which occurred in *Redevelopment Agency of the City of Long Beach v. First*

---

[74] Kate Ramunni, *Storefront Churches Creating Parking Woes*, NEW HAVEN REGISTER, Feb. 17, 2015, at A1.

[75] SCOTT THUMMA & DAVE TRAVIS, BEYOND MEGACHURCH MYTHS: WHAT WE CAN LEARN FROM AMERICA'S LARGEST CHURCHES (2007) 12.

[76] The most important example of acquisition cost property taxation is California's Proposition 13. *See* HELLERSTEIN ET AL., *supra* note 34, at 269; YOUNGMAN, *supra* note 34, at 237.

Christian Church of Long Beach.[77] If churches were taxed on their original acquisition costs, instead of fighting about replacement costs, a church and the tax collector would look at the original purchase price or construction cost of the church. Once set, that number would thereafter be the basis for taxing the church.

While these approaches would obviate the valuation-related entanglement inherent in enforcing property taxation against churches, these theoretical approaches would also increase borderline entanglement as religious groups and tax collectors would tussle at the boundaries of exemption. For example, under a system which distinguishes unique church structures entitled to tax exemption from fungible buildings taxed even though used for church purposes, potential taxpayers and the tax collector would often dispute the side of the line on which particular properties would fall: A church could claim that it had started in an easily valued, abandoned shopped center but, by virtue of improvements to the property, the church's location had become a specialized church building, exempt from taxation.

Moreover, these alternative approaches to valuation would not eliminate the second major source of church-state entanglement in the enforcement of ad valorem property taxes, liquidity problems. Property taxes are payable whether or not the property owner has the cash to pay the tax. To enforce unpaid property taxes, such unpaid taxes give rise to a lien against the taxed property.[78] At some point, if an illiquid property owner does not discharge his property tax obligation, the tax collector enforces this lien by foreclosure. Foreclosure causes a forced sale of the property for which the taxes have not been paid.[79]

Many churches and synagogues are wealthy, well-endowed institutions which would have little difficulty paying property taxes, if such taxes were assessed against their buildings or land. But many religious institutions are not affluent entities with much cash to pay taxes.

Some tax collectors might exercise administrative discretion by allowing property tax liens on churches to accumulate, rather than foreclose such liens and force the sale of church buildings. It would be a troubling exercise of discretion if a tax collector were to enforce his liens against secular taxpayers while he abstained from foreclosing on churches and other sectarian properties with similar outstanding bills for unpaid property taxes. It would be equally troubling if the tax collector allowed

---

[77] 140 Cal. App. 3d 690 (1983, 2d App. Dist., Div. Two).

[78] *See, e.g.*, Code of Ala. § 11-51-6 ("Cities and towns shall have a lien for taxes upon all property assessed for taxation which shall be superior to all other liens, except liens for taxes held by the state and county.").

[79] *See, e.g.*, Conn. Gen. Stat. § 12-172 ("Such lien, during its existence, may be enforced by levy and sale of such real estate if such person has complete title thereto or of his interest in such real estate if he does not have complete title thereto.").

some churches to defer the payment of property taxes while he insisted that other congregations pay promptly.

Thus, in the final analysis, the property taxation of churches involves problematic issues of enforcement entanglement, both in terms of valuation and the imposition of tax obligations upon illiquid churches which lack the cash to pay tax. The universal property tax exemption of churches, condoned by the Court in *Walz*, avoids this church-state entanglement.

Enforcing income taxation is also a highly entangling activity. Applying the income tax to churches and other religious institutions would require the tax collector to delve into church practice and religious doctrine, resulting in much enforcement-related entanglement between church and state.

Consider the fundamental rule of the income tax that a taxpayer deducts its "ordinary and necessary expenses"[80] to determine its net, taxable income. A classic judicial elaboration of this standard for deductibility is Justice Cardozo's much-cited opinion in *Welch v. Helvering*.[81] That opinion confirms the ambiguities inherent in the "ordinary and necessary" test for income tax deductibility:

> Here, indeed, as so often in other branches of the law, the decisive distinctions are those of degree and not of kind. One struggles in vain for any verbal formula that will supply a ready touchstone. The standard set up by the statute is not a rule of law; it is rather a way of life. Life in all its fullness must supply the answer to the riddle.[82]

It is hard to envision a more entangling activity than an IRS or state revenue agent auditing a church to determine whether "life in all its fullness" makes church outlays "ordinary and necessary." If the auditor simply accepts the church's own declaration that an expense is "ordinary and necessary" in light of church doctrine, no income would be left to tax since the church may plausibly label all of its activities and outlays as necessary for its religious mission and thus deductible for income tax purposes. If instead the auditor were to evaluate independently the necessity and ordinariness of church expenses, many entangling inquiries would arise: Is necessity and ordinariness to be assessed in the context of a church's particular beliefs or practices or by looking to some objective, universal standard of religious doctrine and practice? How deeply is the auditor to peer into a church's theology to determine whether the church's outlays implement that theology or not? How does the

---

80 I.R.C. § 162(a), 26 U.S.C. § 162(a).

81 290 U.S. 111 (1933).

82 *Id.* at 114–115.

tax auditor identify the definitive statement of the church's beliefs and practices to apply the "ordinary and necessary" test for income tax deductibility?

Similar church-state enforcement entanglement would arise in the context of another important rule of the income tax: Gifts are excluded from income.[83] The definitive judicial construction of that rule commands an assessment of the donor's intent to determine if the donor gave out of "detached and disinterested generosity."[84] Only if a contributor gives from such altruistic motives is his contribution a "gift," excludable from the donee's gross income.

Churches and other religious institutions depend heavily upon donations from their congregants and other supporters. If churches and other sectarian entities were subject to general income taxes, these entities would be required to assess each donor's intent to determine whether her donation constitutes an income tax–free gift or is includible in the church's gross income as a payment for services rendered. On audit, the IRS or state tax agency would be required to review those intentions, donor by donor. Ultimately, a court could be called upon to determine if particular donations were given out of "detached and disinterested generosity" or out of less altruistic concerns, making such donations income to the church receiving them.

The *Hernandez* case, discussed in chapter three,[85] indicates how intrusive this enforcement process would be. In *Hernandez*, the U.S. Supreme Court sustained the IRS's disallowance of a charitable deduction for Mr. Hernandez's payment for auditing services from the Church of Scientology. Such payments, the Court concluded, do not constitute charitable donations, but rather "were part of a quintessential *quid pro quo* exchange: in return for their money, petitioners received an identifiable benefit, namely, auditing and training sessions."[86]

If churches were subject to income taxation on their basic religious activities, all gifts to churches would be subject to similar scrutiny to determine if they were truly "gifts," given for altruistic reasons, or payments for "an identifiable benefit." This enforcement inquiry would intrude the tax collector deeply into religious doctrine and practice.

Consider in this context the donor who believes that his contributions to his church will open for him the gates of heaven. Is eternal salvation a benefit which turns this donor's contribution from a gift into taxable income for the church receiving the contribution? Or consider the grandparent who, thrilled with her grandson's bar mitzvah or confirmation, sends a check to the synagogue or church after the

---

[83] I.R.C. § 162(a), 26 U.S.C. § 162(a).

[84] *Commissioner v. Duberstein*, 363 U.S. 278, 286 (1960).

[85] *See supra* at 47–49.

[86] *Hernandez*, 490 U.S. at 691.

event. Is this a tax-free gift to the church or a tip, includable in the synagogue's or church's gross income for services rendered?[87]

These problems are not isolated cases at the margins but, rather, reflect the extensive church-state entanglement inherent in enforcing the income tax against religious institutions. If the general income tax applied to churches or other religious entities, it would be necessary to classify donations to such entities as gifts or income. Such classification would intrude the tax collector into religious practice and doctrine as he peers into the minds of individual donors to determine if they gave altruistically or from self-interest.

As *Hernandez* demonstrates, the Code's charitable deduction requires entangling inquiries about religious benefits to determine if a donation to a church or other religious institution is a deductible contribution or a nondeductible payment for services. Congress and the state legislatures have plausibly limited this form of enforcement entanglement by exempting churches and other religious entities from general income taxation, thus obviating another tax-related venue which would require entangling inquiries about religious benefits.

Just as the deductibility problem could be resolved by accepting all church outlays as "ordinary and necessary," the gift-or-income problem could be solved by declaring all payments to churches as gifts, excludable from the churches' respective gross incomes. However, this approach would eviscerate the tax as applied to churches since, under this approach, most church receipts would automatically be declared gifts, leaving no income to tax.

As I discuss in chapter eight,[88] an alternative is to declare all church receipts as income. This approach would eliminate the entanglement involved in separating tax-free gifts from items of income. However, this approach would exacerbate the entanglement flowing from the "ordinary and necessary" deduction inquiry since churches would be incented to increase their deductions if all of their receipts were deemed to be income for tax purposes. It would also raise constitutional and Religious Freedom Restoration Act (RFRA) concerns if gifts to most donees are income tax–free to them while church and religious donees must report equivalent gifts as income.[89]

On balance, the federal and state income tax exemptions for religious institutions (along with other nonprofit philanthropic enterprises) reasonably avoid the church-state enforcement entanglement which would flow from the income taxation of

---

[87] Treas. Reg. § 1.61-2(a)(1), 26 C.F.R. §1.61-2(a)(1) ("tips" are income). *See also Olk v. United States*, 536 F.2d 876, 879 (9th Cir. 1976), cert. denied, 429 U.S. 920 (1976) ("Tokes, like tips" are income).

[88] *See infra* at 239.

[89] *See infra* at 239–240.

churches and other sectarian entities on their religious activities. These exemptions entail revenue forgone, but it is plausible for the state and federal governments to eschew this (perhaps modest) revenue to avoid enforcement entanglement.

D. SALES, PAYROLL, AND REAL ESTATE CONVEYANCE TAXES: LESS PRONE TO ENFORCEMENT ENTANGLEMENT

In contrast to ad valorem property taxes and general income taxes, sales, payroll, and real estate conveyance taxes generate less enforcement entanglement. These taxes are typically assessed on cash transactions. The presence of cash obviates the church-state entanglement stemming from valuation disputes and taxpayer illiquidity. No doctrinal issues complicate the enforcement of the sales, payroll, and real estate taxes. It is thus understandable that these less entangling taxes are more frequently imposed upon churches and religious institutions than are property and income taxes, which would entail greater enforcement entanglement if applied to churches.

Consider sales taxation in the context of a gift shop run by a church. When a congregant buys a retail item from this shop for $5, no valuation problem enmeshes the church and the tax collector. A $5 item is being sold for cash. There is also no liquidity challenge in this context. If the sales tax rate is 5 percent, the buyer of this $5 item must come up with an additional quarter to pay the sales tax. If the buyer doesn't have the quarter, he can cancel his sale or the shop can sell the item to him for $4.75 and thereby free a quarter to pay the sales tax.

Thus, the typical cash retail sale by a church gift shop engenders little enforcement entanglement between that church and the tax collector. The purchase price for the property the church sells is self-valuing, and the buyer has cash to pay the tax. It is thus understandable that many states impose sales taxes in this setting.

The situation is similar when a church purchases tangible personal property at retail. A cash purchase price paid by a church establishes the value for sales tax purposes. The church has the liquidity to make a cash purchase. Some of that cash can be used to pay the sales tax.

Less enforcement entanglement does not mean no enforcement entanglement. If the church gift shop collects sales tax on its retail sales, it must report those sales and remit to the appropriate agency the taxes collected. The tax collector may audit those reports and inspect the shop's records to test the accuracy of those reports.

A noncash barter transaction poses, in the context of the sales tax, the same kind of valuation and liquidity challenges as does ad valorem property taxation. Suppose, for example, that a church's gift shop exchanges a painting for a book. Under the typical sales tax statute, this barter exchange is a taxable transaction because, if it weren't, the sales tax could be avoided through such barter.

At one level, the valuation and liquidity problems look manageable in this barter example: The cash price at which the church gift shop offered the painting to third parties provides evidence of the painting's value. Unless the book is a Guttenberg Bible and the painting is a Picasso, the cash required to pay a typical sales tax is not great in this barter context. Moreover, most transactions between a church gift shop and its customers will be cash sales.

Were U.S. sales tax rates, now relatively low by international standards, to rise to the levels of European or Canadian VAT rates, taxing barter sales might become more challenging. For the foreseeable future, however, the possibilities of valuation- and liquidity-based enforcement entanglement seem manageable, indeed, de minimis, when sales taxes apply to the purchases and sales of church and other religious institutions.

The enforcement of sales taxation can also entail interpretive disputes. Among the most common of these is whether a purchase is a taxable retail transaction or is a purchase for resale, not subject to sales tax.[90] No choice—whether to tax or to exempt the church—is completely disentangling.

On balance, retail sales taxation involves less possibilities for church-state enforcement entanglement than does ad valorem property taxation since cash sales are self-valuing and occur when the buyer has the cash to pay tax. It is thus not surprising that many states, even as they exempt churches and other sectarian entities from annual ad valorem property taxes, impose sales tax when such religious institutions buy or sell (or both).

It is also understandable that the U.S. Supreme Court in *Swaggart Ministries*[91] unanimously held that California's sales tax did not excessively entangle church and state. I will argue in chapter seven[92] that many states could broaden their sales taxation of purchases and sales by religious institutions. These are largely self-valuing cash transactions. Imposing sales tax on church purchases and sales obviates borderline entanglement as there is no borderline to police when there is no exemption. The criterion of economic neutrality indicates that economically similar transactions should be taxed similarly. Revenue concerns further buttress the case for taxing churches' sales and purchases.

Comparable considerations counsel that real estate conveyance taxation carries minimal risk of church-state enforcement entanglement: Since taxable real estate

---

[90] HELLERSTEIN ET AL., *supra* note 34, at 706–716.

[91] *Jimmy Swaggart Ministries v. Board of Equalization*, 493 U.S. 387 (1990). *See supra* at 16–18.

[92] *See infra* at 206–211.

transfers typically involve purchases and sales of buildings for cash, there are neither valuation nor liquidity issues when a religious entity buys or sells real property. Tax collectors and courts need not evaluate church doctrine or practice to enforce conveyance taxes.

Suppose, for example, that the church involved in *Redevelopment Agency of the City of Long Beach v. First Christian Church of Long Beach*[93] had voluntarily sold its church building to a developer in a conventional cash transaction. In that situation, there would have been no substantial risk of entanglement in enforcing California's "documentary transfer tax."[94] The arm's-length price agreed upon by the church and the developer would have fixed the amount to be taxed. The consideration, paid in cash, would have created the liquidity to pay the tax.

The occasional noncash real estate conveyance of a church property does create potential valuation and liquidity challenges. Suppose, for example, that the Long Beach church, instead of selling its site to a developer for cash, had exchanged that site for another parcel owned by the developer. Taxing this in-kind exchange would have engendered liquidity challenges since no cash would have changed hands. Thus, the buyer and/or the seller would have been required to use cash from other sources to pay the California documentary tax triggered by this noncash transaction.[95] In this barter setting, the tax collector would find himself entangled with the church in enforcing the tax, both to determine the amount of tax and to collect the tax. Such entanglement explains why a few states, while generally taxing churches' real estate conveyances, exempt certain noncash transfers which might enmesh the state and the church in valuation and liquidity controversies.[96]

Nevertheless, the prospects of cash-free church-related real estate swaps are not daunting. Hence, it is understandable that most states imposing real estate transfer taxes assess such taxes on all purchases, exchanges, and sales by religious entities: There is little danger of church-state enforcement entanglement when a cash transaction values the property being sold and engenders the liquidity to pay the transfer tax. There is no borderline entanglement when there is no exemption whose borderlines require policing. If real estate sales are proper occasions for raising funds for the public fisc, a church's sale or purchase of real estate is such an occasion.

For reasons which will now be familiar to the reader, the federal taxes which finance Social Security and Medicare also entail little enforcement entanglement

---

93 140 Cal. App. 3d 690 (1983, 2d App. Dist., Div. Two).

94 Cal. Rev. & Tax Code § 11901 et seq.

95 Under Cal. Rev. & Tax Code § 11912, the California documentary tax "shall be paid by any person who makes, signs or issues any document or instrument subject to the tax, or for whose use or benefit the same is made, signed or issued." The parties' deal would thus reflect the need for them to pay the tax.

96 *See supra* at 101–103.

between church and state. While some forms of noncash compensation are subject to these payroll taxes,[97] FICA taxation in practice generally requires the employer to withhold a percentage of its employees' cash wages and to match this withholding with an equal cash contribution by the employer.[98] Applying the FICA taxes to the cash wages paid by sectarian institutions and their employees consequently involves neither liquidity nor valuation challenges which would entangle the IRS and the sectarian employer complying with its FICA tax obligations.

Moreover, no doctrinal quandaries arise when churches are subject to FICA taxation since that tax provides no deduction for "ordinary and necessary" expenses or has any similar deduction which would require an entangling assessment of church mission. It is thus unsurprising that most churches routinely withhold and pay FICA taxes with little church-state friction.

E. THE ENTANGLING TAXATION OF UNRELATED BUSINESS INCOMES

The unrelated business income tax (UBIT) challenges my argument that the federal government and the states impose upon churches those taxes which entail relatively less enforcement entanglement. The UBIT is highly entangling.

As we saw in chapters three[99] and four,[100] both the federal government and thirty-eight states tax the unrelated business incomes of eleemosynary institutions including religious institutions. In contrast, nine states with general corporate income taxes do not tax the unrelated business incomes of nonprofit entities.

The chief argument for taxing the unrelated business incomes of churches, charities, schools, and similar organizations is unfair competition. From this vantage, it is inequitable to permit philanthropic institutions to conduct money-making

---

[97] Most employer-provided fringe benefits are excluded from the FICA tax base. *See, e.g.*, I.R.C. §§ 3121(a)(17) through 3121(a)(20), 26 U.S.C. §§ 3121(a)(17) through 3121(a)(20) (excluding from the FICA definition of "wages" most employer-provided fringe benefits). However, some noncash fringe benefits trigger both FICA and income taxation. If, for example, an employer gives an employee a larger than permitted discount on products or services, the excess discount is subject to both income taxation and FICA taxation. I.R.C. § 132(c), 26 U.S.C. § 132(c) (limiting a "qualified employee discount" to the employer's "gross profit percentage."). To take one possible case, a church employee would have noncash income if the church gift shop sells to him a Bible below the church's cost. This noncash income would be subject to both income and FICA taxation.

[98] The mechanics of FICA taxation are described *supra* at 53–55. As noted there, most economists distinguish between the legal form of the FICA tax, which imposes equal tax liability on the employer and the employer, and the economic incidence of the tax, generally agreed to fall upon the employee in the form of a wage reduction for the amount of the employer's nominal FICA tax obligation.

[99] *See supra* at 49–50.

[100] *See supra* at 98–99.

businesses free of income taxation while their for-profit competitors, running the same or similar businesses, must pay income taxes on their earnings. For example, issues of fairness are alleged to arise if a megachurch can earn tax-free income from a health club for current and prospective members while a commercial competitor pays tax on the net income it derives from conducting the same health club activities. Thus,

> [t]he primary objective of adoption of the unrelated business income tax was to eliminate a source of unfair competition by placing the unrelated business activities of certain exempt organizations upon the same tax basis as the nonexempt business endeavors with which they compete.[101]

As I discuss in chapter eight,[102] most commentators dismiss this fear of unfair competition: A tax-exempt owner maximizes its profits by charging the same (higher) prices as its taxpaying competitors. Nevertheless, the federal government and thirty-eight states have responded to the perception of unfair competition by adopting UBITs.

UBITs generate considerable church-state entanglement. At the borderlines, determining whether any particular business is "unrelated" to a church's tax-exempt mission enmeshes the church and the tax collector in difficult quandaries about the church's religious purpose and activities. Once a religious entity's business is deemed "unrelated" to the entity's calling, enforcing the income tax against that business is as intrusive as is implementing the income tax against any other business.

Consider first the considerable potential for borderline entanglement in determining whether any particular business is "unrelated" to a church's exempt purposes.[103] For example, many churches today reach younger persons by operating coffeehouses.[104] Restaurants have long been common in Young Men's Christian Association (YMCA) and Jewish Community Center (JCC) facilities.

---

101 Treas. Reg. § 1.513-1(b), 26 C.F.R. § 1.513-1(b).

102 *See infra* at 241–242.

103 Evelyn Brody & Marcus Owens, *Nonprofit Oversight Under Seige: Exile to Main Street: The I.R.S.'s Diminished Role in Overseeing Tax-Exempt Organizations*, 91 Chi.-Kent L. Rev. 859 (2016) ("unrelated business activity" is an "ambiguous concept[]"); Michael Fricke, *The Case Against Income Tax Exemption for Nonprofits*, 89 St. John's L. Rev. 1129, 1136 (2015) ("From this definition alone, a host of questions arises regarding exactly what types of revenues are subject to the UBIT.").

104 *See, e.g., C.H. Red Inc. v. Tippecanoe County Assessor*, 2014 STT 195-17 (Ind. Bd. Tax Rev. 2014) (failure to show "sufficiently direct relationship" between religious purposes and coffeehouse); private letter ruling 201645017 (nonprofit corporation operating coffeehouse denied tax-exempt status under Internal Revenue Code Section 501(c)(3)). *Cf. How to Start Guide—Set Up—Starting a Successful Church Coffee Shop or Café*, Coffee 4 Missions, http://www.coffee4missions.com/how-to-guide-building-a-successful-church-café/

Are these coffee shops and restaurants "unrelated" to the exempt purposes of the sectarian institutions operating them? That inquiry requires the tax collector and ultimately the courts to determine the nature of these institutions' respective missions and to assess the appropriate means of effectuating those missions. This inquiry thrusts the tax collector and the courts into questions of religious identity and practice. When Congress extended to churches the unrelated business income tax, it identified myriad types of businesses conducted by churches, including

> chains of religious bookstores, hotels, factories, companies leasing business property, radio and TV stations, newspapers, parking lots, record companies, groceries, bakeries, cleaners, candy sale businesses, restaurants, etc.[105]

Some churches will retort that these operations are related to their religious missions and that accordingly these churches should not be taxed on the profits such operations generate. For example, a religious TV station can plausibly be characterized as an extension of a church's ministry.[106] To conclude otherwise, the IRS or a state tax department must monitor the station's programming and determine whether or not such programming is related to the church's ministry. These are deeply entangling inquiries.

Once a business is classified as "unrelated" to religious purposes, taxing that business's income is as intrusive as is taxing the income of an identical business operated by a for-profit owner. If a church's commercial-style coffee shop is determined to be unrelated to the church's religious activities, the UBIT taxes the income of that coffee shop no differently than the income of a Starbucks store. Hence, the tax collector (and ultimately the judiciary) must determine, among other issues, whether the shop's expenses are "ordinary and necessary,"[107] whether the compensation paid by the shop to its employees is "reasonable,"[108] and whether sales receipts are being accurately and timely reported for income tax purposes.[109] Just as these inquiries enmesh the tax collector and the secular coffee shop, they enmesh the tax collector

---

("Starting or setting up a church run coffee shop or café is becoming standard fare in today's churches across America.").

105 *Ocean Pines Association, Inc. v. Commissioner*, 135 T.C. 276, 285 (2010) (quoting H. Rept. 91-413 (Part I) as reprinted in 1969 U.S.C.C.A.N. 1645).

106 *See, e.g., Christian Voice of Central Ohio v. Testa*, 147 Ohio St. 3d 217 (2016) (a closely divided court held that a Christian radio broadcasting station qualified for property tax exemption as a facility "used exclusively for public worship" under Ohio Rev. Code Ann. §5709.07(A)(2)).

107 I.R.C. § 162(a), 26 U.S.C.§ 162(a).

108 I.R.C. § 162(a)(1), 26 U.S.C.§ 162(a)(1).

109 The basic Code provision on issues of timing is I.R.C. § 446, 26 U.S.C. § 446.

and the church coffee shop being taxed under the UBIT as an unrelated business of the church.

The upshot is a classic tax policy trade-off among contending criteria: Is it better to avoid borderline and enforcement entanglement by not taxing churches' unrelated business incomes? Or is it more appropriate to assure fair competition (or the perception of fairness) by taxing such unrelated business income? Is significant revenue obtainable by taxing the incomes of churches' unrelated businesses? It is sensible for different states to make these decisions for themselves and unsurprising that, while most states tax churches' unrelated business income, nine do not and thus avoid the entanglement flowing from UBIT taxation.

F. THE ENTANGLING TRADE-OFFS OF UNEMPLOYMENT COMPENSATION

Like the Texas sales tax exemption at issue in *Texas Monthly*, the religious-based exemptions permitted by FUTA and utilized by forty-nine states' unemployment compensation statutes are narrow. These limited exemptions involve entangling borderline inquiries to determine if they apply. In particular, these statutory exemptions are limited to a "church" or to an "association or convention" of churches and thus require the administrator of the unemployment compensation system and ultimately the courts to assess whether particular entities are churches. Similarly entangling is the borderline determination whether an individual is exempt from unemployment coverage as "a duly ordained, commissioned or license minister of a church in the exercise of his or her ministry or [is] a member of a religious order in the exercise of duties required by such order."

On the other hand, these narrow coverage exemptions spare the enforcement entanglement which would often result from applying the "misconduct" and "good cause" standards when terminated employees of religious entities claim unemployment compensation benefits. In some instances, administering these employment termination standards would involve neutral, secular criteria. Whether a terminated church employee claiming unemployment compensation has embezzled from his employer or assaulted a fellow employee, for example, would not require an inquiry into religious practice or doctrine. However, when employees are fired by religious and church employers, the presence *vel non* of "misconduct" or "good cause" can be a deeply entangling inquiry, mandating an intrusive assessment of religious practice or teachings. Excluding churches, associations of churches, and clergy from paying unemployment taxation avoids these entangling enforcement-related inquiries when employees are terminated.

Consider in this context *Bishop Leonard Regional Catholic School v. Unemployment Compensation Board of Review*,[110] decided by Pennsylvania's Commonwealth Court. The employee in *Bishop Leonard* was a teacher of secular subjects in a Catholic grade school. This teacher married a divorced man in the Presbyterian Church and was fired for violating Catholic doctrine by her marriage. While the parochial school was entitled to exemption from the Keystone State's unemployment compensation law, it had elected coverage under that law.[111] When she was fired because of her marriage, the teacher claimed unemployment compensation. The parochial school resisted this claim, arguing that the teacher's marriage constituted "willful misconduct"[112] because the teacher knowingly violated the school's policy that all teachers adhere to "the official teachings, doctrine, or laws of the Catholic Church."[113]

A divided court agreed with the school, finding that the school's policy was "reasonable"[114] and that the teacher's violation of this reasonable rule constituted conduct which "directly reflected on her ability to perform her assigned duties and adversely affected the interest of" the Catholic school for which she had worked.[115] The court's dissenters argued that this outcome engendered "excessive entanglement in matters of religion"[116] such as the court's determination that the school's dogma-based employment policy was "reasonable."[117]

Similarly instructive is the opinion of New York's court of appeals *In the Matter of Klein*,[118] another case brought by a teacher of a secular subject whose employment was terminated by a religious school. In *Klein*, the Jewish school fell outside the coverage of New York's unemployment compensation statute.[119] The former teacher asserted that the school's religion-based tax exemption and her consequent inability to collect unemployment benefits violated the First Amendment of the U.S. Constitution.

New York's highest court disagreed. Central to the court's reasoning was the secular purpose of the challenged tax exemption. By excluding religious employers from the system of unemployment compensation, that tax exemption obviates the entangling determinations of religious doctrine and practice which may result when the

---

[110] 140 Pa. Commw. 428 (1991).

[111] *Id.* at 441–442.

[112] 43 P.S. § 802(e).

[113] 150 Pa. Commw. at 431, 434.

[114] *Id.* at 437.

[115] *Id.* 435–436.

[116] *Id.* 444.

[117] *Id.*

[118] 78 N.Y.2d 662 (1991).

[119] *Id.* at 665.

employees of sectarian employers can claim unemployment compensation. As the *Klein* court explained, excluding religious entities from the unemployment compensation system and its taxes

> minimizes governmental intrusion into religious affairs by avoiding the necessity of scrutinizing a religious organization's tenets each time a teacher or other employee is discharged for reasons related to the group's religious mission.[120]

The U.S. Court of Appeals for the First Circuit came to a similar conclusion in another unemployment compensation case highlighting the trade-off between enforcement entanglement and borderline entanglement. In *Rojas v. Fitch*,[121] Rhode Island's Department of Employment and Training determined that the Salvation Army is an exempt church for purposes of the Ocean State's unemployment compensation statute.[122] An employee terminated by the Salvation Army challenged the constitutionality of that tax exemption on First Amendment grounds similar to those asserted by the former employee in *Klein*.[123] Like New York's court of appeals, the First Circuit upheld the church exemption, *inter alia*, because this exemption "eliminates the need for the government to review employment decisions made on the basis of religious rationales."[124]

On the other hand, the church tax exemption itself had earlier caused borderline entanglement when Rhode Island's Department of Employment and Training had to determine if the Salvation Army was a "church" falling within the boundaries of that exemption.

It takes little imagination to perceive other possibilities for church-state entanglement in the administration of the unemployment compensation system. Is there "just cause" for quitting his position when a clergyman who favors (or opposes) same-sex marriage is forbidden (or required) by his congregation to perform such marriages? Is it "misconduct" justifying termination when a minister announces from the pulpit that, as a matter of conscience, she has decided that a particular church doctrine is wrong? Deciding these questions would entangle the administrators of a state's unemployment compensation system and ultimately the courts in questions of religious doctrine and practice.

Exempting churches and clergy from unemployment taxation eliminates these kinds of entangling inquiries in the administration of the unemployment

---

120 *Id.* at 669.

121 127 F.3d 184 (1st Cir. 1997).

122 *Id.* at 185 (n.1).

123 78 N.Y.2d 662 (1991).

124 *Rojas*, 127 F.3d at 188.

compensation system. Such exemption engenders offsetting entanglement at the borders of exemption to determine which employers and employees are churches and ministers and thus excluded from paying unemployment tax. Here again there are no entanglement-free alternatives.

The statutory exemptions for churches, associations of churches, and clergy do not eliminate all religious-based enforcement entanglement in the context of unemployment compensation. Religious individuals who work for secular employers often pose questions of benefit eligibility which raise entangling questions of church doctrine and practice. One of the U.S. Supreme Court's most important First Amendment cases arose in such a setting. In *Employment Division, Department of Human Resources of Oregon v. Smith*,[125] two members of the Native American Church were counselors at a private drug rehabilitation center. After they took peyote at a church ceremony, these employees were subsequently fired for "misconduct" and denied unemployment compensation. The U.S. Supreme Court sustained that denial against First Amendment challenge.

Smith provoked controversy which still continues. *Smith* has generated voluminous commentary[126] and precipitated the federal Religious Freedom Restoration Act of 1993 (RFRA),[127] which, in turn, became the model for state RFRAs.[128]

Exempting churches, associations of churches, and clergy from unemployment taxation protects the administrators of the unemployment compensation system and, ultimately, the courts from having to make the kinds of decisions at issue in *Smith*, namely, when does religiously motivated behavior constitute "misconduct" or "just cause."

Oregon's unique choice[129] to eschew religious exemptions for unemployment compensation taxation accepts enforcement-related church-state entanglement when

---

[125] 494 U.S. 872 (1990).

[126] *See, e.g.*, Marci A. Hamilton, God vs. the Gavel: Religion and the Rule of Law 126 (2005); Garrett Epps, Peyote vs. The State: Religious Freedom on Trial 113–117 (2009).

[127] P.L. 103-141, codified at 42 USCS § 2000bb-1(b).

[128] *See* Edward A. Zelinsky, *Indiana's RFRA Statute: A Plea for Civil Discourse*, http://blog.oup.com/2015/04/indiana-rfra-statute-civil-discourse/.

[129] Oregon's legislature abolished unemployment compensation exemptions for churches in 2005. 2005 Ore. Laws 218, § 1. In *Salem College & Academy, Inc. v. Employment Division*, 298 Ore. 471 (1985), Oregon's supreme court initially held that the religious freedom clauses of the Oregon Constitution forbid the extension of exemption to church-operated religious schools while simultaneously denying such exemption to religious schools which operate independently of any church. In *Employment Division v. Rogue Valley Youth for Christ*, 307 Ore. 490 (1989), Oregon's supreme court, relying on *Salem College*, subsequently held that the Oregon Constitution forbids the exemption of churches from unemployment compensation taxation unless such exemption also extends to nonchurch religious organizations. The court held that all religious organizations (including churches) must pay Oregon unemployment compensation tax. The 2005 legislation codified that result by removing from Oregon's unemployment compensation statute the exemption for churches and

the terminated employees of religious employers claim unemployment compensation payments. In return, Oregon's courts and administrators are spared borderline entanglement since there are no religious exemptions, the borders of which require delineation. Thus, Oregon need not decide if the Salvation Army is a church[130] since Oregon does not exempt churches from its unemployment compensation system. On the other hand, if a church employee claims to have religious-related "good cause" for quitting or if a sectarian employer asserts religious-based misconduct by an employee, the administrator of Oregon's unemployment system and ultimately Oregon's courts must resolve entangling controversies about religious doctrine and practice—as did Pennsylvania's Commonwealth Court in *Bishop Leonard*.[131]

By permitting churches and other religious entities (along with secular exempt employers) to elect coverage under their respective states' unemployment programs, state legislatures empower these organizations to reverse the policy embodied in FUTA and forty-nine state statutes. If a church waives its exemption, it then either pays the regular state unemployment compensation tax or reimburses the state fund for actual unemployment benefits paid to the church's former employees. In return, employees of the electing church become eligible for unemployment compensation payments with the enforcement entanglement such eligibility entails when administrators and courts must decide claims of "misconduct" and "good cause" in religious contexts.

Churches rarely elect to pay unemployment compensation taxation.[132] This reluctance may simply be a matter of cost. On the other hand, churches may perceive that choosing to participate in state unemployment systems intrudes unacceptably into their institutional autonomy when administrators and judges wade into church practice and doctrine to determine if a church employee had "good cause" to quit or if the church had "misconduct" grounds to fire her.

---

ministers. Professor Epps views the *Salem College* decision as an important factor in the Oregon attorney general's subsequent decision to pursue the *Smith* litigation to the U.S. Supreme Court. Garrett Epps, Peyote vs. The State: Religious Freedom on Trial 113–117 (2009).

130 *Cf. Rojas v. Fitch*, 127 F.3d 184 (1st Cir. 1997).

131 140 Pa. Commw. 428 (1991).

132 *The Guide to Negotiating Pastor Compensation (2013)*, published by the Ministers Missionaries Benefit Board, provides detailed advice for clerical compensation packages, including insurance, flexible spending accounts, parsonage allowance, and deferred compensation, https://www.mmbb.org/docs/MMBB Compensation Guide.pdf. However, this comprehensive handbook does not mention the church's option to elect unemployment compensation coverage. Similarly, the model employment agreement of the National Association of Congregational Christian Churches mentions such important topics as medical, retirement, and disability employment for the clerical employee. However, this agreement also does not raise the possibility that the employing church will elect unemployment compensation coverage. http://www.naccc.org/uploads/6/0/0/9/6009825/a_suggested_minister-church_agreement-covenant.pdf.

G. ENTANGLEMENT, SUBSIDIZATION, TAX POLICY CRITERIA, AND THE NORMATIVE TAX BASE

In contrast to my analysis which emphasizes that tax exemption can minimize church-state enforcement entanglement, the opponents of sectarian tax exemptions characterize such exemptions as subsidies. From this premise, it is a short step to conclude that religious subsidies in the form of tax exemptions violate the First Amendment. For example, as we shall see in chapter six,[133] the opponents of the income tax exclusion of parsonages and of parsonage allowances attack that exclusion as unconstitutional, both because the exclusion entangles and because it subsidizes. Important judicial statements reinforce the narrative that all tax exemptions are subsidies. These include Justice Douglas's *Walz* dissent ("tax exemption is a subsidy"),[134] Justice Brennan's *Texas Monthly* plurality opinion ("every tax exemption constitutes a subsidy"),[135] Justice Reed's dissent in *Murdock* ("a tax subsidy"),[136] and Justice Roberts' dissent in *Follett* ("Follett will enjoy a subsidy for his religion").[137]

Chief Justice Burger's majority opinion in *Walz* undermines the characterization of all sectarian exemptions as tax subsidies. *Walz* points to a plausible, nonsubsidizing rationale for religious exemptions, namely, a legislative decision to avoid the enforcement-related entanglement which arises when the state taxes religious institutions and actors.

The characterization of any tax provision as a subsidy is only compelling if there is first established a normative baseline of taxation from which that provision is deemed to subsidize. Only when such a baseline is established can the "subsidy" moniker be meaningfully applied to provisions which deviate from that baseline.

Walz indicates that a normative income tax may properly contain religious exemptions to avoid enmeshing church and state in the inherently intrusive enforcement of the tax law. From the baseline of minimizing enforcement-related church-state entanglement, a tax exemption for sectarian institutions and actors is not a subsidy but, rather, is part of a normative tax, reflecting the nonsubsidizing choice to incur the problems of borderline entanglement rather than the costs of enforcement entanglement.

---

[133] *See infra* at 166–167.

[134] *Walz*, 397 U.S. at 704.

[135] *Texas Monthly*, 489 U.S. at 15.

[136] *Murdock*, 319 U.S. at 130.

[137] *Follett*, 321 U.S. at 581.

In a seminal statement of this perspective, Professor Boris Bittker observed over a generation ago:

> The assertion that an exemption is equivalent to a subsidy is untrue, meaningless, or circular, depending on context, unless we can agree on a "correct" or "ideal" or "normal" taxing structure as a benchmark for which to measure departures.[138]

Despite all of the ink which has subsequently been spilled on this topic,[139] no one has ever refuted Professor Bittker's insight that a tax exemption can only be convincingly labeled as a subsidy if there is prior agreement on the contours of a normative tax from which to measure subsidization. Such agreement requires the identification and assessment of the criteria which should guide tax policy.

Consider, for example, the exclusion under the federal income tax of the income from self-performed services.[140] Consider, in particular, the failure of the Internal Revenue Code to tax the income my neighbor generates by growing his own tomatoes in his home garden.

Those tomatoes constitute an "economic benefit"[141] to my neighbor. He could readily realize the cash value of that benefit by selling his tomatoes at the local farmers market. When he instead eats those tomatoes, my neighbor's consumption constitutes income according to the widely accepted Haig-Simons definition of income, a definition conventionally summarized as equating income with the sum of an individual's savings and his consumption.[142]

---

[138] Boris I. Bittker, *Churches, Taxes and the Constitution*, 78 YALE L.J. 1285, 1304 (1969).

[139] Much of the subsequent writing in this area has occurred under the heading of tax expenditure analysis. *See* Edward A. Zelinsky, Winn *and the Inadvisability of Constitutionalizing Tax Expenditure Analysis*, 121 YALE L.J. ONLINE 25 (2011); Edward A. Zelinsky, *James Madison and Public Choice at Gucci Gulch: A Procedural Defense of Tax Expenditures and Tax Institutions*, 102 YALE L.J. 1165, 1168–1171 (1993); Edward D. Kleinbard, *The Congress Within the Congress: How Tax Expenditures Distort Our Budget and Our Political Processes*, 36 OHIO N.U.L. REV. 1, 4 (2010).

[140] *See, e.g.*, MICHAEL A. LIVINGSTON & DAVID S. GAMAGE, TAXATION: LAW, PLANNING AND POLICY 126–127 (2nd ed. 2010) 126–127 ("no one really expects the imputed income from goods or services to be taxed . . .").

[141] *United States v. Drescher*, 179 F.2d 863, 865 (2d Cir. 1950).

[142] The much-celebrated Haig-Simons definition of income includes as one of its components "the market value of rights exercised in consumption." This indicates that my neighbor has income when he eats his home-grown tomatoes. Indeed, the Haig-Simons definition suggests that my neighbor has income as his tomatoes mature and thereby increase "the value of the store of property rights" represented by those tomatoes. HENRY SIMONS, PERSONAL INCOME TAXATION 50 (1938). For discussion of the Haig-Simons definition of income, *see* WILLIAM A. KLEIN, JOSEPH BANKMAN, DANIEL N. SHAVIRO, & KIRK J. STARK, FEDERAL INCOME TAXATION 48–49 (15th ed. 2009).

The Code confirms that "gross income means all income from whatever source derived"[143]—with no exception for homegrown tomatoes. Similarly, the leading judicial definition of income—"accessions to wealth, clearly realized, and over which the taxpayers have complete dominion"[144]—makes no exception for the tomatoes raised by my neighbor.

Concern for economic neutrality reinforces the case for taxing the income my neighbor receives from his homegrown tomatoes. Not taxing homegrown produce favors those who raise their own vegetables over those of us who earn taxable cash wages with which we purchase our vegetables at the supermarket. We end up at the same economic place—having consumed vegetables—but only the wage earner pays income tax.

Nevertheless, few, if any, think that my neighbor should report on his Form 1040 the value of his homegrown tomatoes or that the IRS should collect federal income tax on account of such tomatoes. Such tax policy criteria as valuation, taxpayer liquidity, public acceptability, and administrability[145] counsel that, notwithstanding the strong theoretical argument that homegrown tomatoes generate income, the Code's definition of income should not be pressed that far.

Does it make sense to characterize the failure to tax homegrown tomatoes as a tax subsidy? Professor Bittker's insight indicates "no." Imputed income and income from self-performed services are excluded from the income tax base, not to subsidize but because such exclusion is a proper feature of a baseline tax, considering such tax policy criteria as taxpayer liquidity, valuation, public acceptability, and administrability.

Tax policy invariably involves choices among these often-conflicting criteria, none of which can ever be achieved in toto. Before labeling any particular item as a "subsidy," that item must first be characterized as part of the normative tax base, a base determined by assessing the offsetting goals of tax policy. Only after such an assessment can the exemption of that item convincingly be deemed a "subsidy."

Thus, before Internal Revenue Code Section 107 and its exclusion from gross income of parsonage housing can be labeled as a tax "subsidy," it is necessary to agree that a normative income tax should include the value of in-kind housing and cash housing allowances provided to "minister[s] of the gospel." If Section 107 appropriately manages the enforcement-related entanglement of church and state, then the exclusion from income of clerical housing and parsonage allowances, like the

---

143 I.R.C. § 61(a), 26 U.S.C. § 61(a).

144 *Commissioner v. Glenshaw Glass Co.*, 348 U.S. 426, 431 (1955).

145 Edward A. Zelinsky, *For Realization: Income Taxation, Sectoral Accretionism and the Virtue of Attainable Virtues*, 19 CARDOZO L. REV. 861, 879 (1997).

exclusion of self-performed services, is part of a normative baseline tax rather than a tax subsidy.

The same is true of any exemption, exclusion, or deduction under any tax system. An exemption, exclusion, or deduction can convincingly be labeled a "subsidy" only if, after identifying and assessing the often-conflicting criteria of tax policy, there is agreement on the normative baseline from which such exemption, exclusion, or deduction departs.

In contrast, statements like Justice Brennan's plurality opinion in *Texas Monthly* reflexively declare that "[e]very tax exemption constitutes a subsidy"[146] and that any tax exemption aimed solely at religious entities and actors unconstitutionally subvents religion. From these premises, Section 107 subsidizes religion in violation of the Establishment Clause.

It is undoubtedly true that, confronted with the choice of being taxed or being exempt, exempt is better.[147] However, Professor Bittker's insight is that the economic benefit of tax exemption to the exempted party does not automatically justify the label "subsidy." Exemption is not per se subsidization. In the context of church-state relations, tax exemption can have the secular, rather than the subsidizing, purpose of minimizing church-state enforcement entanglement.

Consider again in this context the dissents in *Murdock* and *Follett*. The implicit premise of the minority's position is that the municipal licensing ordinances challenged in those cases establish normative taxes so that any deviation from the mandate of those ordinances constitutes a subsidy. The dissenters' unstated premise confronts, without answering, the concerns of the Court's majority: If the challenged ordinances unacceptably intrude upon the exercise of First Amendment rights by excessively burdening religious solicitation, those ordinances cannot constitutionally establish a baseline from which deviations can be deemed subsidizing. An unconstitutional tax cannot serve as a normative baseline.

Thus, the *Murdock/Follett* minority reasoned circularly when it characterized the judicially created exemption for religious canvassers as a "subsidy." If one starts with the premise that the challenged municipal ordinances constitute a normative tax standard, it indeed creates a subsidy to exempt from their coverage religious solicitors. However, the premise that the ordinances can constitutionally serve as a normative baseline for taxation assumes away the majority's concern that, as a First Amendment matter, Free Exercise considerations preclude the application of these ordinances and their fees to religious solicitors. If such concerns forbid localities from assessing license fees from sectarian canvassers, tax statutes imposing such fees

[146] *Texas Monthly*, 489 U.S. at 14.

[147] With apologies to Mae West. ("I've been poor and I've been rich. Rich is better.").

violate the First Amendment and, hence, cannot constitutionally serve as a baseline for measuring subsidization.

The opinions of the *Murdock/Follett* minority highlight another reason why the Court's subsequent case law often focuses upon the simultaneous extension *vel non* of tax benefits to secular as well as religious institutions. If exemptions, exclusions, or deductions do constitute subsidies, subsidies restricted to religious entities and activities raise troubling Establishment Clause issues. Some would view a subsidy underwriting only religious activity as the paradigmatic target at which the Establishment Clause is aimed. If, on the other hand, tax provisions characterized as subsidies extend to broad categories of nonprofit institutions, it is arguably not religion as such being subsidized, but eleemosynary activity in general.

Similarly, the implicit premise of Justice Brennan's *Texas Monthly* opinion is that the normative sales tax base is a tax on all sales; hence, to exclude from taxation sales of religious literature is a subsidizing departure from this normative tax base. This, in turn, raises the question whether "all sales" is a constitutionally proper tax base from which to measure subsidizing deviations or whether, as a First Amendment matter, it is normatively proper for Texas to define its sales tax base to accommodate religious activity.

That Texas' sales tax exemption for religious literature constitutes a "subsidy" is a conclusion, not an analysis. That conclusion depends upon whether such an exemption entangles church and state unacceptably, or whether exemption is required or permitted to prevent such entanglement. If exemption is constitutionally mandated or permitted, the exemption is not a "subsidy" but, rather, implements a constitutionally proper tax base.

H. WHY ENTANGLEMENT MATTERS

Existing patterns of church taxation and exemption, while not perfect, are largely sensible. Some taxes, in particular, annual ad valorem property taxation and general income taxation, would generate substantial church-state entanglement if they were enforced against churches and other religious institutions. The broad exemptions typical of these taxes minimize borderline entanglement since some sectarian institutions can qualify for tax exemption as charitable or educational organizations. When this happens, the tax collector and some sectarian entities need not dispute the nature of religion since these religious entities qualify for exemption under either of the secular headings. While many characterize tax exemptions as the subsidization of the eleemosynary sector, these exemptions minimize the church-state enforcement entanglement which would result if religious property and entities were taxed.

Accordingly, such exemptions of religious property and income are properly part of a normative tax system rather than subsidies.

These observations suggest a line of further inquiry: Why does entanglement matter? Why should the minimization of entanglement be a central constitutional value under the First Amendment's religious clauses? The U.S. Supreme Court has, over the years, given two answers to this line of inquiry. In *Lemon*, the Court observed that disputes along sectarian lines can be particularly bitter and, thus, by implication especially unhealthy for the body politic. In Chief Justice Burger's words, the state statutes invalidated in *Lemon* threatened "[p]olitical fragmentation and divisiveness on religious lines."[148]

The Chief Justice's statements continue a long tradition warning of the dangers of sectarian contention. George Washington similarly commented that "[r]eligious controversies are always productive of more acrimony and irreconcilable hatreds than those which spring from any other cause."[149] From this vantage, the state should refrain from imposing upon churches taxes which are more difficult to enforce since such taxes will engender disputes between the polity (in the person of the tax collector) and churches. Conversely, taxes with less potential for church-state entanglement can be more readily imposed since they carry less danger of "divisiveness on religious lines."

The Supreme Court has also framed concern about church-state entanglement as protecting the autonomy of religious institutions. Again, Chief Justice Burger's warnings in *Walz* and *Lemon* are instructive. The New York property tax exemption, he wrote for the Court, preserves "the autonomy and freedom of religious bodies."[150] Conversely, the state aid programs at issue in *Lemon* were invalidated in part because those programs necessitated "comprehensive, discriminating, and continuing state surveillance" of religious schools to ensure that the programs' conditions were being satisfied.[151]

Whatever its value in other settings, the metaphor of separating church and state is not helpful in tax contexts. Taxing churches leads to enforcement entanglement between the tax collector and the churches being taxed. Exempting churches leads to borderline entanglement as the tax collector and sectarian institutions dispute the boundaries of exemption. The call to "separate" church and state cannot avoid this dilemma. In the tax context, there is no disentangling alternative, no way to completely separate church and state.

---

148 *Lemon*, 403 U.S. at 623.

149 Laurence H. Winer & Nina J. Crimm, God, Schools, and Government Funding: First Amendment Conundrums 15 (2015) (quoting George Washington).

150 *Walz*, 397 U.S. at 672.

151 *Lemon*, 403 U.S. at 619.

Nevertheless, the separationist tradition usefully counsels respect for the internal autonomy of religious institutions. If entanglement cannot be eliminated, it can be minimized to avoid impairing the self-governance of churches and other religious bodies. Some taxes, like ad valorem property taxation and general income taxation, would generate much church-state enforcement entanglement if applied to religious institutions. It is thus unsurprising that these taxes, pregnant with possibilities of enforcement-related church-state entanglement, generally do not apply to sectarian entities. In contrast, levies with less potential for such entanglement, such as the FICA payroll and sales taxes, are more commonly imposed on churches and other religious organizations.

Two other reasons counsel concern about tax-related entanglement: institutional competence and administrative discretion. As we have seen,[152] enforcing certain taxes against churches would require the tax collector and the courts to assess religious doctrine. The interpretation of religious doctrine is beyond the institutional competence of secular courts and tax collectors.

Consider again the possible application of the income tax to church activities. This would require the tax collector and ultimately the courts to determine which church outlays are "ordinary and necessary"[153] and thus deductible for purposes of determining the church's taxable income. Such a determination would force the tax collector and the judiciary to assess religious doctrine and practice to gauge whether particular expenses are "ordinary and necessary" to implement such doctrine and practice. This would take both the IRS (and state tax departments) and the judiciary well beyond their respective fields of institutional competence.

Instructive in this context is the role the courts have defined for themselves in church governance disputes. A common fact pattern in these situations is that a group secedes from a congregation and asserts ownership of assets, such as a church building, simultaneously claimed by another congregation or by an ecclesiastical hierarchy. Or churches enter into employment and other commercial contracts and the parties have a contractual dispute.

To avoid unwarranted church-state entanglement in such settings, the courts eschew questions of church doctrine and practice. When religious bodies are embroiled in asset or contract controversies, the courts will "apply neutral principles of secular law to the dispute at hand" but will not decide issues of religious doctrine or practice.[154] As the U.S. Supreme Court said in its seminal decision, *Watson*

---

[152] *See supra* at 134–137.

[153] I.R.C. § 162(a), 26 U.S.C. § 162(a).

[154] *Little v. First Baptist Church*, 475 U.S. 1148, 1149 (1986) (Marshall, J., dissenting from denial of certiorari). *See also Hosanna-Tabor Evangelical Lutheran Church & Sch. v. EEOC*, 132 S. Ct. 694, 704–705 (2012); *Jones*

v. Jones,[155] civil magistrates are "incompetent judges of matters of faith, discipline, and doctrine . . ."

These considerations of institutional competence caution against subjecting churches to those forms of taxation which would require the tax collector and the courts to assess "faith, discipline, and doctrine." Secular courts lack the competence to decide if particular church outlays are "ordinary and necessary" for income tax purposes. Similarly, the courts lack the competence to decide, in the unemployment compensation context, issues of clerical "misconduct" or "good cause" for terminating employees on religious grounds.

A final concern cautioning against church-state tax entanglement is the prospect of administrative discretion being used to hurt or advance religious interests. Different taxes confer different degrees of discretion upon the tax collector. The property taxation of churches would confer considerable leeway upon assessors to value specialized, single-use church structures. Given the inherent uncertainties of such valuation,[156] an assessor could favor a particular denomination by taxing its church building at the lower end of the possible values. Conversely, a property tax assessor could hurt a disfavored sect by assessing its church building at the upper end of the potential values. The collector's discretion to help or hinder particular religious groups is eliminated if the holdings of all such groups are exempt from property taxation.

On the other hand, there are fewer opportunities for the collector to exercise discretion in the context of sales and payroll taxes, taxes typically imposed on easily valued cash transactions. There is accordingly less opportunity for administrative discretion when religious institutions are subjected to taxation on their sales, purchases, and payrolls. Similarly, real estate conveyance taxation, usually triggered by cash sales, imparts less enforcement discretion to the tax collector and thus engenders less danger of the collector favoring or burdening particular congregations or sects.

---

v. Wolf, 443 U.S. 595 (1979). A recent application of this approach is *Congregation Jeshuat Israel v. Congregation Shearith Israel*, 2016 U.S. LEXIS 65518 (D. R.I. 2016). In its *Memorandum, Findings of Fact, Conclusions of Law, and Order*, the U.S. District Court for the District of Rhode Island adjudicated a dispute over real and personal property between two Jewish congregations. The District Court relied on neutral principles of secular law including the law of charitable trusts and the law of bailment. For a scholarly critique of the law in this area, *see* Michael W. McConnell & Luke W. Goodrich, *On Resolving Church Property Disputes*, 58 ARIZ. L. REV. 307 (2016).

[155] 80 U.S. 679, 732, 13 Wall. 679 (1872) (quoting the decision of the Supreme Court of Pennsylvania in *German Reformed Church v. Seibert*).

[156] *See supra* at 128–134.

I. CONCLUSION

Either taxing or exempting churches and other sectarian entities involves entanglement between church and state. In the tax context, there are no disentangling alternatives. Some taxes entail more church-state entanglement than do other taxes. Different tax provisions entail different types of entanglement. Taxation engenders enforcement-related entanglement when the tax collector collects revenue from religious taxpayers, often by intrusive means. Tax exemptions generate borderline entanglement, as churches and other sectarian actors claim exemption from taxation while tax collectors police the boundaries of exemption and sometimes reject those claims. Tax policy invariably involves trade-offs among conflicting goals, such as revenue-generation, administrability, valuation concerns, liquidity considerations, economic neutrality, and public acceptability. None of these criteria can ever be achieved in toto.

When tax laws impact churches and other sectarian entities, the minimization of church-state entanglement should be an important, often controlling, goal. But such entanglement can never be eliminated in its entirety, any more than any other legitimate objective of tax policy can ever be obtained perfectly. Tax exemptions which minimize church-state entanglement should not be reflexively denounced as subsidies since such exemptions can serve a legitimate secular purpose—minimizing church-state enforcement entanglement—and thus can properly be part of normative tax systems.

On balance, our federal system of decentralized lawmaking minimizes tax-related entanglement of church and state reasonably well. The taxes widely levied against sectarian entities—sales, payroll, real estate conveyance taxes—entail less enforcement entanglement while the taxes from which religious institutions are exempted—property, income, unemployment compensation taxes—would entail more church-state entanglement if they were applied against the church.

However, as the following two chapters demonstrate, there is room for improvement in important respects.

6

PARSONAGES, PARSONAGE ALLOWANCES, AND THE RELIGIOUS EXEMPTIONS FROM SOCIAL SECURITY TAXES AND THE HEALTH CARE MANDATE

IN THIS CHAPTER, we revisit the property and income tax status of parsonages and parsonage allowances. The states' property tax treatment of parsonages illustrates many themes of this book: the trade-off between enforcement entanglement and borderline entanglement, the diversity with which the states make this trade-off, and the virtue of our system of decentralized, federalist decision-making, which allows the individual states to make different assessments of the trade-offs inherent in taxing or exempting parsonages. Moreover, the states' property tax treatment of parsonages confirms that tax exemptions should not automatically be labeled as subsidies. The property tax exemption of parsonages serves the nonsubsidizing purpose of minimizing enforcement entanglement between church and state. The offsetting costs of exemption are revenue forgone and borderline entanglement between the tax collector and the church as institutions claim property tax exemption for the housing they provide to their clergy and as the collector and, ultimately, the courts police those claims for exemption.

The income tax treatment of parsonages and parsonage allowances is likely to be controversial in the years ahead. The Internal Revenue Code excludes from clergymen's gross incomes both the in-kind value of parsonages and cash parsonage allowances. Opponents of these exclusions view them as unconstitutional, alleging both that they entangle and that they subsidize. In contrast, I conclude that the Code's income tax exclusions for parsonages and parsonage allowances permissibly implement the nonsubsidizing choice to incur the problems of borderline entanglement rather than confront the difficulties of enforcement entanglement. This is a reasonable choice in a world of imperfect trade-offs between entangling alternatives.

However, as a matter of tax policy, the income tax exclusion of cash parsonage allowances stands on weaker ground than does the exclusion of housing provided to "minister[s] of the gospel" in kind. The church-state enforcement entanglement inherent in taxing the value of church-provided housing is potentially acute given the valuation and liquidity problems of taxing such noncash income. In contrast, the taxation of cash parsonage allowances involves no challenges of valuation or of taxpayer liquidity. Taxing cash parsonage allowances would be less entangling as a constitutional matter and more administrable as a matter of tax policy than would be the taxation of housing provided to clergy in kind.

At the end of this chapter, I observe that the constitutional controversy over Code Section 107 also implicates the sectarian exemptions of the federal FICA and self-employment taxes as well as the religious exemptions of the tax-based federal health care mandate. My analysis of these tax exemptions is the same: They are constitutionally permitted to avoid enforcement entanglement between the IRS and sectarian actors and institutions. The cost of this reduced enforcement entanglement is borderline entanglement at the boundaries of exemption. While these tax exemptions are constitutionally permitted, they are not constitutionally compelled.

A. THE PROPERTY TAX STATUS OF PARSONAGES

As we saw in chapter two, the constitutions of South Carolina,[1] Virginia,[2] Texas,[3] and Wyoming[4] exempt from property taxation parsonages as well as other church

---

[1] S.C. CONST. art. X, § 3(c) ("There shall be exempt from ad valorem taxation: all property of all public libraries, churches, parsonages and burying grounds . . .").

[2] VA. CONST. art. 10, § 6(a)(2) ("[T]he following property . . . shall be exempt from taxation . . . : Real estate and personal property owned and exclusively occupied or used by churches or religious bodies for religious worship or for the residences of their ministers.").

[3] TEX. CONST. art. VIII, § 2(a) ("[T]he legislature may, by general laws, exempt from taxation . . . actual places of religious worship, also any property owned by a church or by a strictly religious society for the exclusive use as a dwelling place for the ministry of such church or religious society . . .").

[4] WYO. CONST. art. 15, § 12 ("The property of the United States, the state, counties, cities, towns, school districts and municipal corporations, when used primarily for a governmental purpose, and public libraries, lots with the buildings thereon used exclusively for religious worship, church parsonages, church schools and public cemeteries, shall be exempt from taxation, and such other property as the legislature may by general law provide.").

property. By statute, Alaska,[5] Arkansas,[6] West Virginia,[7] and Kansas[8] extend their respective constitutional property tax exemptions for religious and church properties to include parsonages. Nebraska's supreme court has exempted parsonages from property taxation through case law interpreting the Cornhusker State's exemption for "religious" properties.[9]

In contrast, the courts of Ohio,[10] Pennsylvania,[11] and Utah[12] have interpreted those states' constitutional property tax exemptions as leaving parsonages taxable.

As we saw in chapter four, the states which lack constitutional provisions exempting religious properties from property taxation also treat parsonages diversely. By statute, Connecticut exempts from property taxation the land and structure of the parsonage of "any religious organization and actually used by its officiating clergymen."[13] Washington State's statute extends churches' property tax exemption to "a parsonage, convent, and buildings and improvements required for the maintenance and safeguarding of such property."[14] The Washington State statute also provides that a tax-exempt "parsonage and convent need not be on land contiguous to the church property."[15]

Addressing one of the key issues in this area of the law—What exactly is a parsonage?—the Washington Supreme Court[16] held that the church-owned home occupied by the "ordained district superintendent" of the Pacific Northwest Annual

---

[5] ALASKA STAT. § 29.45.030(b)(1). *See also Evangelical Covenant Church v. Nome*, 394 P.2d 882, 885–886 (1964) (holding that a church's second home used by an "assistant or lay pastor" qualifies as property tax parsonage).

[6] ARK. CODE ANN. §26-3-303.

[7] W. VA. CODE § 11-3-9(a)(6).

[8] KAN. STAT. ANN. § 79–201, Seventh.

[9] *Nebraska Annual Conference of United Methodist Church v. Scotts Bluff County Board of Equalization*, 243 Neb. 412, 419 (1993).

[10] *Gerke v. Purcell*, 25 Ohio St. 229, 248–249 (1874); *Faith Fellowship Ministries, Inc. v. Limbach*, 32 Ohio St. 3d 432, 435 (1987). Ohio's courts have upheld the property tax exemption of church custodian's apartments as "incidental to the primary use of the building for public worship." *In re Bond Hill-Roselawn Hebrew School*, 151 Ohio St. 70, 75 (1949). *See also St. Paul's Evangelical Lutheran Church v. Board of Tax Appeals*, 114 Ohio App. 330 (1955).

[11] *See, e.g., Connellsville Street Church of Christ v. Fayette County Board of Assessment Appeals*, 838 A. 2d 848 (Pa. Commw. Ct. 2003).

[12] *State Lake County v. Tax Commissioner*, 548 P.2d 630 (1976). Utah subsequently amended its constitution to more broadly require the property tax exemption of "religious" property. UTAH CONST. art. XIII, § 3(1)(f). The Utah courts have not revisited the property tax status of parsonages under this more expansive terminology.

[13] CONN. GEN. STAT. § 12–81(15).

[14] WASH. REV. CODE § 84.36.020.

[15] *Id.* This provision revises an earlier Washington State statute which had been interpreted as requiring a tax-exempt parsonage to be located on the same parcel as the church. *Anna D. Foley v. Oberlin Congregational Church of Steilacoom*, 67 Wash. 280 (1912).

[16] *Pacific Northwest Annual Conference of the United Methodist Church v. Walla Walla County*, 82 Wash. 2d 138 (1973).

Conference of the United Methodist Church[17] was not a tax-exempt parsonage since this superintendent "ministers to the entire district and not directly to any specific congregation."[18] From this vantage, a supervisor is not a pastor.

Iowa's supreme court decided that the Hawkeye State's property tax statute does not exempt from taxation a single-family residence owned by and adjacent to a synagogue since the janitor who lived in this separate structure was "nonecclesiastical personnel."[19] The Iowa court noted that it might have decided differently had the janitor occupied an apartment in the synagogue or had the occupant of the separate residential structure been a member of the clergy.[20]

Hawaii exempted from taxation "[p]roperty used for church purposes, including incidental activities, parsonages and church grounds."[21] Idaho's statutory exemption from property taxation includes "any and all residences used for or in furtherance of [religious, educational, or recreational] purposes."[22] Under Idaho's previous statute,[23] Idaho's supreme court had held taxable the home used by the president of the Idaho Boise Mission of the Latter-Day Saints[24] and the residence occupied jointly by the bishop of the Roman Catholic Diocese of Boise and a priest/administrator of that diocese.[25] Like Washington's supreme court,[26] Idaho's supreme court reasoned that these individuals' respective homes were not tax-exempt parsonages since these individuals served in supervisory, rather than pastoral, capacities, exercising overall administrative responsibility for a large geographical jurisdiction rather than "minister[ing] to a specific localized congregation."[27] The new Idaho statute overturns these decisions by extending property tax exemption to "any and all residences used for or in furtherance of" religious purposes.[28]

Maine exempts from property taxation "[h]ouses of religious worship, including vestries, and the pews and furniture within them" as well as "property owned and

---

[17] *Id.* at 139.

[18] *Id.* at 142.

[19] *Congregation B'Nai Jeshurun v. Board of Review of the City of Des Moines, Iowa*, 301 N.W. 2d 755, 759 (Iowa 1981).

[20] *Id.*

[21] HRS § 246-32(b)(3) (repealed). Similar exemptions are today established in the county codes of the Aloha State. *See, e.g.*, Hawai'i County Code 1983 (2016 Edition, as amended) § 19-77(b)(3) (exempting from taxation "[p]roperty used for church purposes including incidental activities, parsonages, and church grounds . . .").

[22] Idaho Code § 63-602B(1).

[23] *Id.* § 63-602B(1) prior to amendment by Act of March 2, 2007, ch. 83, § 1, p.95.

[24] *The Corporation of the Presiding Bishop of the Church of Jesus Christ of Latter-Day Saints v. Ada County*, 123 Idaho 410 (1993).

[25] *Ada County Assessor v. Roman Catholic Diocese of Boise*, 123 Idaho 425 (1993).

[26] *Pacific Northwest Annual Conference of the United Methodist Church v. Walla Walla County*, 82 Wash. 2d 138 (1973).

[27] 123 Idaho at 430.

[28] Idaho Code § 63-602B(1).

used by a religious society as a parsonage up to the value of $20,000, and personal property not exceeding $6,000 in value . . ."[29]

Maryland's statute[30] extends property tax exemption to "a parsonage or convent." Maryland's Court of Special Appeals held[31] that a church-owned home did not qualify for tax exemption as a parsonage because the main function of the minister living in the house was to organize new congregations, rather than to serve an existing "identifiable parish."[32] A Maryland apartment complex housing volunteers who work in the Washington, D.C., temple of the Latter-Day Saints was held[33] to be a tax-exempt convent.

Massachusetts extends property tax exemption to "houses of religious worship" including their "pews," "furniture," and "parsonage[s]."[34] Massachusetts also grants tax exempt status to "the official residences" of the "district superintendents" and the "district executives" of several specific churches, including the United Methodist Church and the Baptist General Conference of New England.[35] These residences of supervising clergy, not recognized as parsonages in other states, are tax exempt in the Bay State. Moreover, the Massachusetts statute explicitly confers property tax exemption upon "the official residence occupied by a person who has been designated by the congregation of a Hebrew Synagogue or Temple as the rabbi thereof."[36]

Nevada exempts from property taxes parsonages "owned by some recognized religious society or corporation."[37] New Hampshire exempts from property taxation "parish houses, church parsonages occupied by their pastors, convents [and] monasteries."[38]

The Oregon courts' decisions about the property tax status of parsonages have been particularly fact-specific. Most of a residence owned by a Jehovah's Witnesses congregation[39] was held taxable because "neither church doctrine nor practical necessity require[d the church leader] to live in the residence."[40] In contrast, a parish

---

29 36 MAINE REV. STAT. § 652G.

30 MD. TAX-PROPERTY CODE ANN. § 7-204.

31 *East Coast Conference of the Evangelical Covenant Church of America, Inc. v. Supervisor of Assessments of Prince George's County*, 40 Md. App. 213 (1978).

32 *Id.* at 218.

33 *B. Marie Green, Supervisor of Assessments of Montgomery County v. Church of Jesus Christ of Latter-Day Saints*, 430 Md. 119 (2013). *See also Supervisor of Assessments of Baltimore County v. Trustees of Bosley Methodist Church Graveyard*, 293 Md. 208, 218–219 (1982) (caretakers' homes were not tax exempt since they were not used for actual religious worship).

34 MASS. GEN. LAWS ANN. ch. 59, § 5, cl. 11.

35 *Id.*

36 *Id.*

37 NEV. REV. STAT. ANN. § 361.125(1)(a).

38 N.H. REV. STAT. ANN. 72:23III.

39 *Washington County Assessor v. West Beaverton Congregation of Jehovah's Witnesses, Inc.*, 18 Or. Tax 409 (2006).

40 *Id.* at 421.

rectory[41] in Oregon was fully tax exempt because, as a matter of Roman Catholic doctrine and actual practice, the rectory was "reasonably necessary" to accomplish the church's religious purposes.[42] Distinguishing this case, another Catholic rectory in Oregon was held taxable because there was insufficient use of the rectory for religious as opposed to residential purposes and because the rectory was also too far from the church to be tax exempt.[43]

Vermont extends property tax exemption to "parsonages."[44] Subject to a 10-acre limitation, Wisconsin grants tax exemption to "property owned and used for housing for pastors and their ordained assistants, members of religious orders and communities, and ordained teachers, whether or not contiguous to and part of other property owned and used by such associations or churches . . . while such property is not used for profit."[45]

This diverse pattern of often granular decision-making illuminates several of the themes of this book: There is no perfect approach to the taxation or exemption of parsonages, just imperfect trade-offs which reasonable lawmakers and judges can assess differently. Exempting parsonages, like other similar sectarian exemptions, entails borderline entanglement as tax assessors and, ultimately, courts must determine, at the boundaries of exemption, whether or not particular residences qualify as "parsonages" eligible for property tax exemption. Taxing parsonages involves enforcement entanglement as parsonages (like other real estate) must be valued and as churches must raise the cash to pay the resulting property tax. It is unpersuasive to reflexively denounce the tax exemption of parsonages as subsidization because such exemption serves the nonsubsidizing purpose of minimizing the church-state enforcement entanglement inherent in property taxation.

The strongest case for taxing a parsonage arises when the residence in question is a fungible home which just happens to house clergy. A typical suburban house owned by a church for its minister poses no more valuation difficulties than does any other suburban house which it resembles. For these fungible properties, there will typically be comparable sales of similar properties to guide the valuation process. On the other hand, a parsonage can be a unique, difficult-to-value structure. Think, for example, of the archbishop's home at St. Patrick's Cathedral. There is no obviously workable line to distinguish between easily valued parsonages and hard-to-value parsonages. Even when parsonages are easily valued, fungible homes, liquidity

[41] *Roman Catholic Archdiocese of the Archbishop of Portland in Oregon v. Department of Revenue*, 13 Or. Tax 211 (1995).

[42] *Id.* at 213.

[43] *St. Mary Star of the Sea Catholic Church, Astoria v. Clatsop County Assessor*, 2015 Ore. Tax LEXIS 49 at *23.

[44] 32 Vt. Stat. Ann. §§ 3802(4) and 3832(2).

[45] Wis. Stat. Ann. § 70.11(4)

challenges remain if a church lacks cash to pay property tax—just as any other cash-strapped property owner has trouble paying his tax.

On the other side of the ledger, the property tax can be characterized as a payment for local government services. A church-owned house receives the same public services—police, fire, sanitation, other public works—as any other house. These municipally furnished benefits suggest that the same property taxes should attach to a church-owned residence as are paid by its neighbors which receive the same public services. Taxation is ultimately about revenue.

It is not surprising that different states have resolved these trade-offs differently. A virtue of our system of decentralized, federalist decision-making is that the states can experiment with various formulas and can assess differently the choices inherent in taxing or exempting properties such as parsonages.

B. THE INCOME TAX TREATMENT OF PARSONAGES AND PARSONAGE ALLOWANCES: CODE SECTIONS 107 AND 119

As we saw in chapter three, Section 107[46] of the Internal Revenue Code excludes from the gross income of a "minister of the gospel"

(1) the rental value of a home furnished to him as part of his compensation; or
(2) the rental allowance paid to him as part of his compensation, to the extent used by him to rent or provide a home and to the extent such allowance does not exceed the fair rental value of the home, including furnishings and appurtenances such as a garage, plus the cost of utilities.

Cash payments excluded from a clergyman's gross income pursuant to Section 107(2) have come to be denoted as "parsonage allowance."[47]

To qualify for the Section 107 exclusion, a recipient of in-kind housing or of a cash parsonage allowance must be a "minister of the gospel." In addition, the regulations construing Section 107 specify that the clerical recipient must receive his housing or cash allowance as compensation for performing services "ordinarily" associated with a religious ministry. In particular, the Treasury regulations restrict the Section 107 exclusion to the value of a home or of a parsonage allowance which constitutes "remuneration for services which are ordinarily the duties of a minister of the

[46] 26 U.S.C. § 107.
[47] *See, e.g., Warren*, 114 T.C. at 343, 346.

gospel."[48] Such duties "include performance of sacerdotal functions, the conduct of religious worship, the administration and maintenance of religious organizations and their integral agencies, and the performance of teaching and administrative duties at theological seminaries."[49]

Under this entangling standard, an ordained rabbi was denied the parsonage allowance exclusion because his service as "the national director of Interreligious Affairs for the American Jewish Committee" "was not a ministerial function" for purposes of Section 107.[50] Likewise, a Baptist minister employed by the Christian Anti-Communism Crusade was denied the Code's housing-related exclusion because "the preaching of anticommunism [is not] the conduct of religious worship."[51] The Treasury regulations similarly conclude that a clergyman is not performing services in the exercise of his ministry when he teaches "history and mathematics" at a secular university.[52]

In contrast, the regulations indicate that duties as a university chaplain "which include the conduct of religious worship, offering spiritual counsel to the university students, and teaching a class in religion" constitute services in the exercise of a ministry.[53] Also according to the Treasury regulations, a minister performs services in the exercise of his ministry when he works full-time for "the N Religious Board to serve as director of one of its departments . . . The N Religious Board is an integral agency of O, a religious organization operating under the authority of a religious body constituting a church denomination."[54] Moreover, a minister undertakes services in the exercise of his ministry when he is assigned full-time by his church "to perform advisory service to Y Company in connection with the publication of a book dealing with the history of M's church denomination."[55] Much of this regulatory framework implements Code Section 1402(c)(5)'s limited ministerial exemption from the federal self-employment tax[56] and is incorporated by reference[57] for purposes of Code Section 107.

To be excludable from gross income under Section 107(2), a cash parsonage allowance must be designated as such "in an employment contract, in minutes of or in a

[48] Treas. Reg. § 1.107-1(a), 26 C.F.R. § 1.107-1(a).

[49] *Id.*

[50] *Tanenbaum v. Commissioner*, 58 T.C. 1 (1972).

[51] *Colbert v. Commissioner*, 61 T.C. 449, 456 (1974).

[52] Treas. Reg. § 1.1402(c)-5(c)(2), 26 C.F.R. § 1.1402(c)-5(c)(2).

[53] Treas. Reg. § 1.1402(c)-5(b)(2)(iii), 26 C.F.R. § 1.1402(c)-5(b)(2)(iii).

[54] Treas. Reg. § 1.1402(c)-5(b)(2)(iv), 26 C.F.R. § 1.1402(c)-5(b)(2)(iv).

[55] Treas. Reg. § 1.1402(c)-5(b)(2)(v), 26 C.F.R. §1.1402(c)-5(b)(2)(v).

[56] I.R,C. § 1402(c)(5), 26 U.S.C. §1402(c)(5).

[57] Treas. Reg. § 1.107-1(a), 26 C.F.R. § 1.107-1(a) ("In general, the rules provided in § 1.1402(c)-5 will be applicable to such determination.").

resolution by a church or other qualified organization or in its budget, or in any other appropriate instrument evidencing such official action."[58] In addition, the allowance must be used "(1) for rent of a home, (2) for purchase of a home, and (3) for expenses directly related to providing a home."[59] Outlays for "food and servants" do not qualify for exclusion.[60] The parsonage allowance cannot "exceed the fair rental value of the home, including furnishings and appurtenances such as a garage, plus the cost of utilities."[61]

Although in-kind housing and cash parsonage allowances provided to ministers are excludable from such ministers' gross incomes for income tax purposes, such housing and allowances are subject to the self-employment tax.[62]

In contrast to Section 107 and its exclusion for in-kind housing and cash parsonage allowances limited to "minister[s] of the gospel," Code Section 119[63] provides a general income tax exclusion for housing furnished in kind by all employers to their respective employees. To qualify for this broader exclusion from gross income, "lodging" must be "furnished" to "an employee . . . by or on behalf of his employer for the convenience of the employer."[64] In addition, to qualify for the Section 119 exclusion, "the employee [must be] required to accept such lodging on the business premises of his employer as a condition of his employment."[65]

Unlike Section 107, which excludes from gross income both in-kind housing and cash parsonage allowances furnished to "minister[s] of the gospel," "Section 119 applies only to []lodging furnished in kind."[66]

The opponents of Section 107 have attacked Section 107 as unconstitutional, asserting that Section 107 both entangles and subsidizes.[67] It is more compelling to

---

58 Treas. Reg. §1.107-1(b), 26 C.F.R. § 1.107-1(b).

59 Treas. Reg. § 1.107-1(c), 26 C.F.R. § 1.107-1(c).

60 *Id.*

61 I.R.C. § 107(a)(2), 26 U.S.C. § 107(a)(2) as amended by the Clergy Housing Allowance Clarification Act of 2002, P.L. 107–181, 116 Stat. 583 generally effective for years starting on or after January 1, 2002.

62 I.R.C. §1402(a)(8), 26 U.S.C. § 1402(a)(8). *Cf.* the limited ministerial exemption of I.R.C. § 1402(c)(5), 26 U.S.C. §1402(c)(5).

63 I.R.C. Section 119(a), 26 U.S.C. § 119(a).

64 *Id.*

65 I.R.C. Section 119(a)(2), 26 U.S.C. § 119(a)(2).

66 *Commissioner v. Kowalski*, 434 U.S. 77, 84 (1977) (quoting S. Rep. No. 1622, 83d Cong., 2d Sess., 190 (1954) as reprinted in 1954 U.S.C.C.A.N. 4621, 4826).

67 Meridith Satz, *Re-interpreting the Parsonage Exclusion: Constitutional Challenges and the Agency Response in the Wake of* Freedom From Religion Foundation, Inc. v. Lew, 67 ADMIN. L. REV. 751 (2015); Edward A. Zelinsky, *Do Religious Tax Exemptions Entangle in Violation of the Establishment Clause? The Constitutionality of the Parsonage Allowance Exclusion and the Religious Exemptions of the Individual Health Care Mandate and the FICA and Self-Employment Taxes*, 33 CARDOZO L. REV. 1633, 1652 (2012); *Warren v. Commissioner*, 282 F.3d 1119 (9th Cir. 2002); *American Atheists, Inc. v. Shulman*, 21 F. Supp. 3d 856 (E.D. Ky., N. Div. 2014); *Freedom From Religion Foundation, Inc. v. Geithner*, (E.D. Calif., Sacramento Div.), Tax Analysts Doc.

understand Section 107 as a congressional choice to accept the problems of borderline entanglement rather than embrace enforcement-related entanglement in the income tax treatment of clerical housing.

C. REPEALING SECTION 107: SWAPPING BORDERLINE ENTANGLEMENT FOR ENFORCEMENT ENTANGLEMENT

The opponents of Internal Revenue Code Section 107 argue that Section 107, rather than minimizing entanglement, itself enmeshes the federal tax collector and religious institutions. These opponents marshal credible support for their concerns since policing the borders of Section 107's income tax exclusion involves entangling concerns about eligibility for that exclusion. In a complaint challenging the constitutionality of Section 107, the Freedom From Religion Foundation (FFRF) succinctly observed that, "to administer and apply" Code Section 107,

> the IRS and the Treasury must make sensitive, fact-intensive, intrusive, and subjective determinations dependent on religious criteria and inquiries, such as whether certain activities constitute "religious worship" or "sacerdotal functions;" whether a member of the clergy is "duly ordained, commissioned, or licensed;" or whether a Christian college or other organization is "under the authority of" a church or denomination . . . These and other determinations result in "excessive entanglement" between church and state contrary to the Establishment Clause.[68]

This passage actually challenges not Section 107 itself but the Treasury Regulations which implement it. The regulations are the source of such concepts as "religious worship,"[69] "sacerdotal functions,"[70] and "duly ordained, commissioned, or licensed."[71] However, even if there were no regulations, defining "minister of the gospel" would, as a statutory matter, entail the kind of borderline entanglement which troubled Justice Harlan in *Walz* and which proved controlling for the *Texas Monthly*

2009-23144, complaint at para. 35; *Gaylor v. Lew*, Case No. 16-CV-215-bbc (W.D. Wisc.) Tax Analysts Doc. 2017-994 (opinion and order).

[68] *Freedom From Religion Foundation, Inc. v. Geithner*, (E.D. Calif., Sacramento Div.), Tax Analysts Doc. 2009-23144, complaint at para. 35.

[69] Treas. Reg. § 1.107-1(a), 26 C.F.R. § 1.107-1(a).

[70] *Id.*

[71] Treas. Reg. § 1.1402(c)-5(a)(2), 26 C.F.R. § 1.1402(c)-5(a)(2). *See also* Treas. Reg. § 1.107-1(a), 26 C.F.R. § 1.107-1(a) ("In general, the rules provided in § 1.1402(c)-5 will be applicable to such determination.").

plurality, namely, the need to define who is and who is not a minister, eligible for exemption.

Viewed in isolation, those who attack Section 107 on entanglement grounds mount a powerful case. Difficult issues arise when policing the boundaries of that provision to determine who is eligible for Section 107's income tax exclusion of in-kind housing and cash parsonage allowances. However, for two reasons, Section 107 and its borderline enforcement quandaries cannot be viewed in isolation. First, if Section 107 is overturned by the courts (or repealed by Congress), much housing provided to clergy will generate taxable income to them. This will create enforcement entanglement as the IRS collects housing-related taxes from these clergypersons. Second, if Section 107 is stricken as unconstitutional, many religious institutions and the clergy receiving employer-provided housing will default to the general provisions of Code Section 119.[72] The upshot will be other borderline entanglement problems determining whether clerical employees are eligible for Section 119's income tax exclusion for employer-furnished lodging.

Invalidating Section 107 would cause the federal income taxation of many clergymen who receive currently nontaxable housing from their churches. Taxation is inherently intrusive. It inflicts compliance costs upon taxpayers and engenders conflict between taxpayers and the tax collector. If, for example, the rental value of church-provided housing must be included in a clergywoman's income, that value must be calculated so that the clergywoman can report it on her Form 1040. Such rental values may not be easily determined, particularly if the parsonage is a unique structure.

This would cause enforcement-related conflict among the IRS, the religious institutions furnishing housing to their clerical employees, and the ministers receiving employer-provided housing. In such a context, the relationship between the tax collector and the taxpayer would, per Chief Justice Burger's formulation from *Lemon*, constitute "comprehensive, discriminating, and continuing state surveillance"[73] as ministers are taxed on the housing provided to them.

The enforcement entanglement arising from the income taxation of the value of church-provided housing would be acute. There would be valuation disputes among the IRS, religious employers, and clerical employees as to the fair rental value of church-owned housing. The clergy receiving such noncash housing-based compensation might be illiquid and thus lack the funds to pay tax on this noncash compensation. In Section 107, Congress has plausibly decided that these

[72] Indeed, Section 119 today governs the income tax status of housing provided by religious employers to those employees who do not qualify as "minister[s] of the gospel" for purposes of Section 107.

[73] *Lemon*, 403 U.S. at 619.

enforcement-related valuation and liquidity problems, while acceptable for purposes of the self-employment tax,[74] should be avoided in the context of the income tax.

In short, abolishing Section 107 would not eliminate church-state entanglement. By making church-provided housing taxable, the invalidation of Section 107 would replace the borderline entanglement of that provision (determining who is eligible for the exclusion) with enforcement entanglement (making sure the correct income tax is paid on clerical housing). It was plausible for Congress in Section 107 to choose the quandaries of borderline entanglement over the prospect of enmeshing the IRS, religious institutions, and clergy in the enforcement of the income taxation of such housing. In this setting as in other questions of taxing or exempting the church, there is no disentangling alternative.

D. SWAPPING ONE BORDERLINE ENTANGLEMENT FOR ANOTHER: SECTION 107 VS. SECTION 119

If the courts were to invalidate Code Section 107 on First Amendment grounds or if Congress were to repeal Section 107, some (perhaps much) housing provided to clergy would then be subject to Code Section 119 and its general income tax exclusion for employer-provided housing furnished in kind. Section 119 entangles church and state at the borderlines of exemption, as does Section 107. In particular, Section 119 and its general lodging exclusion require four entangling inquiries to assess at the boundaries of Section 119 whether that provision applies.

First, who is an "employee"? Section 119 only excludes employer-provided housing if the recipient of such housing is an "employee." As Professor Dyer has pointed out, some clergy are employees of their congregations, others are clearly not, and yet others "fall anywhere within that broad range."[75] Determining whether any particular clergyman is an "employee" for purposes of Section 119 necessitates an entangling assessment of the practices of the clergyman's particular church.

Second, is housing provided "for the convenience of the [religious] employer"? Assessing this criterion of Section 119 requires examination of the policies of the religious institution furnishing housing to ascertain whether the institution provides housing to its clerical employee "to enable him properly to perform the duties of his employment"[76] or, rather, to compensate such employee. This, in turn, compels

[74] I.R.C. § 1402(a)(8), 26 U.S.C. § 1402(a)(8).

[75] Boyd Kimball Dyer, *Redefining "Minister of the Gospel" to Limit Establishment Clause Issues*, 95 Tax Notes 1809, 1811 (2002).

[76] Treas. Reg. § 1.119-1(b), 26 C.F.R. § 1.119-1(b).

an intrusive inquiry into the purposes of those who govern the religious employer, including possible inquisition into their internal deliberations.

Third, what is the particular church's "business"? Section 119 only excludes the value of lodging employers provide on their respective "business premises." This element of the statute necessitates a determination of the employing church's "business," which, in turn, requires the IRS to assess the church's policies and practices. Consider, for example, the members of a religious order who live at a homeless shelter they operate for their order. Is maintaining this shelter the order's "business" for purposes of Section 119?

Fourth, what are the church's "premises"? Consider a rabbi expected to entertain his congregants on a regular basis at the home provided to him by the congregation and to hold study groups there. Is this home the "premises" of the congregation for purposes of Section 119?

Thus, striking Code Section 107 under the First Amendment's Establishment Clause or repealing Section 107 legislatively would not end the entangling borderline inquiries the IRS (or state tax collectors)[77] must make of churches which provide housing to their ministers. Rather, striking Section 107 would shift the focus from the entangling borderline questions posed by Section 107 (Is a clergyman a "minister of the gospel"?) to the similarly entangling borderline inquiries posed by Section 119 (Is a clergyman an employee? Is housing provided for his religious employer's convenience? Is this housing part of the church's "business premises"?).

Congress could plausibly have chosen as less intrusive and more easily administered the borderline entanglement posed by Section 107 rather than the borderline entanglement posed by Section 119. Consequently, Section 107 and its income tax exclusion of church-provided housing can be understood as part of a normative income tax rather than be dismissed as subsidization of the church.

Michael L. Gompertz disagrees. Calling on the courts to strike Section 107 as unconstitutional, Mr. Gompertz argues that "there is usually no business need for the minister to live on church property,"[78] that "the requirements of section 119 would almost never be met" by clergymen,[79] and that "it would not be difficult for the IRS to determine whether section 119 is applicable to a clergyman."[80]

---

77 Many state income tax laws incorporate Internal Revenue Code Section 107 or a version of it. *See, e.g.*, CAL. REV. & TAX. CODE § 17131.6 (incorporating a modified version of I.R.C. § 107 into California's income tax statute).

78 Michael L. Gompertz, *Lawsuit Challenges Income Tax Preferences for Clergy*, 128 TAX NOTES 81, 2010 TNT 130-3 (July 8, 2010) at § B(3).

79 *Id.*

80 *Id.*

In making these assessments, Mr. Gompertz *sub silentio* engages in the kind of entangling inquiries he criticizes in the context of Section 107. To determine that "there is usually no business need for the minister to live on church property," Mr. Gompertz must define the business of the church, must determine the needs of that business, and must decide the contours of the church's property. These inquiries under Section 119 enmesh the church and the tax collector as much as (perhaps more than) the determination whether a clergyman is a "minister of the gospel" for purposes of Section 107.

Confronted with these choices, Congress plausibly selected Code Section 107 to manage the entanglement between church and state in the context of housing provided to clergymen. That choice is not inevitable nor does it eliminate entanglement between the IRS and religious institutions. Section 107 eliminates church-state enforcement entanglement for income tax purposes by excluding church-provided housing from clergymen's incomes. The trade-off is borderline entanglement, as the IRS and sectarian actors joust over the boundaries of Section 107's exclusion from clerical gross incomes.

However, striking Section 107 would not eliminate entanglement between church and state either. Rather, invalidating Section 107 would, in some cases, replace entanglement at the borders of Section 107 with enforcement-related entanglement of church and state as the IRS would collect the income taxes attributable to church-provided housing. In other instances, repealing Section 107 would shift the enmeshing inquiries about eligibility for exemption from the entangling inquiries posed at the boundaries of Section 107 to the similarly entangling questions at the borders of Section 119.

E. A BROADER POSSIBILITY: NEITHER SECTION 107 NOR SECTION 119 APPLIES TO RELIGIOUS EMPLOYERS

Consider another possibility, namely, that the Establishment Clause of the U.S. Constitution forbids both Section 107 and the application of Section 119 to churches and their personnel. At first blush, this expansive construction of the First Amendment eliminates both the entangling inquiries necessary to patrol the borders of Section 107 and the entangling inquiries needed to police eligibility for Section 119. Under this alternative, neither provision of the Internal Revenue Code would apply to religious employers or their personnel.

For three reasons, this approach is ultimately unsatisfactory. First, troubling Free Exercise[81] concerns arise if Section 119 is construed as available to all employers

[81] "Congress shall make no law . . . prohibiting the free exercise thereof . . ." U.S. Constitution, Amendment I.

except religious institutions. "[T]he protections of the Free Exercise Clause pertain if the law at issue discriminates against some or all religious beliefs or regulates or prohibits conduct because it is undertaken for religious reasons."[82] Such discrimination against religious belief and conduct would occur in violation of the First Amendment's Free Exercise Clause if Section 119 is interpreted as benefiting all employers except sectarian entities.

Second, if, in a world without Code Section 107, the courts also declare that Code Section 119 cannot apply to religious institutions and their employees or if Congress legislates to that effect, it would then be necessary to determine which institutions and employees fall within this Section 119 ban by virtue of their sectarian nature and which do not. Again, entangling borderline inquires would arise if the IRS were required to determine which employers are religious (and thus outside the purview of Section 119) and which are secular (and thus covered by that provision). The prospect of eliminating church-state entanglement again proves illusory.

Third, if neither Section 107 nor Section 119 precludes the income taxation of the value of housing provided to clergy, then the IRS, to enforce that taxation, must intrude into internal church autonomy to ensure that ministers include in their gross incomes the value of the housing provided to them. The upshot would be the enforcement entanglement against which Chief Justice Burger cautioned in *Walz* and *Lemon*, that is, continuing government intervention into internal church operations. As I have been emphasizing, taxation—particularly the taxation of hard-to-value, illiquid income provided in kind—is inherently intrusive.

At the end of the day, the search for disentangling tax alternatives is unavailing, both in the context of the general relationship between the modern state's tax system and contemporary religious entities and, more specifically, in the context of the tax treatment of church-provided housing for their clergy. When taxes and churches collide, there are no disentangling alternatives, only imperfect trade-offs between different forms of entanglement. If the current regulations under Section 107 were jettisoned, it would still be necessary to decide at the borders of Section 107 who is a "minister of the gospel" for purposes of that provision and who is not. If Section 107 itself were stricken as violating the First Amendment's Establishment Clause, similar borderline issues would arise to determine if Section 119 applies to church-provided housing.

Were the housing provided by churches to their ministers to be income taxed, the resulting enforcement of the Code against churches and their employees would produce the entanglement inherent in the relationship between the tax collector and taxpayers. The IRS's enforcement activity would impair the autonomy of

---

82 *Church of Lukumi Babalu Aye v. City of Hialeah*, 508 U.S. 520, 532 (1993).

religious entities by intruding the IRS into such entities' internal operations. If neither Section 119 nor Section 107 excluded from clerical incomes the rental value of employer-provided housing, there would be both enforcement entanglement (as the IRS taxes housing provided in kind to clergy) and borderline entanglement (to determine which employers are secular and therefore remain covered by Section 119 and its income tax exclusion).

The two factors cited by Chief Justice Burger in *Lemon* reinforce the conclusion that Section 107 is a plausible pick from among the imperfect choices available. First, like the property tax exemption upheld in *Walz*, Section 107's exclusion for in-kind housing and cash parsonage allowances is long-established. Congress added what is now Section 107(1) to the Internal Revenue Code in 1921.[83] Section 107(2) was enacted in 1954.[84] While there is no precise yardstick to determine when laws are old enough to merit *Lemon*'s history-based presumption of constitutionality, Section 107 is not a recent addition to the federal tax statute.

Moreover, unlike the Rhode Island and Pennsylvania laws which required annual appropriations from those states' respective legislatures, Section 107 is a classic tax provision, embedded into a permanent tax Code.[85] There is accordingly less formal[86] opportunity for religiously divisive legislative battles over Section 107 than there is with a prototypical spending program, dependent on annual appropriations.

Reinforcing these *Lemon* factors is the reality that taxing noncash income (like church-supplied housing) is particularly intrusive. The IRS and taxpayers often dispute the value of such in-kind income. The taxpayers receiving noncash income must find cash from other sources to discharge their tax liabilities.

In short, Section 107 is a constitutionally permitted means of managing the entanglement problems inherent in the income tax treatment of the housing churches provide to "minister[s] of the gospel." In the modern tax setting, there is no way to disentangle megachurches from megagovernments. Section 107 is a plausible, though not an obligatory, choice from among the imperfect alternatives available. In a world of trade-offs, Section 107 embodies the constitutionally permissible

---

83 § 213(b)(11) of the Revenue Act of 1921, 67th Congress, 1st Session, 42 Stat. 227, 238.

84 House Ways and Means Committee Report, No. 83-1337, 83rd Cong., 2nd Session, 1954 U.S.C.C.A.N. 4017, 4040.

85 Edward A. Zelinsky, *Are Tax "Benefits" Constitutionally Equivalent to Direct Expenditures?*, 112 Harv. L. Rev. 379, 400–403 (1998).

86 In practice legislatures tend to make budgeting changes at the margins, using the prior year's spending as an accepted baseline. The classic statement of budgetary incrementalism is Aaron Wildavsky, The Politics of the Budgetary Process 13 (1964) ("Budgeting is incremental. The largest determining factor of the size and content of this year's budget is last year's budget. Most of the budget is a product of previous decisions.") (italics omitted). For Professor Wildavsky's later comments on budgetary incrementalism, *see* Aaron Wildavsky, The New Politics of the Budgetary Process 405 (1988).

acceptance of the need to police the borderlines of a tax exemption rather than embrace the enforcement entanglement inherent in taxing the housing churches furnish to their ministers.

To the contrary is Justice Brennan's plurality opinion in *Texas Monthly*. For Justice Brennan (and others), any tax exemption restricted to religious institutions or actors is a subsidy which contravenes the Establishment Clause. From this vantage, Section 107 is an unconstitutional subvention targeted exclusively at religion.

A key problem with the *Texas Monthly* plurality opinion is its contention that, by eliminating the Texas sales tax exemption for religious publications, the Court abolished entanglement between church and state. Not so. *Texas Monthly* merely shifted church-state entanglement from the eligibility determinations at the borders of the sales tax exemption to enforcement entanglement as the state collected tax from religious publications. In the context of the sales taxation at issue in *Texas Monthly*, the enforcement entanglement is relatively manageable since cash sales are self-valuing and generate cash to pay the tax.

But the challenges of taxing in-kind income (like employer-provided housing) are more difficult because of valuation and liquidity predicaments. Thus, in the final analysis, Internal Revenue Code Section 107 is saved from First Amendment challenge by *Walz* and *Walz*'s approval of religious tax exemptions as permitted means of minimizing enforcement entanglement between church and state. Section 107 is a plausible choice for income tax purposes given that no disentangling alternative exists.

F. SECTION 107(2) AS A MATTER OF TAX POLICY

That Section 107 is constitutionally permitted does not mean that Section 107 is compelling as a matter of policy. In terms of tax policy, there is no persuasive case for Section 107(2) and its exclusion of cash parsonage allowances. In First Amendment terms, taxing cash income is less entangling than is taxing equivalent in-kind compensation. When taxing cash, there are no valuation issues and the taxpayer has the liquidity to pay the tax.

The normative[87] arguments for excluding in-kind fringe benefits from employees' gross incomes depend upon such tax policy criteria as valuation, liquidity, administrability, and public acceptability. In light of valuation and liquidity concerns, it

[87] For more on the distinction between normative income tax provisions, designed to implement the proper tax base, and subsidizing provisions, intended to encourage particular activities, *see supra* at 148–152.

is difficult for the IRS (or a state tax collector) to enforce the income taxation of in-kind benefits.

In addition, the taxation of noncash income is poorly understood by taxpayers and often resented by them. The public acceptability of any particular tax provision is an important consideration in a democracy whose tax system requires taxpayers to self-report their respective incomes. From a First Amendment perspective, taxing cash compensation (like a cash parsonage allowance) enmeshes the taxpayer and the tax collector less than does the taxation of otherwise equivalent in-kind income.

These considerations underpin the tax policy argument for excluding from employees' gross incomes the value of employer-provided housing furnished in kind. However, these considerations do not justify Section 107(2) and its exclusion from gross income of cash parsonage allowances. Such allowances raise neither valuation nor liquidity issues since the ministers receiving housing allowances are paid in cash and can defray their tax liabilities from such cash. The IRS can more easily enforce the taxation of cash income than of in-kind income. Taxing parsonage allowances would not offend the popular intuition equating income with cash since such allowances take the form of cash.

The historic justification for Section 107(2) was to establish tax parity between ministers receiving tax-free housing in kind and ministers receiving cash parsonage allowances.[88] Since the former pay no income tax on the lodging provided to them in kind, Congress decided in 1954 that the latter should not report as gross income the housing provided to them in the form of cash allowances.

However, the Code does not create equivalent tax parity between an employee who is provided tax-free housing by his employer under Section 119 and an otherwise similar employee who is paid cash compensation and must purchase his own residential accommodations with after-tax dollars. There is no compelling argument for establishing tax parity among those ministers who receive in-kind housing and those who receive cash housing allowances. The Code creates no similar parity for secular employees receiving taxable cash and secular employees receiving nontaxable employer-provided lodging.

The best retort is that repealing Section 107(2) and its income tax exclusion for parsonage allowances will cause churches to furnish to their clergy tax-free in-kind lodging rather than taxable cash allowances. If Congress repeals Section 107(2), the argument goes, a church previously paying a cash parsonage allowance to a minister

---

[88] House Ways and Means Committee Report No. 83-1337, 83rd Cong., 2nd Session, 1954 U.S.C.C.A.N. 4017, 4040 ("Your committee has removed the discrimination in existing law by providing that the present exclusion is to apply to rental allowances paid to ministers to the extent used by them to rent or provide a home.").

to rent his home could, after such repeal, pay the rent itself and then provide the rented home to the minister in kind and income tax free.

Such behavior will occur at the margins if Congress repeals Section 107(2). By the same token, at the margins, some employers today provide housing to afford their employees the Section 119 exclusion and would not provide that housing if Section 119 were repealed. As long as some in-kind fringe benefits are tax-favored, employers have an incentive to offer such benefits to their workers in lieu of cash compensation.

Yet another possible retort is that my proposal to retain the Section 107(1) income tax exclusion for parsonages provided in kind but repeal Section 107(2)'s exclusion for cash parsonage allowances would violate the federal Religious Freedom Restoration Act of 1993 (RFRA)[89] as well as any state RFRA that would apply to a state following this tack.[90] RFRAs purport to return the law to pre-*Smith*[91] standards under which the government may "substantially burden a person's exercise of religion" only if such burden furthers "a compelling government interest" through "the least restrictive means."[92] Taxing cash parsonage allowances, the argument would go, is such a forbidden burden.

This argument should not succeed in light of such decisions as *Lee*,[93] *Jimmy Swaggart Ministries*,[94] and *Hernandez v. Commissioner of Internal Revenue*.[95] These decisions affirm that

> the broad public interest in maintaining a sound tax system is of such a high order [so that] religious belief in conflict with the payment of taxes affords no basis for resisting the tax.[96]

Under this strongly pro-fisc position, the government would have a compelling interest in taxing cash parsonage allowances along with other cash income. Taxing cash income is the least restrictive means of taxing cash income. The Court of Appeals of Indiana has recently come to a similar conclusion, holding that *Lee* precludes a RFRA defense to criminal charges of income tax evasion.[97]

---

89 P.L. 103-141, 107 Stat. 1488, codified as amended at 42 USCS § 2000bb-1(b).

90 For an example of a state RFRA, *see* KY. REV. STAT. § 446.350.

91 *Employment Division, Department of Human Resources of Oregon v. Smith*, 494 U.S. 872 (1990).

92 42 USCS § 2000bb-1(b); KY. REV. STAT. § 446.350.

93 *United States v. Lee*, 455 U.S. 252 (1982).

94 *Jimmy Swaggart Ministries v. Board of Equalization*, 493 U.S. 378 (1990).

95 *Hernandez v. Commissioner of Internal Revenue*, 490 U.S. 680 (1989).

96 *Lee*, 455 U.S. at 260.

97 *Tyms-Bey v. State of Indiana*, 69 N.E. 3d 488 (Ind. Ct. App. 2017), transfer denied without published opinion, 2017 Ind. LEXIS 370 (S. Ct. of Ind.).

Ironically, the amendment to Section 107(2)[98] which Congress adopted in 2002 during *Warren* to strengthen the case for Section 107(2) had the opposite effect. The 2002 amendment makes Section 107(2) less persuasive as a matter of tax policy by requiring the determination of "the fair rental value" of the minister's home. This entangling limit, now embodied in the statute, increases the compliance costs of the church and of the minister, who must ascertain this limit annually. This limit also compounds the enforcement burden on the IRS, which, when auditing, must ascertain this limit as well. This increase in taxpayer compliance costs and in the IRS's enforcement burden was unfavorable, as was the greater church-state entanglement flowing from factual disputes under amended Section 107(2) about particular church-provided homes' "fair rental value[s]."

Important voices call for the amendment of Section 107(2) to place a dollar cap on that section's exclusion and/or to limit the parsonage allowance exclusion to one residence per minister.[99]

Despite the merits of those proposed reforms, they do not address the underlying unpersuasiveness of the cash parsonage allowance exclusion as a matter of tax policy: Cash compensation is easy to measure and tax.

In short, the exclusion from clerical gross incomes of parsonage allowances is a constitutionally permitted choice, given the imperfect trade-offs in this area, but is not constitutionally compelled. As a matter of tax policy, Section 107(2) is inadvisable since cash parsonage allowances pose neither valuation nor liquidity challenges for taxpayers or the tax system. Even if parsonage allowances were included in clergymen's gross incomes, clergy earning modest compensation would pay little or no federal income tax in light of the standard deduction, personal exemptions, and earned income credit.[100] These provisions keep most low-income taxpayers from paying federal income taxes—although, reflecting another imperfect trade-off, Congress generally requires clergy to pay self-employment tax on the value of their church-provided housing, whether such housing is furnished in cash or in kind.[101]

---

[98] *See* the Clergy Housing Allowance Clarification Act of 2002, Pub. L. No. 107-181, 116 Stat. 583 (amending I.R.C. § 107).

[99] *See* Former Senate Finance Committee Ranking Member Grassley Staff Memo on Review of Media-Based Ministries, BNA TaxCore, Vol. 11, No. 5, LEXSTAT TAXCORE A0C5V9G4K8, Jan. 7, 2011; Evangelical Council For Financial Accountability (ECFA), *ECFA to Lead Independent Commission on Major Accountability and Policy Issues for Churches and Other Religious Organizations*, Jan. 7, 2011; Laura Saunders, *Tax Relief for Clergy Is Questioned*, Wall St. J., Aug. 23, 2011, at C1. The U.S. Court of Appeals for the Eleventh Circuit has held that Section 107(2) in its present form already only excludes from income a parsonage allowance for a single residence. *Commissioner v. Driscoll*, 669 F.3d 1309 (11th Cir. 2012), cert. denied, 133 S. Ct. 358 (2012).

[100] I.R.C. §§ 32, 63(c) and 151, 26 U.S.C. §§ 32, 63(c) and 151.

[101] I.R.C. § 1402(a)(8), 26 U.S.C. § 1402(a)(8).

G. THE CONSTITUTIONALITY OF THE RELIGIOUS EXEMPTIONS FROM THE SOCIAL SECURITY TAXES AND THE INDIVIDUAL HEALTH CARE MANDATE

The constitutional controversy surrounding Code Section 107 has broad implications. If Section 107 unconstitutionally entangles church and state, so do the two religious exemptions from the federal individual health care mandate, as do the religious exemptions from the self-employment and FICA taxes. If Section 107 is constitutionally permissible in light of the trade-off between borderline entanglement and enforcement entanglement, so too these other exemptions are imperfect but constitutionally acceptable choices. The latter is the more compelling conclusion given the absence of disentangling alternatives.

Consider first the entangling borderline inquiries required by Internal Revenue Code Section 1402(g) and its sectarian exemption from the self-employment tax. As observed in chapter three,[102] Section 1402(g) applies if an individual is "conscientiously opposed" to insurance. To so qualify, an individual must be a "member of a recognized religious sect." The determination whether this threshold is met requires three borderline inquiries enmeshing the IRS and the individual claiming this exemption: that individual's membership status in a "sect," the "religious" nature of the "sect" of which he is a member, and the "recognized" status of that religious sect. Once this threshold is crossed, eligibility for exemption under Section 1402(g) further requires examination of the "established tenets or teachings of such sect," as well as a determination that the individual asserting exemption is "conscientiously opposed to acceptance of the benefits of any private or public insurance."

Viewed in isolation, these inquiries (like the similarly entangling borderline questions raised by Section 107) enmesh along religious lines the IRS and the individual claiming exemption from the self-employment tax under Code Section 1402(g). However, at the second step of the analysis, the inevitability of tax-related entanglement recurs: If Section 1402(g)'s religious exemption is stricken on First Amendment grounds or is repealed by Congress, the entangling borderline inquiries required to determine eligibility at the boundaries of Section 1402(g) would be replaced by governmental intrusions into religious individuals' personal autonomy as the IRS enforces the self-employment tax against individuals who oppose social insurance on religious grounds.

If the self-employment tax applies to an individual, the IRS must audit to assess his compliance with that tax. The audit process is inherently intrusive. If the IRS

[102] *See supra* at 55–56.

finds that an individual fails to pay the self-employment tax, the IRS collects the tax from this individual and possibly assesses fines against such individual for his non-payment. If (absent Code Section 1402(g)) an individual declines to pay the tax and fines as a matter of religious scruple, the IRS would be required to proceed against this individual's income and assets to collect a tax which violates this individual's religious beliefs.

Thus, if Section 1402(g) were to be declared unconstitutional or were to be repealed by Congress, the IRS's focus would shift from the borderline inquiries raised by the Section 1402(g) exemption (e.g., Is an individual a "member of a recognized religious sect"?) to the intrusions into personal autonomy which are inherent in enforcing any tax. Borderline entanglement will have been traded for enforcement entanglement.

These observations about Internal Revenue Code Section 1402(g) apply in the context of the individual health care mandate, which is described in chapter three[103] and which incorporates that Code section. Policing individuals' eligibilities for this sectarian exemption from the federal health care mandate will require entangling inquiries at the borders of exemption to determine whether an individual claiming the exemption is a "member" of a "recognized religious sect."[104]

Absent this exemption and its borderline entanglements, there would be church-state conflict in forcing individuals religiously opposed to health insurance to carry such insurance. If, as the FFRF and American Atheists maintain,[105] Section 107 requires excessive entanglement between church and state, so too this religious exemption from the federal health care mandate violates the Establishment Clause as that exemption incorporates Code Section 1402(g). For First Amendment purposes, the questions necessary to assess an individual's eligibility for mandate exemption via Section 1402(g) are indistinguishable from the inquiries under Section 107 to which the FFRF and American Atheists object.

However, nullifying the mandate exemption would not eliminate religious entanglement between the IRS and individuals who reject health insurance on sectarian grounds. Rather, repealing this exemption would again transform the nature of the entanglement. The enmeshing borderline inquiries necessary to determine eligibility for mandate exemption under Section 1402(g) would be replaced by the intrusions needed to enforce the health care mandate against those religiously opposed to it.

---

[103] *See supra* at 57–59.

[104] I.R.C. § 5000A(d)(2), 26 U.S.C. § 5000A(d)(2), incorporating I.R.C. § 1402(g), 26 U.S.C. § 1402(g).

[105] *American Atheists, Inc. v. Shulman*, 21 F. Supp. 3d 856 (E.D. Ky., N. Div. 2014); *Freedom From Religion Foundation, Inc. v. Geithner*, (E.D. Calif., Sacramento Div.), Tax Analysts Doc. 2009-23144, complaint at para. 35.

In short, if Section 107 unconstitutionally entangles the IRS with religious entities and actors in violation of the First Amendment, so too does Code Section 1402(g), which requires similar determinations of religious practice and belief to ascertain if that section applies. More convincingly, Section 1402(g) (both for the self-employment tax and for the health care mandate) embodies the constitutionally permitted choice to accept the borderline entanglements of eligibility determinations to avoid enforcement entanglements. Given the inevitable trade-offs in these areas, it is constitutional to allow Congress to pick between the problems of enforcement entanglement and the difficulties of borderline entanglement. There is, again, no disentangling alternative in tax contexts.

Similar observations pertain to Section 1402(e)'s exemption from the self-employment tax. As discussed in chapter three,[106] Section 1402(e) exempts from the self-employment tax "a duly ordained, commissioned, or licensed minister of a church or a member of a religious order" or "a Christian Science practitioner" if such minister, member, or practitioner "is conscientiously opposed to, or because of religious principles [ ]is opposed to, the acceptance . . . of any public insurance." The IRS and those claiming eligibility for this exemption are enmeshed in such boundary-defining questions as the claimants' ministerial status and the "religious principles" to which such claimants adhere. Without this exemption in the Code, there would be no such borders to contest. Instead, the IRS would enforce the self-employment tax against individuals despite their religious opposition to "public insurance" such as the Social Security system financed by the self-employment tax.

Two of the regulatory provisions explicitly challenged by the FFRF as excessively entangling under Code Section 107 implement the Section 1402(e) exemption from the self-employment tax. Specifically, the FFRF brands as unconstitutional in the context of Section 107 the need for the IRS to determine "whether a member of the clergy is 'duly ordained, commissioned, or licensed,'"[107] as well as the need for the IRS to ascertain "whether a Christian college or other organization is 'under the authority of' a church or denomination."[108]

The first of these tests ("duly ordained, commissioned, or licensed") comes from Code Section 1402(e) and is repeated in the regulations implementing that section.[109] The second of these tests ("under the authority") derives from the regulations implementing the Section 1402(e) exemption from the self-employment

---

[106] *See supra* at 56.

[107] *Freedom From Religion Foundation, Inc. v. Geithner*, (E.D. Calif., Sacramento Div.), Tax Analysts Doc. 2009-23144, complaint at para. 35.

[108] *Id.*

[109] Treas. Reg. § 1.1402(c)-5(a)(2), 26 C.F.R. § 1.1402(c)-5(a)(2).

tax.[110] Both of these tests are incorporated by reference into the regulations under Section 107.[111]

If, as the FFRF contends, these regulatory tests unconstitutionally entangle church and state in the context of Section 107, they also unconstitutionally entangle in the context of Section 1402(e), the Internal Revenue Code provision under which these tests are directly promulgated. By the same token, if these borderline tests are reasonable choices in the context of Section 1402(e) (as I conclude they are), these tests are equally reasonable choices for purposes of Section 107. These tests opt for the problems of borderline entanglement over the quandaries of enforcement entanglement.

Consider as well the other exemption from the federal health insurance mandate for members of a "health care sharing ministry."[112] A member of such a ministry need not carry "minimum essential coverage" if the ministry's adherents "share a common set of ethical or religious beliefs and share medical expenses . . . in accordance with those beliefs."[113]

Paradoxically, this exemption from the individual health care mandate is both less and more susceptible to constitutional challenge than is the religiously narrow health care mandate exemption which incorporates Code Section 1402(g).

On the one hand, the health care ministry exemption applies not just to ministries based on "religious beliefs" but also to health care ministries bottomed on "ethical," presumably secular, "beliefs." Thus, this exemption looks less like the narrow Texas sales exemption, restricted to religious publications and stricken in *Texas Monthly*, and resembles more the broader New York property tax exemption, available to secular philanthropic properties and upheld in *Walz*.

On the other hand, the health care ministry exemption from the federal coverage mandate is a recent innovation to the Internal Revenue Code and thus lacks the *Lemon*-based presumption of history. The purely religious exemption from the federal health care mandate incorporates Section 1402(g), which was added to the Code in 1960.[114] Since Section 1402(g) has been part of the federal tax law for over half a century, it is entitled under *Lemon* to a presumption of constitutionality by virtue of its age.

That history-based presumption should also apply to the health mandate exemption incorporating Section 1402(g). The religious mandate exemption based on Section 1402(g) is an incremental extension of prior law. This exemption

---

110 Treas. Reg. § 1.1402(c)-5(b)(2), 26 C.F.R. § 1.1402(c)-5(b)(2).

111 Treas. Reg. § 1.107-1(a), 26 C.F.R. § 1.107-1(a) ("In general, the rules provided in § 1.1402(c)-5 will be applicable to such determination.").

112 I.R.C. § 5000A(d)(2)(B), 26 U.S.C. § 5000A(d)(2)(B).

113 *Id.*

114 Social Security Amendments of 1960, P.L. No. 86-778 § 105(c), 74 Stat. 924.

acknowledges that, just as those religiously opposed to social insurance should not be required to pay the self-employment tax financing Social Security, they should not be required to comply with the federal obligation to carry health insurance.

In contrast, the mandate exemption for members of qualifying health care ministries makes no reference to Section 1402(g) or to any other prior law. Like the Rhode Island and Pennsylvania statutes invalidated in *Lemon*, this mandate exemption is a new enactment which enjoys no history-based presumption of constitutionality.

Hence, the broader implications of the constitutional challenge to Section 107 and the income tax exclusion established by that section: If the critics are correct that this exclusion for church-provided housing and housing allowances violates the First Amendment by impermissibly entangling the IRS and religious institutions and personnel, so too the First Amendment proscribes the similar religious exemptions of the FICA and self-employment taxes, as well as the religious exemptions of the tax-based federal health insurance mandate.

I conclude otherwise. Given the inherent trade-offs in the tax context between borderline entanglement and enforcement entanglement, these religious exemptions are permissible responses to the inexorable problems of church-state entanglement under modern tax systems. It is not persuasive to reflexively dismiss these exemptions as subsidies. These exemptions serve the nonsubsidizing purpose of avoiding enforcement entanglement, at the price of borderline entanglement as the IRS and taxpayers contend over eligibility at the boundaries of exemption.

These FICA, self-employment, and health mandate exemptions are (like Code Section 107) not constitutionally required. Congress can constitutionally opt for the problems of church-state enforcement entanglement by eschewing these kinds of exemptions.

Instructive on this point is the aftermath of *United States v. Lee*,[115] discussed in chapter one. Mr. Lee, it will be recalled, was a member of the Old Order Amish religion and employed other members of his faith to work on his farm and in his carpentry shop.[116] He did not pay the FICA tax[117] imposed on employers nor did he withhold the FICA tax[118] employers are required to retain from their employees' wages. Mr. Lee's noncompliance with the FICA tax stemmed from his religious beliefs forbidding participation in public insurance like Social Security.[119]

---

[115] 455 U.S. 252 (1982). *See supra* at 22–23.

[116] *Lee*, 455 U.S. at 254.

[117] I.R.C. § 3101, 26 U.S.C. § 3101.

[118] I.R.C. § 3111, 26 U.S.C. § 3111.

[119] *Lee*, 455 U.S. at 257.

Ruling against Mr. Lee, the U.S. Supreme Court held that the federal "Government's interest in assuring mandatory and continuous participation in and contribution to the social security system is very high."[120] That interest, the *Lee* Court concluded, outweighed Mr. Lee's offsetting interest in protecting his religious beliefs:

> Because the broad public interest in maintaining a sound tax system is of such a high order, religious belief in conflict with the payment of taxes affords no basis for resisting the tax.[121]

If Mr. Lee had no employees, he would have qualified under Code Section 1402(g)'s sectarian exemption from the self-employment tax. Section 1402(g), the *Lee* Court held, is a congressional "effort toward accommodation,"[122] which plausibly "drew a line"[123] between, on the one hand, employers who religiously oppose Social Security but must pay FICA tax and, on the other, self-employed persons who reject Social Security on religious grounds and were consequently excused from paying the self-employment tax.

Lee, written by Chief Justice Burger for himself and seven of his colleagues,[124] follows the trail of permissive accommodation marked by *Walz*. In cases like Mr. Lee's, Congress chose not to accommodate. In the framework of this book, Congress elected in Mr. Lee's case for the problems of enforcement entanglement—making Mr. Lee pay FICA tax for himself and his employees despite their religious objections to Social Security. Congress thereby avoided the quandaries of borderline entanglement—determining whether Mr. Lee was eligible for a sectarian exemption from paying the Social Security tax.

Subsequent to *Lee*, Congress reversed this choice and enacted the religious exemption of Section 3127[125] to overturn *Lee*. Section 3127 now exempts from FICA taxation employers and employees described in Section 1402(g), that is, employers and employees who are "member[s] of a recognized religious sect" and who, by reason of their adherence to the "established tenets or teachings of such sect," are "conscientiously opposed to acceptance of the benefits of any private or public insurance."[126]

---

[120] *Id.* at 258–259.

[121] *Id.* at 260. In *Employment Division, Department of Human Resources of Oregon v. Smith*, 494 U.S. 872, 880 (1990), the Court cited *Lee* for the proposition that the First Amendment does not require exemption from "a neutral, generally applicable regulatory law that compel[s] activity forbidden by an individual's religion."

[122] *Lee*, 455 U.S. at 260, n.11.

[123] *Id.* at 261.

[124] Justice Stevens concurred in a separate opinion. *Id.* at 261.

[125] I.R.C. § 3127, 26 U.S.C. § 3127.

[126] I.R.C. § 1402(g), 26 U.S.C. § 1402(g).

Thus, today Mr. Lee and those sharing his religious opposition to Social Security need neither withhold nor pay FICA taxes.

Since Code Section 3127 incorporates Section 1402(g), its constitutional status, like the constitutional status of the federal health mandate exemption also incorporating Section 1402(g), depends upon the constitutional status of Section 1402(g) itself. If Section 1402(g) entails excessive religious entanglement in violation of the Establishment Clause of the First Amendment, so too these provisions which subsume Section 1402(g) entangle excessively. On the other hand, I contend that Section 1402(g) is constitutionally permissible, as there are no disentangling alternatives when the modern tax system interacts with the contemporary religious community. From this vantage, Section 3127 (which incorporates Section 1402(g)) similarly survives First Amendment scrutiny.

Section 3127 covers situations where both an employer and her employees object on religious grounds to Social Security. Internal Revenue Code Section 3121(b)(8)(B),[127] in contrast, applies when a sectarian employer objects to the payment of FICA taxes but the employer's employees do not share those objections. Under Section 3121(b)(8)(B), these employees are treated as though they are self-employed and thus pay the federal self-employment tax while the religiously objecting employer is excused from paying the FICA taxes it would otherwise owe.

Section 3121(b)(8)(B) highlights again the inexorable choice between borderline entanglement and enforcement entanglement. To be eligible for FICA tax exemption under Section 3121(b)(8)(B), an employer must be a church or "church-controlled organization" which "is opposed for religious reasons to the payment of the" employer FICA tax. Determining qualification for this exemption enmeshes church and state in religiously sensitive inquiries at the boundaries of exemption: Is a particular employer a church or "church-controlled"? Is the church's opposition to FICA taxation "for religious reasons"?

However, repealing Section 3121(b)(8)(B) would entangle church and state as well. Absent Section 3121(b)(8)(B), the IRS must enforce FICA taxation against churches doctrinally opposed to such taxation. Again, the choice Congress confronts is between imperfect alternatives, that is, the enmeshment of church and state in determining qualification for exemption or the entanglement of church and state as the IRS enforces FICA taxation against churches opposed to such taxation. In First Amendment terms, Section 3121(b)(8)(B), like the other exemptions of the FICA and self-employment taxes, is a reasonable, though not a compelled, choice to incur the difficulties of patrolling the borders of sectarian tax exemption rather than incur the costs of enforcing taxation against those religiously opposed to it.

---

127 I.R.C. § 3121(b)(8)(B), 26 U.S.C. § 3121(b)(8)(B).

H. A FINAL WORD ON *LEMON*

Among the important contemporary First Amendment controversies is the status of what Justice Kennedy labeled "the so-called *Lemon* test."[128] Justice Scalia, in a memorable attack on *Lemon*, observed that "[t]he secret of the *Lemon* test's survival, I think, is that it is so easy to kill. It is there to scare us (and our audience) when we wish it to do so, but we can command it to return to the tomb at will."[129] Others are more supportive of *Lemon*.[130]

My approach to this debate will, at this point, not surprise the reader: Entanglement, one of the three *Lemon* factors, is not a useful criterion in the tax context, as there are no disentangling alternatives in that context. Whatever the value in other settings of entanglement as a criterion for First Amendment decision-making, entanglement provides no purchase in judicial evaluation of tax exemptions for religious actors and institutions.

The invariable choice under the modern tax system is to tax sectarian actors and institutions and thereby incur the problems of enforcement entanglement or to exempt such actors and institutions and thereby incur the quandaries of borderline entanglement. Church-state entanglement can sometimes be minimized in the tax setting, such as by adopting broader exemptions which include secular as well as sectarian exemption categories. Similarly, there is less church-state enforcement entanglement taxing the church if the event to be taxed is easily valued and produces the cash to pay tax. Conversely, there is more enforcement entanglement if a tax requires doctrinal assessments such as determining whether particular religious outlays are "ordinary and necessary."[131]

At the end of the day, there is no perfect way in the modern world to avoid some measure of tax-related entanglement between contemporary government and the contemporary church. As I discuss in chapter eight,[132] the resulting choices are best made by legislators, not judges.

---

128 *Salazar v. Buono*, 130 S. Ct. 1803, 1812 (2010).

129 *Lamb's Chapel v. Ctr. Moriches Union Free Sch. Dist.*, 508 U.S. 384, 399 (1993) (Scalia, J., concurring) (parenthesis in original).

130 *See, e.g.*, Marci A. Hamilton, *Justice Sandra Day O'Connor (Ret.): The Endorsement Factor*, 43 ARIZ. ST. L.J. 349 (2011).

131 I.R.C. § 162(a), 26 U.S.C. § 162(a).

132 *See infra* at 223–229.

I. CONCLUSION

The diversity with which the states treat parsonages illustrates that there is no perfect approach to the property taxation (or not) of parsonages, just trade-offs which reasonable lawmakers and judges can assess differently. Exempting parsonages, like other similar sectarian exemptions, creates borderline entanglement as tax assessors and, ultimately, courts must determine, at the boundaries of exemption, whether or not particular residences qualify as "parsonages" eligible for property tax exemption. Taxing parsonages generates enforcement entanglement as parsonages (like any other real estate) must be valued and as churches must raise the cash to pay the resulting property tax. It is unpersuasive to reflexively denounce the tax-exemption of parsonages as subsidization. Such exemption can serve the nonsubsidizing purpose of minimizing the enforcement entanglement inherent in property taxation.

The controversy over the constitutionality of Code Section 107 is wide-ranging in its implications. If, as contemporary opponents of Section 107 argue, the income tax exclusion that section grants to "minister[s] of the gospel" unconstitutionally entangles church and state, so too do the equivalent religious exemptions from the federal health care mandate and from the FICA and self-employment taxes. Ultimately, this argument is also unpersuasive.

In the contemporary tax context, extensive contact between tax systems and religious institutions is inexorable, whether religious institutions and personnel are taxed or exempted. In the tax setting, there are no disentangling alternatives.

Section 107 and its exclusion from gross income for clerical recipients of in-kind housing and parsonage allowances are constitutionally permitted, though not constitutionally required, responses to the problems of entanglement inherent in the relationship between the modern government and the modern church. Similarly, the Code's sectarian exemptions from the individual health coverage mandate and from the Social Security taxes are acceptable, though not obligatory, means under the First Amendment of managing the inevitable tensions between the tax system of the contemporary state and the religious community.

It is unpersuasive to simply characterize these (and similar) tax exemptions as subsidies. Exemption can properly be part of a normative tax base when such exemption serves a nonsubsidizing purpose. Code Section 107 serves such a nonsubsidizing purpose, namely, minimizing the enmeshment of church and state which would flow from the income taxation of parsonages provided in kind and of cash parsonage allowances.

The constitutionality of the parsonage allowance exclusion does not imply the exclusion's advisability as a matter of tax policy. Since such allowances are paid to "minister[s] of the gospel" in cash, there is, as a matter of tax policy, no convincing reason to exclude such allowances from ministers' gross income. Such cash housing allowances pose neither valuation difficulties nor liquidity issues for clerical taxpayers. However, in First Amendment terms, Section 107 is a permissible constitutional choice for managing the inevitable entanglement between church and state under modern tax systems.

7

OTHER ISSUES FOR THE FUTURE

Churches' Lobbying, Campaigning, and Sales Taxation

IN THIS CHAPTER, I discuss two additional issues likely to be controversial in the years ahead. The first of these is the Internal Revenue Code's prohibitions on political campaigning and substantial lobbying by tax-exempt organizations, including churches. After reviewing these prohibitions and the controversy they have engendered, I propose a new statutory safe harbor for the internal communications of churches. This limited safe harbor would protect in-house church discussions from both Section 501(c)(3)'s ban on substantial lobbying and from that section's prohibition on political campaigning. Under this proposed amendment to the Internal Revenue Code, churches would, along with other tax-exempt institutions, otherwise remain subject to the Code's bars on campaigning and lobbying. These statutory bars properly deter the diversion of income tax–deductible resources to campaigning and lobbying.

The second issue I discuss in this chapter is the future of the sales tax. Many states should expand the sales tax obligations of churches and other religious organizations, both as sellers and as buyers of tangible personal property. The sales tax entails less entanglement than other forms of taxation such as ad valorem property taxation because sales taxes are typically triggered by cash purchases. Cash transactions are self-valuing and occur when cash is available to pay the sales tax. Hence, the sales tax obligations of sectarian sellers and buyers can be expanded with relatively modest

Taxing the Church. Edward A. Zelinsky.

church-state enforcement entanglement flowing from that expansion. Revenue considerations as well as concerns about economic neutrality buttress the argument for expanding the sales tax obligations of sectarian entities as purchasers and as sellers.

At first blush, these two issues—churches' internal communications, their sales tax liabilities—are unrelated. However, both reflect the centrality of entanglement concerns to the relationship between the contemporary church and the contemporary tax system. Entanglement considerations counsel greater protection than current law provides for speech within churches. Entanglement considerations similarly indicate that the sales tax obligations of sectarian institutions should be expanded.

In conventional terms, the former is a "pro-church" recommendation while the latter is "anti-religious." I suggest a different vantage and hope that the reader who disagrees with my particular recommendations will nevertheless be persuaded of the centrality of entanglement concerns in assessing both these topics.

A. SECTION 501(C)(3)'S BANS ON SUBSTANTIAL LOBBYING AND POLITICAL CAMPAIGNING

As we saw in chapter three,[1] the Internal Revenue Code prohibits all tax-exempt Section 501(c)(3) institutions, including churches and other religious entities, from "substantial[ly] . . . carrying on propaganda, or otherwise attempting, to influence legislation."[2] In addition, Section 501(c)(3), through what is often denominated as "the Johnson Amendment," forbids tax-exempt organizations, including churches, from "participat[ing] in, or interven[ing] in, (including the publishing or distributing of statements), any political campaign on behalf of (or in opposition to) any candidate for public office."[3] Unlike the ban on "substantial" lobbying, Code Section 501(c)(3)'s prohibition on campaigning makes no allowance for insubstantial campaign activity by a tax-exempt entity.

The Code's prohibitions on political lobbying and campaigning have been controversial, particularly as applied to churches.[4] Liberals claim that conservative churches flout the statutory bar on political activity to support Republican candidates.[5]

---

[1] *See supra* at 45.

[2] I.R.C. Section 501(c)(3), 26 U.S.C. Section 501(c)(3).

[3] *Id.* (parentheses in original).

[4] Lloyd Hitoshi Mayer, *Politics at the Pulpit: Tax Benefits, Substantial Burdens, and Institutional Free Exercise*, 89 B.U. L. REV. 1137, 1138 (2009).

[5] *See, e.g., The Rise of the Religious Right in the Republican Party*, THEOCRACY WATCH, http://www.theocracywatch.org; Jasper L. Cummings Jr., *Deducting Political Expenditures*, 153 TAX NOTES 847, 853 (2016) ("There is a fair chance that most of that political activity is in the segment of churches that entered politics in a big way in the form of the Moral Majority beginning in the late 1970s.").

Conservatives retort that liberal churches, particularly African-American churches, campaign on behalf of Democrats.[6] Objective evidence suggests that both of these criticisms have validity.[7] Moreover, some church groups openly defy Section 501(c)(3)'s ban on political activity.[8]

Revenue Ruling 2007-41[9] is the IRS's current interpretation of the statutory prohibition on political campaigning by Section 501(c)(3) organizations. The IRS understands this prohibition on political activity as requiring the IRS to intrude deeply into churches' internal operations to monitor and evaluate the comments of church personnel. According to that ruling, for example, a minister, while free to make statements as an individual, cannot endorse a candidate for public office at "an official church function, [or] in an official church publication."[10] Thus, a minister's statement supporting a candidate from the pulpit, in a church's newsletter to its parishioners, or on a church website[11] can potentially cost his church its tax-exempt status.

Moreover, according to the IRS, a prohibited endorsement need not be explicit. For example, without expressly backing a candidate, a church (or other nonprofit organization) can lose its tax-exempt status under Section 501(c)(3) by making itself available as a forum to one candidate but not to another "during the ... campaign."[12] Since candidates today campaign nonstop,[13] this standard effectively requires the IRS to scrutinize churches' year-round activities to ensure that churches do not implicitly endorse candidates by granting them selective access to the church as a forum.

These administrative rules carve out a safe harbor for incumbents. Current officeholders can be invited to attend and speak at functions sponsored by churches and other 501(c)(3) entities as long as no explicit reference is made to the incumbent's re-election.[14]

---

6 *See, e.g.*, *Many Black Pastors "Extensions of Democratic Party,"* ONE NEWS NOW (Mar. 9, 2015), http://onenewsnow.com.

7 Pew Research Center, MANY AMERICANS HEAR POLITICS FROM THE PULPIT (Aug. 8, 2016).

8 Samuel D. Brunson, *Dear IRS: It Is Time to Enforce the Campaigning Prohibition, Even Against Churches*, 87 U. COLO. L. REV. 143, 145 (2016) (discussing "Pulpit Freedom Sunday"); Ellen P. Aprill, *Why the IRS Should Want to Develop Rules Regarding Charities and Politics*, 62 CASE W. RES. L. REV. 643, 673–674 (2012); Nathan J. Richman, *Grassley Questions Namorato on Sermon Letter*, TAX NOTES TODAY, 2015 TNT 164-2 (discussing the Alliance Defense Fund's "Pulpit Initiative,"); Mayer, *supra* note 4, at 1140.

9 Rev. Rul. 2007-41, 2007-1 C.B. 1421.

10 *Id.* at situation 5. *See also id.* at situation 6 (candidate endorsement offered at "an official organization meeting ... constitutions political campaign intervention.").

11 *Id.* at situation 21.

12 *Id.* at situation 9.

13 *See, e.g.*, NORMAN J. ORNSTEIN & THOMAS E. MANN, THE PERMANENT CAMPAIGN AND ITS FUTURE 17, 220 (2000).

14 Rev. Rul. 2007-41 at situations 10 and 11.

A skeptical interpretation of this safe harbor is that the IRS thereby accommodates the senators and representatives who approve its budget. A less jaundiced explanation is that this safe harbor recognizes a legitimate need to permit incumbent officeholders to make routine appearances in their respective constituencies. Either way, challengers are potentially disadvantaged by this administrative rule since there is no equivalent safe harbor protecting a church's (or other nonprofit organization's) tax-exempt status if it invites only a nonincumbent candidate to speak.

Moreover, according to the IRS in Rev. Rul. 2007-41, the "issue advocacy" of a tax-exempt group may "function[] as political campaign intervention"[15] and thus cost the group its tax-exempt status. Whether such issue advocacy is permitted is a fact-based determination with all of the uncertainties that implies. Among the relevant considerations identified by the IRS is whether the issue being addressed by the 501(c)(3) entity "is a prominent issue in a campaign that distinguishes the candidates."[16] Under this fact-based standard, a minister's sermon could jeopardize her church's tax-exempt status if, on the Sunday before an election, the minister supports or opposes abortion rights, same-sex marriage, gun control, the death penalty, or the Confederate flag should the IRS determine this subject to be "a prominent issue" in a current electoral campaign.

Unlike the Internal Revenue Code's prohibition on "substantial" lobbying, the Code's ban on political campaigning by tax-exempt entities is absolute. On the Sunday before the 1992 presidential election, Branch Ministries placed an advertisement in the *Washington Times* and in *USA Today*, urging Christians to vote against then-governor Bill Clinton.[17] In *Branch Ministries v. Rossotti*,[18] the U.S. Court of Appeals for the D.C. Circuit held that these two ads were sufficient to trigger the ban on campaigning by tax-exempt organizations.

Code Section 4955, enacted as part of the Revenue Act of 1987,[19] imposes an excise tax on the campaign expenditure of any Section 501(c)(3) organization including any church or other religious tax-exempt entity.[20] This excise tax applies both to the entity[21] and to any manager of the entity who knowingly agrees to such

---

[15] *Id.*

[16] *Id.* at situation 16.

[17] *Branch Ministries v. Rossotti*, 211 F.3d 137, 140 (D.C. Cir. 2000).

[18] *Id.*

[19] The Revenue Act of 1987 also added to the Code two procedural provisions addressing "flagrant" campaign participation by Section 501(c)(3) organizations. Revenue Act of 1987, P.L. 100-203, 101 Stat. 1330. I.R.C. Section 6852 authorizes an immediate assessment of the excise tax imposed by Section 4955 if there is "a flagrant violation of the prohibition against making political expenditures." I.R.C. Section 7409 authorizes an injunction against a 501(c)(3) entity to stop it from continuing to "flagrantly" participate in a political campaign. I.R.C. §§ 6852 and 7409, 26 U.S.C. §§ 6852 and 7409.

[20] I.R.C. § 4955, 26 U.S.C. § 4955.

[21] I.R.C. §§ 4955(a)(1) and 4955(b)(1), 26 U.S.C. § 4955(a)(1) and 4955(b)(1).

campaign expenditure unless the manager did not act "willful[ly]" and had "reasonable cause."[22] The excise tax established by Code Section 4955 gives the IRS a method to enforce the statutory ban on campaign expenditures short of formally revoking the offending group's tax-exempt status.[23]

While Section 501(c)(3)'s prohibition on campaign expenditures is absolute, that section's ban on lobbying applies only to "substantial"[24] lobbying by a tax-exempt entity. This statutory ban on substantial lobbying, like the prohibition of all campaigning by tax-exempt organizations, requires fact-based enforcement determinations by the IRS and, ultimately, the courts. Under the relevant Treasury regulations, a tax-exempt organization engages in statutorily prohibited lobbying if the organization "(c)ontacts, or urges the public to contact, members of a legislative body for the purpose of proposing, supporting, or opposing legislation; or (a)dvocates the adoption or rejection of legislation."[25] Thus, a minister's comments in a sermon could jeopardize the church's tax-exempt status if those comments are construed as "advocat[ing] the adoption or rejection of legislation."[26] Under these rules, the U.S. Court of Appeals for the 10th Circuit upheld the revocation of the tax-exempt status of Christian Echoes National Ministry as the church had "attempt[ed] to influence legislation through an indirect campaign to mold public opinion."[27]

In response to the uncertainty of determining whether lobbying is "substantial" or not, Congress in the Tax Reform Act of 1976 added Sections 501(h) and 4911 to the Internal Revenue Code. Section 501(h)[28] allows most public charities to elect a safe harbor calculation to determine if the electing charity's lobbying is substantial or not.

---

22 I.R.C. §§ 4955(a)(2) and 4955(b)(2), 26 U.S.C. § 4955(a)(2) and 4955(b)(2).

23 Strictly speaking, any participation in a political campaign causes the participating organization to lose its tax-exempt status under I.R.C. Section 501(c)(3). However, the language of Section 4955 contrasts with the language of Section 4912, discussed *infra*. Section 4912 imposes an excise tax on an organization which has lost its tax-exempt status "by reason of making lobbying expenditures." Section 4955 contains no equivalent language. The most natural reading of the two sections side by side is that Section 4912 applies when a previously tax-exempt entity has lost its tax exemption but that Section 4955 can apply without such a formal loss being declared by the IRS. Compare I.R.C. § 4912(a), 26 U.S.C. § 4912(a) with I.R.C. § 495a), 26 U.S.C. § 4955(a).

24 I.R.C. § 501(c)(3), 26 U.S.C. § 501(c)(3).

25 Treas. Reg. § 1.501(c)(3)-1(c)(3)(ii), 26 C.F.R. § 1.501(c)(3)-1(c)(3)(ii).

26 *Id.*

27 *Christian Echoes National Ministry, Inc. v. U.S.A.*, 470 F.2d 849, 855 (10th Cir. 1972).

28 I.R.C. § 501(h), 26 U.S.C. § 501(h). For purposes of Sections 501(h) and 4911, "lobbying expenditures" are an exempt entity's total outlays attempting to influence legislation including communications with government officials and efforts to influence public opinion. I.R.C. §§ 501(h)(2)(A), 4911(c)(1), 4911(d)(1), 26 U.S.C. §§ 501(h)(2)(A), 4911(c)(1), 4911(d)(1). "Grass roots expenditures" are the subset of these outlays devoted to influencing public opinion. I.R.C. §§ 501(h)(2)(C), 4911(c)(3), 26 U.S.C. §§ 501(h)(2)(C), 4911(c)(3). Under Section 4911, an exempt organization's "exempt purpose expenditures" are the organization's total annual outlays for the purposes for which the organization is tax exempt exclusive of the organization's fundraising costs. I.R.C. § 4911(e)(1), 26 U.S.C. § 4911(e)(1).

A public charity which has made the Section 501(h) election calculates its exempt purpose expenditures and then takes a percentage of those expenditures to determine its nontaxable lobbying amount and its lobbying ceiling amount for the year.[29] For example, if a school which has made the 501(h) election makes annual exempt purpose expenditures of $400,000 on its educational activities, the school's lobbying taxable amount for the year is 20 percent of that figure, that is, $80,000.[30] If the school's exempt purpose expenditures are instead $600,000, its lobbying taxable amount is 20 percent of the first $500,000 plus 15 percent of the balance for a total of $115,000.[31]

To see the operation of Sections 501(h) and 4911, suppose that the school with a lobbying taxable amount of $80,000 actually spends $50,000 in that year on lobbying. This is a no-harm-no-foul situation: Since the school's lobbying outlays are less than its ceiling amount ($120,000), the school's lobbying is insubstantial for purposes of Section 501(c)(3) and the school's tax-exempt status. Moreover, no excise tax is due since the school's lobbying outlays are less than its lobbying nontaxable amount ($80,000).

Assume instead that the school spends $100,000 this year on lobbying. In that case, the school's exemption remains secure because its lobbying outlays are still less than the lobbying ceiling amount of $120,000. However, the school now owes tax under Section 4911 of $5,000, that is, 25 percent of the excess of $100,000 over $80,000.

Suppose finally that this school spends $125,000 on lobbying. In this case, the school's lobbying, since its exceeds the lobbying ceiling amount of $120,000, can cause loss of the school's tax-exempt status if the school "normally" exceeds the lobbying ceiling amount. Even if this high level of lobbying expenditures is an isolated, rather than a normal, case, the school owes the 25 percent excise tax on the amount

---

[29] I.R.C. §§ 501(h)(2)(B), 4911(c)(2), 26 U.S.C. §§ 501(h)(2)(B), 4911(c)(2).

[30] I.R.C. § 4911(c)(2), 26 U.S.C. § 4911(c)(2).

[31] *Id.* An organization's lobbying ceiling amount is 150 percent of its lobbying nontaxable amount. I.R.C. § 501(h)(2)(B), 26 U.S.C. § 501(h)(2)(B). Its grass-roots nontaxable amount and its grass-roots ceiling amount are 25 percent of the equivalent lobbying figures. I.R.C. § 4911(c)(4), 26 U.S.C. § 4911(c)(4). For all organizations electing under Section 501(h), the lobbying nontaxable amount is capped at $1 million. I.R.C. § 4911(c)(2)(A), 26 U.S.C. § 4911(c)(2)(A).

If a public charity makes the Section 501(h) election, as long as its "lobbying expenditures" are "normally" less than its "lobbying ceiling amount" and its "grass roots expenditures" are "normally" less than its "grass roots ceiling amount," the public charity remains tax exempt under Section 501(c)(3). I.R.C. § 501(h)(1), 26 U.S.C. § 501(h)(1). If, however, a public charity which has made the Section 501(h) election makes more lobbying expenditures than its "lobbying nontaxable amount" or makes more "grass roots expenditures" than its "grass roots nontaxable amount," Section 4911 imposes an excise tax of 25 percent on the excess. I.R.C. §§ 4911(a), 4911(b), 26 U.S.C. § 4911(a), 4911(b).

of its lobbying outlays ($125,000) over the school's nontaxable lobbying amount ($80,000).

Churches and auxiliaries and conventions of churches are not allowed to make the 501(h) safe harbor election.[32] At first blush, denying churches the Section 501(h) safe harbor option appears hostile to churches' interests. Why deny churches an option available to other tax-exempt entities? However, the legislative history of the 1976 law indicates that churches asked to be denied this option. The General Explanation of the Tax Reform Act of 1976[33] states that, during the legislative process, churches had "indicated a concern that if a church were permitted to elect the new rules (of Section 501(h)), then the Internal Revenue Service might be influenced by this legislation even though the church in fact did not elect."[34]

Suppose, for example, that a church routinely spends $400,000 on its sacerdotal activities and "normally" spends $125,000 on lobbying. If Section 501(h) applied to the church, the church would lose its tax-exempt status because of its lobbying. As described by the General Explanation, some churches were concerned that the IRS and the courts, in this example, would automatically assume that the church's lobbying was "substantial" even if the church had not made the Section 501(h) election.

To accommodate this concern, churches and church auxiliaries and conventions cannot make the Section 501(h) safe harbor election. Moreover, Code Section 501(h)(7)[35] specifies that the standards established by Section 501(h) to identify when lobbying is substantial have no relevance to the lobbying activities of those eleemosynary entities which cannot or do not elect Section 501(h)'s safe harbor for lobbying outlays.[36]

Thus, Section 501(h) plays no role in determining whether or not a church's lobbying is substantial. While churches cannot elect Section 501(h)'s safe harbor on lobbying expenses, a nonchurch religious organization with sufficient public support to qualify as a public charity can make this election.[37]

If a public charity (but not a church) skips the Section 501(h) election and loses its tax-exempt status because of substantial lobbying, a 5 percent excise tax applies to the public charity's lobbying expenditures.[38] This excise tax applies both to the

---

[32] I.R.C. § 501(h)(5), 26 U.S.C. § 501(h)(5).

[33] Staff of the Joint Committee on Taxation, *General Explanation of the Tax Reform Act of 1976*, 94th Cong. (Comm. Print 1976).

[34] H.R. Rep. No. 94-1210 (1976), at 12 (Conf. Rep.).

[35] I.R.C. § 501(h)(7), 26 U.S.C. § 501(h)(7).

[36] *See also* Dean M. Kelley, Why Churches Should Not Pay Taxes 79–83 (1977) (discussing church opposition to Section 501(h)).

[37] I.R.C. § 501(h)(4)(E), 26 U.S.C. § 501(h)(4)(E).

[38] I.R.C. § 4912, 26 U.S.C. § 4912.

public charity[39] and to any manager of the public charity who knowingly agreed to such lobbying expenditures unless such manager did not act "willful[ly]" and had "reasonable cause."[40]

Section 501(c)(3)'s prohibitions on campaigning and substantial lobbying engender considerable enforcement-related entanglement between church and state. The IRS, to enforce these prohibitions, must monitor and evaluate church activities and the statements of church personnel to determine if such activities and statements constitute explicit or implicit campaigning or amount to "substantial" lobbying.

This enforcement is a deeply entangling enterprise. Insofar as the IRS is enmeshed with secular nonprofit institutions as the IRS scrutinizes their activities and communications, this enforcement-related entanglement might be considered acceptable: The Free Exercise clause does not protect secular nonprofit organizations in the implementation of their respective missions. However, the IRS's monitoring and evaluation of internal church communications intrudes deeply into "the autonomy and freedom of religious bodies"[41] protected by the First Amendment.

B. THE CONTROVERSY

No commentator is completely happy with Section 501(c)(3)'s prohibition on political campaigning by tax-exempt entities. Even legal scholars who are supportive of this prohibition call for technical modifications to the prohibition or for better enforcement of the prohibition.

Professor Roger Colinvaux concludes that the ban on campaigning by tax-exempt entities "serves important purposes"[42] with "no easy alternative."[43] He identifies five rationales for the prohibition of political campaigning by tax-exempt entities:

> (1) Congress wants charities to focus on core charitable activity; (2) Congress wants a charitable sector untainted by partisan flavor; (3) Congress does not want to subsidize political activity through exemption; (4) Congress wants to protect charities from political capture; and (5) Congress does not think political activity is charitable activity.[44]

---

[39] I.R.C. § 4912(a), 26 U.S.C. § 4912(a).

[40] I.R.C. § 4912(b), 26 U.S.C. § 4912(b).

[41] *Walz*, 397 U.S. at 672.

[42] Roger Colinvaux, *The Political Speech of Charities in the Face of Citizens United: A Defense of Prohibition*, 62 Case. W. Res. 685, 755 (2012).

[43] *Id.* at 756.

[44] *Id.* at 711.

Professor Laura Chisolm would also retain the prohibition on campaign activity by 501(c)(3) groups.[45] However, she would enable such groups to form and maintain political action committees (PACs) under Code Section 527[46] as long there is "formal and fiscal separation" between any tax-exempt institution and its respective PAC.[47]

Professor Ellen Aprill urges the IRS to develop more detailed administrative rules to implement Section 501(c)(3)'s prohibition on political campaigning by tax-exempt institutions.[48] Attorney Kelley S. Shoop argues that the Code's ban on tax-exempt entities' political campaigning "should [be] more actively enforce[d]."[49]

Dean Donald B. Tobin supports the ban on campaigning by tax-exempt entities but also calls for more effective enforcement.[50] The ban, he argues, is good for both churches and society as a whole. Viewing the income tax treatment of Section 501(c)(3) groups as a subsidy, Dean Tobin contends that

> [s]ubsidizing the entry of churches into politics artificially increases the power of religious institutions in society and poses serious problems for our current system of governance. This may allow churches, or their followers, to be over-represented in political debates and political life.[51]

Dean Tobin also views the ban on campaign activity as good for churches. If churches can campaign, they will be "co-opted" and intimidated "by powerful politicians or political parties."[52] Moreover, if churches can campaign, politicians will prefer some churches (those supporting them) over others (those opposing them) while churches themselves will become internally divided over which candidates to support.[53] To strengthen enforcement, Dean Tobin proposes that the 501(c)(3) prohibition on political campaigning by tax-exempt entities be administered by "an independent commission."[54]

---

45 Laura Brown Chisolm, *Politics and Charity: A Proposal for Peaceful Coexistence*, 58 GEO. WASH. L. REV. 308 (1990).

46 I.R.C. § 527, 26 U.S.C. § 527.

47 Chisolm, *supra* note 45, at 363.

48 Aprill, *supra* note 8, at 664.

49 Kelly S. Shoop, Note, *If You Are a Good Christian You Have No Business Voting for This Candidate: Church Sponsored Political Activity in Federal Elections*, 83 WASH. U. L.Q. 1927, 1948 (2005).

50 Donald B. Tobin, *Political Campaigning by Churches and Charities: Hazardous for 501(c)(3)s, Dangerous for Democracy*, 95 GEO. L.J. 1313 (2007).

51 *Id.* at 1326.

52 *Id.* at 1322–1323.

53 *Id.* at 1323–1324.

54 *Id.* at 1359–1361. Some of the commissioners would be selected by the president; others would be picked by the leader of the opposition party in the Senate; yet other commissioners would be randomly chosen "IRS career employees in the Exempt Organizations Division of the IRS who had ten or more years of experience at the IRS." *Id.* at 1361.

Professor Samuel Brunson advances three reasons for stricter enforcement of the 501(c)(3) ban on churches' political campaigning.[55] First, "the IRS should enforce the law as written."[56] Second, enhanced enforcement of Section 501(c)(3) would make Congress accountable for "the law it has written."[57] Finally, such enforcement would give affected churches standing "to place the constitutionality of the prohibition in front of the courts."[58]

Many legal scholars are troubled that the Code's bar on political campaigning intrudes into church autonomy. These scholars propose fundamental alternatives to current law to reduce that intrusion. These pundits also emphasize the rights of ministers and church members to communicate freely among themselves without scrutiny by the tax collector. Central to this critique of the Code's ban on churches' campaigning is the celebration of the historic role of churches as participants in important political movements in American life. The alternatives advanced by these observers touch upon issues which are now familiar to the reader, namely, the trade-off between enforcement entanglement and borderline entanglement; whether relief should be provided narrowly to churches or more broadly to religious organizations or most broadly to all eleemosynary institutions. These proposals demonstrate, again, that in this area there are no ideal solutions, only imperfect trade-offs among competing and legitimate values.

Professor Buckles, for example, would repeal Section 501(c)(3)'s blanket ban on participation in political campaigns. He would replace that ban with an excise tax in the Internal Revenue Code on the "political campaign expenditures" of tax-exempt organizations which are not "independently controlled."[59] While his proposed definition of "political campaign expenditure" would largely track current law, Professor Buckles would provide a safe harbor "for any expenditure related to any oral communication made primarily between an [exempt] organization and its members in person."[60] Thus, a minister's, rabbi's, or imam's verbally delivered sermon would be immunized from scrutiny of its content, but a written statement in a church newsletter would not be protected by this safe harbor for campaign activity.[61] For this

---

[55] Brunson, *supra* note 8, at 171.

[56] *Id.*

[57] *Id.*

[58] *Id.*

[59] Johnny Rex Buckles, *Not Even a Peep? The Regulation of Political Campaign Activity by Charities Through Federal Tax Law*, 75 U. CIN. L. REV. 1071, 1074 (2007).

[60] *Id.* at 1109.

[61] An interesting issue under this proposal is whether a sermon retains its status as protected "oral" communication with members if the sermon is videotaped and placed on the church's website. A similarly interesting issue is whether, in the case of a megachurch with multiple locations, a sermon delivered at the main church location is still "oral" communication when it is simultaneously broadcast to the church's satellite locations.

purpose, the determination of a 501(c)(3) entity's independence would be based on the rules currently applicable to private foundations.[62]

Professor Buckles' proposal to amend the Internal Revenue Code eliminates one of the most entangling enforcement inquiries under current law, that is, the IRS's monitoring and evaluation of pulpit communications to determine if such communications constitute political campaigning. His proposal would also minimize borderline entanglement since his safe harbor for independently authorized campaign expenditures would apply to all independently governed 501(c)(3) organizations. Thus, to administer his proposal, there would in specific cases be no need to determine if a particular independently governed organization is a "church" since this organization might qualify as "religious" or as charitable or educational.

On the other hand, Professor Buckles' proposal would leave many houses of worship subject to his recommended excise tax on political campaigning. Numerous synagogues, for example, would not satisfy Professor Buckles' criteria for independent governance since often a majority of a synagogue's board members are officers of and substantial contributors[63] to the synagogue. Similarly, a prototypical family-based entrepreneurial church would not qualify as independently governed under this proposal since the church founder and the founder's family often dominate the church's governing board.

Under Professor Buckles' proposal, political campaign expenditures by these non-independently governed entities would trigger a punitive tax based on the highest federal income tax rate increased by 20 percent. Under current tax rates,[64] this penalty would be 59.6 percent of the political campaign expenditure of any 501(c)(3) group which is not independently governed or the political campaign expenditure of an independently governed 501(c)(3) entity if the expenditure were influenced by inside directors.

However, there would be no consequences if a majority of the independent directors of an independently governed tax-exempt entity approved a political campaign

62 Under Professor Buckles' proposal, to qualify as an independently governed entity, a majority of the board overseeing the entity must not be officers, employees, "substantial contributors," or a family member of such an officer, employee, or contributor. If an entity satisfies this initial test of independent governance, a campaign expenditure by the entity must, as a procedural matter, only be authorized by its independent directors without the participation of the minority of nonindependent directors.

63 For this purpose, Professor Buckles would incorporate the definition of a "substantial contributor" used in Section 507(d)(2) in the context of private foundations. In particular, Internal Revenue Code Section 507(d)(2) defines an individual as a "substantial contributor" if the individual and her spouse cumulatively contribute more than $5,000 in any year and if such cumulative contributions constitute more than 2 percent of total contributions received by the donee institution. I.R.C. § 507(d)(2), 26 U.S.C. § 507(d)(2).

64 Under Internal Revenue Code § 1, the current highest income tax bracket for individuals is 39.6 percent. Internal Revenue Code § 1, 26 U.S.C. § 1.

expenditure, and there would be no penalty for any in-person communication among church members.

Consider in this context an iconic moment in American history: Martin Luther King Sr.'s switch of his support in the 1960 presidential election from Richard M. Nixon to John F. Kennedy.[65] Rev. King announced that he now supported Kennedy (despite Kennedy's Catholicism) because of Kennedy's telephone call to Mrs. Coretta Scott King. In that call, Kennedy had expressed concern for the safety of Martin Luther King Jr., recently arrested by the Atlanta police and being held in a Georgia state prison.

Under Rev. Rul. 2007-41,[66] this endorsement, had it been made from the pulpit, could have cost Rev. King's church its tax-exempt status under Section 501(c)(3). However, as an oral communication with the church's members, a statement from the pulpit would have been protected by the safe-harbor Professor Buckles proposes for internal church communications. On the other hand, if Rev. King Sr. had allowed this statement to be videotaped and replayed on Atlanta's television stations, the relevant issue under the Buckles proposal would have been whether there was an "expenditure" (such as Rev. King's salary), which had been authorized by independent directors who compromised a majority of the church's board.

In contrast to Professor Buckles' proposal, I would not focus on the governance of the church but rather would emphasize the dichotomy between internal church communications and resource-diverting activity. I would also create special rules only for churches, understanding that a narrowly drawn exemption will entail borderline entanglement determining whether entities are or are not churches eligible for the safe harbor I suggest. That is a cost I would accept to protect the autonomy of internal church communications.

Unlike Professor Buckles, Attorney David S. Miller[67] would retain the Code's general ban on political campaigning by all Section 501(c)(3) organizations. However, Attorney Miller would create a statutory safe harbor available to all such organizations. Attorney Miller's safe harbor would be similar to Code Section 501(h)[68] but, unlike Section 501(h), would not be elective. Under Attorney Miller's proposal to amend the Code, campaigning by an organization with a single employee or a single independent contractor would be deemed de minimis if that employee or contractor spends less than 15 percent of her time on campaigning.[69] For a 501(c)(3)

---

[65] THEODORE WHITE, THE MAKING OF THE PRESIDENT 321–323 (1960).

[66] Rev. Rul. 2007-41, 2007-1 C.B. 1421.

[67] David S. Miller, *Reforming the Taxation of Exempt Organizations and Their Patrons*, 67 TAX LAW. 451 (2014).

[68] I.R.C. § 501(h), 26 U.S.C. § 501(h).

[69] Miller, *supra* note 67, at 506.

organization with two or more employees or independent contractors, the statutory safe harbor would apply as long as less than 10 percent of their collective time were devoted to political campaigning.[70] A second test to qualify for this safe harbor would require the tax-exempt entity to spend no more than the lesser of $5,000 or 10 percent of its nonsalary budget on political campaigning.[71]

Thus, an occasional sermon addressing political campaign issues or an isolated candidate endorsement like Rev. King's would be protected by Attorney Miller's safe harbor since relatively little of the minister's time would be involved in these isolated statements. Similarly, a newspaper ad like the pre-election advertisement paid for by Branch Ministries would pass muster if the cost were $5,000 or less and that advertisement represented all of the church's nonsalary campaign expenditures for the year.

If a tax-exempt organization's campaign outlays exceeded these safe harbor limits, Attorney Miller would apply an excise tax to these expenditures. In addition, the IRS could seek the revocation of tax-exempt status for political campaigning, though Attorney Miller believes that, under his approach, this power of revocation "would be applied sparingly."[72]

In contrast to the Buckles and Miller proposals to amend the Internal Revenue Code to provide political campaign safe harbors to all Section 501(c)(3) entities, Professor Lloyd Hitoshi Mayer concludes that some "[h]ouses of worship . . . have a strong argument that [the federal Religious Freedom Restoration Act (RFRA)] requires an exception to the [campaigning] prohibition in the unique context of in-person sermons during regular worship services."[73]

Professor Mayer also suggests that the RFRA and the First Amendment's Free Exercise Clause might protect "the internal religious communications of houses of worship"[74] from Code Section 501(c)(3)'s prohibition on campaigning.

Professor Mayer's vantage, protecting sermons and possibly other internal church communication, requires us to again revisit the issue which troubled the *Texas Monthly* plurality, namely, the borderline entanglement flowing from a narrowly drawn exemption for religious entities. In this case, the exception Professor Mayer would craft is narrow, since it would apply only to churches, not to nonchurch religious organizations or to any secular entities. My proposal is similarly narrow.

---

70 *Id.*

71 *Id.*

72 *Id.* at 507.

73 Mayer, *supra* note 4, at 1142.

74 *Id.* at 1216.

Attorney Deirdre Dessingue takes a particularly nuanced view of the relationship between religion and politics.[75] The church loses its "distinctive prophetic voice" when it intervenes in partisan politics.[76] On the other hand, she writes,

> [c]hurches have a played a pivotal role in every important political struggle since (and including) national independence: the abolition of slavery, gambling, child labor, prostitution, temperance, the death penalty, the war in Vietnam, abortion, and civil rights.[77]

From this premise, she calls for a fundamental contraction of the Code's prohibition on churches' political campaigning:

> The prohibition should be limited to explicit endorsements of or opposition to political candidates and other clear and unambiguous support, financial or otherwise. Discussion of issues should never constitute prohibited political activity.[78]

The views of Professor Allan J. Samansky are similar.[79] He calls for "a more liberal interpretation of the ban against campaigning by churches."[80] "[C]hurches and religious leaders should have virtually complete freedom to communicate with their congregations."[81] However, Professor Samansky would not permit "official endorsement by a church."[82] He would also keep current law for other tax-exempt organizations, arguing "that there are convincing arguments for treating churches differently from other section 501(c)(3) organizations when interpreting and applying the prohibition against intervening in campaigns."[83]

Professors Nina J. Crimm and Laurence H. Winer urge Congress to amend Section 501(c)(3) to permit all tax-exempt organizations, secular and religious, to engage in both "internal" and "external political campaign speech."[84] However, donors to any

---

75 Deirdre Dessingue, *Prohibition in Search of a Rationale: What the Tax Code Prohibits; Why; to What End?*, 42 B.C. L. Rev. 903 (2001).

76 *Id.* at 925.

77 *Id.* at 923 (parenthetical in original).

78 *Id.* at 928.

79 Allan J. Samansky, *Tax Consequences When Churches Participate in Political Campaigns*, 5 Geo. J.L. & Pub. Pol'y 145 (2007).

80 *Id.* at 151.

81 *Id.* at 165.

82 *Id.* at 178.

83 *Id.* at 152.

84 Nina J. Crimm & Laurence H. Winer, Politics, Taxes, and the Pulpit: Provocative First Amendment Conflicts 327 (2011).

organization engaging in such speech would lose the charitable deduction under Internal Revenue Code Section 170 for their contributions to that organization.[85]

From the foregoing, it is fair to say that no commentator is satisfied with the status quo. Those favoring the current statute call for better enforcement and more objective interpretive guidelines of Section 501(c)(3)'s ban on political campaigning. Critics view the Code's current prohibitions on campaigning and substantial lobbying by tax-exempt entities as intruding unacceptably into internal church autonomy.

The proponents of Section 501(c)(3) in its current form score their heaviest points when they raise the prospect of tax-deductible resource diversion. Without some restraints, nonprofits could easily become conduits for funneling income tax–deductible resources into political campaigning and lobbying. This is an outcome no one should favor.

Critics of the status quo occupy their strongest ground when they seek to protect internal communications within congregations. Current law intimately entangles church and state insofar as the Code now requires the IRS to monitor and evaluate discussions within congregations to ascertain if those discussions constitute campaigning or lobbying. Had the 501(c)(3) bans on campaigning and substantial lobbying been aggressively enforced in the past, American life would have been diminished. Such causes as abolitionism and civil rights were deeply anchored in America's churches.

Taking this debate into the 115th Congress, Representative Walter B. Jones Jr. of North Carolina has introduced legislation to repeal the Johnson Amendment in its entirety.[86] Senator James Lankford of Oklahoma and Representative Steve Scalise of Louisiana have proposed to amend Section 501(c)(3) to permit any tax-exempt organization to make any kind of statement "in the ordinary course of the organization's regular and customary activities in carrying out its exempt purpose" as long as such statement does not entail the organization "incurring . . . more than de minimis incremental expenses."[87] President Donald Trump, reiterating the position he took during the presidential campaign,[88] has pledged to "get rid of and totally destroy the Johnson Amendment."[89] The Jones proposal would leave intact Section 501(c)(3)'s prohibition on substantial lobbying activities by tax-exempt organizations while the safe harbor created by Lankford-Scalise legislation would immunize a tax-exempt organization's statements from the Section 501(c)(3) ban on substantial lobbying.

---

[85] *Id.*

[86] H.R. 172 (115th Cong., 1st sess.).

[87] S. 264 and H.R. 781 (115th Cong., 1st sess.).

[88] David Sherfinski, *Donald Trump's Push to Repeal Johnson Amendment Buoys Religious Freedom Advocates*, WASH. TIMES, Aug. 14, 2014.

[89] Abby Phillip, *Trump Asks for Prayers for Arnold Schwarzenegger's Ratings at National Prayer Breakfast*, WASH. POST, Feb. 2017. On May 4, 2017, President Trump further expressed his opposition to the Johnson Amendment in a *Presidential Executive Order Promoting Free Speech and Religious Liberty*, https://www.whitehouse.gov/the-press-office/2017/05/04/presidential-executive-order-promoting-free-speech-and-religious-liberty.

C. A PROPOSAL TO PROTECT INTERNAL CHURCH COMMUNICATIONS

I would resolve this debate by amending the Internal Revenue Code to create a statutory safe harbor protecting internal church communications from both the ban on political campaigning and the ban on substantial lobbying. No inference or presumption should arise as to activity or expression outside the proposed statutory safe harbor. This proposal would achieve a better balance by sheltering the internal expressive autonomy of churches while continuing to deter the use of churches and other tax-exempt organizations to divert tax-deductible resources into political activity. This limited statutory safe harbor would reduce the possibilities for enforcement entanglement since the IRS would no longer be required to monitor and evaluate internal church communications for their content.

Contrary to the recommendations of some commentators,[90] I would not treat "official" or "explicit" endorsements differently from other internal church discussions. A ban on express endorsements would require the IRS to continue to scrutinize in-house church communications. My proposal instead reduces the church-state enforcement entanglement which arises when the tax collector must monitor in-house church discussions. Such monitoring would continue if "official" and "explicit" endorsements remain off limits to tax-exempt churches. For this same reason, I disagree with the proposal of Professors Crimm and Winer, which would require the IRS to police churches (and other nonprofit entities) to determine if they engage in "political" speech.

Little of substance would be gained by outlawing "official" or "explicit" endorsements since skilled speakers can make their meanings clear without using those labels. A rhetorician as adroit as Rev. King Sr. could have effectively communicated his support for Kennedy's candidacy while eschewing terms like "official" and avoiding an express endorsement. To reduce church-state enforcement entanglement, the safe harbor protecting in-house church communication should be a true safe harbor, immunizing from IRS scrutiny all internal church discussions including any "official" or "explicit" endorsements of particular candidacies or causes.

My proposal also reflects the conclusion that, in entanglement terms, it is artificial to treat separately the Section 501(c)(3) ban on campaigning and that section's ban on substantial lobbying. Both prohibitions, in their current forms, raise the same question about the autonomy of church communications: Should the IRS be obligated to police discussions within religious congregations to enforce the limitations of Section 501(c)(3)? When a minister delivers a pro-life or pro-choice sermon, that

---

[90] Dessingue, *supra* note 75, at 928; Samansky, *supra* note 79, at 178.

sermon can, depending on the circumstances, be characterized under current law as a lobbying effort to mobilize public opinion or as political campaigning to support or oppose particular candidates. Either way, it is deeply entangling for the tax collector to be monitoring and evaluating this sermon.

To reduce enforcement entanglement between the IRS and churches, all pulpit communications (even "official" and "explicit" statements and endorsements) should be excluded from both the ban on political campaigning and the ban on lobbying. Commentators like Professor Colinvaux and Attorney Dessingue correctly observe that churches (including synagogues, mosques, and other such religious institutions) forfeit their distinctive voices when they become overtly partisan. But these congregations, not Congress, are responsible for protecting their respective voices. The revised statute should discourage the diversion of tax-exempt resources into campaigning and lobbying while safeguarding internal church discussions from church-state entanglement. Churches must themselves maintain their unique voices transcending partisanship.

My proposal raises an important issue at the borderline of the suggested exemption for in-house church communications: What is the pulpit in the digital age? This inquiry in turn raises two subquestions: What is a church? What, in a world of electronic media, are internal, pulpit-like communications?

As we saw in chapter three, many provisions of the Internal Revenue Code already pose the entangling borderline question whether particular institutions are churches or not. For example, the Code places churches into the public charity category rather than classifying them as private foundations.[91] In procedural terms, the Code excuses "churches, their integrated auxiliaries, and conventions or associations of churches" from filing annual returns[92] and from obtaining IRS confirmation of their tax-exempt status.[93] Similarly, the Code extends special audit protections to "any organization claiming to be a church"[94] and to "any convention or association of churches."[95] Church retirement plans receive more lenient treatment under the Code than do the retirement arrangements of nonchurch employers.[96] My proposal for a safe harbor for in-house church communications would create another potentially contentious

---

91 I.R.C. §§ 170(b)(1)(A)(i) and 509(a)(1), 26 U.S.C. §§ 170(b)(1)(A)(i) and 509(a)(1).

92 I.R.C. § 6033(a)(3)(A)(i), 26 U.S.C. § 6033(a)(3)(A)(i).

93 I.R.C. § 508(c)(1), 26 U.S.C. § 508(c)(1).

94 I.R.C. § 7611(h)(1)(A), 26 U.S.C. § 7611(h)(1)(A).

95 I.R.C. § 7611(h)(1)(B), 26 U.S.C. § 7611(h)(1)(B).

96 I.R.C. §§ 401(a) (flush language at end of section), 411(e)(1)(A), 414(d), 26 U.S.C. §§ 401(a) (flush language at end of section), 411(e)(1)(A), 414(d); ERISA § 4(b)(1), 29 U.S.C. § 1003(b)(1). *See Advocate Health Care Network v. Stapleton*, 2017 U.S. LEXIS 3554.

borderline between churches, entitled to the protection of such safe harbor for their in-house messaging, and nonchurches, not entitled to such protection from the Section 501(c)(3) bans on campaigning and substantial lobbying.

We again see that, in this area, there are no ideal solutions, just imperfect trade-offs. Through a safe harbor for in-house church communications, I propose to reduce the enforcement entanglement inherent in the IRS's policing of internal church discussions. That safe harbor would protect churches' in-house conversations from both the Section 501(c)(3) prohibition on campaigning and that section's prohibition of substantial lobbying. The resulting reduction of enforcement entanglement would come at a cost, namely, borderline entanglement as the IRS would monitor the boundaries of a safe harbor limited to internal church discussions to determine which organizations are (and are not) churches entitled to the protection of their internal messaging from IRS review.

Borderline entanglement could be mitigated by expanding the proposed safe harbor for in-house communications to cover the internal discussions of all religious organizations or, even more broadly, to cover in-house communications among all 501(c)(3) entities. However, I would not enlarge the proposed safe harbor to reach beyond internal church discussions. Supporters of current law correctly cite the danger that 501(c)(3) groups can be used to divert tax-deductible donations into campaigning and lobbying. Responding to this concern, my proposed statutory safe harbor should be limited to the internal communications of churches. This would leave the current statutory bans intact for all 501(c)(3) groups other than churches and would continue to apply those bans to churches outside the context of churches' internal communications.

In particular cases, it would be a challenge under my proposal to separate internal church communications protected by the suggested statutory safe harbor from other church activity. In today's world of the Internet and electronic media, the church's pulpit is not as clearly demarcated as it was in an earlier age. The line between internal communications and external outreach is not as clear today as it once was.

For example, a preacher in a megachurch may simultaneously broadcast her sermon to different locations at which the church conducts services. Those broadcasts will often be available to the world at large. Similarly, a minister may place her sermon on the church's website for the benefit of congregants who did not attend the service at which the sermon was delivered. While steps can be taken to limit the access of outsiders to these electronically transmitted communications, those limits will often be permeable.

The difficulties of distinguishing internal from external communications in the modern age may sometimes be even greater than these examples suggest. If a celebrity preacher, like Rev. Billy Graham or Rev. Rick Warren, today makes a politically salient announcement from the pulpit, that announcement will become known to the world at large moments later. Through social media and television, a celebrity preacher like Rev. Joel Osteen is regularly heard and read by millions each week.[97]

Under my proposed safe harbor for in-house church communications, *Branch Ministries*[98] would remain good law. Consequently, if a preacher's church paid for a newspaper ad or hired a public relations firm to disseminate his announcement beyond the membership of the church, that could constitute campaigning or lobbying and thus potentially trigger the prohibitions of Section 501(c)(3). The facts of *Branch Ministries* would cross the line from protected internal church communications to the diversion of tax-deductible resources to lobbying and campaigning. Hence, the safe harbor would not apply in that kind of situation since the church was reaching beyond its membership.

This approach would require difficult line-drawing problems. But what important legal principle does not, including the Johnson Amendment in its current form? On balance, the best, albeit imperfect trade-off, is to protect internal church communications while otherwise leaving in place the Internal Revenue Code's current prohibitions on tax-exempt organization's political campaign activity and substantial lobbying.

My proposal differs from the Jones bill[99] in two respects. The Jones legislation would apply to all activities of all 501(c)(3) entities. My proposal is narrower and would only immunize from scrutiny churches' internal communications. Moreover, the Jones proposal would leave intact the ban on "substantial lobbying" for all exempt organizations, including churches. My proposal in this respect is broader and would carve a safe harbor from Section 501(c)(3)'s lobbying ban for internal church communications.

The Lankford-Scalise legislation[100] comes closer to my proposal but is still different in important respects. That legislation would protect all Section 501(c)(3) organizations. I suggest that protection just be extended to churches. Since the problem is untoward government intrusion into churches' internal communications, the solution is the protection of such church communications.

Moreover, the Lankford-Scalise bill would permit any kind of statement "in the ordinary course of the organization's regular and customary activities in carrying out its exempt purpose."[101] In contrast, I propose more targeted protection for churches'

---

[97] Http://www.onlinechristiancolleges.com/joel-osteen/.

[98] *Branch Ministries v. Rossotti*, 211 F.3d 137, 140 (D.C. Cir. 2000).

[99] H.R. 172 (115th Cong., 1st sess.).

[100] S. 264 and H.R. 781 (115th Cong., 1st sess.).

[101] *Id.*

internal communications. Under the Lankford-Scalise bill, a nonchurch religious organization could construe its exempt purpose as including communication aimed at the general public. This is too broad a standard and could permit the diversion of tax-deductible contributions to political campaigns. My proposal, in contrast, would protect church autonomy by creating a safe harbor limited to churches' internal communications. While securing the First Amendment rights of churches (and similar congregations such as synagogues, temples, and mosques), my approach would keep a stronger barrier against the potential use of tax-deductible donations for political campaigning. Since the problem is untoward government intrusion into churches' internal communications, the solution should be targeted to the protection of such church communications. My proposal would constitute a better balance of the contending considerations.

I envision the proposed safe-harbor as an amendment to Internal Revenue Code Section 501(c)(3) to provide that internal church communications cannot be deemed campaigning or lobbying. The various states could experiment with different variations of these and other proposals. I would favor such experimentation as part of the desirable diversity with which the states tax and exempt churches and other religious entities in different ways. However, the states, while pursuing varied approaches to the sales and property tax treatment of churches and other religious entities, in practice follow the federal government's policies toward the income tax treatment of churches and other eleemosynary entities.[102] I consequently suspect that a federal safe harbor along the lines I propose would become the state law norm as well.

D. EXPANDING THE SALES TAX OBLIGATIONS OF CHURCHES

An attractive feature of our federal system is that the states can and do experiment with different tax treatments of churches and other religious institutions. As we saw in chapters two[103] and four,[104] within the broad national consensus that church property is tax exempt, the implementation of that exemption varies among the different states, particularly as to the tax status of parsonages and religious facilities such as summer camps. Even greater, as we saw in chapter four,[105] is the diversity of the states' sales tax treatments of churches and religious institutions.

---

[102] Though eight states with corporate income taxes do not apply tax the unrelated business taxable incomes of exempt institutions.

[103] *See supra* at 25–36.

[104] *See supra* at 67–77.

[105] *See supra* at 77–97.

The sales tax is a bulwark of state and local government finance.[106] It is, however, an open question whether the sales tax will be adapted to the challenges of the twenty-first century. Two such challenges are widely acknowledged: The difficulties of collecting sales tax on Internet purchases[107] and the omission of most services from the states' sales tax bases. The states' sales tax bases are now restricted to tangible personal property and a limited number of services.[108] As services constitute an increasing percentage of consumer outlays, the failure to tax most services hobbles sales tax revenues, largely tied to consumers' purchases of tangible personal property.

As they update their respective sales tax statutes to address these challenges, the states should expand the sales tax obligations of churches and other religious organizations, both as sellers and as buyers. Expanding the sales tax liabilities of sectarian entities would enhance state revenues and advance economic neutrality while engendering comparatively little enforcement entanglement. Sales taxes are typically triggered by cash purchases. Cash transactions are self-valuing. A cash purchaser has the liquidity to pay the sales tax triggered by his purchase. No doctrinal issues comparable to the "ordinary and necessary" inquiry of the income tax[109] arise in the context of the sales tax. Thus, unlike the ad valorem property taxation of churches or the taxation of churches' net incomes, expanding the sales tax obligations of sectarian sellers and buyers would generate relatively little church-state entanglement but would yield in an economically neutral manner additional revenue to finance public services, reduce tax rates, or both.

Consider initially the ten states which impose upon churches both the obligation to collect sales tax on the items they sell and the duty to pay sales tax on the items they purchase. In *Jimmy Swaggart Ministries v. Board of Equalization*,[110] discussed in chapter one,[111] the U.S. Supreme Court upheld against constitutional challenge California's sales tax, which in this fashion imposes sales tax obligations on religious entities both as sellers and as buyers.

---

106 Walter Hellerstein, Kirk J. Stark, John A. Swain, & Joan M. Youngman, State and Local Taxation: Cases and Materials 651–652 (10th ed. 2014).

107 *Id.* at 850–866. *See also* David Brunori, *What You Should Know About the Sales Tax*, Tax Analysts Blog (July 20, 2016). On certain states' efforts to tax sales made in electronic commerce, *see* Edward A. Zelinsky, *The Political Process Argument for the Supreme Court to Overrule* Quill, 82 Brook. L. Rev. 1177 (2017); Edward A. Zelinsky, *California's Once and Future "Amazon" Law*, 62 State Tax Notes 83 (2011); Edward A. Zelinsky, *Lobbying Congress: Amazon Laws in the Lands of Lincoln and Mt. Rushmore*, 60 State Tax Notes 557 (2011).

108 Hellerstein et al., *supra* note 106 at 657–658 and 841–852.

109 I.R.C. § 162(a), 26 U.S.C. § 162(a).

110 493 U.S. 378 (1990).

111 *See supra* at 16–18.

As a matter of tax policy, economic neutrality favors taxes with broad bases and relatively low rates since such taxes interfere minimally with market-based economic decisions and are fairest to taxpayers engaging in economically equivalent transactions.[112] Considerations of equity and economic neutrality suggest that all nonprofit institutions, including churches, should pay and collect sales taxes to avoid the economic distortion and inequity which results when some transactions are taxed but economically comparable events are not. If, for example, a church purchases coffee and cake to serve to parishioners after services, that purchase is indistinguishable from the purchase of coffee and cake by these parishioners to consume when they come home from church. In the interests of equity, revenue, and economic neutrality, these two equivalent purchases should be taxed the same way.

The offsetting consideration is the possibility of unacceptable church-state enforcement entanglement when the church is subject to tax. However, when the church pays cash for the coffee and cake to feed its members, the resulting tax is easily determined and the church has the cash to pay the tax. Given prevailing sales tax rates in the United States, at worst, the church can buy a little less cake to pay the tax.

As we saw in chapter four,[113] some states only impose sales tax obligations on churches as sellers while other states just impose sales tax obligations on churches as buyers. A desirable reform would be for more of these states to follow California's path and impose on churches sales tax obligations both as both buyers and as sellers. Short of this, the states can, in the interests of revenue and economic neutrality, significantly simplify and expand churches' sales tax liabilities with little church-state entanglement resulting from that expansion.

Consider, for example, Illinois, which excludes from its sales tax purchases of personal property by "charitable, religious or educational"[114] organizations while generally requiring those organizations[115] to collect tax on their sales of tangible personal property.[116] Despite the general obligation to collect sales tax on its sales, an Illinois religious organization need not collect tax on its sales of tangible personal property to its members.[117] Thus, if an Illinois synagogue's gift shop sells a pair of Sabbath candles to a nonmember for cash, the synagogue collects sales tax while the same cash sale of candles to a member of the congregation is tax free.

---

[112] Edward A. Zelinsky, *For Realization: Income Taxation, Sectoral Accretionism and the Virtue of Attainable Virtues*, 19 CARDOZO L. REV. 861, 892–893, 906–909, 917–918, 931, 958 (1997).

[113] *See supra* at 84–90. Some states condition either form of sales tax immunity on IRS confirmation of tax-exempt status. *See supra* at 90–96.

[114] 35 ILL. COMP. STAT. ANN. 120/2-5(11). There is an identical exemption for purposes of the Illinois use tax. 35 ILCS 105/3-5(4).

[115] 86 Ill. Admin. Code § 130.2005(a)(1)(E).

[116] 35 ILL. COMP. STAT. ANN. 120/1 (seventh paragraph, defining "sale at retail").

[117] *Id.* at subparagraph (1).

Unlike Illinois, other states requiring churches to collect sales tax do not distinguish between sales to members and sales to nonmembers. Rather, these states mandate that churches collect tax regardless of the membership status of the purchaser. Thus, a synagogue in Virginia (unlike a synagogue in Illinois) must collect sales tax if its gift shop sells candles to a member as well as to a nonmember.[118] Illinois' distinction between tax-free sales to members and taxable sales to nonmembers is problematic since the two kinds of sales are economically indistinguishable. Both a sale to a member and a sale to a nonmember are self-valuing cash transactions which entail little church-state entanglement if taxed.

Despite its general obligation to collect sales tax, an Illinois religious organization need not collect tax on "occasional dinners, socials or similar activities" even if "such activities are open to the public."[119] This kind of exception for church-supplied food is more widespread than is the sales tax exemption for sales to members—and is equally hard to justify. For example, Nebraska, like Illinois, requires eleemosynary institutions to collect sales tax on their sales but exempts churches from the obligation to collect sales tax on food "sold by a church at a function of such church."[120] Pennsylvania similarly immunizes from sales taxation food sold by a church "on [its] premises . . . in the ordinary course of its activities."[121]

Just as the distinction between tax-free sales to members and taxable sales to nonmembers is problematic, it is difficult to justify the common sales tax exemption for churches' retail food sales. A church charging for a "dinner[], social[] or similar activit[y]"[122] is no different from a restaurant supplying a meal for the same price. The price the church levies for a ticket to a congregational dinner is transparent while tax can be (and in many states is) added onto that price. Little entanglement would result from taxing these sales. Many states, such as New York, already impose sales tax when nonprofit organizations, including churches, charge for meals.[123] Such taxation produces revenue in an economically neutral manner with little enforcement entanglement.

Yet another area where churches' sales tax collection obligations could be expanded is the arena of casual sales. States typically exempt from taxation casual sales such as transactions at garage sales or at the proverbial neighborhood

---

[118] 23 Va. Admin. Code 10-210-310(I)(1) (Virginia churches "are required to register as dealers, collect the tax from customers (who may include church members, visitors, or other persons outside the church membership")) (parentheses in original).

[119] 35 ILL. COMP. STAT. ANN. 120/1 (seventh paragraph, last sentence).

[120] NEB. REV. STAT. ANN. § 77-2704.10(2).

[121] 61 PA. CODE § 32.21(c)(3)(ii).

[122] 35 ILL. COMP. STAT. ANN. 120/1 (seventh paragraph, last sentence).

[123] 20 NYCRR § 529.7(i)(3), Example 12.

lemonade stand. Such exemptions make sense administratively. It is not cost-efficient to send tax collectors to patrol lawn sales. It is unrealistic to expect high levels of compliance if casual sales are taxed. The taxation of casual sales would strike many rank-and-file taxpayers as inappropriate, flunking the tax policy test of public acceptability. States properly recognize these realities when they exempt casual sales from sales taxation.

It is sensible for a state's casual sale exception to apply to eleemosynary institutions, including churches. If a church cleans out its basement and sells the items it finds, the church should receive the same sales tax–free treatment as would a family conducting an isolated yard sale. However, many states provide broader sales tax exemptions for the casual sales of churches and other nonprofit entities. There is no compelling defense of these broader exemptions for eleemosynary entities' casual sales.

For example, Maine's sales tax statute exempts from taxation any person's casual sales.[124] The statute defines a tax-exempt casual sale as "an isolated transaction" not conducted "in the ordinary course of repeated and successive transactions of like character."[125]

The Maine statute also provides a special exemption for any "civic, religious or fraternal organization" which conducts "a bazaar, fair, rummage sale, picnic or similar event"[126] as long as the organizations' sale activities are not "continuing."[127] This special exemption permits "the sales of candy, light bulbs, novelties or other tangible personal property" for "fund raising campaigns of limited duration."[128]

There is no compelling reason for this additional exemption, which allows religious, civic, and fraternal groups to conduct tax-free sales which are not "casual" under the generally applicable definition, but which qualify as tax free under the special exemption.

Consider, for example, a church conducting a candy sale to raise funds. The candy is typically the same as or similar to the candy purchasable at a commercial store. If this sale does not meet the general test for a tax-free "casual" sale, there is no compelling reason for Maine's more generous exemption limited to philanthropic entities.

To take another case, Ohio exempts from sales taxation any person's "(c)asual sales."[129] In addition, Ohio exempts from tax the sales of tangible personal property

---

[124] 36 MAINE REV. STAT. § 1752(1-D).

[125] *Id.*

[126] *Id.*

[127] Maine Revenue Services, *Sales, Fuel & Special Tax Division, Instructional Bulletin No. 9, Casual and Infrequent Sales* (Oct. 1, 2013), available at https://wwwl.mainegov/revenue/salesuse/Bull910012013.pdf.

[128] *Id.*

[129] OHIO REV. CODE ANN.§ 5739.02(B)(8).

by eleemosynary institutions, including churches, for six or fewer days "in any calendar year."[130] There is no convincing reason why churches and other nonprofits in the Buckeye State are afforded this special sales tax exemption rather than being required to rely on the same casual sales exemption as applies to other sellers.

These kinds of reforms—taxing sales to church members, taxing sales of church-provided meals, taxing sales which fall outside general exemptions for casual sales—are, in the grand scheme of things, small changes. But the nature of the sales tax is that any particular item taxed or exempted will often be small. The sales tax is the cumulative total of such small items.

Consider finally the four states which neither require churches to collect taxes on their retail sales nor pay sales taxes on their retail purchases. These blanket exemptions can be understood as expressions of tax-related symmetry: From this vantage, if churches (and other nonprofit organizations) do not pay income or property taxes, they should not collect or pay sales taxes either. Alternatively, blanket sales tax immunity for churches as buyers and sellers might reflect the judgment that even the minimal church-state enforcement entanglement stemming from sales taxation is too great to justify the taxation of church-related sales and purchases.

I favor a different balance. Requiring churches and other religious entities to collect and pay sales tax makes the tax fairer and more economically neutral by taxing equivalent transactions regardless of the parties involved. It also raises revenue which can be used to finance state services, lower sales tax rates, or both. These benefits can be obtained with minimal church-state entanglement since most sales are self-valuing and involve cash, some of which can and should be diverted to pay the tax.

E. CONCLUSION

The two issues discussed in this chapter—churches' internal communications, their sales tax liabilities—reflect the centrality of entanglement concerns to the relationship between the contemporary church and the contemporary tax system. Entanglement considerations counsel greater protection than current law provides for speech within churches. Entanglement considerations similarly indicate that the sales tax obligations of sectarian institutions should be expanded.

---

130 *Id.* § 5739.03(B)(9)(a).

8

CONSTITUTIONAL AND TAX POLICY ISSUES

IN THIS FINAL chapter, I discuss six important debates about constitutional and tax policy issues in the context of taxing or exempting the church and other religious institutions. The underlying theme of this chapter is that debate about the First Amendment and about tax policy would be enhanced by greater attention to the imperfect trade-offs at play when taxing or exempting churches and other religious entities. Such debate would also be enriched by greater consideration of the policies which Congress and the state legislatures have embraced in response to the relevant constitutional and tax policy concerns.

The first of the constitutional disputes discussed in this chapter is the controversy about the original understanding of the religion clauses of the First Amendment. Whatever the relevance of that history in other contexts, the tax status of churches was not a salient concern in the drafting or enactment of the First Amendment. Consequently, the original understanding of the Establishment and Free Exercise Clauses furnishes no guidance whether to tax or to exempt sectarian institutions and actors.

A second controversial topic is whether the First Amendment should be construed as authorizing judicially created exemptions from laws of general applicability when such laws burden religion. The U.S. Supreme Court created such exemptions in *Murdock*[1] and *Follett*[2] when it relieved Jehovah's Witnesses from municipal licensing fees for their religious solicitation. Per the Supreme Court's more recent decisions in *Lee*[3] and *Jimmy Swaggart Ministries*,[4] the First Amendment today provides no support to sectarian actors and institutions seeking judicially imposed exemptions from generally applicable taxes. Under current law, sectarian groups seeking tax exemptions must obtain such exemptions legislatively. That is proper since legislatures can better make the imperfect trade-offs inherent in taxation than can courts.

A third important controversy has been the criteria, if any, which should guide legislative decision-making in determining the proper relationship between church and state. Some commentators conclude that no overriding theory satisfactorily articulates the correct relationship between church and state. These theory-skeptical commentators argue that the best we can do is to resolve particular controversies as well as possible, acknowledging that there are no ideal choices.

The taxation and exemption of churches and religious entities confirms this cautionary perspective. In the tax context, important criteria should illuminate legislative decisions to tax or to exempt religious institutions and actors. Some taxes, because of the liquidity and valuation challenges they entail, entangle church and state more deeply than do taxes involving self-valuing cash transactions. Other taxes, if applied to sectarian institutions, would require tax collectors and courts to enmesh themselves in religious doctrine and practices. Important tax policy criteria—such as revenue, economic neutrality, public acceptability, administrability—should inform legislative decision-making as well. At the end of the day, the decision to tax or to exempt churches and other religious institutions and actors requires legislative determinations which balance these legitimate and offsetting considerations. These case-specific determinations cannot be reduced to any grand formula.

A fourth significant constitutional debate pertains to the rhetoric of separationism. Even if the original understanding of the First Amendment was quite limited, today that amendment is widely understood in separationist terms. However, the separation of church and state is not a self-defining proposition, particularly in the tax context. Enforcing generally applicable taxes against sectarian entities and individuals does not separate church and state but entangles them. The relationship between the tax collector and the taxpayer is among the most enmeshing

[1] *Murdock v. Pennsylvania*, 319 U.S. 105 (1943).

[2] *Follett v. Town of McCormick*, 321 U.S. 573 (1944).

[3] *United States v. Lee*, 455 U.S. 252 (1982).

[4] *Jimmy Swaggart Ministries v. Board of Equalization*, 493 U.S. 378 (1990).

legal relationships in our society. Opponents of sectarian tax exemptions can credibly claim to be seeking many objectives but separating church and state is not one of these.

After examining these four constitutional controversies, this chapter turns to two topics of tax policy. First, I discuss the general propriety of the income tax–exemption of nonprofit entities. Important commentators argue that it is both feasible and desirable to impose income taxes upon eleemosynary entities when such entities generate profits from their activities. My analysis suggests that, whatever the merits of subjecting hospitals, universities, and similar commercial-style secular philanthropies to income taxation, it would be highly entangling to tax churches on the income derived their basic religious activities. However, the investment incomes of church (and other religious) endowments could be taxed with less enforcement entanglement since the taxation of passive investment incomes such as interest and dividends does not entail the same kinds of entangling inquiries as does the taxation of income from active operations.

I close this chapter by discussing commentators who have challenged and who have supported the unrelated business income tax (UBIT). The UBIT is the most important evidence contradicting my thesis that the federal and state governments today generally exempt churches and other sectarian entities from the taxes with the greatest potential for church-state entanglement. The UBIT is the important case to the contrary, a tax imposed on churches with significant possibilities for church-state entanglement. It is very entangling for the tax collector and the courts to assess whether a particular activity is related or not to a church's mission and for them to then apply to that activity the regular rules of income taxation.

Underlying my discussion of these six topics is the theme that debate about the First Amendment and tax policy would be strengthened by more attention to the considerations at play when taxing or exempting religious entities. Our discussions of both taxes and the U.S. Constitution are diminished when each of these important topics is effectively cabined from the other.

A. THE ORIGINAL UNDERSTANDING OF THE RELIGION CLAUSES OF THE FIRST AMENDMENT: PROHIBITING A NATIONAL CHURCH VS. NONPREFERENTIALISM VS. SEPARATIONISM

The original understanding of the Religion Clauses of the First Amendment is a matter of considerable controversy. Commentators on this topic fall into three broad categories: those contending that the Establishment Clause was originally comprehended in very limited terms, as only prohibiting a national church; those asserting that the First Amendment was initially understood as compatible with governmental assistance provided to all religions on a nonpreferential basis; and those arguing that the First Amendment was interpreted from the beginning as erecting a formidable wall of separation between church and state.

Looking at this debate, I conclude that the tax status of churches was not a salient concern when the First Amendment was drafted and ratified because taxation was not yet systematized and recurring. Thus, the original understanding of the First Amendment, whatever its relevance in other contexts, provides no guidance whether to tax or to exempt sectarian institutions and actors.

Donald L. Drakeman affirms the view that the First Amendment's "original meaning" was quite limited: "to forbid the establishment of a single national religion."[5] Drakeman argues that the adoption of the Establishment Clause was perceived at the time as an event of little import since no one favored the single, established national church which the amendment banned. Outlawing a national church was "noncontroversial,"[6] an "anodyne"[7] measure which aroused no opposition since the First Amendment was understood as merely barring a national church, which no one sought.

Advancing this initial understanding of the First Amendment as a limited prohibition on a national church, Drakeman criticizes the "Virginia-centric"[8] narrative of the amendment propounded by Chief Justice Morrison R. Waite in *Reynolds v. United States*[9] and by Justice Hugo Black in *Everson v. Board of Education*.[10] This narrative portrays the original interpretation of the First Amendment as considerably more robust than a simple prohibition of a single national church. This narrative of the Old Dominion is the source of the "wall of separation" metaphor which has been widely embraced by courts and commentators.

In *Reynolds*, the U.S. Supreme Court affirmed the bigamy conviction of a member of the Church of Jesus Christ of Latter-Day Saints despite his claim that bigamy was his religious duty and was thus protected from criminal prosecution by the First Amendment. Central to *Reynolds* was Chief Justice Waite's invocation of James Madison's "Memorial and Remonstrance,"[11] Thomas Jefferson's letter to the Danbury Baptists,[12] and the Virginia statute guaranteeing religious freedom drafted

[5] Donald L. Drakeman, Church, State, and Original Intent ix (2010).
[6] *Id.* at 262.
[7] *Id.* at 282.
[8] *Id.* at 146.
[9] 98 U.S. 145 (1879).
[10] 330 U.S. 1 (1947), *rehearing denied*, 330 U.S. 855 (1947).
[11] *Reynolds*, 98 U.S. at 163.
[12] *Id.* at 164.

by Jefferson.[13] From these documents, Chief Justice Waite ascribed an expansive reach to the First Amendment. In a particularly influential observation, the Chief Justice opined that Jefferson's "wall of separation between church and State" is "almost . . . an authoritative declaration of the scope and effect of the [First] amendment."[14]

In *Everson*, Justice Black revisited this Virginia-based terrain to buttress a separationist narrative of the origins of the First Amendment.[15] Relying in important part upon the materials invoked in *Reynolds*, Justice Black concluded that the First Amendment goes beyond the limited prohibition of a national church.[16] Rather, Jefferson's wall of separation as embodied in the amendment prevents, *inter alia*, "laws which aid one religion, aid all religions, or prefer one religion over another."[17] Moreover, the wall of separation created by First Amendment means that

> [n]either a state nor the Federal Government can, openly or secretly, participate in the affairs of any religious organizations or groups and *vice versa*.[18]

Drakeman argues that the absence of controversy when the First Congress adopted the First Amendment belies this Virginia-based narrative. Had the proposed amendment been understood then in broad, separationist terms, he argues, the amendment would have provoked considerable debate in the First Congress which enacted it. Instead, the amendment aroused no opposition, suggesting that it was understood as doing no more than forbidding a national church, which no one favored anyway.

Drakeman acknowledges that the concept of religious establishment was, at the time the First Amendment was adopted, "a concept in transition."[19] He nevertheless concludes that the weight of the evidence indicates that the Establishment Clause of the First Amendment was originally comprehended as no more than a noncontroversial prohibition of a single national church. Neither the "brief and desultory" discussion in the First Congress[20] nor the unedifying records from the state ratification debates[21] supports or refutes either the nonpreferentialist interpretation of the First Amendment as permitting generally available assistance to all religions or the separationist construction of the amendment as impeding contact between church and

[13] *Id.* at 163.

[14] *Id.* at 164.

[15] *Everson*, 330 U.S. at 11–16.

[16] *Id.* at 15–16.

[17] *Id.* at 15.

[18] *Id.* at 16 (italics in original).

[19] DRAKEMAN, *supra* note 5, at 228.

[20] *Id.* at 196.

[21] *Id.* at 214–215.

state. There is, according to Drakeman, no convincing evidence of original intent either way. All that remains of the original intent behind the First Amendment is a limited prohibition of a national church.

Professor Robert L. Cord agrees that the First Amendment was originally understood as preventing a national church. However, like other nonpreferentialists, he goes beyond that conclusion. The amendment, Professor Cord argues, was also originally interpreted as compatible with government assistance available to all religions as long as no religion or group of religions is favored over any other.

Central to Professor Cord's case are the religious-focused draft amendments which several states proposed when they ratified the Constitution. Also important to his argument are the early actions of the federal government when the First Amendment was proposed and after the amendment was enacted.

The states which asked for a religious-oriented amendment to the Constitution opposed a national church. However, Professor Cord contends, these states did not reject government assistance to religion available evenhandedly to all. They sought instead to assure "that no particular religious sect or society ought to be favored or established by law in preference to others."[22]

Moreover, in its early history, the federal government distributed assistance to religion in a variety of forms. This aid included the subvention of religious missionaries serving various Native American tribes. From this evidence, Professor Cord concludes, the First Amendment

> was intended to prevent the establishment of a national church or religion, or the giving of any religious sect or denomination a preferred status . . . There appears to be no historical evidence that the First Amendment was intended to preclude Federal governmental aid to religion when it was provided on a nondiscriminatory basis. Nor does there appear to be any historical evidence that the First Amendment was intended to provide *absolute separation or independence* of religion and the national state. The actions of the early Congresses and Presidents, in fact, suggest quite the opposite.[23]

Professor Cord points as well to presidential Thanksgiving proclamations infused with religious rhetoric[24] and to congressionally authorized chaplains for Congress and the military.[25] He further rejects the separationist narrative advanced in

---

[22] Robert L. Cord, Separation of Church and State: Historical Fact and Current Fiction 161 (1982) (quoting North Carolina's and Rhode Island's proposed amendments to the Constitution).

[23] *Id.* at 15.

[24] *Id.* at 51.

[25] *Id.* at 53.

Reynolds and *Everson*, citing early federal appropriations for the propagation of religious teaching for Native Americans.[26] It is, Professor Cord contends, impossible to reconcile President Jefferson's approval of such appropriations with the Establishment Clause if the First Amendment had been understood as erecting a strict wall of church-state separation. From these sources, Professor Cord concludes that the historical purpose of the First Amendment was "to prohibit Congress from establishing a national religion or putting one religion or religious sect in a preferred status."[27] The amendment was not intended to prevent assistance generally available for all religions as long as no "single religion, religious sect, or religious tradition" was given "a legally preferred status."[28]

In contrast, Professor Leonard W. Levy is a strong separationist.[29] Professor Levy, like Drakeman and others,[30] views the legislative debates in the First Congress as "brief, listless and unclear."[31] Professor Levy argues further that seven states at the time the First Amendment was adopted had establishments which were not exclusive to a single sect. Rather, these states' establishments entailed general public support for many or all Protestant denominations. Hence, when the First Amendment prohibited federal laws "respecting an establishment of religion," this was understood as forbidding all federal support for any religion even when such support is evenhanded, applicable to multiple or all religions:

> After the American Revolution seven of the fourteen states that comprised the Union in 1791 authorized establishments of religion by law. Not one state maintained a single or preferential establishment of religion. An establishment of religion meant to those who framed and ratified the First Amendment what it meant in those seven states, and in all seven it meant public support of religion on a nonpreferential basis. It was specifically this public support on a nonpreferential basis that the establishment clause of the First Amendment sought to forbid.[32]

---

[26] *Id.* at 58.

[27] *Id.* at 160.

[28] *Id.* at 214.

[29] Leonard W. Levy, The Establishment Clause: Religion and the First Amendment (2nd ed. 2007).

[30] *See, e.g.*, Fergus M. Bordewich, The First Congress: How James Madison, George Washington, and a Group of Extraordinary Men Invented the Government 115 (2016) (The First Congress' debate about the Bill of Rights "was remarkably short, snappish, and driven by the politics of the moment . . ."); Nina J. Crimm & Laurence H. Winer, Politics, Taxes, and the Pulpit: Provocative First Amendment Conflicts 159 (2011) ("the sparse congressional record of the First Congress . . .").

[31] Levy, *supra* note 29, at 133.

[32] *Id.* at xxii.

Professor Levy supports Jefferson's "wall of separation" as the most compelling original characterization of the First Amendment:

> Despite continuing complaints about the wall of separation between government and religion, that is the policy embodied by the establishment clause. The Constitution erected that wall.[33]

Like Mr. Drakeman, Professor Levy is critical of a narrow focus on the history of church-state relations in Virginia.[34] Other states' histories "are equally important."[35] These histories, Professor Levy asserts, reveal that, when the First Amendment was adopted, a religious establishment meant, not a single, European-style exclusively financed church, but support for religion more generally:

> An establishment of religion in America at the time of the framing and ratification of the Bill of Rights meant government aid and sponsorship of religion, principally by impartial tax support of the institutions of religion, all the churches.[36]

Hence, he concludes, when the First Amendment declared that Congress could make no laws "respecting an establishment of religion," those adopting and ratifying this language comprehended it as preventing any federal aid to religion, even aid distributed nonpreferentially.[37]

The first two interpretations of the original understanding of the First Amendment—the amendment simply prohibited a national church or also condoned public aid distributed to religion nonpreferentially—do not challenge the network of church-related tax exemptions that exists today. That network does not constitute a single, forbidden national church. Those exemptions apply nonpreferentially to all religions.

Moreover, the documents which are central to the Virginia-based, separationist narrative do not challenge those tax exemptions either. These documents do not

---

[33] *Id.* at 245.

[34] *Id.* at 75.

[35] *Id.*

[36] *Id.* at 76.

[37] While Professor Levy is solidly in the separationist camp, he is critical of those he views as overly dogmatic in pressing the separationist cause: "forebearance is sometimes better than disputation or litigation." *Id.* at 243. Professor Levy, for example, believes that the U.S. Supreme Court was wrong in *Board of Education of Kiryas Joel Village School District v. Grumet*, 512 U.S. 687 (1994), to declare unconstitutional a public school district the boundaries of which were drawn around a village of Jews who are members of the Satmar Hasidic sect. LEVY, *supra* note 29, at 253–256.

indicate that either Jefferson or Madison viewed tax exemption as undermining (or buttressing) the wall of church-state separation. Indeed, there is no indication that Jefferson or Madison thought about tax exemption when they wrote these now-iconic documents. This is not surprising since, when these documents were written, taxation was not as systematic as it is today. The modern sales and income taxes lay well in the future and property taxation was then not as routinized as it currently is. Thus, tax exemptions for sectarian institutions were not as salient as they are today.

Consider first Jefferson's letter to the Danbury Baptists.[38] That short (three paragraph) epistle says nothing about taxing churches or, for that matter, says nothing about any particular issue of public policy. The letter quotes the Establishment and Free Exercise Clauses and asserts that, by adopting the First Amendment, "the whole American people" built "a wall of separation between Church & State."[39] Jefferson neither tells the Danbury Baptists that this wall requires their church to pay tax nor tells them that this wall guarantees their church tax exemption to separate it from the state.

Madison's lengthier "Memorial"[40] similarly provides no explicit guidance on the taxation or exemption of churches. To the extent the "Memorial" is suggestive on the subject of tax exemption, the "Memorial" intimates that the tax exemption of churches is compelled. "Religion," Madison declares, "is wholly exempt from" the "cognizance" of "Civil Society."[41] Since "Religion" is "exempt from the authority of the Society at large, still less can it be subject to that of the Legislative Body."[42] The bar against public support for religion is absolute since minor, apparently de minimis, subventions for religion can lead to full-blown subsidy of the sectarian:

> [T]he same authority which can force a citizen to contribute three pence only of his property for the support of any one establishment, may force him to conform to any other establishment in all cases whatsoever . . .[43]

Madison wrote these oft-quoted words before the modern "Legislative Body" provided to churches the panoply of public services which are common today, for example, police and fire protection to church buildings and Social Security coverage to nonclerical church employees.[44] Perhaps Madison would have written these words

---

38 Thomas Jefferson, *Letter to the Danbury Baptists*, Jan. 1, 1802, http://www.loc.gov/loc/lcib/9806/danpre.html.

39 *Id.*

40 James Madison, *Memorial and Remonstrance against Religious Assessments*, June 20, 1785, http://press-pubs.uchicago.edu/founders/documents/amendI_religions43.html.

41 *Id.*

42 *Id.*

43 *Id.*

44 Municipal police and fire departments as we know them today were first established well into the nineteenth century. Boston is generally credited with having established the first modern municipal police

differently in such a world. Perhaps not. Perhaps "exempt[ion] from the authority . . . of the Legislative Body" implied for Madison exemption from all taxation, though later in his life Madison criticized Kentucky's tax exemption for churches.[45] In any event, the "Memorial," if accepted as an authoritative statement of the original understanding of the First Amendment, provides no explicit direction on the taxation or exemption of churches and other sectarian institutions. The tax exemption of churches was, at the time of the "Memorial," not the prominent issue it would later become.

Much of the Virginia Religious Freedom Act[46] is a lengthy preamble expressing sentiments similar to those of Jefferson's letter and Madison's "Memorial": "[T]o compel a man to furnish contributions of money for the propagation of opinions which he disbelieves is sinful and tyrannical."[47] The statute's operative language declares that "no man shall be compelled to frequent or support any religious worship, place, or ministry whatsoever, nor shall be enforced, restrained, molested, or burthened in his body or goods, nor shall otherwise suffer on account of his religious opinions or belief[s] . . ."[48] The statute neither requires the taxation of religious entities nor declares that tax exemption constitutes forbidden "support" of churches.

It is not surprising that these Virginia-based documents do not address the taxation or exemption of churches. At the time these documents were written, the modern sales and income taxes lay well in the future. Property taxation was then not as systematic as it is today. As Professor Stephen Diamond observes, "routine, annual taxation did not become a feature of American fiscal life until after the economic crisis of 1837."[49] In a similar vein, John W. Whitehead notes that, during the Founding era, "notions concerning tax exemption for religious groups were not extensively developed in a formalized way."[50] Similarly, Professor John Witte Jr. indicates that the criticism of church tax exemptions "as vestiges of religious establishment" dates

department in 1838. Gary Potter, *The History of Policing in the United States*, Part 1, EASTERN KENTUCKY UNIVERSITY: POLICY STUDIES ONLINE (June 25, 2013), http://www.plsonline.eku.edu/insidelook/history-policing-united-states-part-1. Cincinnati is generally credited with having created the first modern fire department in 1853. *Cincinnati Fire Department: First in the Nation*, CITY OF CINCINNATI, http://www.cincinnati-oh.gov/fire/history/. These developments occurred well after Madison wrote his *Memorial and Remonstrance against Religious Assessments* in 1785.

[45] LEVY, *supra* note 29, at 124.

[46] ACT FOR ESTABLISHING RELIGIOUS FREEDOM (Jan. 16, 1786), http://www.calhum.org/files/uploads/program_related/TD_VA_Statute_of_Religious_Freedom.pdf.

[47] *Id.*

[48] *Id.*

[49] Stephen Diamond, *Efficiency and Benevolence: Philanthropic Tax Exemptions in 19th-Century America*, *in* PROPERTY-TAX EXEMPTION FOR CHARITIES: MAPPING THE BATTLEFIELD 119 (Evelyn Brody ed., 2002).

[50] John W. Whitehead, *Tax Exemption and Churches: A Historical and Constitutional Analysis*, 22 CUMBERLAND L. REV. 521, 538 (1992).

"from the 1810s onward"[51]—well after the adoption and ratification of the First Amendment. It is thus unsurprising that the history of that amendment provides no explicit guidance about churches' tax-exempt status. That exempt status was not then as salient as it would later become.

Moreover, the First Amendment as adopted only precluded Congress from enacting laws "respecting an establishment of religion." The application of the First Amendment to the states lay in the distant future[52] as did the modern federal income tax and the Social Security tax.[53] There was no reason for the drafters or ratifiers of the First Amendment to concern themselves with state taxes or with federal taxes they could not have imagined.

In short, the search for the original understanding of the First Amendment neither supports nor undermines tax exemption for churches and other sectarian institutions. Whatever the relevance of that history in other contexts, whether to tax or exempt churches was not a concern in the drafting or enactment of the First Amendment. The original understanding of the First Amendment furnishes no guidance whether to tax or to exempt sectarian institutions and actors.

B. EXEMPTING CHURCHES FROM LAWS OF GENERAL APPLICABILITY: THE RELATIVE MERITS OF JUDICIAL AND LEGISLATIVE DECISION-MAKING

Professor Marci Hamilton argues that the courts should enforce laws of general applicability against churches and religious entities rather than exempt sectarian institutions and actors on First Amendment grounds. If churches or other religious actors are to be relieved from otherwise generally applicable laws, she contends, legislatures, not courts, should do the exempting:

> [M]ost laws should govern religious conduct, and the only legitimate exceptions occur when the legislature has determined that immunizing religious conduct is consistent with public welfare, health, and safety.[54]

---

[51] John Witte Jr., *Tax Exemption of Church Property: Historical Anomaly or Valid Constitutional Practice?*, 64 S.Cal. L. Rev. 363, 381 (1991).

[52] The U.S. Supreme Court applied the First Amendment to the states in *Cantwell v. Connecticut*, 310 U.S. 296, 303 (1940).

[53] The modern federal corporate income tax was adopted in 1909. Corporation Excise Tax Act of 1909, 36 Stat. 11, ch. 6 (Aug. 5, 1909). The modern federal income tax for individuals was adopted in 1913. Revenue Act of 1913, 38 Stat. 114, 166 § II-A (Oct. 3, 1913). The federal FICA tax was adopted in 1935. Social Security Act, Pub. L. 74-271, Title VIII (Aug. 14, 1935).

[54] Marci A. Hamilton, God vs. the Gavel: The Perils of Extreme Religious Liberty 32 (2014) (hereinafter Hamilton, Perils).

> Each day there are more reasons to embrace the Supreme Court's reasoning in *Employment Division v. Smith* and the principle that religious conduct must be governed by the same laws that govern the rest of us. At the same time, the argument for permissive accommodation remains strong—so long as the legislature takes into account the larger public good. Forbidding religious exemptions altogether would be tyranny, but granting them as of right is anarchy.[55]

As this passage indicates, Professor Hamilton strongly defends the U.S. Supreme Court's decision in *Employment Division, Department of Human Resources of Oregon v. Smith*,[56] introduced in chapter five.[57] *Smith* involved two members of the Native American Church who were counselors at a private drug rehabilitation center in Oregon. When they took peyote at a church ceremony in violation of state law, these individuals were fired for "misconduct" and were subsequently denied unemployment compensation. The U.S. Supreme Court sustained this denial against First Amendment challenge because "an individual's religious beliefs [do not] excuse him from compliance with an otherwise valid law prohibiting conduct that the State is free to regulate," such as drug use.[58]

The consumption of peyote, even for religious sacramental purposes, violated Oregon's drug laws.[59] The Free Exercise Clause, the *Smith* Court declared, does not excuse compliance with such "a generally applicable law"[60] just because an individual violating the law is religiously motivated.

Consider again in this context *Murdock*,[61] *Follett*,[62] *Jimmy Swaggart Ministries*,[63] and *Lee*.[64] As we saw in chapter one,[65] *Murdock* and *Follett* were the U.S. Supreme Court's initial confrontations with the First Amendment in the tax context. In these two cases, a divided Court struck on First Amendment grounds generally applicable municipal license fees for solicitation insofar as such license fees applied to Jehovah's Witnesses. Professor Hamilton's analysis and *Smith* indicate that *Murdock* and *Follett* were wrongly decided as the Court should not have carved First Amendment

---

[55] Marci A. Hamilton, God vs. the Gavel: Religion and the Rule of Law 310–311 (2005) (hereinafter Hamilton, Rule of Law).

[56] 494 U.S. 872 (1990). *See also* Hamilton, Perils, *supra* note 54, at 329 (criticizing "the Chicken Little quality of the post-*Smith* hysteria.").

[57] *See supra* at 146.

[58] *Smith*, 494 U.S. at 878–879.

[59] *Id.* at 876.

[60] *Id.* at 878.

[61] 319 U.S. 105 (1943).

[62] 321 U.S. 573 (1944).

[63] 493 U.S. 378 (1990).

[64] 455 U.S. 252 (1982).

[65] *See supra* at 1–4.

exceptions for religious solicitations from these generally applicable municipal license fees.

In contrast to *Murdock* and *Follett*, in both *Jimmy Swaggart Ministries* and *Lee* the Court later[66] unanimously sustained generally applicable tax laws when they were enforced against religious institutions and actors. In *Jimmy Swaggart Ministries*, the Court upheld California's sales tax as applied to the transactions of a sectarian ministry. In *Lee*, the Supreme Court confirmed Mr. Lee's obligation to withhold and pay the same FICA taxes as other employers despite Mr. Lee's sincere, religiously motivated opposition to public insurance programs like Social Security.

These later two decisions indicate that, to use Judge Noonan's felicitous phrase, the U.S. Supreme Court is no longer of a "*Murdock* mind."[67] In the tax setting, *Lee* and *Jimmy Swaggart Ministries* indicate that a *Smith* mindset now prevails judicially instead: As the U.S. Supreme Court currently construes the First Amendment, that amendment does not give religious actors or institutions constitutional protection from generally applicable taxes.

One can envision situations where tax laws which nominally apply to a broad range of taxpayers in practice narrowly burden religion or particular religions. Suppose, for example, that a city or state were to impose a higher sales tax rate on meals furnished in restaurants which do not feature pork on their menus. On its face, this higher sales tax would be formally neutral and would apply to any religious or secular restaurant which offers its patrons beef, lamb, or chicken but not pork. Despite its formal applicability to all restaurants, most of us would, as a substantive matter, perceive a higher sales tax on restaurants which do not serve pork as a pretextual burden imposed in violation of the First Amendment upon the religious practices of kashrut and halal.

However, in *Lee* and *Jimmy Swaggart Ministries* the challenged taxes were genuinely of general applicability. In these contexts, the First Amendment today does not exempt religious actors and institutions from such taxes.

On both procedural and substantive grounds, Professor Hamilton's pro-*Smith* analysis supports the Supreme Court's decision in *Lee* and *Jimmy Swaggart Ministries* to shut the courthouse door to religious persons seeking constitutional relief from tax laws of general applicability. As a procedural matter, she argues, litigation is dominated by the sectarian plaintiffs who petition for exemption. A court typically "only consider(s) the claims of the parties."[68] In contrast, the legislative

---

[66] *See supra* at 16–18 and 22–23.

[67] JOHN T. NOONAN JR., THE LUSTRE OF OUR COUNTRY 193 (2000).

[68] HAMILTON, PERILS, *supra* note 54, at 333–334 ("courts may only consider the claims of the parties before them and only the record introduced by the parties. To a significant degree, the parties control the court's (and especially the less experienced clerk's) worldview. Their facts—and only their facts—are relevant in the case.") (parenthetical in original).

process permits broader interests and considerations to affect outcomes. "[I]n the state legislatures," Professor Hamilton writes, "more voices can be heard."[69]

As a substantive matter, she argues, the potentially freewheeling legislative process can produce better results than can the more constrained procedures used by courts:

> The judicial process is a packaged affair with strict limitations on the latitude of the judge to make policy determinations. In contrast, the legislative process is at its very best when it engages in wide-ranging debate and investigation that can determine social policy out of a universe of options.[70]
>
> No court, deciding the issue in the context of a single case, is competent to take into account all of the interests that need to be considered. The final accommodation is a complicated equation that calls for legislative reasoning regarding what the law should be and not just an interpretation of a law.[71]

Consequently, Professor Hamilton concludes that

> [e]xempting religious conduct from neutral, general laws must be (1) duly enacted by a legislature, not decreed by a court; (2) must be debated under the harsh glare of public scrutiny; and (3) must be consistent with the larger public good.[72]

On the other hand, public choice theory cautions that the legislative process is not always "at its very best" and is often captured by narrow interests.[73] Indeed, according to Professor Hamilton, this is what happened when religious groups, with no real opposition or discussion, quickly stampeded Congress and many state legislatures into adopting Religious Freedom Restoration Acts (RFRAs) to overturn the *Smith* standard that laws of general applicability are enforceable against religious persons like everyone else.[74]

Some who oppose exemptions for religious groups undoubtedly perceive that they have stronger voices as litigants and amici in courts rather than as minor players

---

69 *Id.* at 92.

70 *Id.* at 333.

71 HAMILTON, RULE OF LAW, *supra* note 55, at 173–174. *See also id.* at 297. ("By comparison, the legislature has unlimited latitude to frame the issues over which it has power, to determine the extent of its investigation, and to take a position.").

72 *Id.* at 275.

73 Edward A. Zelinsky, *James Madison and Public Choice at Gucci Gulch: A Procedural Defense of Tax Expenditures and Tax Institutions*, 102 YALE L.J. 1165 (1993).

74 HAMILTON, RULE OF LAW, *supra* note 55, at 181–182.

in the legislative process. This would seem to be the premise of the litigation-based tactics of anti-religion groups like the Freedom From Religion Foundation (FFRF) and American Atheists, namely, that they can better advance their agendas in courthouses[75] than in the halls of the legislatures.

However, Professor Hamilton counters that amici "rarely" appear at the trial level.[76] This is a significant limitation because most litigation is resolved in the trial courts. Even if litigation continues to an appeals court, what happens in the trial court can be influential, if not decisive, as the case goes up the court system. Most obviously, the facts of the case are determined by the trial judge and are rarely overturned on appeal.[77]

Like Professor Hamilton, Professor Alexander Bickel was skeptical about judicial decision-making, though for different reasons. Professor Bickel was concerned about the "counter-majoritarian difficulty"[78] when unelected judges exercise the power of judicial review to strike as unconstitutional statutes adopted by elected legislators. However, Professor Bickel's skepticism was tempered by two strengths he perceived in judicial decision-making. First, Professor Bickel concluded that the courts, immunized from immediate political pressures and operating more deliberately and reflectively than legislative bodies, are better institutions for making principled decisions:

> [C]ourts have certain capacities for dealing with matters of principle that legislators and executives do not possess. Judges have, or should have, the leisure, the training, and the insulation to follow the ways of the scholar in pursuing the ends of government. This is crucial in sorting out the enduring values of a society, and it is not something that institutions can do well occasionally, while

---

[75] *Warren v. Commissioner*, 282 F.3d 1119 (9th Cir. 2002); *American Atheists, Inc. v. Shulman*, 21 F. Supp. 3d 856 (E.D. Ky., N. Div. 2014); *Freedom From Religion Foundation, Inc. v. Geithner*, (E.D. Calif., Sacramento Div.), Tax Analysts Doc. 2009-23144, complaint at para. 35; *Freedom From Religion Foundation, Inc. v. Geithner*, 715 F. Supp. 2d 1051 (E.D. Calif. 2010); *Gaylor v. Lew*, Case No. 16-CV-215-bbc (W.D. Wisc.) Tax Analysts Doc. 2017-994 (opinion and order).

[76] Hamilton, Rule of Law, *supra* note 55, at 296 ("It is true that in some cases, outside interests can expand the judge's understanding of the underlying social issues by filing amicus, or friend of the court, briefs, but that is rarely done at the trial level.").

[77] In a federal appellate court, a trial court's "[f]indings of fact, whether based on oral or other evidence, must not be set aside unless clearly erroneous . . ." Fed. R. Civ. P. 52(a)(6). Most states have similarly deferential rules which require appellate courts to generally accept trial courts' factual findings. *See, e.g., In re Estate of Stuchlik*, 289 Neb. 673, 682 (2014) ("an appellate court cannot set [the trial court's] findings aside unless they are clearly erroneous.").

[78] Alexander M. Bickel, The Least Dangerous Branch: The Supreme Court at the Bar of Politics 16 (1962).

> operating for the most part with a different set of gears. It calls for a habit of mind, and for undeviating institutional customs.[79]

Moreover, judicial decision-making, Professor Bickel argued, is more granular. In a particular case, judges can produce better outcomes than do legislators because, in deciding specific cases, judges address particular facts and particular parties:

> Statutes, after all, deal typically with abstract or dimly foreseen problems. The courts are concerned with the flesh and blood of an actual case. This tends to modify, perhaps to lengthen, everyone's view.[80]

Thus, while Professor Hamilton views the parties as limiting the court, Professor Bickel viewed them as providing important context for judicial decision-making.

Consider in this setting a case like *East Coast Conference of the Evangelical Covenant Church of America, Inc. v. Town of Swanzey*,[81] discussed in chapter 4.[82] In that case, New Hampshire's supreme court denied tax exemption to a camp in its entirety as a charitable property, but approved limited exemption for parts of the camp as religious property.[83] Specific buildings, including the chapel, "administrative offices, maintenance center, barn and workshop," the New Hampshire Court held, were "reasonably related" to religious purposes and thus tax exempt.[84] However, the remainder of the camp, including residential facilities, the "dining hall and other recreational facilities" was held to be taxable.[85] The courts, Professor Bickel admonishes, do this type of granular, fact-specific decision-making better than do legislatures.

Professors Laurence H. Winer and Nina J. Crimm[86] favor legislative decision-making in the Establishment Clause context:

> However difficult it might be for a court to engage in overt balancing in evaluating an Establishment Clause claim, a legislature is well situated to do so. Indeed, legislating is all about balancing competing interests and claims.[87]

---

79 *Id.* at 25–26.

80 *Id.* at 26.

81 146 N.H. 658 (2001).

82 *See supra* at 73–74.

83 *Swanzey*, 146 N.H. at 660–664.

84 *Id.* at 663.

85 *Id.* at 664.

86 Laurence H. Winer & Nina J. Crimm, God, Schools, and Government Funding: First Amendment Conundrums (2015).

87 *Id.* at 245.

The current pattern by which the federal and state governments tax and exempt churches and other religious institutions confirm the superiority of legislative, rather than judicial, decision-making in this area. In the tax context, legislatures can better balance the interests and concerns inherent in taxation than can courts.

Tax policy decisions should be guided by such criteria as revenue, administrability, economic neutrality, valuation concerns, liquidity considerations, and popular acceptability.[88] Even when a legislator is properly sensitive to these often-conflicting tax policy criteria, decisions about the design and level of taxes are intrinsically political and arbitrary. Taxation is ultimately about allocating the costs of government among different persons, an inherently political task. Taxation innately entails line-drawing which is necessary but not principled, for example, taxing sales at 5 percent rather than 6 percent. Paradoxically, taxation, while inescapably political and arbitrary, is today also highly technical in nature. In a democracy, this kind of political, often arbitrary, decision-making should occur in elected legislatures, augmented by specialized professional staffs with technical expertise.

Taxation can also involve (or should involve) principled decisions of the sort identified by Professor Bickel as best confided to the courts. But even as to these decisions, Professor Hamilton is right to emphasize the potentially broader participation of different groups and interests in the legislative process.

In a case where a legislature singles out a particular religious minority for disparate treatment, such as the theoretical penalty tax for the refusal to serve pork, the courts' ability to make principled and granular decisions enables them to better protect the minority's rights. However, when a religious group seeks immunity from a tax law which genuinely applies to all relevant taxpayers, that request should be debated in Congress and in the state legislatures—which, under our federal system of constitutional and statutory law, is where such debate occurs today. Legislatures are better positioned than courts to make the choices and trade-offs inherent in taxing and exempting.

C. THE CRITERIA GOVERNING LEGISLATIVE EXEMPTIONS FROM LAWS OF GENERAL APPLICABILITY

Consider again in this context the aftermath of *Lee*: Congress amended the federal FICA statute to give Mr. Lee and other religious opponents of Social Security the tax exemption the U.S. Supreme Court declined to furnish them.[89] Was Congress

---

[88] Edward A. Zelinsky, *For Realization: Income Taxation, Sectoral Accretionism and the Virtue of Attainable Virtues*, 19 CARDOZO L. REV. 861 (1997).

[89] *See supra* at 56.

correct to do so? More generally, when should a legislature extend tax exemption to religious actors and entities and when should it not? Are legislative tax exemptions inherently ad hoc in nature or are there persuasive principles which should guide legislative decision-making when taxing or exempting churches and other religious actors and institutions? I conclude that the trade-offs inherent in taxing and exempting religious persons and actors entail legislative judgments which cannot be reduced to overarching formulas.

As just noted, all choices about taxation are, in important respects, intrinsically political and arbitrary. Taxation is ultimately about allocating the costs of government, an inherently political task. Taxation innately entails line-drawing which is necessary but not principled, for example, taxing sales at 5 percent rather than 6 percent. Paradoxically, taxation, while inescapably political and arbitrary, is also highly technical in nature. Decisions about taxes should also be illuminated by such often offsetting tax policy criteria as revenue-generation, administrability, economic neutrality, and public acceptability. In a democracy, this kind of balancing of contending considerations best occurs in elected legislatures, augmented by professional staff with technical expertise.

Few would condone legislative decision-making utterly without constraint. For example, most of us would object to the theoretical tax which, while formally neutral, effectively targets kosher and halal eating establishments for higher sales tax burdens than are imposed on secular and Christian restaurants. However, this leaves a broad swath within which legislators can and should balance legitimate and conflicting criteria when taxing or exempting religious persons.

Professor Hamilton eschews this situation-specific vantage. Critical to her analysis are her overarching prescriptions that legislatures, as they approach religious persons, should do "no harm" and should promote the "public good": The "no-harm principle"[90] as Professor Hamilton formulates it typically precludes exemptions or exclusions for religious entities or individuals since "the public good requires the deterrence and punishment of harmful actions, regardless of the identity of the actor."[91]

Whatever the value of the "no harm" and "public good" criteria in other settings, they are not helpful when a legislature decides to tax or to exempt religious institutions and actors. For some, any tax exemption is harmful because it subsidizes the exempt person and thereby deprives the government of revenue or requires higher tax rates for those taxpayers not exempted. However, as discussed in chapter 5,[92] the "subsidy" label is conclusory absent prior agreement that taxation is otherwise

---

[90] HAMILTON, PERILS, *supra* note 54, at 16–17.

[91] HAMILTON, RULE OF LAW, *supra* note 55, at 240.

[92] *See supra* at 148–152.

appropriate. It is only compelling to label the tax exemption of religious persons as a subsidy harming the public fisc if it is first assumed that such persons should be taxed—but that is the very question being decided.

The "public good" standard is similarly appealing at first glance but ultimately proves unhelpful in the tax context as well. While the public good is readily identified in many settings, it is often not so easily discerned in the tax context. For some, more ample government revenues are a public good because such revenues pay for more government services. For others, taxes are innately harmful because they divert productive resources from the private sector.

Professors Paul Horwitz[93] and Marc DeGirolami[94] are skeptical of broad theoretical formulas purporting to guide decision-making about the proper relationship between church and state. For these two scholars, there are just particular, often difficult, decisions which must be made as well as possible without the benefit of overarching principles.

Professor Horwitz calls himself a "constitutional agnostic." As such, he doubts the value of such First Amendment approaches as separationism, nonpreferentialism, formal neutrality, substantive neutrality, equality, accomodationism, liberty, endorsement, and coercion.[95] These theories do not obviate the need for "hard or tragic"[96] choices in particular instances when the legitimate claims of the state conflict with the equally legitimate claims of religion. In lieu of such formulas, Professor Horwitz's "constitutional agnosticism" counsels a frame of mind:

> an open and empathetic approach to church-state conflicts, one in which the legislator, whatever his or her own position on matters of religious truth or matters of public policy, at least attempts to enter imaginatively the perspective of the contending groups involved in any such legislation before casting his or her vote.[97]

This approach acknowledges that executives and legislators

> govern amid a play of contending beliefs and interests, and have a strong interest in mediating fairly among those interests. They can achieve that understanding only by trying to make an imaginative leap into the perspectives of

---

93 Paul Horwitz, The Agnostic Age: Law, Religion, and the Constitution (2011).

94 Mark DeGirolami, The Tragedy of Religious Freedom (2013).

95 Horwitz, *supra* note 93, at 225, 232.

96 *Id.* at 222.

97 *Id.* at 156–157.

> the people involved. For executive officials, as for legislators, constitutional agnosticism is the best way not only of achieving sound results, but of achieving them in a way that fully accounts for and responds to the play of interests and perspectives in a pluralistic age.[98]

Professor DeGirolami is similarly skeptical of comprehensive theories of religion and law and instead adopts the case-by-case "method of tragedy and history."[99] This method postulates that

> decision making in this area can never be fully systematized, and that it will be forever burdened by tragic outcomes, results that sacrifice important values whose loss cannot be compensated by the triumph of others.[100]

Commentators on law and religion tend to devote relatively little attention to the tax system, although it is an arena in which church-state tensions are resolved on a regular basis. Perhaps this disinterest reflects a sense that "taxes" are somehow different from other aspects of the legal system.[101] I suggest an additional explanation why commentators on church-state relations often devote comparatively little attention to taxes: Our federal, decentralized tax system generally reaches reasonable (not perfect) accommodations between church and state.

This workable accommodation is, as Professors Horwitz and DeGirolami suggest, not the product of any overriding theory. Rather, it reflects myriad decisions made over time in different, decentralized settings. In the tax context, there are important tax policy criteria which should illuminate legislative decisions to tax or to exempt religious institutions and actors. These decisions entail imperfect trade-offs among legitimate and competing goals. These trade-offs cannot be reduced to grand formulas. Our system of taxing and exempting churches may not satisfy any overarching theory, but it largely (though imperfectly) works in practice.

Tax policy should be influenced by such criteria as revenue, economic neutrality, administrability, valuation concerns, liquidity considerations, and popular acceptability. The prospect of church-state entanglement should similarly guide whether

---

98 *Id.* at 157.

99 DeGirolami, *supra* note 94, at 3.

100 *Id.* at 6.

101 Alice G. Abreu & Richard K. Greenstein, *Tax as Everylaw: Interpretation, Enforcement, and the Legitimacy of the IRS*, 69 Tax Law. 493, 497 (2016) ("This experience of difference—tax exceptionalism—is so prevalent that it extends to the way that tax scholars, most of whom are also taxpayers, think of the tax law. And it has led them to think of tax as different from other fields of law and, in some cases, even as something separate from law.").

to tax or exempt sectarian entities. At the end of the day, balancing these legitimate and offsetting criteria is a matter of legislative judgment which cannot be reduced to a grand formula.

D. THE RHETORIC OF SEPARATIONISM

My analysis counsels skepticism about the rhetoric of separationism in the tax context. Relying on the history of the struggle for religious freedom in Virginia, Professor Philip Hamburger[102] concludes that the First Amendment originally did not mandate "a separation of church and state."[103] Rather, the religious dissenters whose concerns animated the First Amendment sought to bar "government's power to legislate an establishment."[104] This comes close to Mr. Drakeman's interpretation of the original understanding of the First Amendment.[105]

According to Professor Hamburger, the First Amendment became widely interpreted as separating church and state only as the nineteenth century unfolded. Those initially calling for the separation of church and state reflected the forces of secularization.[106] Later, these secular and "anti-clerical" adherents of church-state separation were joined by nativists concerned about the potential political and economic power of the Catholic Church.[107]

The nineteenth-century advocates of separating church and state first called for amending the U.S. Constitution to embody that separation. The most prominent of their proposals was the "Blaine Amendment" discussed in chapter two.[108]

102 PHILIP HAMBURGER, SEPARATION OF CHURCH AND STATE (2002).

103 *Id.* at 1.

104 *Id.* at 107.

105 *See supra* at 216–218.

106 HAMBURGER, *supra* note 102, at 110. (After the adoption of the First Amendment "separation first became popular among relatively secular, political, and anticlerical Americans, even as it remained disreputable among religious dissenters, who continued patiently to seek the rather different religious liberty they had been demanding for so very long.").

107 *Id.* at 193 ("In the middle of the nineteenth century some Americans employed the idea of separation of church and state against Catholicism and thereby made it a popular "American" principle."). *See also id.* at 192 ("fears of church authority and especially of the Catholic Church made separation respectable as an 'American' principle. Accordingly, amid anti-Catholic, nativist demands for conformity to American principles, Americans increasingly assumed that separation was their nation's religious liberty.").

108 *See supra* at 39–40. *See also* HAMBURGER, *supra* note 102, at 297–299. The "Blaine Amendment" would have applied to the states the standards of the Free Exercise and Establishment Clauses. *Cantwell v. Connecticut*, 310 U.S. 296, 303 (1940), achieved this result in 1947 when the U.S. Supreme Court held that "[t]he fundamental concept of liberty embodied in [the Fourteenth] Amendment embraces the liberties guaranteed by the First Amendment." In addition, the Blaine Amendment would have also provided that no resources "for the support of public schools" should "ever be under the control of any religious sect . . . or . . . be divided between religious sects or denominations." HAMBURGER, *supra* note 102, at 298.

According to Professor Hamburger, it was only after their efforts to amend the U.S. Constitution failed that advocates of church-state separation claimed that such efforts were unnecessary after all. The First Amendment, these advocates started to assert, already separated church and state.[109] This separationist interpretation of the First Amendment ultimately prevailed in *Reynolds* and *Everson*.

In an important sense, we today are all separationists:[110] It is hard to envision the U.S. Supreme Court repudiating *Reynolds* or *Everson*. Concern about church-state entanglement is, at its core, concern about keeping the secular and sectarian apart. For the future, church-state separation will, explicitly and implicity, be central to First Amendment dialogue.

However, despite the widespread acceptance of the desirability of separating church and state, the concept of separationism is not self-defining. Separationist rhetoric can be adapted to disparate results. In *Everson*, the separationist narrative led the Court to sustain New Jersey's busing of parochial school students—over the famous objections of Justice Jackson's dissent decrying the inconsistency between that separationist narrative and the Court's conclusion.[111]

We should be skeptical of separationist rhetoric in the tax setting. Consider one final time the debate over the constitutionality of Internal Revenue Code Section 107.[112] Section 107 excludes from the gross income of a "minister of the gospel" his church-provided in-kind housing and his cash parsonage allowance. The opponents of Section 107 contend that this Code provision entangles church and state and that abolishing Section 107 would accordingly separate them.

This critique is credible as to the borderline entanglement generated by Section 107 since those claiming that exemption from gross income necessarily characterize themselves as "ministers of the gospel." The IRS and the state tax commissioners must police and sometimes reject those claims. This is quintessential borderline entanglement as the taxpayer bidding for religious exemption and the tax collector protecting the fisc joust at the boundaries of exemption.

On the other hand, in terms of enforcement, taxing does not separate church and state but, rather, enmeshes them. Taxing in-kind housing, such as a parsonage

---

[109] HAMBURGER, *supra* note 102, at 335 ("advocates of separation focused on constitutional interpretation. They quickly forgot about arguments that an amendment was necessary and claimed instead that American constitutions had already, since their inception, fully guaranteed a separation of church and state.").

[110] With apologies to Thomas Jefferson ("We are all republicans—we are all federalists."). The other famous analogue ("We are all Keynesians now.") was written by Professor Milton Friedman, though it is often attributed to Richard Nixon.

[111] *Everson v. Board of Education*, 330 U.S. 1, 19 (1947) (Jackson, J., dissenting) ("The case which irresistibly comes to mind as the most fitting precedent is that of Julia who, according to Byron's reports, 'whispering "I will ne'er consent,"—consented.'").

[112] I.R.C. § 107, 26 U.S.C. § 107. *See supra* at 165–173.

in which a minister lives, is particularly entangling, both because of valuation issues (what is the use of a unique home worth?) and liquidity questions (in-kind income does not put cash in the taxpayer's hands to pay tax). Taxing cash parsonage allowances is also entangling—all taxation is to some degree—but is less so since neither a valuation quandary nor a liquidity issue arises when there is cash income to tax.

For the indefinite future, we will in important part conduct First Amendment discussions in terms of church-state separation. However, we should be skeptical about unqualified claims concerning separationism in the tax context. Enforcing generally applicable taxes against sectarian entities and individuals does not separate church-state, but entangles them as the tax collector administers the law and as the taxpayer complies with it. The relationship between the tax collector and the taxpayer is among the most enmeshing legal relationships in our society. Opponents of sectarian tax exemptions can credibly claim to pursue many goals, but separating church and state is not one of these.

E. TO TAX OR EXEMPT THE PROFITS OF NONPROFITS

As commentators discussed these four constitutional topics, tax policy scholars simultaneously debated the proprietary of continuing to exempt nonprofit corporations from federal income taxation. In a seminal article in 1976, Professor Boris Bittker and Attorney George K. Rahdert[113] advanced two defenses of the Internal Revenue Code's exemption of nonprofit institutions from income taxation. First, nonprofit institutions, they argue, do not have income "in the normal sense" of the term.[114] Consequently, determining a nonprofit organization's income "would be a conceptually difficult, if not self-contradictory task."[115] Second, according to Bittker and Rahdert, assuming that a nonprofit organization's income can be calculated, there is no proper way to determine the appropriate tax rate at which such organization should pay tax on this income:

> [N]onprofit organizations engaged in "public service" activities, broadly conceived, should be wholly exempted from income taxation, because they do not realize "income" in the ordinary sense of that term and because, even if they did, there is no satisfactory way to fit the tax rate to the ability of the beneficiaries to pay.[116]

113 Boris I. Bittker & George K. Rahdert, *The Exemption of Nonprofit Organizations from Federal Income Taxation*, 85 YALE L.J. 299 (1976).

114 *Id.* at 328.

115 *Id.* at 307. *See also id.* at 312 ("any attempt to treat charitable activity as a 'business' is self-contradictory.").

116 *Id.* at 305.

Professor Henry Hansmann subsequently criticized the Bittker-Rahdert analysis on several grounds. He started with the increasing resemblance of many nonprofit corporations (which do not pay federal income tax) with profit-making corporations (which do):

> Nonprofit firms now commonly provide goods and services in direct competition with profit-seeking firms, and in many cases increasingly resemble their for-profit competitors in their manner of organization and operation.[117]

This analysis implies that the term "nonprofit" corporation is a misnomer. A philanthropic corporation can earn a profit by generating current revenues exceeding its current expenses. A philanthropy, notes Professor Hansmann, is merely forbidden by the "nondistribution constraint" from paying such profit to shareholders. A nonprofit corporation must ultimately use its profits for its philanthropic purposes rather than pay such profits to equity owners as dividends.[118]

Professor Hansmann further observes that so-called "commercial nonprofits" "receive little or no income from donations, but rather derive all or nearly all of their income from the sales of goods or services that they produce."[119] The income of these essentially commercial enterprises can be taxed in the same way that the income of their for-profit competitors is taxed. Hospitals are a prime example of the equivalence between commercial nonprofits and their competitors which pay federal income tax.[120]

As to "donative organizations" which receive much of their revenues from contributions, such contributions can be treated "as sales receipts" "appropriately includable in gross income."[121] The "cost of the services, such as disaster relief, rendered by donative nonprofits would then be deductible, analogously to ordinary business expenses."[122] Thus, Professor Hansmann—contrary to the Bittker-Rahdert analysis—concludes that

> without much difficulty we can extend to nonprofits the general principles of tax accounting commonly applied to profit-seeking firms.[123]

---

[117] Henry Hansmann, *The Rationale for Exempting Nonprofit Organizations from Corporate Income Taxation*, 91 Yale L.J. 54 (1981).

[118] *Id.* at 56.

[119] *Id.* at 59.

[120] *Id.* at 89.

[121] *Id.* at 61. *See also id.* at 85 ("We need simply view the donations that the firms receive as the price that the public is prepared to pay for the services that the firms produce.").

[122] *Id.* at 61.

[123] *Id.* at 62.

While there are plausible arguments for subsidizing eleemosynary activity through the Section 170 deduction for charitable contributions, Professor Hansmann tells us, the only credible rationale for exempting nonprofit corporations from income taxation is "to compensate for difficulties that nonprofits have in raising capital" since nonprofits cannot issue stock to shareholders and thus cannot raise equity capital.[124] Professor Hansmann is skeptical of this rationale for tax-exempting nonprofit enterprises.[125]

Professor Evelyn Brody[126] also highlights the increasing resemblance of nonprofit corporations and profit-making organizations which compete with one another:

> Recent years have brought a revolution in the types and extent of commercial activities undertaken by nonprofits, as well as an influx of proprietary enterprises into traditionally nonprofit fields, such as hospital care and higher education.[127]

As commercial schools and hospitals and their nonprofit competitors look more alike, she argues, it becomes less compelling to tax the former but exempt the latter.[128]

The commercialization of "nonprofit" education becomes increasingly evident as universities sell their patents and intellectual property for ever larger sums[129] and as highly profitable college athletics programs become indistinguishable from commercial athletics.[130]

Professor Daniel Halperin agrees that it is feasible in practice to tax the income of nonprofit corporations: "There is nothing about the nature of the charitable organization that precludes income taxation."[131] However, he concludes that over time such taxation would generate little net revenue for the public fisc. Any surplus earned currently by a nonprofit institution will be spent on the institution's future philanthropic activities. In present value terms, it makes no difference to the

---

124 *Id.* at 72.

125 *Id.* at 92.

126 Evelyn Brody, *Charities in Tax Reform: Threats to Subsidies Overt and Covert*, 66 TENN. L. REV. 687 (1999).

127 *Id.* at 746.

128 *Id.* at 692–693 ("support repealing the tax exemption of nonprofit hospitals. The highly visible and increasingly commercial-looking nonprofit educational institutions would then become the next category of contention."); *id.* at 723 ("extending the commerciality logic might require simply revoking the exemption of nonprofit hospitals . . . health care's pervasive and highly visible commercial taint.").

129 *See, e.g.*, Teresa Watanabe, *UCLA Will Get Hundreds of Millions for Rights to Prostate Cancer Drug*, L.A. TIMES, Mar. 4, 2016.

130 *See, e.g.*, JOE NOCERA & BEN STRAUSS, INDENTURED: THE INSIDE STORY OF THE REBELLION AGAINST THE NCAA (2016); David Wharton, *UCLA's Under Armour Deal for $280 Million Is the Biggest in NCAA History*, L.A. TIMES, May 24, 2016.

131 Daniel Halperin, *Is Income Tax Exemption for Charities a Subsidy?*, 64 TAX L. REV. 283, 284 (2011).

Treasury whether this surplus is tax-exempted today or is spent and deducted in the future.[132]

Either way, this amount destined for eleemosynary purposes is ultimately untaxed. Hence, he argues, the current tax exemption of nonprofits' operating earnings is defensible. Professor Halperin finds more compelling the taxation of the endowment incomes of nonprofit institutions.[133] Others view more favorably the prospect of taxing the incomes of nonprofit organizations.[134]

Suppose that Congress were to impose income taxation upon all hospitals and schools. With these institutions no longer income tax exempt, the income tax exemption of religious entities would look less like the broad property tax exemption upheld in *Walz*, available to an expansive class of eleemosynary institutions. Instead, with all schools and hospitals taxed on their respective incomes, the residual income tax exemption of sectarian organizations would begin to resemble the narrower sales tax exemption struck in *Texas Monthly*, applicable only to religious literature.

In this hypothetical world, the distinction between borderline entanglement and enforcement entanglement would again come to the fore. If schools and hospitals were subject to income taxation while religious institutions remain income tax free, there would be intense pressure at the borderlines separating these categories: Would Notre Dame and Yeshiva University be classified as schools subject to income taxation or would they, as religious institutions, remain tax exempt? What about parochial schools? Similar borderline inquiries would arise as to religious hospitals. Would these hospitals be taxed on their respective incomes because they resemble their secular counterparts or would religious hospitals retain tax-exempt status because of their sectarian sponsorship?

Some of these borderline inquiries would be eliminated if income tax exemption in this new world were limited to churches. In that case, the incomes of religious hospitals and schools would be taxed in the same fashion as the profits of their secular competitors. But then church-state entanglement would arise at the new borderline between income tax–exempt churches and nonchurch religious entities, subject to income taxation. As we have seen in the context of property taxation,[135] there is considerable borderline entanglement in some states as tax collectors and judges must distinguish between exempt church properties and nonexempt religious properties

---

[132] *Id.* at 293–294.

[133] *Id.* at 298.

[134] *See, e.g.*, Michael Fricke, *The Case Against Income Tax Exemption for Nonprofits*, 89 St. John's L. Rev. 1129, 1167 (2015) (proposing "to remove the income tax exemption for nonprofits but to allow them an unlimited deduction for expenses directly related to their charitable purposes . . .").

[135] *See, e.g., supra* at 30–36, 67–77, 143–146, and 151–154.

such as summer camps, printing facilities, and church-provided housing. Similar entanglement would arise if nonchurch religious organizations were taxed on their respective incomes while churches remain income tax free.

Borderline entanglement could be eliminated altogether by subjecting all religious corporations, including churches, to across-the-board income taxation. However, significant enforcement entanglement would then occur as churches' incomes would be assessed and their expenses classified as deductible or not. As I observed earlier,[136] if church income is taxed, the tax collector and the church would be enmeshed along doctrinal lines as the collector would evaluate whether payments to a church are tax-free gifts or are instead taxable payments for services. It would be similarly entangling for the tax collector and the courts to determine if a particular church outlay is "ordinary and necessary"[137] and thus deductible for income tax purposes.[138] This determination would require tax collectors and judges to assess doctrine and religious practice, an inherently entangling task. Is operating a baptismal font "ordinary and necessary"?

Professor Hansmann's argument suggests categorizing all church receipts as taxable. This would eliminate the church-state entanglement which would arise from the tax collector and the courts policing the distinction between tax-free gifts and taxable services. If all church receipts were to constitute gross income, the IRS and the judiciary would not need to assess whether a payer's disbursement to a church was a taxable payment for church-provided services or a nontaxable gift to the church.

However, including gifts and all other receipts in churches' gross incomes would boost such incomes and thereby increase the stakes of the deduction inquiry. Greater gross incomes would incent churches to claim greater deductions for "ordinary and necessary" outlays to offset the additional gross income stemming from the inclusion of gifts in gross income. Again, determining whether church outlays are "ordinary and necessary" would enmesh the tax collector and the courts in internal church affairs and doctrine.

Moreover, the First Amendment, as well as federal and state RFRAs, would prevent federal and state tax systems from singling out churches (or churches and other religious institutions) by only treating the gifts they receive as income. "[T]he protections of the Free Exercise Clause pertain if the law at issue discriminates against some or all religious beliefs or regulates or prohibits conduct because it is undertaken for religious reasons."[139] Such unconstitutional discrimination would result if gifts

---

[136] *See supra* at 135–136.

[137] I.R.C. § 162, 26 U.S.C. §162.

[138] *See supra* at 134–135.

[139] *Church of the Lukumi Babalu Aye, Inc. v. City of Hialeah*, 508 U.S. 520, 532 (1993).

to sectarian institutions were treated as income while gifts to everyone else (including individuals) remained income tax free. In RFRA terms,[140] it would uniquely burden religious entities if gifts to them were declared taxable income while gifts to other donees remained tax free. It is hard discern a compelling government interest in taxing gifts to religious entities if other gifts continued to be income tax free.

Thus, extending income taxation to nonprofit hospitals and schools would potentially trigger a chain of events increasing church-state entanglement. If religious entities were to retain exempt status while hospitals and educational organizations become taxable on their incomes, conflict would arise at the borders of exemption as tax collectors would joust with potential taxpayers over their classification as sectarian and thus tax exempt. If, on the other hand, income taxation were to be extended to churches and religious entities as well as to schools and hospitals, enforcing the tax against sectarian institutions would enmesh these religious institutions and the tax collector. It would be particularly troubling for the IRS and the courts to assess whether religious-related operating expenses are "ordinary and necessary" and consequently deductible for income tax purposes.

Considerably less church-state entanglement would flow from Professor Halperin's suggestion that Congress just tax the endowment incomes of philanthropic organizations. An endowment tax is attracting attention, both in Congress and some state legislatures.[141] Under this limited approach, the operations of religious (and secular eleemosynary) organizations would remain income tax exempt while such organizations' investment incomes would become taxable.

Identifying dividends, interest, royalties, rents, and other forms of passive investment income is a relatively straightforward enterprise which can be conducted in accordance with secular principles of tax law—unlike separating gifts from fee income for religious services rendered, an inquiry which requires assessment of the payer's intent. Similarly, the deduction *vel non* of the costs associated with earning endowment forms of income (e.g., brokerage fees, fees for financial advisers) do not raise the entangling doctrinal inquiries inherent in taxing churches' operating incomes, for example, is an outlay for a particular religious activity "ordinary and necessary"?

[140] 42 USCS § 2000bb-1(b); Ky. Rev. Stat. § 446.350.

[141] *See, e.g.*, Colleen Murphy, *Tax Free College Endowments in Crosshairs as Overhaul Looms*, Daily Tax Report (BNA), Dec. 30, 2016; Timothy W. Martin & Melissa Korn, *Is Taxing Harvard, Yale, Stanford the Answer to High College Costs?*, Wall St. J., May 5, 2016, at C1; Janet Lorin, *Rich Schools Defend Tax-Free Status, Spending of Endowments*, Daily Tax Report (BNA), Apr. 4, 2016; Janet Lorin, *Cash Strapped Connecticut Wants to Tax Yale Endowments*, Bloomberg, Mar. 23, 2016; Tyler S.B. Olkowski, *Study Proposes Excise Tax on Harvard's Endowment*, Harvard Crimson, Apr. 22, 2015 (discussing 2008 proposal for a 2.5 percent Massachusetts endowment tax). Paige Jones, *Massachusetts Bills to Tax College Endowments Elicit Both Support, Backlash*, Tax Notes Doc.2017-53958.

Thus, a Congress or legislature concerned about church-state entanglement could plausibly leave intact the basic income tax exemption for churches (either exempt by themselves or along with other secular philanthropic organizations) while taxing such churches' endowment incomes. Taxing churches' operating incomes raises much more enmeshing enforcement issues than does taxing churches' passive investment incomes. Moreover, taxing all endowments across the board would eliminate any borderline entanglement since there would be no exemption for churches or other religious endowments with boundaries to police.[142]

F. REVISITING THE UNRELATED BUSINESS INCOME TAX (UBIT)

Unsurprisingly, Bittker and Rahdert, who favor the general income tax exemption of eleemosynary institutions, are also UBIT skeptics. In debate about the federal UBIT, they tell us, "the fear of unfair competition between taxable and tax-free enterprises was exaggerated."[143] If, in a pre-UBIT world, a tax-exempt institution purchased a profit-making enterprise, the prices that enterprise charged its customers before it was purchased continued to be the profit-maximizing prices after acquisition by the new tax-exempt owner.[144] Hence, they contend, it was "mysterious"[145] for taxpaying competitors to fear unfair price reductions triggered by the new owner's tax-exempt status. A new tax-exempt owner has the economic incentive to maintain prevailing prices and the profits flowing from them.

Moreover, according to Bittker and Rahdert, the ultimate economic impact of the UBIT falls on the beneficiaries of the organizations paying that tax. The UBIT reduces "the amount that the exempt organization can apply to its charitable or other purposes."[146] Hence, the UBIT's final economic incidence, falling on these beneficiaries, is likely "regressive."[147]

Like Bitter and Rahdert, Professor Hansmann[148] dismisses the unfair competition defense of the UBIT since a tax-exempt entity purchasing a business maximizes the business's profits by charging customers the same competitive, market-based prices as were charged by the prior taxable owner. Thus, in a world without the UBIT,

---

[142] *See* discussion *supra* at 125–128, discussing how across-the-board taxation eliminates borderline entanglement since there is no exemption with boundaries to police.

[143] Bittker & Rahdert, *supra* note 113, at 325.

[144] *Id.* at 319.

[145] *Id.*

[146] *Id.* at 325.

[147] *Id.* at 326.

[148] Henry B. Hansmann, *Unfair Competition and the Unrelated Business Income Tax*, 75 VA. L. REV. 605 (1989).

a nonprofit corporation acquiring a profit-making business would "leave[] undisturbed the price that prevails when only for-profit firms compete, and thereby maximize[] the difference between cost and sales price."[149]

While Professor Hansmann rejects the fairness rationale for the UBIT, he supports the tax on grounds of economic efficiency. Without the UBIT, the endowments of nonprofit entities would eschew investments in the common stock of publicly traded corporations subject to corporate taxation. These endowments would instead concentrate their respective holdings in wholly owned, unincorporated enterprises benefiting from the entities' tax-exempt status.

The dividends of publicly traded corporations are paid net of federal income taxation. Without the UBIT, nonprofit entities would receive the wholly untaxed profits of the unincorporated firms they fully own. Thus, without the UBIT, "nonprofits would have a strong incentive to abandon the current practice of investing in a broad range of common stocks and to pursue instead a strategy of investing in firms that the nonprofits can completely own" and thereby convert such unincorporated firms to income tax–free status.[150]

Moreover, Professor Hansmann asserts, a world without the UBIT is likely to entail less efficient management of the enterprises owned by nonprofit institutions. With no UBIT, eleemosynary institutions would acquire wholly owned business enterprises to avoid the impact of corporate income taxation. The managers of nonprofit institutions would thereby become the ultimate managers of the unincorporated business enterprises purchased by these eleemosynary entities. There is no reason to believe that those running nonprofit organizations oversee well the business operations owned by their organizations.[151]

I have argued that the current system does a reasonable job of exempting churches and religious institutions from the taxes most pregnant with possibilities for church-state enforcement entanglement (ad valorem property taxation, corporate income taxation, unemployment compensation tax) while taxing sectarian entities when there is less possibility of such entanglement (sales taxation, real estate conveyance taxation, FICA payroll taxes). The UBIT is the chief evidence contradicting this argument. The federal UBIT applies to churches and other religious entities as do the UBITs of most states which impose corporate income taxes. As observed earlier,[152] it is highly entangling for the tax collector and the church to determine whether or not

---

[149] *Id.* at 611.

[150] *Id.* at 614–615.

[151] *Id.* at 616–617.

[152] *See supra* at 140–143.

a particular activity, for example, a television station or a coffee house, is "related" to a church's mission.

So far, there is little reported case law reflecting this church-state entanglement. Perhaps the IRS and state tax collectors have been reluctant to enforce the UBIT against churches and religious organizations. Perhaps these sectarian organizations have responded to the UBIT preemptively, by shifting to taxpaying entities those activities which are arguably "unrelated" to their religious missions. The relatively small amounts paid under the UBIT[153] suggest that either or both of these explanations may be true.

G. CONCLUSION

Each of the six debates discussed in this chapter is important in its own right. From my analysis of these debates, an underlying point emerges: Discussion of both the First Amendment and of tax policy would be enhanced by greater attention to the invariable and imperfect trade-offs at play when taxing or exempting churches and to the policies which Congress and the state legislatures have embraced as they balance the relevant constitutional and tax policy considerations. Debate about both the Constitution and tax policy are diminished when each is cabined from the other.

[153] In 2013, the last year for which data is available, all tax-exempt institutions paid a total federal UBIT aggregating $581,003,000. By the standards of the federal budget, this is a small amount. *See* SOI Tax Stats—Exempt Organizations' Unrelated Business Income (UBI) Tax Statistics, Table 1, https://www.irs.gov/uac/soi-tax-stats-exempt-organizations-unrelated-business-income-ubi-tax-statistics. Unrelated Business Income Tax Returns: Number of Returns, Gross Unrelated Business Income, Total Deductions, Unrelated Business Taxable Income (Less Deficit), Unrelated Business Taxable Income, and Total Tax, by Type of Tax-Exempt Organization, Tax Year 2013. *See also* Jael Jackson, *Unrelated Business Income Tax Returns, Tax Year 2012*, http://src.bna.com/mBK.

CONCLUSION

THERE ARE BROAD areas in which churches and, more generally, religious organizations enjoy tax exemption. On the other hand, churches and other religious entities pay more taxes than many believe. Churches and other religious organizations are treated quite diversely by different taxes and by different states. Sometimes churches and other religious entities are taxed in the same fashion as secular organizations and persons. Yet other taxes narrowly exempt churches while taxing nonreligious philanthropic organizations. Still other taxes exempt religious entities along with secular eleemosynary institutions.

Central to my analysis is the concern which has come to be called "entanglement": Either taxing or exempting churches and other sectarian entities entangles church and state. In the tax context, there are no disentangling alternatives. Taxing churches results in enforcement entanglement as the tax collector collects revenue from religious taxpayers, often by intrusive means, and as taxpayers comply with their obligations to pay tax. Exempting churches causes borderline entanglement as churches and other sectarian actors claim the coverage of tax exemption while tax collectors and the courts police the boundaries of exemption and sometimes reject those claims.

The taxes to which churches are more frequently subject—federal Social Security and Medicare taxes, state sales taxes, real estate conveyance levies—generally fall on the less entangling end of the spectrum. The taxes from which religious institutions are exempt—general income taxes, ad valorem property taxes, unemployment taxes—are typically taxes with the greatest potential for enforcement-related entanglement between church and state. The taxes generating the greatest enforcement entanglement are those, like ad valorem property taxation, where the amount of the taxpayer's liability may be difficult to determine and where the taxpayer may lack the cash to pay the tax.

Tax policy invariably involves choices among conflicting and legitimate goals, such as revenue-generation, administrability, public acceptability, economic neutrality, valuation considerations, and liquidity concerns. None of these goals can ever be achieved in toto. When tax laws impact churches and other sectarian entities, the minimization of church-state entanglement should be an important, often controlling, goal. In practice, it frequently is as Congress and the state legislatures generally exempt churches and religious institutions from the taxes with the greatest possibilities of enforcement entanglement. However, in the tax context, church-state entanglement can never be eliminated in its entirety, any more than any other legitimate objective of tax policy can ever be obtained perfectly.

Tax exemption can serve the important nonsubsidizing goal of mitigating enforcement entanglement between church and state. However, tax exemption itself entangles the state and sectarian entities and personnel at the borders of exemption as those entities and personnel claim eligibility for tax exemption and dispute with the state and its agents the boundaries of exemption.

It is unpersuasive to reflexively label any tax exemption, deduction, or exclusion as a "subsidy" prior to agreement upon a normative tax base from which such exemption, deduction, or exclusion departs. Exemptions for religious actors and institutions can be legitimate, nonsubidizing features of a normative tax base when such exemptions minimize enforcement entanglement between church and state. In a world of imperfect choices between entangling alternatives, it is often a plausible, nonsubsidizing choice to exempt sectarian actors and institutions and thereby incur the problems of borderline entanglement rather than enmesh church and state in the difficulties of enforcement entanglement.

However, churches and other sectarian institutions utilize public services, often quite heavily. Such institutions are often wealthy and engage in economically significant transactions, including the purchase and sale of real estate. Such wealth and transactions reflect capacity to pay tax. To the extent possible, taxation should be economically neutral among potential taxpayers and their comparable activities.

Hence, taxing the church or exempting the church involves imperfect trade-offs among competing and legitimate values. On balance, our federal system of decentralized legislation makes these trade-offs reasonably, though there is room for improvement in particular instances.

In a world of trade-offs and imperfect choices, the diversity with which the states tax and exempt the church is, as a normative matter, a strength of our federal system. Multiple solutions emerging from state-by-state choices are often better than a single, uniform rule imposed nationally—though, in important instances, the Internal Revenue Code creates national norms which the states generally tend to follow when taxing or exempting the church. The tax policy trade-offs involved in taxing or exempting churches and other religious entities are best made legislatively.

Discussion of the First Amendment and tax policy would be enhanced by greater attention to the considerations at play when deciding upon taxing or exempting churches and to the various policies which Congress and the state legislatures have embraced balancing these legal and tax policy considerations.

Index